Changing Conceptions of Psychoanalysis

Merton M. Gill, M.D.

Changing Conceptions of Psychoanalysis: The Legacy of Merton M. Gill

edited by

Doris K. Silverman

and

David L. Wolitzky

THE ANALYTIC PRESS

2000 Hillsdale, NJ London

Published by
The Analytic Press, Inc., Publishers
Editorial Offices:
101 West Street
Hillsdale, New Jersey 07642
www.analyticpress.com

Designed and typeset by Compudesign, Charlottesville, VA

Index by Leonard S. Rosenbaum

Library of Congress Cataloging-in-Publication Data

Changing conceptions of psychoanalysis : the legacy of Merton M. Gill / edited by Doris K. Silverman and David L. Wolitzky.
p. cm.
Includes bibliographical references and index.
ISBN 0-88163-235-X
1. Psychoanalysis. 2. Gill, Merton Max, 1914-1994.
I. Silverman, Doris K. II. Wolitzky, David L.

RC506.C455 2000
616.89'17—dc21

00-046903

Printed in the United States of America
10 9 8 7 6 5 4 3 2 1

Contents

Contributors

Steven H. Cooper, Ph.D. is Training and Supervising Analyst, Boston Psychoanalytic Society and Institute, and Clinical Associate Professor of Psychology, Beth Israel Hospital, Harvard Medical School.

Morris N. Eagle, Ph.D. is Professor of Psychology, Derner Institute of Advanced Psychological Studies, Adelphi University, and Faculty, New York University Postdoctoral Program in Psychoanalysis and Psychotherapy.

Lawrence Friedman, M.D. is Clinical Professor of Psychiatry, Cornell University Medical College, and Faculty, New York Psychoanalytic Institute.

John E. Gedo, M.D., as author and editor, has contributed 18 volumes to the psychoanalytic literature.

Irwin Z. Hoffman, Ph.D. is Lecturer in Psychiatry, University of Illinois College of Medicine at Chicago, Faculty and Supervising Analyst, Chicago Center for Psychoanalysis, and author of *Ritual and Spontaneity in the Psychoanalytic Process* (TAP, 1998).

Robert R. Holt, Ph.D. is Professor of Psychology, Emeritus, New York University.

Philip S. Holzman, Ph.D. is Professor of Psychology, Emeritus, Harvard University.

Theodore J. Jacobs, M.D. is Clinical Professor of Psychiatry, Albert Einstein College of Medicine, and Training and Supervising Analyst, New York and New York University Psychoanalytic Institutes.

Otto F. Kernberg, M.D. is Director, Personality Disorders Institute, The New York Hospital-Cornell Medical Center, Westchester Division, and Training and Supervising Analyst, Columbia University Center for Psychoanalytic Training and Research.

Paolo Migone, M.D. teaches in the Department of Psychology, University of Parma, Italy, and is the author of *Terapia Psicoanalitica*.

Doris K. Silverman, Ph.D. is Training and Supervising Analyst and Faculty, Institute for Psychoanalytic Training and Research, and Supervisor and Faculty, New York University Postdoctoral Program in Psychotherapy and Psychoanalysis.

Henry F. Smith, M.D. is Training and Supervising Analyst, Psychoanalytic Institute of New England East, and Associate Editor, *Journal of the American Psychoanalytic Association*.

Robert S. Wallerstein, M.D. is Professor Emeritus and former Chairman, Department of Psychiatry, University of California San Francisco School of Medicine, and Training and Supervising Analyst, San Francisco Psychoanalytic Institute.

David L. Wolitzky, Ph.D. is Director, New York University Psychology Clinic, and Executive Committee Member, Faculty, and Supervisor, New York University Postdoctoral Program in Psychotherapy and Psychoanalysis.

PART I

MERTON GILL'S PLACE IN PSYCHOANALYSIS

Chapter 1

Gill's Influence on Psychoanalysis: An Introduction

David L. Wolitzky and Doris K. Silverman

I

Merton Max Gill was born in Chicago on July 26, 1914 and died there on November 13, 1994. His four score included a remarkable career in psychoanalysis. Gill's influence has been amply evident not only during the nearly half century of his illustrious career but it will endure for many generations. Thus, Gill will have a secure and distinguished place in the history of psychoanalysis. No one stated it more effectively than Wallerstein (1984): "It has been Merton Gill's fate to be an acknowledged leader in (American) psychoanalysis almost from the beginning of his career. An uncommon percentage of his writings have been almost instantly—and justly—hailed for their critical influence at particular points in the history of analysis in America, in relation both to psychoanalytic clinical practice . . . and to psychoanalytic theory formulation" (p. 325). He also cites several publications by Gill that clearly have become classics in the psychoanalytic literature.

It is evident that with Gill's death, psychoanalysis has lost one of its brightest stars. Gill illuminated in a most incisive, lucid manner several key controversies in psychoanalytic theory and practice. Our compilation of these essays in Gill's honor is timely, not merely as a tribute to him, but because the issues he wrote about are central to the current ferment in psychoanalysis.

We have invited contributions from a distinguished group of analysts whose work either reflects Gill's direct influence or who, by virtue of their own theoretical and clinical writings, are in a position to comment on Gill's contributions. Although many of the authors in this volume have an affinity with Gill's views, others will be critical. Gill enjoyed challenging discourse and appreciated a closely reasoned argument even if its author disagreed with him. In fact, we reminded the colleagues who contributed to this volume that the best way to honor Gill's memory would be to write critical and incisive analyses of the kind so characteristic of Gill on issues with which Gill passionately grappled. We hope the reader will agree that our contributors have met this challenge well.

As Hoffman (chapter 3) makes clear in his masterful summary of Gill's many contributions, Gill's work encompassed a variety of domains, including hypnosis, psychiatric interviewing, psychological testing, metapsychology, and clinical theory. We chose to restrict the focus of this volume to the issues that occupied Gill in the last two decades of his career rather than to include papers that span the entire range of his interests and contributions. In the case of Freudian metapsychology, for example, the controversy has virtually disappeared from the analytic literature, and Gill's position on this issue had a dominant influence on its demise.

In recent years, Gill was particularly focused on the nature of the transference and the psychoanalytic situation. Most of the contributors to this volume take up issues related to the concept of transference, the patient/analyst relationship, and the nature of the psychoanalytic situation. These issues continue to be most relevant to the current debates and controversies concerning effective strategies and techniques of psychoanalytic treatment. They also are related to broader philosophical, epistemological considerations. Accordingly, we have included contributions that are germane to these more general concerns (see particularly chapters 5 through 9, by Holt, Eagle, Friedman, Jacobs, and Silverman, respectively).

In the last two decades of his work, Gill repeatedly emphasized that the interpretation of the transference, as he conceived it, was vital for effective treatment and that it should be the defining characteristic of psychoanalysis. He argued that transference was unwittingly overlooked or insufficiently explored in clinical work. Gill's conceptualization of the transference emphasized the interaction of the patient and the analyst as a relationship of mutual influence. Gill forcefully rejected the idea that the analyst had a superior view of the patient's intrapsychic reality and that the transference was a distortion to be judged and corrected by the analyst. He stressed instead the exploration of the plausibility of the patient's construal of the analyst. Gill believed that his view was consistent with a hermeneutic-constructivist position. In addition to embracing this philosophical position, Gill abhorred the notion of distortion because it implied that an analyst who held this view was engaged in an authoritarian manipulation of the patient and would be less likely to acknowledge that the patient was being influenced by something real in the analyst. We know, based on our interactions with him and on his published work, that Gill encountered enough rigidity, arrogance, and pomposity among his analytic colleagues during (and after) his formative analytic years to have little tolerance for an attitude that suggests that the analyst has a lock on the truth. Our information is bolstered by Hoffman's (1996a) remarks in his tribute to Gill during the February 10, 1995 memorial service for Merton:

> I think we have to understand that Merton was on a mission. Something bothered him about the way psychoanalysts worked and thought about their work. . . . Although he couched his concerns in scientific, theoretical terms, I believe that Merton's impression of mainstream psychoanalytic practice violated his sense of values. He felt that analysts had a great deal of power in the analytic situation and that, all too often, they unwittingly abused that power instead of trying to reduce it and/or to exercise it in a fully responsible and helpful way. I think Merton felt that this abuse of power was thoroughly institutionalized and rationalized theoretically so that it became very difficult to bring it to light and subject it to critical scrutiny. Under the guises of the blank screen, of the transference as a simple distortion, of the rule of abstinence, of the claim of analytic neutrality, of a one-person psychology . . . what Merton found was one human being who was in a position of authority blaming another who was in a subordinate position for everything that developed in their relationship that was problematic. Whatever went wrong, the analyst could so easily come up smelling like a rose. But what Merton smelled in this scenario was a rat, a subtle form of domination [pp. 28–29].

Chapter 7 by Friedman and chapter 14 by Wolitzky take up this theme and its implications.

From this perspective, one can appreciate that Gill preferred the notion of plausibility rather than distortion in characterizing the patient's reaction, that he emphasized the coconstruction of the transference, and that he found a two-person, social-contructivist view conceptually appealing. In this connection, he was pleased to quote Racker (1968) who said:

> The first distortion of truth in the myth of the analytic situation is that it is an interaction between a sick person and a healthy one. The truth is that it is an interaction between two personalities in both of which the ego is under pressure from the id, the superego, and the external world; each personality has its internal and external dependencies, anxieties, and pathological defenses; each is also a child with his internal parents; and each of the whole personalities—that of the analysand and that of the analyst—responds to every event of the analytic situation [p. 132].

At the same time, Smith (in chapter 2) cites Gill's comment that "it also reminds me . . . of what I think is one of Sullivan's very interesting remarks where he said: 'There are two anxious people in the room; it is to be hoped that the therapist is the less anxious of the two.'"

Given the views stated above, exclusive reliance on a so-called "one-person" psychology was untenable. In his final book, however, Gill recognized the importance of unconscious fantasy and, therefore, the necessity for both a one-person and a two-person psychology. As he (Gill, 1994) put it, "It remains true that the great discovery peculiar to psychoanalysis, the internal factor in the sense of unconscious fantasy, is the one that psychoanalysis must zealously protect" (p. 28). Richards and Lynch (1996) take up this point in trying to locate Gill's views within the context of contemporary psychoanalytic theory, and Silverman's essay addresses it in this book.

In the broadest sense, this book is about the ways to conceptualize the nature of the psychoanalytic situation, the analytic interaction, and the nature of motivation. Thus, the chapters range over issues such as the optimal ambience of the analytic interaction; the role of interpretation and insight; the conceptualization, function, and handling of the transference; the significance of the analyst as an old and a new object, the proper mode of analytic listening; and the interactive, intersubjective nature of the therapeutic relationship. Each contributor focuses on one or more of these factors in presenting a view of what facilitates or impedes therapeutic change in psychoanalysis. We believe that this collection of essays offers a representative sampling of many of the key current issues in psychoanalytic theory and practice.

Although Gill himself never presented a fully explicit, systematic theory of all the components of the therapeutic action of psychoanalysis, his writings on the subject provide a model of personality change. The model seems to contain the following propositions:

1. The patient and the analyst are in a constant, ongoing interaction in which each participant influences the other.
2. Treatment is effective to the extent that the analyst, right from the start, is attuned to and interprets both the patient's explicit references to his or her experience of the relationship and, especially, indirect allusions to the relationship. He stressed, in particular, the analyst's sense of what the patient senses that the analyst feels toward the patient.
3. He emphasized that these interpretations should focus primarily on the here-and-now transference and address the patient's resistance to both the awareness of the transference and the resolution of the transference.
4. He stressed that the analyst should be (a) especially alert to link the patient's experience of the relationship (a phrase Gill used as a synonym for transference) to some aspect of the analyst's behavior (i.e., to recognize its plausibility) and (b) acutely aware of the interpersonal and intrapsychic meanings to the patient. Gill stressed the transference meanings of the form and content of the interpretation as well as the fact that the analyst made an interpretation. One must keep in mind that interpretation is a form of interaction and that the

analyst must be aware of the "very common phenomenon of the enactment in interpretation of the very issue which is interpreted" (Gill and Hoffman, 1982, p. 91).

5. The ambience of the therapeutic situation is vital.

Thus, it is essential that the analyst believe and convey that the interpretation is offered tentatively and is not presented as a final truth. The analyst must refrain from maintaining a position as the authority who will definitively correct the patient's distorted perceptions.

II

The five sections in Part II (chapter 2) are devoted to appreciations and reminiscences ranging from the mostly personal to the mostly professional/scientific, drawn from different sources. The first three sections (by Wallerstein, Holzman, and Holt) were presented at a memorial service for Merton that was organized by his widow, Ilse Judas, at the Department of Psychiatry, University of Illinois, February 10, 1995. These eulogies, along with several other moving remembrances of Merton, were published in the *Annual of Psychoanalysis* (Winer, 1996). Wallerstein's remarks also appeared as Gill's official obituary in the *International Journal of Psycho-Analysis* (Wallerstein, 1995).

Because the sections in chapter 2 (as well as the material in chapter 3) were not written specifically for this book, they contain inevitable overlap and repetition of biographical details. We ask the reader's understanding of this redundancy.

For many years, Gill was a cherished member of the Rapaport-Klein Study Group, a group of friends and colleagues of David Rapaport and George Klein who met annually at the Austen Riggs Center in Stockbridge, Massachusetts. They presented papers and exchanged views on current issues in research and theory relevant to psychoanalysis. The comments by Friedman (in chapter 2) and the essay by Silverman (chapter 9, also published in *Psychoanalytic Psychology*, 1996) were presented at a memorial tribute to Gill at the June 1995 meeting of the Rapaport-Klein Study Group.

The tributes to Gill from three of his closest friends and colleagues, Robert Holt, Philip Holzman, and Robert Wallerstein, reflect longstanding relationships of mutual affection and respect. Their friendships with Merton, and with one another, date back to their time together at the Menninger Foundation in Topeka, Kansas in the late 1940s and early 1950s. This period can be considered to be the Golden Era of American Ego Psychology, under the leadership of David Rapaport. It included such luminaries, in addition to Holt, Holzman, and Wallerstein, as George

Klein, Margaret Brenman, Lester Luborsky, Benjamin Rubinstein, Roy Schafer, Otto Kernberg, and Sybille Escalona, to name some of the most prominent. With the possible exception of a brief period when Erik Erikson was at the Austen Riggs Center in Stockbridge, Massachusetts, there never has been such a concentration of outstanding psychoanalytic thinkers in one institution. Especially noteworthy is that these psychoanalysts were not content with extending and elaborating Freudian theory but on subjecting it to a most critical reading and analysis and, where possible, on using it as a framework for empirical investigation. It is not surprising that this group produced numerous papers that exposed the limitations and errors in Freudian metapsychology. As Hoffman, Gill's close friend and collaborator in recent years, makes clear, Merton was at the forefront of such critiques. Holt, Holzman, and Wallerstein present portraits of Merton that capture his essential features in a way that will strike a warm and responsive chord in those who had the privilege and good fortune to know him. The material presented by Smith and by Friedman will also convey a good deal about Merton's attitudes and approach to psychoanalysis.

All of the contributors to this volume knew Gill personally. Some had a friendship with him that extended over many decades. Thus, in more informal ways, they are able to comment on some of Gill's personal attitudes and qualities as they influenced the positions he took over the years. In this connection, we should point out that on a few occasions Gill was interviewed in a manner that allowed for an informal, wide-ranging expression of his views (Gill, 1982, 1991; Raymond and Rosbrow-Reich, 1997). We recommend the interested reader read these interviews because they capture directly the nature of his personality, in particular his incisive wit and his hatred of pretension.

We know these eulogies and commentaries do not sufficiently capture the complex, multifaceted aspects of this charismatic man, who was particularly engaging. He was earthy and funny and deeply attached and committed to those he loved and admired. He was biting and brilliant, sensual and seriously intellectual, vibrant and moody. He cared passionately about psychoanalytic issues and devoted himself relentlessly to writing and speaking about his beliefs. With his logical, incisive mind coupled with a sonorous voice and compelling articulate persuasiveness, he commanded great attention and respect in the psychoanalytic community and he attracted a large following of interested students and colleagues.

Part III contains Hoffman's comprehensive overview of Gill's many contributions (chapter 3) followed by a complete bibliography of Gill's writings and a listing of some of his awards (chapter 4). The range and productivity of the man are impressive. Furthermore, as noted above, several of Gill's publications have become classics in the field.

For the most part, the chapters in Part IV can be grouped under several related themes or headings: "Natural Science and the Hermeneutic Orientation: The Debate" (chapter 5, Holt; chapter 6, Eagle; chapter 7, Friedman); "Psychoanalysis as a One-Person and a Two-Person Psychology" (chapter 8, Jacobs; chapter 9, Silverman); "Psychoanalysis and Psychoanalytic Psychotherapy: Critical Differences or Blurring of Boundaries?" (chapter 10, Wallerstein; chapter 11, Migone; chapter 12, Gedo); and "Transference" (chapter 13, Kernberg; chapter 14, Wolitzky; chapter 15, Cooper). The editors offer an introductory commentary on each of the chapters.

Nine of the 11 chapters in Part IV are original contributions; the remaining two contributions (Wallerstein's and Silverman's) are previously published articles directly relevant to Gill's work.

III

In concluding this introduction, we wish to note the nature of our relationship to Gill and our interest in undertaking this project. We both got to know Merton over the many years of our attendance at the meetings of the Rapaport-Klein Study Group. It was inspiring to discuss issues of theory and technique with him and to observe his incisive wit and conceptual clarity in his comments on many presentations. In addition, one of us (DLW) had the good fortune of seeing him regularly during the two years (1970 and 1971) he was on the staff of the Research Center for Mental Health, which at the time was part of the Department of Psychology at New York University. For these two years, Merton was a Special NIMH Fellow focusing on methods for the intensive study of audio-recorded psychoanalyses. Although there were obvious ethical issues to be dealt with, Gill was interested in devising methods to study the differential impact of interpretations, which were (or were not) deliberately focused on the transference. In the context of this work, he would play portions of a tape-recorded analysis and a group of us would rate various aspects of the patient's material. These weekly research meetings afforded me (DLW) an invaluable opportunity to learn how a senior clinician conducted an analysis, an experience that often surpassed what I learned through ordinary supervision. I (DLW) derived enormous benefit from impromptu supervisory sessions with Merton. We discussed clinical and theoretical issues that rarely emerged in my formal control case supervision.

Finally, we note there are a few people who were vitally important in Merton's personal and professional life whose contributions are not reflected in this volume. First and foremost is Ilse Judas, not only Merton's loving and devoted wife for many years, but also a person who staunchly supported and contributed to his intellectual endeavors.

Perhaps no person was as essential to Merton's development as a psychoanalytic theorist as his beloved mentor and close friend, David Rapaport. At a memorial meeting devoted to reminiscences about David Rapaport, Merton was movingly evocative in his recall of the importance of this man in his life. Gill appreciated Rapaport's immersion in Jewish humor, his monumental scholarly interests, his disciplined work ethic, his vitality, and his nourishment of colleagues and students in the field, qualities that had a profound impact on Gill. In their summary of Rapaport's contributions to psychoanalysis and psychology, Gill and his coauthor George S. Klein wrote about colleagues "who owe their intellectual momentum to his ideas" (Gill, 1967, p. 31) and Gill clearly was one of these colleagues.

It was at the Menninger Foundation, under the aegis of Rapaport, that Gill found an affinity with many psychologists, including George Klein, Robert Holt, Philip Holzman, Margaret Brenman, and Roy Schafer, among others. One scholarly outcome of these associations was his collaboration with Rapaport and Schafer on the now classic, two-volume text *Diagnostic Psychological Testing* (Rapaport, Gill, and Schafer, 1945–1946).

Margaret Brenman was a close, life-long colleague who collaborated with him on their pioneering studies of hypnosis. Hartvig Dahl, a dedicated psychoanalytic researcher, had a long, fruitful, intellectual dialogue with Merton. We are confident that Gill certainly would acknowledge his personal and intellectual debt to them as well as to others of whom we may not be aware.

We have reserved for separate mention Merton's close, special relationship to Irwin Z. Hoffman, clearly his most important collaborator in the last two decades of his life. Jointly, they developed a coding scheme to evaluate the patients' allusions to the transference and published papers on this topic as well as on the nature of the analytic situation and the transference. It is apparent that Gill was enormously impressed by and influenced by Hoffman's independent contributions, particularly Hoffman's social constructivist (now called dialectical constructivistism [Hoffman, 1998]) view of the analytic situation. In his interview with Raymond and Rosbrow-Reich (1997), Gill repeatedly praised Hoffman as his mentor in conceptualizing the nature of the psychoanalytic situation. It is therefore especially fitting that we include in this volume Hoffman's previously published, lucid overview of Gill's contributions (Hoffman, 1985, 1996b).

REFERENCES

Gill, M. M. (1967). *The Collected Papers of David Rapaport*. New York: Basic Books.

Gill, M. M. (1982). Merton Gill: An interview. *Psychoanal. Rev.*, 69:167–190.

Gill, M. M. (1991). Merton Gill speaks his mind. *Amer. Psychoanal.*, 25:17–21.

Gill, M. M. (1994). *Psychoanalysis in Transition*. Hillsdale, NJ: The Analytic Press.

Gill, M. M. & Hoffman, I. Z. (1982). Analysis of transference: Vol. II, Studies of nine audio-recorded psychoanalytic sessions. *Psychological Issues*, 54. New York: International Universities Press.

Hoffman, I. Z. (1985). Merton M. Gill: A study in theory development in psychoanalysis. In: *Beyond Freud*, ed. J. Reppen. Hillsdale, NJ: The Analytic Press.

Hoffman, I. Z. (1996a). Creativity and integrity in the final decades. *The Annual of Psychoanalysis*, 24. Hillsdale, NJ: The Analytic Press.

Hoffman, I. Z. (1996b). Merton M. Gill: A study in theory development in psychoanalysis. *Psychoanal. Dial.*, 6:5–53.

Hoffman, I. Z. (1998). *Ritual and Spontaneity in the Psychoanalytic Process*. Hillsdale, NJ: The Analytic Press.

Racker, H. (1968). *Transference and Countertransference*. New York: International Universities Press.

Rapaport, D., Gill, M. M., & Schafer, R. (1945–46). *Diagnostic Psychological Testing*. Chicago: Yearbook Publishers.

Raymond, L. W. & Rosbrow-Reich, S. R. (1997). *The Inward Eye*. Hillsdale, NJ: The Analytic Press, pp. 209–240.

Richards, A. D. & Lynch, A. (1996). Merton Gill: A view of his place in the "Freudian" firmament. *The Annual of Psychoanalysis*, 24. Hillsdale, NJ: The Analytic Press.

Wallerstein, R. S. (1984). The analysis of the transference: A matter of emphasis or of theory reformulation? *Psychoanal. Inq.*, 4:325–354.

Wallerstein, R. S. (1995), *Internat. J. Psycho-Anal.*, 76, Part 2, 399–402.

Winer, J., ed. (1996). *The Annual of Psychoanalysis*, 24. Hillsdale, NJ: The Analytic Press.

PART II

PERSONAL/PROFESSIONAL REMINISCENCES

Chapter 2

Merton M. Gill: Reminiscences

Editors' Introduction: *As noted in our introductory chapter, the five sections of this chapters are tributes to Gill, drawn from several sources.*

Section One: *Merton Max Gill, M.D.*

Robert S. Wallerstein

Merton Gill occupied a unique place in my intellectual and emotional scheme of things: as close friend and colleague, as scientific ideal and moral gadfly, and as research mentor and supporter, albeit—despite mutual wishes that would have had it otherwise—we never worked collaboratively in the same setting. I first met Merton in the early 1950s—now more than four decades ago—when I, at the very start of my career as a psychotherapy researcher, was fashioning, together with some colleagues, what evolved into the very massive and ambitious 30-year-long Psychotherapy Research Project of The Menninger Foundation and was applying to the Foundation's Fund for Research in Psychiatry for my first extramural grant funding. Merton, whom I knew then only through his early writings on psychotherapy and psychoanalysis, which had indeed played a signal role in the conceptual organization of our project, came as one of the site visitors. He was then, at our first meeting, his characteristically incisive, lucid, probing, at times acerbic and uncomfortably probing, but always at the same time, curiously respectful self. After the visit, none of us could be sure of Merton's intellectual take on the project, but in due course, we were informed that we were awarded the grant that helped launch our project on its long career. It was this show of confidence by Merton in what I could produce that continued to mark and help to sustain my whole future research career, as when years later, in 1966, I left Topeka and my active directorship of the still ongoing research program in order to take up my continuing career in San Francisco, and yet somehow still carry out my commitment to the final clinical accounting of the

---

Reprinted by permission from the *International Journal of Psycho-Analysis* (1995, Volume 76, Part 2, pp. 399–402).

work and the results of this psychotherapy research project. That is, my book, *Forty-Two Lives in Treatment*, the chronicle of this 30-year-long research program, was at that time only a dream for the future, and it was Merton's continuing faith that I would not shirk or disappoint this task that not only helped enable me to accomplish it, but required that I do so. Incidentally, it was also Merton who suggested the title of the book, but the account of that amusing vignette would be too long a digression here.

From that first encounter in the early 1950s, Merton and I had become fast friends and intellectual comrades in arms, though he was always also the older one who helped light the conceptual path of our side-by-side pursuit of the science and the research potential of psychoanalysis. I followed all his writings carefully and through his various, at times, drastic, reversals of field, and always learned from them, even when I also, at times, sharply disagreed. It is this ongoing response to Merton's work that prompted me to begin an invited critical appraisal of his 1982 monograph on the *Analysis of Transference*, for a 1984 issue of the journal, *Psychoanalytic Inquiry*, with an admiring paragraph locating him and his influence in American psychoanalysis—in my view—as follows:

> It has been Merton Gill's fate to be an acknowledged leader in (American) psychoanalysis almost from the beginning of his career. An uncommon percentage of his writings have been almost instantly—and justly—hailed for their critical influence at particular points in the history of analysis in America, in relation both to psychoanalytic clinical practice (and its relation to the derivative dynamic psychotherapies) and to psychoanalytic theory formulation (in the ascendancy and then the decline of ego psychology—the apotheosis of metapsychology). Witness the 1954 paper, "Psychoanalysis and Exploratory Psychotherapy," which (together with Edward Bibring's essay of the same year) more than any other contributions from the various panels and symposia of 1952–1954 set our understanding of the nature of psychoanalysis as a therapy, in all its similarities to and differences from the congeries of dynamic psychotherapies elaborated within its framework. Or consider the 1959 paper coauthored with David Rapaport, "The Points of View and Assumptions of Metapsychology," which so concisely defined and capped the full elaboration of the metapsychological points of view including the co-equal placement among them of the adaptive point of view. Consider the 1963 monograph in the *Psychological Issues* series, *Topography and Systems in Psychoanalytic Theory*, the ultimate extension of the metapsychological theory-building advanced over lifetimes by Hartmann and by Rapaport. Or, consider finally, the 1976 paper, "Metapsychology Is Not Psychology," in which Gill joined the revisionist retreat seeking to dismantle the metapsychological edifice and return psychoanalytic theorizing to an experi-

> ence-near focus on just its special or clinical theory—as opposed to the to-be-excised general or metapsychological theory. Curiously, the signal influence of each of these successive landmark contributions has endured despite Gill's own subsequent turning away from and even disavowing positions that he had so persuasively earlier espoused [pp. 325–326].

And so it has also been with the monograph on the *Analysis of Transference*, which was the occasion for the critique from which the remarks I have just quoted are drawn and with the series of papers with his Chicago colleague and collaborator, Irwin Hoffman, on the interactional aspects of the psychoanalytic situation as reflections of a psychoanalytic two-body psychology, eventuating in the now comprehensively articulated constructivist perspective in psychoanalysis propounded by Hoffman, and so I am confident it will be with Merton's final capstone book, *Psychoanalysis in Transition*, which represents the elaboration of the full evolution of Gill's psychoanalytic thinking over the half-century of his active scholarship—a book for which I was writing a review for the *Journal of the American* when his widow, the Chicago psychoanalyst Dr. Ilse Judas, called to notify me of his death.

This lifetime sequence of landmark contributions to our psychoanalytic theoretical and clinical corpus emerged over the course of a professional career lived out in a series of major psychoanalytic centers, from The Menninger Foundation in Topeka, Kansas (1941–48), where Merton received both his psychiatric and psychoanalytic training and coauthored with Margaret Brenman a book on hypnotherapy, and with Rapaport and Schafer the massive two volume *Diagnostic Psychological Testing*, creating a milestone battery of projective psychological diagnostic tests; then through a five-year sequence (1948–53) at the Austen Riggs Center in Stockbridge, Massachusetts, as part of the brilliant galaxy clustered there in those halcyon days, and at the Yale University Department of Psychiatry and the then-fledgling Western New England Psychoanalytic Society and Institute; followed by a decade of combined private practice and organized psychotherapy research in the San Francisco Bay Area (this from 1953–63) where Merton came fully into his own as psychoanalytic clinician, educator, theorist, and systematic psychotherapy researcher; followed then by six years as a Research Career Professor of Psychiatry at the Downstate Medical Center in Brooklyn, New York, and two subsequent years as a special National Institute of Mental Health Fellow at the Research Center for Mental Health at New York University, during which overall span in New York (1963–71) Merton undertook, with a group of collaborators, the systematic microanalytic research study of the entire sequence of hours of an audiotaped and visually observed psychoanalysis that he conducted; and into his finally settled and long career in Chicago from 1971 until his death as an NIMH Research Scientist Awardee and as Professor of Psychiatry at the Abraham Lincoln School of Medicine of the University of Illinois in Chicago where both his later theoretical articles (and revisions) and his continuing research inquiries and fruitful partnership with Irwin Hoffman all took place. Across this peripatetic, but always intensely productive, scholarly career, Merton invigorated and challenged the intellectual life of a succession of psychoanalytic communities—Topeka, Western New England, San Francisco, New York, and finally Chicago—and garnered much recognition and many honors. Among the latter were the I. Arthur Marshall Distinguished Alumnus Award of the Menninger School of Psychiatry in 1976; the Heinz Hartmann Award of the New York Psychoanalytic Society in 1992; and, most recently, one of the 1994 Mary S. Sigourney Awards for Outstanding Contributions to Psychoanalysis, announced to him during his period of terminal illness and accepted posthumously for him by Ilse Judas.

Thus a kaleidoscopic but highly condensed account of Merton Gill the psychoanalyst. But what of Merton Gill, the man and my friend? Merton had one of the sharpest minds and sharpest tongues that I have been privileged to know, but the latter was not invoked in personal attack on people, just on ideas. It is often said of such individuals that they do not suffer fools easily; in Merton's case, it was foolishness he did not suffer easily. To me, the paradigm illustration of Merton in action as incisive thinker and intellectual illuminator took place in the early 1970s when I was the first chairman of the American Psychoanalytic Association's newly created Committee on Scientific Activities and Merton and Heinz Kohut were among the initial group of members. Merton and Heinz would tend to sit opposite each other, flanking me, engaged tenaciously in the committee's first task, the clarification, for ourselves, of how we understood our charge and how we conceived of psychoanalysis as science and of psychoanalytic research as an activity. All of us who were party to the provocative fireworks of those discussions have carried ever since an indelible memory of having participated in a very moving intellectual adventure, and this same capacity continued undiminished until Merton's death. In recent years, our chief contact has occurred through Merton's active participation in the semiannual all-day dialogues within the research consortium that I have organized under the aegis of the American Psychoanalytic Association, the Collaborative Analytic Multi-Site Program of process and outcome psychoanalytic therapy research. Though no longer an active hands-on researcher, Merton was always a most attentive and probing and often disconcerting participant. The group had its most recent usual December meeting in New York shortly after Merton's death, and he was sorely missed, both his contribution and his undaunted spirit.

But Merton was also a kindly and even a sentimental man, endearing and lovable through his often matter-of-fact or even, at times, seemingly gruff demeanor. My wife Judy and I had two occasions of brief travel together in Europe with Merton and his longtime partner Ilse Judas. The first was in Italy in 1969 after the Rome IPA Congress of that year, when we happened to meet in Tuscany and shared some days together with a special highlighted visit to Pisa. The second was in England in 1975 after the London IPA Congress, when we again chanced to meet, this time in York while exploring its magnificent cathedral, and again spent some time together. This was Merton relaxed and carefree and truly happy in ways that were rare to see, and here his gracious, and kindly, and sentimental side could come to the fore.

This was for me an important perspective because, as by now a longtime friend, I had come to know that Merton, with all his accomplishments and all his recognitions and all his honors, also had a difficult and, at times, very painful personal life. He had two earlier marriages that ended unhappily before settling down over the last thirty years with Ilse Judas, whom he had first met when he was a young man in college; she had come to America as a teenage refugee from Hitler and had been taken in and raised by Merton's family in Milwaukee. Throughout his troubled life, Merton was beset by episodes of deep and incapacitating depression, of total despair for himself and for any future, and yet from each of these, he finally bounced back with undiminished resilience and intensity and commitment to a life of the mind at its fullest that was truly a marvel to behold. I have had the occasion and the opportunity to visit with Merton in each of the opposite extremes of his life. He had also over recent years suffered severe and progressive cardiac disease, which led him to cease accepting professional speaking invitations lest the happenstances of his health not permit him to fulfill the commitment at the appointed time.

My own last visit with Merton took place during his final bout of severe illness covering the span of several months. I was visiting in Chicago this past October and knew that Merton had been ill and hospitalized since the summer, and I arranged to visit him, now back in his home, during that Chicago trip. It was less than two weeks before he succumbed, though I had no inkling at the time that death was so imminent. We tried to speak hopefully about the future, I with my eternal optimism, about his return to his active life and to continued participation with our research consortium. I told him what I have said to very few, that I loved him, and I was moved that he expressed the same in return. The next I heard was the telephone call the day of his death. He was one of the heroes of all of American psychoanalysis, not just a hero of mine. I, along with many others, will always miss him. In addition to his wife Ilse Judas, Merton is survived by five children and stepchildren, five grandchildren, and two brothers.

Section Two: *Merton Gill: Teacher, Scholar, Friend*

Philip S. Holzman

The obituary notice in *The New York Times* on November 19, 1994, while respectful, seemed, like all such notices, a bit stony and cold. "Merton Max Gill," it read, "an academic psychoanalyst, died on Sunday at Rush-Presbyterian-St. Luke's Medical Center in Chicago. Dr. Gill, who lived in Chicago, was 80 years old." We are obliged here to fill in the color, the warmth, the intensity, the zealousness, the humor, the uninhibited exuberance, the moodiness, and the sheer brilliance of this man who was first and always my teacher, but also my good friend. And in this process we explore what his life meant for us and for the profession he so passionately served and believed in.

My first encounter with Merton occurred in Topeka in 1946. Some people burst upon the scene with an indelible identifying quality. With Groucho, it was his slouchy walk; with FDR, it was his jaunty smile of confidence. With Merton, it was his resonant, baritone voice that commanded immediate attention. To me, as a 24-year-old student at the Menninger Foundation's newly established School of Clinical Psychology and fresh out of the U.S. Army, Merton's was the instant and immediate stentorian voice of authority, without benefit of any military rank—and with what authority he spoke. But at that time, he also inspired fear in me and in many of my fellow students who took a course in hypnosis from him—until one revealing and defining occasion, when he publicly shamed me. You remember that he and Margaret Brenman were then the reigning experts on hypnotherapy. On that day, we were reviewing the literature on hypnosis, and I had read a paper by du Bois Reymond, which Merton asked me to summarize and comment on in class. Now, in the Army, I was in a company with a lieutenant named du Bois, which he pronounced "du Boys." I proceeded to call du Bois Reymond "du Boys Reymond." Merton stopped me and asked in his deepest stentorian tones, "Du Boys? Du Boys?" The class, of course, broke out into gales of laughter, and I broke into a paroxysm of blushing. I tried to explain the source of my error in pronunciation and added something like, "So I made him more American than he really was." Then Merton hinted a smile of understanding, thus revealing to me a side of him I had not suspected until then. At that instant, I remember feeling that he was softer than he had first come across to me.

Indeed, he was softer, and he was also a very funny man. He could tell jokes extremely well. Merton had few peers in his capacity for telling the ethnic Jewish joke, sometimes told completely in fluent Yiddish, and he

---

Based on a eulogy delivered at a Memorial Service, February 10, 1995, University of Illinois, Department of Psychiatry.

was able to quip and retort spontaneously in ways that highlighted the humor in almost any situation. One quality stands out about his humor. In spite of my initial encounter over du Bois Reymond, his humor was seldom *ad hominem*. He tended not to ridicule people. Rather he ridiculed ideas, positions, and movements, but not people. He was too unyieldingly respectful of people to poke fun at them or their frailties or to retaliate for an attack on him.

It was through the Rapaport-Klein Study Group that I got to know him as a friend and colleague. When David Rapaport was still alive, Merton and I dreamed up the idea of gathering together, once a year, Rapaport's students and colleagues to discuss the widening range of their ideas. The occasion was to have been Rapaport's 50th birthday. But when David died at 49 in December of 1960, we, together with George Klein, pushed this idea into a reality. Every June, we would meet in Stockbridge for two days of exhilarating discussions about psychoanalysis or about ideas that were touched by psychoanalytic thought. Merton's comments inevitably contained his stylistic stamp: they were logical, incisive, and to the point. His points always advanced the discussion, deepened it, and probed its limits, and if there were any slippage in logic on the part of a presenter at these meetings, Merton was usually the first to pounce on the offense, but not the offender, although it might not have seemed that way to some offenders.

To be near Ilse, Merton moved to Chicago in 1971. What a gift to the intellectual life of Chicago's psychoanalytic community that was! Before his move, he used to be clean-shaven, except for an on-again, off-again moustache. Now he sported a beard that gave him the visage of both Hemingway and Freud, a romancer and a visionary, at times that of a Hebrew prophet, but one with twinkling eye and therefore the humor that those stern prophets did not have. I don't know who understood the reason for this transformation, for only a very few were privy to the deeper and the darker secrets of his inner self.

Ann and I and Ilse and Merton, at our house or at Ilse's, shared evenings in lively discussions, sometimes replete with controversy. Ilse showed herself to be a gracious and generous hostess and arranged a number of splendid parties, including a memorable one for Merton's 60th birthday, which brought together many of his friends from all over the country.

He brought with him from New York his burning interest in the process of analysis. He was among the first to advocate the recording of psychoanalytic sessions in order to be able to read and reread them and, by this exposure to objective scrutiny, to understand the nature of the therapeutic process. In his early efforts while still in New York, he tried experimenting with types of interpretations, "correct" and "incorrect," to observe their effects on the process. He soon gave up this method as too manipulative and as quixotic and even antithetical to the therapeutic endeavor. After he had settled in Chicago, Merton began an analysis with

Samuel Lipton, one of the unsung giants of our profession, who had an enormous influence on him. From Sam he learned a new perspective on the centrality of the transference in analytic practice.

We met frequently in those days, and we found that we could talk together about psychoanalytic issues quite apart from psychoanalytic gossip. Both of us were sufficiently versed in and awed by received psychoanalytic doctrine yet sufficiently irreverent and defiant of authority that we could question and probe the doctrine, but each of us in our own way. We decided to meet regularly to discuss the process of psychoanalysis and, especially, Merton's developing ideas about the centrality of the analysis of the transference. The setting for this series of meetings, which lasted until 1977, when I left Chicago, was my house on 57th Street in Hyde Park. We met regularly on Monday evenings. Ann, my wife, prepared lovely dinners, and the three of us dined, sometimes joined by one of our children. The dinners were usually the occasion for discussing politics and our families. Merton spoke with great warmth and respect about his children, and we also shared the latest jokes we had heard.

We rarely spoke about professional issues at the dinner table, but once the two of us retired to the living room, we left the jokes and the outside world behind and immersed ourselves in the recorded psychoanalytic sessions. We poured over them, scrutinizing them for meaning with reference to the relationship that was unfolding between analyst and analysand. The ideas of "resistance to the awareness of the transference" and "resistance to the resolution of the transference" became frequent and familiar as we went through the transcripts. These were heady times, full of immersion in the psychoanalytic dialogue, redolent with the promise of pressing forward to new insights into the complexity of dynamic interactions. In these meetings, Merton developed the ideas, influenced principally by Sam Lipton's spiritual presence, of first clarifying the extratransferential allusions and experiences in order to understand the transference embedded in them. Next, it was important to raise the transference interactions and fantasies to awareness and, third, to work through the transferential dynamic interplay that had been put on the analytic agenda. This emphasis on what has been called "the here and now" received renewed vigor from Merton's formulations.

These discussions gave Merton permission for unbridled release of theoretical formulations that were sheltered from public criticism. They were also fun. Merton made the most of them, fashioning a set of rating scales to give some objective frame to the interpretative gloss on the psychoanalytic transcripts. Our scientific temperaments, however, were not completely congruent. I was no match for Merton's brilliance in penetrating to the essence of the meaning of the psychoanalytic transactions and his articulateness in formulating the dramatic plot that unfolded in the therapeutic interview. He was dazzling, and I learned so much from him that

I scarcely know how to enumerate the many ways he influenced my own therapeutic practice. My own temperament called for a modicum of empiricism to season the theory. Often, at the end of an evening of poring over a transcript, I would urge him to institute a study to find out what difference it made to focus on the resistance to the recognition of the transference, the early heightening of the relationship issues, and the other innovations he formulated. Do these interventions make detectable differences in outcome, however one wanted to measure that event? Merton resisted that call for testing.

We skirmished over the need for extraanalytic verifications and proofs. I would raise Einstein's objection to psychoanalysis that there is always the nagging and persistent doubt about the validity of Freud's bold intellectual constructions. "It is the old song," Einstein wrote, "of the indispensability and at the same time the untrustworthiness of introspections."[1] But Merton would brush that aside. His concern was with the unfolding interpersonal dynamics that illuminated the present and the past, yet he never disparaged my empirical thrust.

I often thought that, if I had stayed in Chicago, we might have instituted such a study because, although Merton was a man who defended his positions vigorously, he was never closed to alternatives. I have seen him many times change his mind when the weight of evidence suggested to him that his previous position may have been wrong. This was the case when he changed his mind about his classic 1958 paper with Rapaport on "The Points of View and Assumptions of Metapsychology" and his 1963 monograph on *Topography and Systems in Psychoanalytic Theory*. His immersion in the labyrinthine complexities of metapsychology and of the psychoanalytic process represented a major part of his intellectual world. The 1958 paper was a *tour de force* of integration, a masterful and concise summary of the sprawling metapsychology, creatively distilled into fewer than 15 pages. The monograph explored the concepts of consciousness, preconscious, and unconscious as systems and their relation to the quality of mental contents and to the issue of the viability of a separate topographic point of view. Then, after having taken these ideas about as far as he could (and perhaps almost anyone could), he became convinced that this kind of metapsychological exploration was not only a dead end, but was the wrong path for psychoanalysis to take. He shifted his position and became highly critical of his previous ideas. When George Klein died, Merton and I produced, in George's memory, *Psychology Versus Metapsychology*, a book that was a commodious critique of metapsychology. Merton's loyalty was to probing for truth, and if he understood that he was wrong, he would change

---

[1] Letter to O. Lobbenberg from A. Einstein, February 12, 1950, in Archives of Hebrew University, Archive # 60341. Permission granted by the Albert Einstein Archives, the Hebrew University of Jerusalem.

accordingly. I consider this quality a defining strength of Merton's intellect.

His efforts were hardy, persistent, and truly heroic, and many was the time that they were accomplished while he was suffering from one of his physical ailments or one of his crippling depressions, from which it surely seemed to him that he might never emerge. Still, during these black periods, his intellect was as rapier sharp as always, and somehow, miraculously, he was able to concentrate on the intellectual topic at hand. Even at the end of his life, his body already subdued by the disease that would soon completely claim him, he produced another major book on his work, one that is sure to be as influential as his previous works. I marvel at the strength, durability, and toughness of his mind.

One of his major characteristics was directness. One could count on him to be plain spoken and candid, in that deep voice that went directly to the point. During one of the seders at Ilse's house, he interpolated an intellectual argument he felt compelled to take up with us. There is a prayer in which the reader praises and thanks God for many things, including having chosen the Jews above all other people. Merton paused after reading this passage about the chosen people and, in his orotund, clear voice—indicating that he was always reflecting on what he was saying—announced to us, "That phrase always made me uncomfortable. I think I can do without it."

He also did not tolerate well exhibitionistic displays of self-promotion and immodesty. It may be said here that he wore his own considerable pride discreetly and with noteworthy dignity. About one person, however, he could almost allow a public acknowledgement of worship, and that was David Rapaport, whom he truly loved and respected. I remember walking through the Stockbridge cemetery with him to visit David's, George Klein's, and Bob Knight's graves. We stopped beside David's grave and glanced at the unique black stone on which were carved the words, "*Mi Chomocha,*" meaning, "Who can be compared with you?" This phrase is the beginning of the Hebrew, "compared with you in the entire universe, O Lord." He turned to me and said, perhaps with more admiration than derision, "Some chutzpa! Hah?"

When I left Chicago, I left behind those memorable Monday evenings with Mert. Although Merton and I continued to see each other at the Rapaport-Klein Meetings and at other meetings, the regularity of our social and scientific encounters diminished.

Now he is gone from our midst. He lived four score years. His was a long life. He accomplished much for the profession he loved. I knew him as a good and wise friend and as an exquisite teacher. It is a mournful occasion to say farewell to such a man, but this sad emotion is mixed with gratitude for his long life, part of which he shared with us. We can rejoice that so many of us were touched by his presence. Although he knew the Hebrew liturgy and could recite the ritual prayers, he shunned religion, and he did not want a Hebrew prayer, even the one of remembrance, said for him. We will not forget this good man, this *Tzadik*, his works, and what he meant to us. I say my farewell to him, with some license, from two lines in W. H. Auden's poem on the death of Yeats:

> Earth, receive an honored guest,
> Merton Gill is laid to rest.

Section Three: *Merton Gill: A Sketch of His Life and Some Reminiscences*

Robert R. Holt

When I first met Mert, in 1946, he was 32 years old—only 3 years older than I—but he seemed much more my senior than that. Only 8 years had passed since he had received his MD from the University of Chicago, where he also did his undergraduate work. After an internship at Michael Reese Hospital, he had gone to Topeka to take a residency at the Menninger Clinic, then a much smaller and less famous place than it has become since. He had first become a staff member and, by 1946, had for a year been Chief of the Outpatient Department and had newly become Assistant Director of the Research Department, David Rapaport's right-hand man. Moreover, he was almost through his psychoanalytic training; he graduated from the Topeka Institute the next year—a pretty rapid rise for someone so young, but no one spoke of Mert as a "boy wonder" or "whiz kid." He was mature for his years, and clearly possessed not only intellectual brilliance but a charismatic personal quality that drew people to him from the beginning.

At first, I knew him only through his participation in the evening lectures, held almost weekly under the auspices of the newly founded Menninger School of Psychiatry. Outside speakers, often of considerable distinction, came through Topeka to speak about their specialties, each time followed by open discussion. One after another, the heavy hitters of the home team would come to bat with comments or critique, some—like Karl Menninger, David Rapaport, and Robert Knight—already with great reputations, others yet to receive renown but equally cogent and articulate, like Margaret Brenman, Sybille Escalona, Milton Wexler, and Lewis Robbins. None of these stars could upstage the young Gill, however. The substance of what he said was always thoughtful and insightful, but it took on added impressiveness from his gift of speaking in well-framed and fluent sentences delivered with flashes of cutting wit in the deep, orotund, mellifluous, bass voice we all recall so well.

I believe that it was Rapaport who finally got us acquainted on a one-to-one basis, but our friendship grew slowly. I found Merton fascinating but not very approachable; he could make you laugh a lot, but there was often a sharp edge to his sense of humor. I suspect now that he was less secure and more defensive than I realized at the time.

The first period of Gill's publications began in Topeka with a few clinical papers and a landmark collaborative study: *Diagnostic Psychological Testing* (Rapaport, Gill, and Schafer, 1945–1946). Mert always tried to make it plain that he knew little about testing and that his collaboration had been limited to two exercises of his psychiatric skills: interviewing the Kansas highway patrolmen who served as the control group for the research, and helping to review the clinical data on the hundreds of mixed psychiatric cases and to assign them to a standard set of nosological categories. (*All* subjects, normal and abnormal alike, had been given the same battery of psychological tests, on which the research was focused.)

His other main collaborator in Topeka was Margaret Brenman-Gibson, who drew him into her exploratory research on hypnosis and hypnotherapy. They published a number of joint papers and an acclaimed book, *Hypnotherapy* (Brenman and Gill, 1947).

To my personal disappointment, as well as that of many others, Mert left Topeka in 1948 to accompany Bob Knight to Stockbridge as part of another exciting institutional renaissance, at the Austen Riggs Center, along with Margaret Brenman, Roy Schafer, Alan Wheelis, and Erik Erikson. (Rapaport followed a year later.) The work on hypnotherapy continued, culminating in a second, more definitive book, *Hypnosis and Related States* (Gill and Brenman, 1959), which made notable theoretical, as well as clinical, contributions.

Considerably before that, however, Gill had moved on to the Yale Medical School's Department of Psychiatry, where he began another collaborative research project, this time on the initial psychiatric interview (Gill et al., 1954). While still in Stockbridge, he had become one of the founding members of the Western New England Psychoanalytic Society. He became a training analyst in its institute in 1950, as well as vice president and then president of the society.

In 1953, he moved to Berkeley, where he settled for a decade. I'll skip over this period, since I was mostly far away. But one of the best things about my year in Palo Alto (1960–61) was the opportunity to see Mert fairly often, exchanging manuscripts and having stimulating talks about our mutual fascination with metapsychology. I recall with special pleasure a beach outing with Mert and his second wife Charlotte, with little Ben and his two older half-brothers Rod and Kim (whom Merton adopted). It was one of many occasions on which I could see the warmth and kind firmness with which he interacted with his children. He maintained frequent contact with all five of them, including two daughters from his first marriage, whatever his fallings out with their mothers.

David Rapaport's sudden death that year also brought us together in joint efforts to handle the immediate practical aftermath and the longer task of surveying his literary remains and preparing to publish much of it, as well as the immediate project of organizing a memorial volume, *Motives and Thought* (Gill, 1967b), to which Merton contributed a paper.

Let me say a little about the working relationship between Gill and Rapaport. Both men had an unusual capacity for collaborative work, which is possible only between mature persons who are capable of subordinating individual competitive ambitions to the requirements of an intellectual challenge. There can be no question that Gill was fully able to write important contributions completely on his own; his bibliography attests to that. Nevertheless, it also contains an unusual number of substantial pieces of work done in partnership with one or more colleagues. Nowhere was Mert's special talent for teamwork more evident than in the work he did with his mentor, that extraordinary intellect and remarkable human being, David Rapaport. When they were not in the same institution, they continued a warm and close personal relationship, with a steady exchange of long letters and phone calls, punctuated by working visits. Those would typically be intensive weekends of sitting together until late into the night over notes and manuscripts, full of vigorous argument and productive work, but with a great deal of often uproarious comic relief. Those who were privileged to hear the exchange of jokes between these two legendary raconteurs have never forgotten it. A notable product of this long-distance collaboration was the groundbreaking paper, "The Points of View and Assumptions of Metapsychology" (Rapaport and Gill, 1959).

Rapaport's tragically untimely death in 1960 interrupted a major undertaking, which Gill (1963) completed alone, a further rational reconstruction and extension of metapsychology. It was followed by a masterly summary of Rapaport's contributions (Gill and Klein, 1964) and his editing of a massive collection of Rapaport's papers (Gill, 1967a).

In 1963, a move to New York inaugurated a new period of Mert's professional life, first at the Downstate Medical Center of the State University of New York, where his research was in collaboration with Justin Simon and other medical psychoanalysts. Starting in 1969, to the delight of George Klein, myself, and our staff at the Research Center for Mental Health (RCMH), he spent two years at New York University as a Special NIMH Fellow. During these New York years, his research focused on the intensive study of the process of psychoanalysis via tape recording. He devised a technique of making the huge data base of a recorded analysis (whether fully transcribed or not) usable by means of nested summaries. He would listen to the tape of an hour, then dictate a carefully planned abstract of the entire proceeding and an even briefer precis using a controlled vocabulary of key words. These documents made it possible to review many hours quickly to find necessary data for a specific study, a method that has enabled several other people to do good research using his cases. His two reports on this work (Gill et al., 1968; Simon et al., 1970) join a small, but valuable, corpus of reflections on clinical research methods, which he published over a period of about four decades.

During his two years at NYU, Mert intensified his friendship with me, but even more so with George Klein, a camaraderie that dated back to Topeka days. George and I had gone there as Rapaport's students and proteges and, beginning in 1953, had developed the RCMH as a center of empirical and theoretical research on psychoanalytic psychology. Gill joined at a time when Hartvig Dahl had begun a new line of work on the analytic process using tape recordings; now George became actively involved. The focus was a regularly meeting working group, which I and a few others joined, where we discussed work in progress. Mert was trying the audacious idea of experimentally introducing into an ongoing analysis deliberately off-target interpretations, followed by "correct" ones at a long enough interval to compare effects. He was able to do so with such conviction that "blind" observers could not tell which interpretations were appropriate and which inappropriate.

Since the death of our mentor, Rapaport, we had been going through a period of fundamental questioning of the Freudian metapsychology in which all three of us had been so thoroughly drilled. I don't know to what extent George and I infected Mert with our skepticism; basically, however, we were all responding to real problems with the texts, for which only David had always been able to find an extenuation or explanation. George was writing a series of revisionist theoretical papers at the time of his sudden and early death in 1970, which was, of course, a heavy blow to the NYU working group. Gill and Leo Goldberger undertook the editorial task of making a publishable book (Klein, 1976) from George's manuscripts, and with Phil Holzman, Mert organized and edited a posthumous *Festschrift* in George's honor. That collection contains "Metapsychology Is Not Psychology," Gill's (1976) first explicit turning away from the endeavor to salvage and rehabilitate this general or nonclinical theory of psychoanalysis, toward what he hoped might be a hermeneutic science.

That was only one of several instances in which Mert had the courage and intellectual integrity to admit that he had been wrong, even that a line of work was fundamentally flawed, despite the fact that he had devoted many years to it. In my estimation, anyone who has the guts to admit error on an important theoretical or metatheoretical point displays the kind of intellectual heroism often attributed to Freud. But this is only one of the qualities that endeared Merton Gill to those who were fortunate enough to be his friends. He was steadfastly loyal, absolutely reliable, unfailingly helpful, and emotionally supportive—no wonder he was such a fine therapist!

My wife Joan and I cherish the memories of one time when we had an opportunity to be steadily together with Mert and Ilse for a little over a week. They accepted our invitation to spend some summer vacation time with us in our house in Truro toward the end of August 1971. There was plenty of time for good conversation, enjoying the beauties of Cape Cod together, relaxing on the beach, and enjoying good food—especially when Ilse displayed an unsuspected talent for baking.

That fall, Chicago welcomed the return of a prodigal son (though I mean it in the sense of his being extremely abundant and generous, rather than profligate), if not with a fatted calf, then at least with another professorship of psychiatry at the Abraham Lincoln School of Medicine, plumped out with a Research Scientist Award from NIMH. That was to be his last move.

To go back to our shared vacation, I remember being struck at the time by the developmental change in Mert over the many years I had known him. From being the kind of brilliant young man who simultaneously attracts people and frightens them away by a mordantly witty tongue, he had become a wise, maturely loving and beloved person of remarkable benevolence, who made no effort to conceal his own human vulnerability. At times, to be sure, he could still be a rascal, a clown, even a curmudgeon. He lived life fully, knowing the depths of despair and depression, as well as the heights of love and widely acclaimed achievement. But he never seemed impressed with himself, always wryly self-deprecatory and aware of his own limitations.

In November 1983, he wrote to me: "We get older and the damn flesh asserts itself at the very time when we feel we should, and can, use what we have learned to justify what we were given—and I don't mean to belittle the pleasure in showing what we can do as well as to stick out our tongues at fate. I will be 70 next summer and I think from time to time that I don't want to 'go quietly into the night.'" As his body began to give out in the final decade, he faced his mortality with his usual ironic humor. He went through enough misery in those final months for all of us to be glad he is released from it, despite our personal grief.

REFERENCES

Brenman, M. & Gill, M. M. (1947), *Hypnotherapy: A Review of the Literature*. New York: International Universities Press.

Gill, M. M. (1963), *Topography and Systems in Psychoanalytic Theory. Psychological Issues*, Monogr. No. 10. New York: International Universities Press.

Gill, M. M., ed. (1967a), *The Collected Papers of David Rapaport.* New York: Basic Books.

Gill, M. M. (1967b), The primary process. In: *Motives and Thought: Psychoanalytic Essays in Memory of David Rapaport*, ed. R. R. Holt. *Psychological Issues*, Monogr. 18/19. New York: International Universities Press, pp. 259–298.

Gill, M. M. (1976), Metapsychology is not psychology. In: *Psychology vs. Metapsychology: Psychoanalytic Essays in Memory of George S. Klein*, ed. M. M. Gill & P. S. Holzman. *Psychological Issues*, Monogr. No. 36. New York: International Universities Press, pp. 71–105.

Gill, M. M. & Brenman, M. (1959), *Hypnosis and Related States: Psychoanalytic Studies in Regression.* New York: International Universities Press.

Gill, M. M. & Klein, G. S. (1964), The structuring of drive and reality: David Rapaport's contributions to psychoanalysis and psychology. *Internat. J. Psycho-Anal.*, 45:483–498. (Also in Gill, 1967a)

Gill, M. M., Newman, R., Redlich, F. C. & Sommers, M. (1954), *The Initial Interview in Psychiatric Practice.* New York: International Universities Press. (Published with phonograph records)

Gill, M. M., Simon, J., Endicott, N. A. & Paul, I. H. (1968), Studies in audio-recorded psychoanalysis. 1. General considerations. *J. Amer. Psychoanal. Assn.*, 16:230–244.

Klein, G. S. (1976), *Psychoanalytic Theory: An Exploration of Essentials*, ed. M. M. Gill & L. Goldberger. New York: International Universities Press.

Rapaport, D. & Gill, M. M. (1959), The points of view and assumptions of metapsychology. *Internat. J. Psycho-Anal.*, 40:1–10.

Rapaport, D., Gill, M. M. & Schafer, R. (1945–46), *Diagnostic Psychological Testing* (2 vols.). Chicago: Yearbook Publishers (out of print). Also see: Rapaport, D., Gill, M. M. & Schafer, R. (1968), *Diagnostic Psychological Testing* (revised edition by R. R. Holt). New York: International Universities Press.

Simon, J., Gill, M. M., Fink, G., Endicott, N. A. & Paul, I. H. (1970), Studies in audio-recorded psychoanalysis: 2. The effect on the analyst. *J. Amer. Psychoanal. Assn.*, 18:86–101.

Section Four: *A Personal View of Gill's Paradigm*

Lawrence Friedman

What follows is a tentative and, I emphasize, very personal view of Gill's paradigm. I know he developed his later ideas in collaboration with Hoffman, and in many respects he simply depended on Hoffman's thinking, but I am looking at Gill's paradigm as an expression of Merton's own mission and not commenting on their joint work, per se, still less the philosophy of constructivism.

In public debate Gill was certainly the most vivid and possibly the most eloquent analyst of my time. His rhetoric was a special blend of prickliness and courtliness. His sharply pointed, perfectly phrased comments animated many a dull meeting, dazzling us with wit and polish that I had imagined to be the exclusive virtue of an earlier era. His prose is graceful and respectful of the reader. It can only have been his thoroughness and precision that prompted Karl Menninger to accuse him of making something boring out of a lively subject. Liveliness can be bought at the expense of accuracy. Gill was too thoughtful for that; he had too much respect for his profession, his colleagues, his interlocutors, and everyone who would correspond with him. He was never too ill or too busy to try to reach an understanding with anyone who wished to argue with him. One rarely sees such passion outside of politics or religion. And as to practice, I have been awed by his incredibly selfless dedication to difficult patients .

Gill is known for his forthright (and therefore educational) switchbacks on previously held positions. Like Sandor Ferenczi he was more interested in finding the truth about treatment than in nursing a magnum opus. But, in fact, he was never as one sided or unqualified in his successive theories as has been alleged, and as even he sometimes came to believe. In fact, it seems to me that he was unusually careful in his formulations. His reputation for going to extremes was probably earned by the vigor of his opposition. He knew most clearly what was wrong, so to speak, knew it from direct experience, and knew how to express it crisply.

As a thinker, Gill is generally associated with seven tenets: (1) Psychic structure is a continuum—a continuum of ego and id, impulse and defense. (2) Psychoanalysis is distinguished from psychotherapy by the induction of regression and the resolution of the transference by interpretation alone. (3) Metapsychology is pseudo-biology. (4) The resistance is mainly fear of plausible transference. (5) The analyst is never a blank screen. (6) Psychoanalysis is not distinguished from psychotherapy by its use of regression; but rather by its fearless scrutiny, especially of transference. (7) [With Hoffman] The analyst lacks authority on the relationship, and should enjoy a freer but more tentative expressiveness.

Despite the zig-zags in his advocacy, I think one can catch sight of a common thread that might lead to a useful characterization of his final paradigm.

To begin with, I think Gill was what in common language is called a realist, and what philosophers call a nominalist. He did not want implacable, smug abstractions to stand between him and experience.

For instance, he thought that Freudian structures were too categorical. Such rigidity is not realistic, he argued, nor theoretically coherent. Mental activity is not so easily tagged. It's more like a continuum from less to more refined meanings, feelings that are more and less concealed. Mental events don't assemble under the flag of ego or id. They are ego-ish when compared to something id-ish, and id-ish when compared to something more ego-ish; impulse in relation to what's more defensive, defense in relation to what's more impulsive. (He anticipated Brenner in this.)

Along the same lines, Gill thought that analysts were using a fake biology in the form of metapsychology to assign meanings to pseudo-anatomical compartments, thus unrealistically tearing them out of the unitary, living web of meaning that we see in clinical work. In real life, as Merton saw it, what actually goes on in the consulting room is hermeneutic conversation. Again, it is a single network of relationships among meanings that analysts *really* think about, not universal, physical-ish groupings.

Having thus objected to mental structures and metapsychology as abstract labels ripped out of the real network of human meaning, it was natural for Gill to add "transference" and "resistance" to his list of misleading abstractions. If you get up close to a real treatment, you realize that transference is not a phase of analysis, or a type of hallucinatory experience, unconnected to the whole interaction. And as to resistance, it cannot be abstracted from the treatment event, since resistance is not an abstract force; it is whatever the patient is disavowing in his relationship to the analyst at every moment. Analysts who wait for Transference or Resistance to come on stage like the ghost of Hamlet's father are, like Hamlet, chicken-hearted cowards frittering away the time for action.

It is not surprising that Gill's nominalism would eventually summon the whole, traditional picture of treatment to judgement. He found in it something even more pernicious than fake psychic structures, something worse than pseudobiological-metapsychology, something more dishonest than Resistance-with-a-capital-R. It is the custom of packaging the analyst's actions as a taken-for-granted, null class of events, a neutral backdrop for the patient's gratuitous displays of unprovoked affect. Gill said that you will never understand what the patient is experiencing, let alone enable him to express it, if you think that you're doing something abstract, called analysis, rather than doing something individual and personal that warrants a personal reaction. Gill knocked analytic treatment right off its Platonic pedestal, and when you pick up the pieces, it's just an analyst and a patient reacting to each other. The analyst is doing something, not conducting something.

Since the analyst's personal behavior registers in the patient's preconscious, Gill's focus had the important effect of calling overdue attention to the preconscious as the site of analytic work. To see what had been logged in that register, the analyst would have to cultivate the patient's view as a plausibility, en route to determining not truth or distortion, but the patient's customary bias. Nominalism thus encouraged egalitarianism and cooperativeness.

That ethical posture had other roots, as well, that blossomed especially in his last work. I have suggested as one motive that Gill wanted to be realistic—even immediate—with patients: so for theory, he chose a continuum rather than abstract structures, and for practice, a personal interaction rather than a psychoanalytic "situation." But, further, I think Gill felt that technical abstractions were not only unwarranted reifications, but also tools that analysts use to intimidate and manipulate patients. One sees here the second motive in Gill's work, which became dominant at the end: his hatred of manipulation. When the analyst pigeonholes behavior as "impulse" or "defense," as a shift of energy, as a resistance to treatment, or as a transference projection, not only is he thinking badly, according to Gill; his typecasting is preventing the patient from recognizing what's being done to him. Gill saw that many analytic traditions amount to a kind of gaslighting, a professional bullying. It is not just that abstractions are false; they also coerce patients by prejudging them.

Gill seems to have subscribed to a Nietzschean truth: To assume that you "know" about someone ahead of time guarantees that you will manipulate him—it is already a manipulation of him. Gill's skepticism of abstract items and his preference for continuous immediacy now joined forces with his hatred of intimidation and manipulation, and he was ready for his final battle.

His last enemy was nothing less than all the foreknowledge that goes unquestioned by the analyst. He waged war against unreflective, unchallenged routines, everything that forecloses a new meaning at a new moment with a new individual. He challenged smug assumptions because they coerced the patient's meanings. But it wasn't a precious concern with individuality that absorbed Gill. He was not an existentialist. He believed that analysis was a general process that should be investigated by consensual study. He believed in tracking down hidden truths—painful truths when necessary. He was an innovator in psychoanalytic documentation and a leader in psychoanalytic research. He considered psychoanalysis a form of science. I think Irwin Hoffman's philosophy of social constructivism offered him a way of coming freshly to the patient and remaining open minded, without having to restrain his exposure of subterfuge. I think he was drawn to constructivism because it respected individuality without mystifying it. Gill, I think, hated mystification. The point was not to celebrate individuality, but to avoid manipulating, bullying, and fooling people. And "people" includes analysts. For Gill was no more willing to be coerced than to be coercive. That's how he differed from some other antiauthoritarian theorists. I think he saw those others as masochistically reversing the old bullying and allowing themselves to be uselessly stifled. It is difficult, indeed, to imagine a theory so powerful that it would persuade Merton Gill to allow himself to be stifled. Social constructivism permitted both parties to thrive.

Although Gill would doubtless have continued to describe analysis as a quest for understanding, I get the impression that, at the end, another definition was almost as important to him: psychoanalysis is the continuous effort to interact without manipulating. Just as Kohut thought of understanding mainly as a way to restore the empathic bond, so, I suggest, Gill's honest probing of the interaction was mainly intended to clean up subtle coercion and restore integrity to the relationship. Gill's final definition of psychoanalysis was embodied in the mantra: *Nothing* remains unanalyzed. And why is everything to be analyzed? Not to dissolve it; the transference does not end. And not to accumulate knowledge; that's too vague an aim. The fundamental reason that nothing should remain unanalyzed is so that every interpersonal *force* will be *undermined* by reflection, rather than being *reenforced* by a silent assumption.

Gill felt personally responsible for carrying forward Freud's work in Freud's manner, that is, without sycophancy or compromise. I think he did it. He made logical sense out of the structural theory. He rescued Freud's transference and resistance paradigm from reification. And, finally, he made an honest man of Freud in regard to one vital treatment promise. It would have brought down Gill's formidable wrath on me for saying so, but say it I must: In his final years, Gill was busy polishing up Freud's blank screen.

We all know that, for Gill, the blank-screen metaphor was the Devil himself. But in its origin, the blank screen meant that the analyst would be the only person in the world who did not impose a fixed role and relationship on his partner. What Gill did was to catch Freud cheating on this promise, and he found that analysts had been cheating on it ever since. The way they did it is by hiding their actions in a sealed envelope called the blank screen. In effect, Gill recognized that, to be truly dedicated to the *goal* of the blank screen, the analyst would have to stop pretending that he *is* one, and, instead, continuously *analyze* his unavoidable impact.

In a way, the same thing applies to technique; customary analytic technique pretends to be a kind of blank action. In his later work Gill pointed to the great, nominalist truth that in personal reality there is no technique, just this analyst and that patient. It is only by sleight of hand that the analyst makes some actions seem to materialize out of a timeless, nether-world called technique, when, in fact, the analyst is actually doing a something to someone at some time.

Thus, Gill was angry with me for talking about how "The Analyst" behaves, and he scolded me for imagining what this means to "The Patient." "You don't know that," I heard him say, in effect. "You have to look and see. Talking to us in this room, you don't know the analyst; you don't know the patient; and you don't know the moment." It startled me to realize that my picture of the analyst as *not* a blank screen offended Gill as much as other people's picture of the analyst *as* a blank screen. And then I realized why: It is pictures drawn ahead of time—*any* pictures—that prejudice the issue. I realized that in Gill's eyes, my antecedent, supposedly superior knowledge makes me a manipulator rather than an inquirer. In other words, by presuming to know ahead of time, I was not being blank enough to receive on my screen whatever the therapeutic moment would create. I was bound to paste an unquestioning image of myself onto the interaction and then dishonestly claim I was just reading what's there. [Gill also suspected that I was trying to rid myself of the characteristics I was describing and thus make myself invisible, or else that I automatically assumed that if patients accused me of manipulating them, they must be right.]

Gill was at the forefront of a major movement in psychoanalysis. Its agenda involves confronting the reality of treatment events, stripping away protective self-images from the analyst, and refocusing on the bite and crunch of effective therapy (which usually lies in the newly freed negative feelings about the analyst's behavior).

In Gill's paradigm the analyst is wary of all fixed, abstract knowledge and keeps an open mind about every level of work, from the expectations of daily routine, through the grand theory of the mind, on up to the notion of a preestablished reality.

This paradigm is modeled on ordinary conversation; a wish to communicate is assumed as its baseline. The work is mutual and cooperative in conception, but unpredictable as experienced. The analyst calls out when he spots a muffled communication, and he leans over backward to catch uncomfortableness in the relationship. A strenuous effort is made to examine all the inputs to the patient's situation. The idea behind the treatment is that one's sense of things is obscured by fixed assumptions, and is clarified when both parties note how they mutually weave meanings together.

What about technique? Technique joins other eternal truths in the dust bin. It comes down to "just analyze!" Some older analysts used to say that, too. But the reason they scorned technique was they fancied themselves to be intuitive knowers and "just analyze" for them meant "keep reading out the id," whereas Gill despised technique as a manipulative pretension, and his "just analyze" meant demystifying and deconstructing personal impacts.

In short, Gill's last paradigm is a rigorous attempt to rid analysis of the element of manipulation. There are several such projects today, but few so consistently seek to neutralize manipulation on the levels of both action and thought; few so consistently deconstruct performatives (as Havens calls them) by both analyst and patient.

To what end, we might ask? Obviously the goal can no longer be to point out distortion—not even to point out bias among a range of possibilities. The final goal can only be to provide an experience of mutual freedom and fearlessness, to show how meanings come about, and to foster a coherent and autonomous life.

Section Five: *Arguments with Merton*

Henry F. Smith

Editor's Introduction: *The May 1997 meeting in San Diego of the American Psychoanalytic Association included a panel chaired by Henry Smith that was devoted to Gill's views on transference. As Smith tells us, it had originally been intended as a meet-the-author session to discuss Gill's 1994 book* Psychoanalysis in Transition, *but unfortunately Gill died before that session could take place.*

In offering us his Introduction to that panel on transference, Smith appreciatively conveys Merton's lucid and feisty intellectual and personal style. He closes his account with the transcript of several excerpts taken from an audiotape of Merton in a workshop in 1994.

Merton was not the easiest of men. Not long ago Glen Gabbard (1996) chaired a panel on "Hate in the Analytic Setting." Introducing the panelists, he joked that he had assembled the four most hated figures in psychoanalysis. As the discussion period opened, Merton stood up from the audience and indignantly asked, if these were the most hated men in psychoanalysis, why had he not been included?

For Merton, argument was often the beginning of respect. Our friendship, which was regrettably brief, began, it seemed, when I criticized him in a paper I had written. It turned out he agreed with my criticism and responded some time later with an all-out attack on a paper of mine. I told him I took his salvo as the opening of a friendship, which I hoped was not too large a leap of inference. But I also pointed out that he had based his attack on a misconception about my patient.

His next letter began, "My face is red!" He was always quick to acknowledge when he was wrong. Then he wrote, "No, you are not making too large a leap of inference when you regard this as the opening of a friendship. Another one for the archives: I was present when David Rapaport and Heinz Hartmann drank [to their friendship]. Because I loved Rapaport and it meant so much to him, I was quite moved."

Merton did not suffer fools gladly. When I asked him to chair a two-day clinical workshop on process and technique, I asked if he would choose someone for the case presentation. It was always easier if consultants selected their own presenters. To my dismay, he said, "No, I'll trust you to pick someone," and then he added with that gesture that fell somewhere between a compliment and a cuff on the cheek, "Just make sure it's not some schmuck who doesn't know what the fuck is going on."

Few analysts have made as many seminal contributions to the theory and practice of analysis over five decades as did Merton Gill, beginning with his training at Menninger in the early 1940s, where he met David

Rapaport; through his stint at Austen Riggs and Yale; the decade he spent as a training analyst in San Francisco; and finally, after a brief stop in New York, his return to Chicago, the city where he was born, for the final two-and-a-half decades of his life. It was a journey that took him from the most classical of positions to an integration of the interpersonal, the hermeneutic, and the contructivist into psychoanalysis.

In reviewing his early papers, we cannot help but be dazzled by the clarity of his thinking. Some of his thoughts became the emblems of an era, and they endure even to this day, especially and curiously, as Wallerstein (1997) has pointed out, those views he later disavowed. I am thinking of his oft quoted 1954 definition of psychoanalysis: "Psychoanalysis is that technique which, employed by a neutral analyst, results in the development of a regressive transference neurosis and the ultimate resolution of this neurosis by techniques of interpretation alone" (Gill, 1954, p. 775). He later said he disagreed with everything he wrote in that paper. So, you see, he not only argued with others, he argued constantly with himself; and he always won, especially when he changed his mind. If his most recent position was that analysis is analysis no matter what the frequency or position of the patient, back in 1954, in advocating frequent sessions, he was pursuasive and startlingly evocative: "The frequency of visits . . . [is] necessary to keep open the wounds into the unconscious" (Gill, 1954, p. 778).

There are several points of note in these shifts. Like many of us, Merton was addicted to analysis, and he was always trying to define it, do it right, and do it better. Sometimes his enthusiasms went to excess. He spoke about this in a recent interview (Raymond and Rosbrow-Reich, 1997). Asked if his feeling of engagement was different now than when he worked more traditionally, Merton said, "Yes, it's very different. It's not a different form of engagement. It's a greater engagement. I carry things to extremes. When I was a classical analyst, I thought, 'Look, you're not supposed to have a relationship with the patient. Okay, I won't say hello and I won't say goodbye.' And I didn't. Now I think that's nuts. But I tried it," adding that now, "if I don't feel related to a patient, something is very wrong" (pp. 211–212).

In recent years Gill became passionately interested in the analysis of the transference in the here-and-now, or the patient's experience of the analytic relationship—he used the two interchangeably, something many have found conceptually troubling. He advocated early interpretation of the transference with particular attention to the transference as a plausible construction on the part of the patient, rather than a distortion. More recently with Irwin Hoffman he was exploring the cocreated nature of the transference.

But if Merton could take diametrically opposed positions from one decade to another, like Freud he never entirely pulled up his earlier stakes. Both characterologically and intellectually he was restless, and in that perpetual argument with himself he could often see the virtues of several sides at once. Whether this made him an eloquent spokesman for what is currently called the "dialectics" of analysis (for the inherent tensions and contradictions in analytic work and for the nondichotomous intertwining of the intrapsychic and the interpersonal) or whether it made him appear confused, someone who seemed to be taking extreme positions at certain times and at others trying to do it all, is a judgment that only history can make.

Regardless of that judgment, however, as his life came to a close, Merton did not lose touch with his earlier allegiances. Thus, in his final book he (1994) wrote, "It remains true that the great discovery peculiar to psychoanalysis, the internal factor in the sense of unconscious fantasy, is the one that psychoanalysis must zealously protect" (p. 28).

In this regard I want to return to the interview I mentioned and give you a flavor of Merton's continual balancing of one side and then the other, reminiscent in some ways of Freud. Thus, he begins one part of the discussion, "My hope is . . . that analysis is slowly . . . beginning to recognize that it is a dyad, and that that's at the heart of understanding it." Then he adds, "which is not to deny the centrality of a one-person psychoanalysis as well. That's a mistake I made for quite a while. As I began to see what was wrong with a one-person analysis, in my usual impetuous, exaggerated way, I threw away the one-person analysis in favor of a two-person analysis." He then digresses with an aphorism, illustrating the one-person case, "The human body is not created by social intercourse but by sexual intercourse. . . . The prominence that is progressively being given to the social aspects of the human psyche unfortunately is leading some former analysts to abandon the centrality of the body." Then he shifts again, "By the way, something that occurred to me not long ago that is an insight of some consequence is that Freud's change from the first anxiety theory to the second one in 'Inhibitions, Symptoms, and Anxiety' was a hermeneutic shift. . . . Whereas the first theory said repression of libido leads to anxiety, the second theory [said] anxiety leads to repression. How much more sense, intuitive sense, the second theory makes. If you're nervous, if you're frightened, you try to forget it. . . . The change is a hermeneutic turn. . . . I mean . . . the body is very important in terms of what it means, not *qua* the body." Then he shifts back again, "But . . . it's not just . . . the meaning of the body, it's the body too." And finally he stops to reflect on his own process of thinking: "If I talk . . . I suddenly realize that I don't understand that or that I've been, in my impetuous way, too—if you'll forgive the expression—cock-sure about what I think. I'll think about it some more" (Raymond and Rosbrow-Reich, 1997, pp. 227–229). That was it, he never stopped thinking about it some more—and then some more and then some more.

For Gill, the patient and the analyst were either *in* a relationship, or they were not. Challenging the resistance to that relationship was his primary consideration in technique, an approach that brought him into constant conflict with self psychology. In these latter years Merton was critical of analyses that seemed to him intellectualized and sterile, in which the engagement with the analyst did not deepen, and in which there seemed to be a kind of resistance built into the very frame of the analysis itself. He wanted to increase the immediacy of the work and improve the results. This theme has a long history, heard, for example, in Ferenzci, in Strachey, and in the Kleinian literature more generally, where much attention has been paid to the here and now and to the nature of the object relationship expressed in the patient's transference.

But it is also in keeping with current trends, a common ground, if you like, of interest in authenticity, aliveness, and engagement, and it subtends much of the contemporary literature on enactment and subjectivity. Some of these interests are used to argue the advantages of one theory over another, or one technical device over another. I question whether this is a useful approach. However consequential theory may be to practice, there are many aspects of technique and many common goals that transcend different theories and different technical approaches. Thus, authenticity, affective engagement, and immediacy, together with the analyst's level of activity and spontaneity are not limited to one school of analysis or another. There are engaged and unengaged patients and analysts of all pursuasions. While some resistances may be better addressed with one technique or another, the process of resistance itself, in the patient and in the analyst, will always rise to the challenge and adapt, often imperceptibly, to the theory and technique of the analyst (Smith, 1997).

Furthermore, with every shift in technique, we need to ask not only what is gained and what is lost for the patient, but also how does the change benefit the analyst? Notice that Gill characteristically acknowledged the influence of his own impulsiveness and his own impatience. To pursue allusions to the transference inevitably increases the *analyst's* sense of relatedness. So, if it is hard to argue with Merton's goal that the patient and the analyst be more engaged, what if the patient is doing the best he or she can? Are we becoming intolerant of resistances, especially the narcissistic sort, and of the patient's need *not* to engage us, to make more solitary self-discoveries? (Smith, 2000) As Arlow (1991) says, the analyst is not the most important person in the patient's life. How should the analyst deal with his or her own wishes for engagement?

It is around this issue of impatience that Hoffmann (1996) has begun to diverge from Gill, saying that a patient and an analyst may need more time to work their way out of certain transference-countertransference dilemmas, and that it may take longer than Gill would like to assess the quality of the work. While Gill never gave up his belief in the mutative value of interpretation alone, Hoffmann has come to consider that noninterpretive interactions are in a kind of dialectical tension with interpretations of the transference that enhances the mutative potential of both.

It seems to me we can distinguish many contemporary approaches to analysis according to their views of unconscious processes and of unconscious fantasy, both in the generation of neurosis and as a focus of technique. If Merton acknowledged the importance of unconscious fantasy, he nevertheless admitted that, while he tried to be "alert" to it in his listening, he truly privileged the attention he gave to the patient's experience of the analyst. These are not mutually exclusive foci, but any of us can readily verify that, as the analyst selects one aspect of the work for attention, the patient follows our lead, and before long the work takes on a somewhat different shape and structure. As the focus changes, the data changes, the narratives change, and soon another analyst's work can sound very foreign to our ears. The current climate is filled with many such disparate voices. At the same time my sense is that those aspects of the transference that patients bring with them, and that they replicate in relationship after relationship, exert an insistent pull on the analyst, demanding analytic attention regardless of one's theoretical allegiance. What is common to different approaches, then, and what is unique may vary at different levels of abstraction and at different times in the work.

In trying to resolve the conflicts in contemporary analysis and in his own intellectual history, Merton (1995) spoke about a dialectic between what he called the innate and the experiential. He said, "I believe that both the classical and the relational points of view do indeed take both [the innate and the experiential] into account, probably more equally in practice than in theory" (p. 90).

Before closing I want you to hear Merton say it himself. I have recorded a bit of what we heard in that clinical workshop three years ago, although the quality of the tape unfortunately does not match the quality of the experience he gave us.

This is May 1994, six months before he died:

(For those of you who are reading this, each of the following exerpts is in Gill's voice with its familiar cadences.)

Selection 1:

By the way, we don't give enough attention to the fact that to tell a patient that to be in analysis you have to come four or five times a week, and you're going to lie on a couch, is a manipulation of the transference if there ever was one, because we have a tendency to think of that as just a neutral following out of the appropriate rituals and rites, but in fact the transference is being "manipulated." And, in particular, since I presume some of you came here because you wanted to see how seriously I really mean putting the analysis of the transference in the here and now in the center of the proceedings, I will oblige you by saying, "Yes I really mean it, and this is an example of it."

Selection 2:
If you're going to inhibit flagging something because you're afraid the patient will experience it in a particular way, that's a manipulation of the transference. Not that you can avoid manipulating the transference. By definition you are manipulating it all the time. My argument only is that you do your damnedest to be aware that that is true and to deal with it as much as you can.

Selection 3:
There's no beginning of an interaction. Interaction exists *ab initio*. There's no beginning and no end.

Selection 4:
We all have our own temperaments, and they influence the way in which we work. I'm an impatient person. I don't want to hang around. And as I grow older I have less time to hang around. And you have to become even more impatient. So it is my responsibility to be aware, in so far as I possibly can, of the degree to which that influences me.

Selection 5:
You're always interrupting the free associations, or you *should* always be interrupting them. Whatever you *say* is an interruption of the free associations. I don't understand free association to mean the patient just talks and talks and talks, and you just listen and listen and listen [Laughter]. Analysis, I repeat, is a conversation. It should be a coherent account. The difference between so-called free association and ordinary social intercourse is that *more* is told in free association than otherwise. It is a fuller, more complete account of a person's mental content, because in ordinary social context we omit various things that we feel is impolite or improper to say.

Selection 6:
. . . and if you want me to justify the equation of speaking of transference and the patient's experience of the relationship I can do that, but it would take a little time.

Selection 7:
(Merton was asked, if he were the analyst, would he say anything to the patient under discussion about the distance in the patient's relationship to the analyst?): I would say something about the state of the relationship, but I wouldn't just say that it's because the patient feels unengaged. I would say to that, the patient experiences *me* as unengaged, and that I believe that that is significantly related to the fact that *he* feels unengaged. I would take responsibility for it, too.

Selection 8:
We all have our own hierarchies of what we think is central in human relationships. My own feeling is so strongly that it's a matter of whether there *is* a relationship or not; *that* is superordinate in the hierarchy.

Selection 9:
In an argument with Kernberg he once called me a Sullivanian, and he thought he was insulting me [Laughter].

Selection 10:
If you're asking me about interpersonal and intrapsychic, I believe that that is an unfortunate antinomy—that would be a long, large discussion. I believe that is not a good way of putting it at all, [rather] that they influence each other. I don't want to be seen as privileging the one or the other. In fact, one of my objections to the so-called relational development in current psychoanalysis is that it seems to me that it *does* privilege the relational, despite the talk about the fact that of course the intrapsychic—whatever *that* means—is also a factor, so I don't want to be seen as privileging it (the relational). But in the analytic situation I must admit that, in my view, if there is evidence to me that there isn't a *relationship*, that is what requires first attention. And obviously there are powerful, intrapsychic reasons for that being the case. . . . In my view, if the two participants are not engaged with each other, it is not an analytic situation.

Selection 11:
Patients are not stupid. One of the most important things that Racker said is: we have this myth that there's a healthy analyst and a sick patient, and it's a myth. As Racker put it, there are two human beings, both of whom are struggling with ids, egos, and superegos. It also reminds me of what I think is one of Sullivan's very interesting remarks where he said, "There are two anxious people in the room; it is to be hoped that the therapist is the less anxious of the two." I won't inhibit a second thing that Sullivan said that I think is priceless. He said, "The supply of interpretations far exceeds the demand" [Laughter].

In losing Merton we lost a passionate explorer, challenger, defender, and lover of analysis. In this latter generation of American psychoanalysts he was one of the giants. As you listen to our panelists, try to listen, as Merton would have, for what is and is not going on between the analyst and the patient, and try to listen for what is gained and what may be lost with a particular analyst's theoretical orientation and clinical focus. If we can imagine Merton rising from his seat in the audience to chastise us once again and to argue, as he did so gloriously over the years, we will have achieved our goal this afternoon.

REFERENCES

Arlow, J. A. (1991). Two-Day Workshop on Process and Technique, Fall meeting, American Psychoanalytic Association, New York, December.

Gabbard, G. O. (1996). *Love and Hate in the Analytic Setting*. Northvale, NJ: Aronson.

Gill, M. M. (1954). Psychoanalysis and exploratory psychotherapy. *J. Amer. Psychoanal. Assn.*, 2:771–797.

Gill, M. M. (1994). *Psychoanalysis in Transition*. Hillsdale, NJ: The Analytic Press.

Gill, M. M. (1995). Classical and relational psychoanalysis. *Psychoanal. Psychol.*, 12:89–108.

Hoffman, I. Z. (1996). Merton M. Gill: A study in theory development. *Psychoanal. Dial.*, 6:5–53.

Raymond, L. W. & Rosbrow-Reich, S. (1997). *The Inward Eye*. Hillsdale, NJ: The Analytic Press.

Smith, H. F. (1997). Creative misreading: Why we talk past each other. *J. Amer. Psychoanal. Assn.*, 45:335–357.

Smith, H. F. (2000). Countertransference, conflictual listening, and the analytic object relationship. *J. Amer. Psychoanal. Assn.*, 48:95–128.

Wallerstein, R. S. (1997). Merton Gill, psychotherapy, and psychoanalysis. A personal dialogue. *J. Amer. Psychoanal. Assn.*, 45:233–256.

PART III

MERTON GILL: THEORETICIAN AND PSYCHOANALYST

Chapter 3

Merton M. Gill: A Study in Theory Development in Psychoanalysis

Irwin Z. Hoffman

Editors' Introduction: *In this reprinted essay, Irwin Z. Hoffman, Gill's closest collaborator in their work on transference, presents a masterful, comprehensive summary of Gill's contributions to psychoanalysis, including his early pioneering of hypnosis with Margaret Brenman, his work on psychiatric interviewing, on psychodiagnostic testing (with David Rapaport and Roy Schafer), his writings on metapsychology and psychoanalytic theory, and his theoretical, clinical, and research work on transference. The range and depth of Gill's scholarship is clearly illuminated by Hoffman.*

Merton Max Gill was born in Chicago in 1914. He was the second of three boys. For business reasons, the family soon moved to Milwaukee. In high school, Gill was among the top performers in an oratory club. He was an excellent student and graduated first in his class.

Gill received his Ph.B. (Bachelor of Philosophy) from the University of Chicago in 1934, having majored in psychology. His interest in psychoanalysis developed quite early, inspired, in part, by a reading of Freud's *Introductory Lectures*. By the time he entered medical school at the University of Chicago, he was certain that he wanted to become not only a psychiatrist but also a psychoanalyst. Gill received his M.D. from the University of Chicago in 1938 and went on to do his internship at Michael Reese Hospital from 1939 to 1941.

The original version of this paper was published in J. Reppen (ed.), *Beyond Freud* (The Analytic Press, 1985). A later version appearing in *Psychoanalytic Dialogues* 6:5–53 (1996) is republished here.

In 1941, Gill began his residency at the Menninger Clinic in Topeka, Kansas. Here his psychoanalytic career was launched under the influence of such notable psychoanalysts as Karl and William Menninger and Robert Knight. The most important intellectual influence was that of David Rapaport, the head of the Department of Psychology and subsequently of the Department of Research, with whom there quickly developed a very strong reciprocal bond. Gill became involved initially, along with Roy Schafer, in Rapaport's work on diagnostic psychological testing (Rapaport, Gill, and Schafer, 1945–1946, 1968). Later, he collaborated closely with Rapaport on the development of psychoanalytic metapsychology. At Topeka, Gill was also introduced by Margaret Brenman to hypnosis, a technique that was useful in treating the many war-related cases of traumatic neurosis at that time. This was the beginning of a 16-year collaborative investigation of hypnosis and related phenomena. Gill also met George Klein and Robert Holt, among others, at the Menninger Clinic.

After graduating from the Topeka Psychoanalytic Institue in 1947, Gill, along with Rapaport and Brenman, moved to Stockbridge, Massachusetts, to join Knight, who had become the director of the Austen Riggs Center. At Riggs, between 1948 and 1950, Gill continued his work on hypnosis and on metapsychology. From 1950 to 1953, Gill was at Yale, where he collaborated with Newman and Redlich in writing *The Initial Interview in Psychiatric Practice* (1954). While at Yale, he was appointed training analyst at the Western New England Psychoanalytic Institute.

Gill moved to Berkeley, California, in 1953, where he had a private practice and an appointment as training analyst at the San Francisco Psychoanalytic Institute. Supported by a grant from the Foundations Fund for Research in Psychiatry, Gill continued his collaboration with Brenman (Gill and Brenman, 1959) and with Rapaport (Rapaport and Gill, 1959). He met with Rapaport three or four times each year to exchange ideas and to go over papers and drafts of chapters for the book they were writing. Gill also teamed up with Timothy Leary to do research on psychotherapy, an effort that led to a coding scheme designed to give a comprehensive account of the psychotherapeutic process (Leary and Gill, 1959). Toward the end of this period in California, Gill collaborated with the neuropsychologist Karl Pribram in a study of Freud's *Project for a Scientific Psychology*. This work was shelved, however, and was not prepared for publication until many years later (Pribram and Gill, 1976).

Rapaport's untimely death in 1960 was a great personal loss for Gill. Soon after, he completed the monograph they had begun together (Gill, 1963) and began collecting Rapaport's papers (Rapaport, 1967). With George Klein, he also wrote a summary of Rapaport's contributions (Gill and Klein, 1964). Later he contributed a paper on the primary process to Robert Holt's collection of essays in Rapaport's honor (Gill, 1967).

In 1963, as the recipient of a lifetime Research Career Award from the

National Institute of Mental Health, Gill moved to Brooklyn, where he became Research Professor in Psychiatry at the Downstate Medical Center of the State University of New York. He also began in earnest to record psychoanalysis for research purposes, although he had done a good deal of recording previously in his studies of hypnosis and psychotherapy.

From 1968 to 1971 Gill was a Fellow at the Research Center for Mental Health at New York University. Here, he rejoined Klein and Holt, both of whom further influenced Gill's thinking on psychoanalytic metapsychology.

In 1971, soon after Klein's death, Gill returned to Chicago, where he became a professor of psychiatry at the University of Illinois at the Medical Center and a supervising analyst at the Chicago Institute for Psychoanalysis. With Leo Goldberger, he edited George Klein's (1976) book for publication. In 1976, he and Philip Holzman edited a collection of papers in Klein's memory dealing with the controversy that surrounded psychoanalytic metapsychology. In this volume, Gill (1976) published his own full-scale critique of metapsychology, calling into question much of what he himself had written over the years. In Chicago, changes in Gill's thinking about the psychoanalytic process were further stimulated by Samuel Lipton's ideas, particularly Lipton's distinction between technique and the personal relationship in psychoanalysis (Lipton, 1977a) and his close attention to various forms of resistance to the transference (Lipton, 1977b). Here, Gill (1979, 1982) crystalized his own revised view of psychoanalytic technique and the beginnings of a method for systematically studying its application (Gill and Hoffman, 1982b).

Among the most important influences on Gill's thinking were his own experiences as a patient with several analysts. These experiences left him with a deep sense of the difference that the personality of the analyst can make in the analytic process, as well as of the differences attributable to varying points of view on technique. Gill's convictions were informed and inspired by a wide range of experiences as an analyst, as an analysand, and as an intimate co-worker with many of the most seminal psychoanalytic thinkers of our time.

The Scope of Gill's Contributions

Merton Gill's contributions to psychoanalytic thought encompass a wide range of interrelated issues that are fundamental to the development of psychoanalysis as an intellectual and professional discipline. One of the extraordinary things about the corpus of Gill's work is that it embodies some of the major tensions in the field, with Gill himself standing among the leading spokespersons on both sides of a fundamental controversy. Thus, it was not unusual for Gill in 1984 to find himself differing sharply with someone who cited "Gill, 1954" to buttress his or her own position. Similarly, no critique of the earlier Gill is more thoroughgoing and unsparing than that which is stated or implied in Gill's later contributions.

At the heart of this movement in the history of Gill's ideas lies the renunciation of psychoanalytic metapsychology. In this respect, Gill's intellectual history is closely related to those of other students and colleagues of David Rapaport who moved away from the perspective of this extraordinary, charismatic teacher even while continuing to reflect his inspiration in the energy, rigor, and imagination of their own work (Holt, 1965, 1976; Klein, 1976; Schafer, 1976). Despite the striking commonalities among the members of this group, Gill's intellectual metamorphosis is especially noteworthy because he was probably the closest to Rapaport of his students. It was Gill who took it upon himself to collect Rapaport's papers (Rapaport, 1967). It was also Gill who completed the ambitious theoretical project that began with the landmark paper on the metapsychological points of view that he and Rapaport wrote together (Rapaport and Gill, 1959) and that culminated with the publication of *Topography and Systems in Psychoanalytic Theory* (Gill, 1963), most of which was written by Gill himself after Rapaport died. With Klein, as noted earlier, Gill also wrote an extraordinary summary of Rapaport's contributions (Gill and Klein, 1964). It is a tribute to Gill's intellectual independence and courage that he, too, finally broke with Rapaport and became one of the most thoughtful and careful critics of psychoanalytic metapsychology.

In this essay, Gill's contributions are reviewed in relation to three fundamental tasks or challenges that are critical for psychoanalysis and that are brought into sharper focus in Gill's work. The first is the challenge of determining and describing the nature of psychoanalysis as a discipline. I include under this heading Gill's contributions to metapsychology as well as his later critique of metapsychology and his argument against the natural science framework that psychoanalytic metapsychology utilizes. To include Gill's early contributions under this heading is to take a questionable liberty, since Gill was not raising questions about psychoanalysis as a discipline while he was immersed in elaborating its theoretical structure within a natural science frame of reference. Only with hindsight can one argue that seeds of the later critique were sown, paradoxically, by the very thoroughness of the earlier work. In this respect I am taking my cue from Gill himself, who said of Rapaport, "It was the clarity, brilliance, and persistence with which he pursued the implications of metapsychological theory that exposed its structure and problems" (quoted in Reppen, 1982, p. 169).

The second challenge is that of defining the nature of the psychoanalytic situation itself and the optimal psychoanalytic technique. What are the distinguishing features of psychoanalysis as compared with other therapies? How does psychoanalytic theory of technique take account of the fact that the analyst is a person who inevitably bears a personal relationship to the patient? This concern was central for Gill throughout his career, as was a variant of this question, one that lies on the interface of the metatheoretical and the clinical-theoretical areas, namely, what are the implications of the fact that psychoanalysis is a discipline in which the human mind is simultaneously the subject and the object of investigation? In his clinical contributions, too, we find a major shift in Gill's position. Unlike the shift in his metatheoretical perspective, however, there are relatively clear and direct precursors of Gill's later ideas on psychoanalytic treatment in his earlier work.

Finally, we have the challenge of subjecting psychoanalysis as a mode of therapy to some kind of systematic observation and empirical test, despite the requirements of confidentiality and the enormous complexity of the whole phenomenon. On this matter Gill was unwavering throughout his career. He insisted that the propositions of psychoanalysis must be verifiable according to the usual criteria of science. It was his conviction that to reject the notion that psychoanalysis is a natural science is by no means to reject the notion that it is indeed a science. Or, to approach the matter from the other side, Gill felt that to claim that psychoanalysis is a hermeneutic discipline is not to relinquish its scientific accountability.

It is somewhat artificial to separate Gill's contributions into these three areas because of the extent of their interrelationship. This is particularly true with respect to Gill's later work. Over the years, Gill's ideas developed into an increasingly coherent and internally consistent position. His metatheory, his clinical theory, and his attitude toward research developed into a unified perspective on psychoanalysis. What Gill had to say later in his career about research in the psychoanalytic situation followed logically from what he had to say about the nature of the psychoanalytic situation itself and about the essence of psychoanalytic technique. The clinical viewpoint, in turn, bears a close relationship to his critique of metapsychology and his espousal of a rigorous hermeneutic position for psychoanalysis. This conceptual integration was absent in Gill's earlier work; the contributions to metapsychology were either unrelated to the concurrent clinical contributions or bore a strained relationship to them. Similarly, the research focus was only partially related to the metapsychological investigations or to clinical psychoanalysis.

As noted earlier, Gill's later perspective amounts to a telling critique of his earlier ideas. In this overview of Gill's contributions, a bias will be evident in that the earlier work will be considered in the light of its relationship to later developments in Gill's thinking. This approach automatically risks diminishing the intrinsic value of certain earlier positions and contributions because they will appear either as germinal vis-à-vis what comes later or as unworthy of further development in their own right. No history is unbiased, however, and I would be hard pressed to look at Gill's earlier work in any other way because, in some important respects, I shared his later perspective and had the good fortune to collaborate with him on aspects of its development. What follows is a selective review of Gill's extensive writings (particularly through 1984) that draws primarily on books and papers that seem to represent culminations or crystalizations of phases of his work and thought.

Contributions to Psychoanalytic Metatheory

Gill's Immersion in Metapsychology

Rapaport and Gill (1959) set out to complete a program that they believed Freud left unfinished, namely, the spelling out of "that minimal set of assumptions upon which psychoanalytic theory rests" (p. 1). They group these assumptions under five headings that, they propose, constitute the basic *points of view* of psychoanalytic metapsychology. These points of view are at the highest level of abstraction in the theory (Gill, 1963, p. 153). Presumably, to be complete, a psychoanalytic explanation of any psychological phenomenon must include reference to all five points of view. According to Rapaport and Gill (1959), these points of view are the *dynamic* (having to do with force), the *economic* (having to do with energy), the *structural* (having to do with "abiding psychological configurations"), the *genetic* (having to do with origins and development), and the *adaptive* (having to do with relationship to the environment). The genetic and adaptive points of view are additions to those explicitly formulated by Freud. The structural point of view refers specifically to the division of the mental apparatus into the systems of id, ego, and superego, and replaces the topographic point of view insofar as the latter refers specifically to the division of the mental apparatus into the systems of unconscious (Ucs.), preconscious (Pcs.), and conscious (Cs.). Rapaport and Gill argue that, although he moved in this direction, "Freud never explicitly replaced the topographic point of view of metapsychology by a structural one" (p. 2).

The Elucidation of Theoretical Inconsistencies

Gill's contributions to psychoanalytic metapsychology bear the stamp of Rapaport's influence both in style and substance. In *Topography and Systems in Psychoanalytic Theory* (1963), Gill's most extensive metapsychological work (see Ross, 1965, and Spence, 1964, for synopses and reviews), we find a scrupulous attention to Freud's writings. Often, quotations and page citations on some aspect of the subject are followed first by a highlighting of internal inconsistencies and then by a creative attempt at integration, including whatever reformulation seems necessary or useful. This kind of careful exegesis of Freud's writings, one of Rapaport's legacies (Gill and Klein, 1964), invariably underscores the complexity of Freud's thinking and the elusiveness of what Freud "really meant" by such terms as "ego," "id," "primary process," "secondary process," and even "metapsychology" itself. The elusiveness is, in itself, a tribute to Freud's scientific temperament. It reflects his refusal to become comfortable with formulations that are simplistic, incomplete, or inconsistent with other theoretical propositions and with clinical data.

Apfelbaum (1966) is critical of Gill for implying that the contradictions in Freud are avoidable and that it is, in principle, possible to develop a more coherent and internally consistent account of the systems of the mind. He writes, "One aim of Gill's monograph is to give the *coup de grace* to the topographic model, so as finally to settle the issue from what point of view the mental systems are to be established. Gill finds in Freud's unwillingness to drop this model a difficulty of Freud's rather than a difficulty inherent in the structural approach itself" (p. 467). In point of fact, however, Apfelbaum does Gill something of a disservice here in that Gill's monograph, quite in the spirit of Freud's writings on the subject, raises as many questions as it answers about psychic structures.

Indeed, Gill's discussion shatters any illusion one might wish to maintain that the replacement of the topographic model by the structural model does away with internal inconsistencies within the various subsystems of the mind. Gill diligently follows Freud in his attempt to localize various properties of mental content in one or another subsystem. He examines each of the dimensions with which Freud was struggling: the relationship of contents to consciousness, the condition of their energy, their mode of functioning, whether or not they employ neutral energy, and, finally, whether they are associated with the repressed or the forces of repression. For the sake of scientific elegance, it would have been convenient if unconsciousness, free energy pressing for immediate discharge, primary process (that is, drive-organized ideas), absence of neutral energy, and contents that are considered to be repressed had all been located in one system. Conversely, consciousness, inhibited or bound energy, secondary process, neutral energy, and the forces of repression, ideally, would all be correlated and form a second major system. That the repressing forces—the defenses—could themselves be unconscious was decisive in leading Freud partially to discard the topographic model, that is, the criterion of consciousness for defining systems. Instead, Freud chose to group together the repressed in the system-id and the repressing forces in the system-ego. As Gill (1963) notes, however,

> Freud's solution of the difficulties of the topographic system leaves unresolved a number of issues relating to these difficulties. Even if the relationship to consciousness is dropped as a criterion of mental sys-

> tems, it is still necessary to account for the exceptions to parallelism between the relationship of contents to consciousness and their mode of organization and kind of cathexis; and a division of the repressed and repressing into id and ego fails to account for the similarity between them indicated by the fact that they are both dynamically unconscious [p. 51].

It is noteworthy that Gill's extraordinary effort to reconcile these contradictions ends up with his raising a significant question about the validity of the structural model itself insofar as it connotes a set of internally consistent, relatively well-demarcated systems of the mind. There seems to be no end to the "exceptions to parallelism" that are exposed by clinical experience. Perhaps one of the most important and bold contributions of Gill's (1963) monograph is the blurring of the distinction between id and ego:

> I favor, then, a definition in which id and ego are conceived of as a hierarchical continuum of forces and structures existing at all levels of the hierarchy.
>
> Such a solution argues that Freud's resolution of the fourth difficulty of the topographic systems was *not a good one,* because, by putting force into one system and counterforce into another, it obscured the existence of a hierarchy of force-counterforce integrations, and while conceptualizing counterforce in structural terms, did not do the same for force. The recognition of this hierarchy, furthermore, makes it clear that, on any particular level of the hierarchy, force and counterforce, despite their antithesis, show similarities in mode of functioning, energy employed, and energy regulated [pp. 146–147; italics added].

Gill's emphasis on continua of types of mental activity throughout might be regarded as a forerunner of his later holistic approach, which places the whole person at the center of the theory. This change will be discussed further later on. The main point I wish to make here is that one comes away from *Topography and Systems* with anything but the sense that the whole notion of systems has been salvaged and clarified. Indeed, whether it is useful to think at all in terms of discrete psychological systems, at least in accord with the various criteria that Freud was juggling, seems questionable and is explicitly challenged by Gill.

The Depreciation of Consciousness

In *Topography and Systems*, Gill (1963) discusses the considerations that argue for discarding the topographic perspective as a metapsychological point of view. Central to his thesis is the idea that "the relationship [of contents] to consciousness can be subsumed under the five metapsychological points of view" (p. 159). Gill takes pains to emphasize that to demonstrate that "a topographic point of view in metapsychology is unnecessary" is not to "belittle the importance of the relation of contents to consciousness and of consciousness as such." On the contrary, topographic conceptions retain "an important place in psychoanalysis, both clinically and theoretically" (p. 148).

This disclaimer, however, is unconvincing. To say that the topographic status of a mental event, which encompasses its phenomenological status, can be "subsumed under" (p. 159) the other points of view, or is "explicable in terms of the more basic hypotheses" (p. 159) associated with them, or can be "accounted for" (p. 61) in their terms is to denigrate consciousness as a source of explanation in the theory. Elsewhere, Gill and Klein (1964) indirectly acknowledge as much when, speaking of Rapaport, they state that "he observed that with the replacement of Freud's topographic systems by the tripartite model of ego, id, and superego, consciousness was reduced in importance" (p. 493). Applying Gill's (1976) own critique of metapsychology, I believe that the idea that topographic considerations are reducible to the other points of view follows from the mistake of assuming that quasi-neurophysiological concepts describable in terms of the dimensions of natural science are of a higher order or are more abstract than psychological concepts. That this is the mistaken assumption underlying the exclusion of a topographic point of view may be obscured by the fact that the view itself can be framed largely in natural science terms. Such terms, however, are applicable primarily to the preconditions for the emergence of conscious experience, not to the impact of consciousness itself on the organization of experience and behavior. We can see this clearly if we examine the terms of Gill's (1963) discussion of the clinical importance of consciousness (chapter 9) and compare it with the terms of his argument against the inclusion of the topographic perspective among the basic metapsychological points of view (chapter 10). In the first discussion, for example, Gill speaks of the hypothesis that "insight plays a vital role in changing behavior" (p. 151). In the second discussion, Gill argues that "access to consciousness is determined by competition among external forces, among internal forces, and between external and internal forces" (p. 155). To apply Gill's later critique (1976, 1977a), the first of these statements is framed in psychological terms, whereas the second is framed in quasi-neurophysiological terms. According to Gill in 1976, only the first is relevant to psychoanalytic theory, but in 1963 the first statement was regarded as subordinate to the second in line with the assumption that psychological phenomena must be explained by antecedent neurophysiological conditions.

One is left, then, with this non sequitur: the *preconditions* of consciousness can be described in terms of the economic, structural, dynamic, genetic, and adaptive points of view. Therefore, the difference that consciousness *makes* in experience and behavior is subsumable under these points of view. The rejoinder may be that even the changes that follow from consciousness, or, more particularly, from insight, may be describable in terms of the other points of view. We find such a formulation in the following statement by Gill (1963): "The sense organ Cs. plays the highest role in the hierarchy of regulations of psychic functioning, increasing the cathexis of contents to which the attention cathexis is directed, bringing about an advance in synthesis of the contents which excite it, and making possible the cathecting even of contents which give rise to unpleasure" (p. 158).

The weakness of this argument is transparent, since consciousness is reduced to some sort of sensory apparatus, and it is not at all clear how a sensory apparatus can "direct" anything. Moreover, to the extent that it does direct ensuing processes, it is not at all evident how this element of control could be described without reference to consciousness itself, that is, by referring only to the interactions among various other forces. The fact is that the directive properties of the system Cs. carry us inescapably into the realm of human intention and into the universe of discourse in which intention, meaning, and self-conscious reflection have their proper place. Among the critics of psychoanalytic metapsychology, Klein (1976) probably was the clearest and most emphatic on this issue.

The restoration of consciousness in psychoanalytic theory does not in any way imply a denigration of the crucial role of unconsciously motivated actions. However, terms like intention and meaning, which Gill came to regard as the proper terms for psychoanalytic discourse, are, to begin with, categories of conscious experience. These categories are then attributed to phenomena that lie outside the realm of conscious experience but that nevertheless act to a significant degree "as if" they were conscious. As Gill (1977a) wrote: "Let it be recalled that Freud insisted that only on the assumption that unconscious psychological processes must be understood in the same terms as conscious ones, except for the fact of consciousness itself, could one fill in the gaps in conscious life and construct a coherent, meaningful psychological continuity" (pp. 585–586).

In the end, Gill himself equivocated about the demotion of the topographic perspective from the level of formal point of view to the level of clinical theory. He concluded *Topography and Systems* (1963) with a telling disclaimer: "It is of course also possible that with some future redefinition or reclassification of the metapsychological points of view a topographic point of view will be included. The issue is, after all, one of definition" (p. 169). Nevertheless, it is a measure of the degree to which Gill uncritically adopted the natural science frame of reference of metapsychology that in his major theoretical contribution to it he slights the point of view that is most useful clinically and that is closest to the data of the psychoanalytic situation and of interpersonal experience generally. Implicit in the holistic "person point of view" that Gill (1983b) was later to adopt as the supraordinate point of view of psychoanalysis, and implicit also in the theory of technique that Gill came to advocate is a recognition of the fundamental importance of the topographic point of view and of consciousness in psychoanalytic explanation.

The Depreciation of Object Relations

Another indicator of the depth of Gill's immersion in metapsychology was his relative neglect of internal and external objects in his discussion of the systems of the mind. Freud's superego provides the basis for a bridge from a mechanistic model, in which the forces of the id are harnessed by the apparatuses of the ego, to one in which the person's experience is seen as shaped by his or her interactions with others. Yet not only is the person as such virtually absent from Gill's account of mental processes in 1963, but so are other persons, which is merely the other side of the same coin.

The systems of the mind, in the framework of classical metapsychology, house and process various stimuli from within and from without. Presumably, the stimuli that are associated with encounters with other human beings, who are perceived eventually as whole persons, are the most important in determining the quality of experience, behavior, and development. Freud's concept of the superego (even though it may derive its power from the forces of the id) theoretically requires attention to object relations—that is, to the meaning of interpersonal encounters as opposed to impersonal stimuli as they impinge on the individual. As Apfelbaum (1966) points out, ego psychology tended systematically to underemphasize the superego precisely because it is not readily accounted for in a mechanistic model:

> The omission of the superego on a level of formal theorizing by Hartmann, Rapaport and Gill further illustrates the point that the structural approach, as they have developed it, no longer refers to the study of the interrelations of id, ego and superego, but to formulations having to do with "the control of structure over drive." To put this another way, the structural approach now refers to the construction of a psycho-analytic model which relies wholly on explanation in terms of energy and structure. A dynamic conception such as the superego is

> not congenial to this model since it cannot be rendered in these terms [pp. 460–461].

Apfelbaum goes on to praise Melanie Klein, Erikson, Zetzel, and Winnicott for their focus on the superego and the corollary understanding that "the nature of the ego is determined at all times by its relations with internal and external objects" (p. 461). This view is consistent with Gill's later critique of metapsychology, which grew out of a hermeneutic position. For Gill, this position is inseparable from a relational perspective.

The Seeds of the Later Critique

Gill's metapsychological contributions pull simultaneously toward the deepest possible immersion in a natural science framework and toward the extrication of psychoanalytic theory from it as an inappropriate universe of discourse. As counterpoint to Gill's depreciation of consciousness and his underemphasis of object relations, we find a surfacing of fundamental questions that jeopardize the entire way of thinking entailed by psychoanalytic metapsychology. In the first place, the internal contradictions are so cumbersome, and the moves necessary to resolve them so convoluted and so distant from the data that they allegedly comprehend, that the viability of the whole project seems precarious. In the end, as we have seen, Gill's proposals are actually quite radical in that they challenge the validity of existing attempts to define clearly demarcated subsystems in the mind and argue instead for an emphasis on continua (see Gill, 1967). Freud (1923) himself said that "the ego is not sharply separated from the id; its lower portion merges into it" (p. 24). Gill (1963, p. 141) goes beyond Freud, however, encouraging an almost complete erosion of the boundaries between the two systems. His position actually foreshadows a retreat from the notion of a primary source of energy and force having a prepsychological, quasi-organic basis. *The infusion of the id with the properties ordinarily reserved for the ego represents a pull away from drive theory as conceptualized in traditional metapsychological terms. At the same time, the infusion of the ego with the motivational properties ordinarily reserved for the id pulls away from the notion of a rational agency in the mind that has access to the outside world uncontaminated by subjectivity.* Thus, although it was clearly not part of his intent, Gill, in 1963, had already laid the groundwork for the dissolution of the sharp dichotomy of subjectivity and objectivity that characterized Freud's epistemology and that so colored his clinical theory. Moreover, Gill's redefinition of the id represents a precursor of his later attack on the "energy-discharge point of view" as distinct from the "person point of view" in psychoanalysis (Gill, 1983b).

The Repudiation of Metapsychology

Gill's movement away from metapsychology had to be a painful process, given his closeness to Rapaport. He did, however, have the support of Schafer and Klein, among others. Klein, in particular, had a strong influence on Gill's thinking. Gill's (1976) critique of metapsychology further develops Klein's (1973) original notion that psychoanalytic theory is characterized by a mingling of terms from two universes of discourse, the psychological and the biological, and that the two must be disentangled before psychoanalytic theory can develop in any useful way.

The reversal of Gill's position on the value of classical metapsychology for psychoanalysis is reflected in a dramatic way in the book he wrote with Pribram on Freud's *Project for a Scientific Psychology* (Pribram and Gill, 1976). Here, Pribram and Gill elaborate on metapsychology as a theoretical model for neuropsychological investigations. In a certain sense, this effort is in keeping with Gill's claim that metapsychology is, in fact, in a different universe of discourse than is psychoanalytic psychology. It also carries the implication, however, that the development of psychoanalysis itself will be promoted by investigations that focus on "brain-behavior-experience interfaces" (p. 168). In a conclusion that was added around the time of publication, more than 10 years after much of the collaborative work was completed (Gill, personal communication), there is an unusually candid statement of sharp disagreement on this issue between the two authors. The book concludes with this provocative comment:

> Where we differ is that Gill feels that psychoanalysis must go its own way and that means purging it of its natural science metapsychology, while Pribram welcomes psychoanalysis back into the natural sciences. Pribram doubts that the differing views of the two authors are really, in the long run, incompatible, while Gill finds them irreconcilable [p. 169].

The format of Gill's (1976) tour de force on metapsychology is once again in the Rapaport tradition in that it begins with a detailed examination of Freud's writings in order to clarify the implications of Freud's theoretical propositions. In particular, Gill does psychoanalysis an inestimable service by documenting Freud's continuing tendency to gravitate toward neurophysiology despite his many disclaimers and his acceptance, at times, of psychoanalytic psychology as a science in its own right. Repeatedly, as Gill shows, Freud betrayed an underlying feeling that the phenomena of psychology must be explained by neurophysiology.

It is important to emphasize that Gill is not rejecting theory as such, including the whole hierarchy of concepts that characterize a fully developed theory, ranging from concepts that are close to the data to those that are more distant and more abstract. That he was rejecting theory is a common misunderstanding that goes hand in hand with the idea that the survival of Freud's metapsychology is equivalent to the survival of analytic theory itself. Rather, Gill is arguing that concepts having to do with space, force, energy, and the like are not on a higher level of abstraction than are those that are clinically derived and that are framed in strictly psychological terms. Instead, the former are hypotheses about the neurophysiological correlates of psychological phenomena. What is wrong here is not only that they happen to be bad neurophysiology (Holt, 1965), but that they are intended as concepts of a higher order than are those of the clinical theory.

In fact, Gill is not even entirely rejecting the metapsychological points of view. He argues, for example, that although the terms of the economic point of view so consistently reify the notion of quantities of energy and force that they should be discarded, the other points of view, especially the structural and dynamic, might be salvageable if reformulated in psychological terms. Gill (1976) concludes his critique of metapsychology with a statement that is much milder than the title, "Metapsychology is Not Psychology," suggests:

> Metapsychological propositions and clinical propositions that are purely psychological must be disentangled and examined on their appropriate grounds. For this reason, despite the argument that there is no direct connection between metapsychology and psychology, the present state of affairs in psychoanalytic theory is such that it makes no sense to say globally that one accepts or rejects metapsychology [pp. 103–104].

Following Klein and Schafer, Gill insists that not only is the quasi-neurophysiological theory of metapsychology detrimental to the development of psychoanalysis, but so is any "metatheory" that implies that psychological phenomena must be explained in terms of mechanisms known from another universe of discourse. Thus, it is not surprising that Gill rejects the attempt to substitute the model of the computer and information theory (Peterfreund, 1971) for traditional metapsychology. Information theory is seductive because it seems, on the surface, to be addressing the problem of meaning itself, thereby avoiding the pitfall of traditional metapsychology. Gill (1977a), however, claims that the terms of information theory are either being used in an informal, nontechnical way, in which case they amount to "no more than a restatement of psychoanalytic propositions in technical sounding terms like 'feedback' and `match and mismatch'" (p. 591), or else they are being used in a technical sense, which means they are located in a natural science frame of reference. Once again, in other words, the assumption is being made that psychoanalytic theory building must subsume the phenomena of self-conscious human experience under the rubric of an allegedly more general set of phenomena in which the person as agent is absent. Gill's point is that the very exclusion of the person identifies information theory as one that deals with a different universe of discourse than psychoanalysis rather than as one that is at a higher level of abstraction.

Gill is arguing for a theory that assumes the existence of the person as "a unitary human agent conceived of as initiating and in that sense responsible for pursuing humanly meaningful aims" (Reppen, 1982, p. 179) and that proceeds to identify patterns and regularities among such aims and the adaptations that accompany them. To a certain extent, especially with respect to the content of basic human motives, he leaves open the question of what will evolve from a purely clinical, person-oriented psychoanalytic theory. Gill (1977a) was loathe to give up the central importance of drives in development:

> The close association in our literature between the concept of peremptoriness, instinctual drives, and psychic energy apparently leads many to believe that the abandonment of the concept of psychic energy amounts to giving up the idea of instinctual drives. That is simply not true. What is true is that the biological phenomena related to instinctual drive cannot be directly translated into the realm of psychoanalytic psychology, but become relevant there only in terms of their meaningfulness [p. 593].

There are indications in Gill's writings, however, of a questioning of the concept of the primacy of instinctual drives, even if recast in psychological terms. Thus, for example, he describes as "fateful" the theoretical step Freud took when he conceptualized conflict between the systems of the mind in terms of forces seeking expression and those opposed to such expression. Gill (1978) explains that this step "opened the way to designate a special class of motivations as the ones seeking expression in contrast to that class of motivations which sought to keep them from expression. The class seeking expression was referred to as the instinctual impulses and those were in turn related to bodily needs, in particular sexual" (p. 484). The emergence of the structural theory did nothing to change this basic distinction between the two types of motivation, Gill continues:

> Though [Freud] had thus disposed of the error of assuming that defensive processes had ready access to consciousness while the processes defended against did not, he was still left with a class distinction between processes seeking expression and processes seeking to prevent such expression.

> An alternative scheme would have been to conceptualize the contending processes as equally striving for expression and to sever the idea of processes seeking expression from any special relationship to the body, but such a scheme would have violated his conception of a hierarchy of psychic processes with the base of the hierarchy constituted by the somatic "drives" [pp. 484–485].

Although Gill does not explicitly draw the implications, his position certainly is consistent with the kind of theorizing that George Klein (1976) undertook. Freed of the encumbrance of metapsychology, Klein set forth a revised view of human sexuality and proposed other types of "vital pleasures" that have a kind of irreducible status.

Gill's New Metatheory: An Epistemological Position

It is true, nevertheless, that Gill himself refrained from formulating specific notions of the fundamental motives that organize behavior and experience. He devoted most of his attention to psychoanalytic theory of technique, complete with lower level concepts, such as types of communications by the patient and types of interventions by the analyst (Gill, 1982; Gill and Hoffman, 1982b), and higher level concepts, such as resistance to awareness of transference, resistance to the resolution of transference, and propositions about the interrelationships among all of these (Gill, 1979, 1982). At the highest level of abstraction we find a bridge to the new metatheoretical perspective that Gill adopted. Although in some of his writings he equated metapsychology with Freud's energy discharge model, Gill (1983b) also stated that he regarded as a "cogent objection" the idea that "any system of thought must have a `meta' organizing principle, whether implicit or explicit" (p. 525). The organizing principle that Gill believed should replace Freud's basic concept of energy discharge is "the person point of view." For Gill, the term person connotes both the *agency* of the subject of analytic investigation and treatment and the subject's *social* nature.

What appear to have been left out of Gill's theory of technique are propositions about the content of the issues that one would expect to be sources of conflict for the individual and that would become the objects of resistance. Gill's theory of technique, in this particular sense, is content free. But it is important to recognize that this absence of attention to content is not merely the reflection of Gill's particular area of interest. There is, rather, something intrinsic to Gill's position that is resistant to generalizations about the content of human motivation. This feature lies at the heart of what evolved as Gill's epistemology and, at the same time, is the organizing principle at the apex of the hierarchy of concepts that constitute his theory of technique. This is the principle of perspectivism or constructivism;[1] the meaning of any emotionally significant experience is actively organized by the person according to a particular perspective that he or she brings to bear in interpreting it. This position is necessarily skeptical of or actively critical of propositions about universal motives, since such propositions may imply a transcendence of perspectivism—a revelation, one might say, of the motivational factors that generate perspectives in the first place. A perspectivist position, by definition, does not allow for the possibility of such transcendence. This is not to say that perspectivists may not, for heuristic purposes, posit the existence of certain basic motives, but they would naturally be skeptical about the applicability of such motives to any particular culture, subculture, individual, or individual at a certain moment in time.[2]

The definition of perspectivism just given does not refer explicitly to one important feature of the principle—its social basis. People's perspectives develop and are sustained or eroded in the context of their interactions with other persons. In analysis, according to Gill, one never reaches a point where one discovers something that comes solely from the patient, independent of the influence of other persons. Instead, one finds specific interactions out of which certain perspectives emerged that colored subsequent interactions. In these interactions, the patient, with the participation of the other persons involved, constructed an identity, a social world, and a way of living with other people, which the patient perpetuates in subsequent encounters. This way of being with others is not the only way available to the patient, although he or she may subjectively experience it as such.[3]

There is one basic human tendency or motive that Gill's perspectivism can accommodate, and that is the universal human tendency to make sense of experience in an interpersonal context. The need for meaning and the need for other people are inextricably intertwined. Gill gravitated toward theories, such as Bowlby's, that emphasize human attachment as the basic motive in the hierarchy of human motives (Gill, 1983b; see also Eagle, 1981). He shied away from considering the seeking or construction of

---

[1] I have chosen the term constructivism in my own writing (Hoffman, 1991, 1992b, c), but Gill generally used the terms perspectivism and constructivism interchangeably, which is how they are used in this essay.

[2] It is important to recognize that theory building is not precluded from a constructivist point of view and that healthy skepticism is not the same as nihilism.

[3] The emphasis on social interaction has practical utility in the psychoanalytic situation. However, I do not believe it precludes theorizing about what the individual brings to relationships, both in terms of internalized structures derived from experiences with others and in terms of innate tendencies that are relatively free of social influence. This is the view that Gill (1994, e.g., pp. 18–28) adopted himself in his last book, in which he insists that psychoanalysis requires an integration of "one-person" and "two-person" points of view.

meaning as primary motives (see Basch, 1977) because, for him, interpersonal human relatedness was paramount. However, Gill's epistemology and his emphasis on human interaction can readily be integrated.

Gill's theory of technique can be viewed, in effect, as the clinical application of his epistemology. This is not, of course, a reflection of the way in which the theory of technique evolved. On the contrary, Gill moved from particular clinical experiences, as an analysand and as an analyst, toward a deep conviction about a way of working with people that he felt would be most conducive to change. If anything, his epistemology grew out of his clinical theory. Once the epistemology is articulated, however, it is not difficult to go back and see its reflection in the theory of technique.

Gill sees the psychoanalytic situation as one in which two people interact and continually try to establish the meaning of that interaction as one of them experiences it. Gill's focus on the here-and-now can be viewed, in part, as an intensive molecular study of the process by which meaning is constructed by one human being—the patient—in interaction with another—the analyst. This process is understood to be liberating precisely because it entails a movement by the patient from an absolute view of his or her predicament, which is dominated by the neurotic or obstructing transference, to a perspectivist view, which allows for the realization of latent potentialities. Such change is born of an emotionally meaningful interpersonal experience in which patient and analyst work together to extricate themselves from the repetitive patterns that the neurotic transference and countertransference impose, as if these patterns defined the only ways in which the two participants could relate. Before giving a fuller account of Gill's later theory of technique, let us go back and review the clinical contributions that antedate it and that, in varying degrees, contain the seeds of its development.

The Clinical Contributions

As noted earlier, unlike the integral relationship between his later theory of technique and his later metatheoretical position, there is only a partial connection between Gill's earlier clinical contributions and his metapsychological contributions. In discussing this second aspect of Gill's work, I will focus on three main areas of clinical contribution: hypnosis, the initial psychiatric interview, and psychoanalytic technique.

Studies of Hypnosis and Related States

Gill's research and writing on hypnosis bring together many of his major areas of interest. Unlike his work on the initial interview (Gill, Newman, and Redlich, 1954), which maintains a strictly clinical focus throughout,

Gill's discussion of hypnosis includes the ambitious attempt to synthesize empirical observations and clinical theory, on one hand, with classical metapsychology, on the other. Consistent with a value that runs through all of Gill's professional life, however, the work on hypnosis was inspired by an interest in developing an approach that could be applied usefully to deal with a pressing clinical problem—in this instance, that of traumatic neurosis during World War II.

The publication of *Hypnosis and Related States* (Gill and Brenman, 1959) represented the culmination of his collaboration with Brenman on a wide range of studies, which involved the participation of many outstanding clinicians, including Knight, Karl Menninger, and Schafer. Over time, the authors' interest in the clinical application of hypnosis evolved into a much broader task, which was to understand regressive states generally, including those encountered in the usual psychoanalytic situation.

The entire complex project employed a combination of methods, including observation of hypnosis in psychotherapeutic situations, experimental procedures, and even the use of anthropological data gathered by Bateson and Mead (1942) in their study of trance states in Bali. The work by Gill and Brenman (1959) is a model of clinical research; not only are many methods used and systematically compared, but the authors are extraordinarily diligent in openly discussing the process of the research and the thinking that went into each piece of work that they undertook. Hypotheses and findings are always accompanied by candid discussion of uncontrolled variables affecting the authors' sense of confidence in their own hunches and conclusions. Systematic quantitative studies are supplemented by a wealth of rich clinical material throughout.

The studies of hypnosis include a fascinating oscillation between the poles of the strictly psychological and the biopsychological. Significantly, and in accord with Gill's later work, Gill and Brenman (1959) state: "For many years we found ourselves accumulating two apparently independent bodies of data from our observations of the hypnotic state, but were unable to discern any theoretical bridge between them. The observations of 'altered ego function' and of 'transference phenomena' seemed to us to be in quite separate realms of discourse" (p. xix).

However, in sharp contrast to Gill's later psychoanalytic focus, which is deliberately confined to the realm of "transference phenomena" in the broad sense (that is, the realm of the interpersonally meaningful), Gill and Brenman considered the integration of the two realms of discourse to be of great importance. Although, to be sure, the subject matter in this instance was hypnosis and not psychoanalysis or psychoanalytic theory per se, the authors were operating with a psychoanalytic perspective and the work itself was undertaken in the spirit of a psychoanalytic investigation, as the subtitle, *Psychoanalytic Studies in Regression*, makes clear.

Thus, it is legitimate to contrast Gill's implicit perspective on psychoanalysis as a discipline in this book with his later viewpoint. The earlier work epitomizes a contribution born of the view that psychoanalysis can and should be a general psychology. What makes this possible, Gill and Brenman argue, is the development of ego psychology as represented in the work of Hartmann, Kris, Loewenstein, and Rapaport. As a result of the efforts of these theorists, it is possible, the authors claim, to investigate the effects on the ego of various kinds of environmental factors, including the presence or absence of various quantities of "stimulation." The authors state as the "basic theoretical premise of their book" that "hypnosis is a particular kind of regressive process which may be initiated either by sensory motor-ideational deprivation or by the stimulation of an archaic relationship to the hypnotist" (p. xx). It is not that Gill would later argue that only the meaning of the relationship to the patient is necessary to describe or explain the phenomenon of hypnosis, and that the effects of stimulus deprivation as such are unimportant. He would assert, however, that an investigation defined as *psychoanalytic* would be confined to and would be designed to maximize what could be understood about that aspect of the phenomenon having to do with its meaning to the participants.

Another issue that sharply divides Gill's point of view in his work on hypnosis from his later perspective is the role of regression in the psychoanalytic process. For Gill in the 1960s, there was little doubt that an induced regression lay at the heart of the process. His intensive investigation of hypnosis and related regressive states was undoubtedly fueled in part by the assumption that anything learned about regression in hypnosis would not only have clinical utility in itself, but would also further the understanding of psychoanalytic treatment. Gill and Brenman (1959, pp. 117, 134–135, 329) cite and agree with Macalpine's (1950) conceptualization of the psychoanalytic process as a kind of slow-motion hypnotic procedure. Hypnosis also has in common with psychoanalytic treatment the fact that, ideally, the regression is not a total one ("regression proper") but rather a partial one, which "a subsystem of the ego" undergoes in keeping with Kris's concept of regression in the service of the ego. This regression is brought about in hypnosis as well as in analysis by a combination of impersonal factors (such as stimulus deprivation) and interpersonal factors (such as promotion of a submissive, dependent attitude). Although the regression itself, in either case, is not spontaneous but induced, the particular form that the regression takes bears the stamp of each patient's history and neurotic conflicts. Important points of agreement and disagreement between Gill's earlier view of transference and his later view are well illustrated in the following statement from *Hypnosis and Related States:*

> We know in general that when a "transference interpretation" is made, it should in fact be an interpretation which shows the patient that his response is not appropriately geared to the actual behavior of the therapist, but is in fact an expression of something ancient in himself which he has brought to the situation. We must now ask ourselves what is our position in this connection if we introduce a technique (hypnosis) which implicitly states, "By dint of what I am doing you will find yourself able to do things you otherwise cannot and unable to do things you otherwise can." In short, if we take a position which implies superior power, how can we ask the patient to analyze the irrational, transference aspect of his being hypnotizable at all? Yet we have done this, usually in the face of bitter resistance from our patients, some of whom, as we have seen, said they would prefer to give up the use of hypnosis entirely rather than analyze its meaning for them. As one might expect, despite what one might call the "reality provocation" of inducing hypnosis, it has been possible to tease out the specifically personal projections of each individual and, on the basis of what the hypnotic relationship seemed to mean to him, to make use of these in the treatment.
>
> Yet is this qualitatively different from the non-hypnotic standard psychoanalysis where we ask the patient to lie down while we sit up, where we arrogate to ourselves the privilege of responding or not as we see fit, where we ask the patient to let us see him completely though he cannot see us, and finally where from time to time we tell him what is "really" going on? Does not all of this too imply that we regard ourselves as "in charge" of the situation in a uniquely powerful way? Indeed, how commonly this is the lament of the analysand. Yet, the fact remains that each analysand reacts in his own way to this "provocation" too, and reveals his archaic and established patterns of feeling and behavior as transference phenomena [Gill and Brenman, 1959, pp. 369–370].

Clearly, Gill was concerned then as he was later about the influence of the analyst's behavior on the patient's experience of the relationship. Indeed, the strained quality of his effort to reconcile the classical view of transference with his appreciation of the influence that the analyst exerts is striking and seems to almost beg for the new resolution he was later to achieve. Gill eventually ceased to define transference, even with its particular idiosyncratic nuances, as divorced from the way in which the analyst participates in the process. Also, in accord with the perspectivist position he developed, Gill ceased to divide the patient's experience into an aspect appropriate to the present circumstances and one grossly inappropriate to them which comes entirely from the past.

In a major departure from his earlier views, Gill later opposed considering the deliberate attempt to induce a regression to be essential or even desirable in the psychoanalytic situation. He eventually objected, in principle, to any intentional manipulation of the patient regardless of its purpose. What becomes the core of the psychoanalytic process is the exploration of the ways in which the patient is assimilating the advertent and inadvertent influences that the analyst exerts via the analyst's inevitably significant emotional participation in the interaction (Gill, 1982, 1983a). A molecular analysis and explication of the patient's conscious and preconscious way of constructing and construing the immediate interaction with the analyst replaces the induction of a state of mind that is allegedly closer to that of the primary process and the unconscious. Thus, there is no question that Gill abandoned the effort to investigate in a direct way, in the psychoanalytic situation or in any other context, those mental states that appear to be discontinuous with familiar, secondary-process modes of thought. The condensed, often uncanny symbolic richness of the material represented in many of the vignettes in *Hypnosis and Related States* seems to be absent from much of the clinical material Gill published later to illustrate his revised view of analysis of transference (e.g., Gill and Hoffman, 1982a).

It is clear that Gill turned away from the mysteries of hypnotic states, dreams, fugue states, and so on in favor of the seemingly more readily accessible nuances of interpersonal interactions. It would be easy, but also a mistake, however, to assume that Gill's course simply represents a flight from a dangerous and foreign world to a more familiar and safe one. The fact is that although the content and modes of organization of thought in the psychoanalytic discourse that Gill came to encourage may seem familiar or mundane, the type of interaction he sought is rare indeed, and the route toward its achievement is not without its own special psychological perils. Indeed, Gill began to suspect that being caught up with the psychodynamic meaning of symbolic material may represent an escape from the greater anxiety associated with directly confronting what the patient and the analyst are experiencing in their immediate interaction but which is unformulated or unspoken.

It is important not to leave this area without underscoring the important lines of continuity between the ideas presented in Gill's work on hypnosis and his later viewpoint. To begin with, there is the notion of two universes of discourse, as noted earlier, which remain separate throughout *Hypnosis and Related States* despite the authors' determination to integrate them. Second, there is an emphasis on the importance of the relationship throughout and on the element of mutuality in the process. Gill and Brenman (1959) take the position that "hypnosis is at least in part a dovetailing of the unconscious fantasies of the two people involved, and that strictly speaking one should not speak of 'the hypnotic state' but rather of 'the hypnotic relationship'" (pp. 60–61). They spell out the specific form that this reciprocity of roles takes:

> From analysis of the two sets of data, on subject and on hypnotist, it appears to us quite clear that hypnosis is a complex dovetailing relationship between the two participants wherein the overt role taken by the one is the covert fantasy of the other. Thus, while the hypnotist is *overtly* being the powerful figure, whether as a domineering tyrant or a boundless source of "supplies" he is covertly on the receiving end of this power and/or bounty in his fantasy. . . .
>
> As we have seen, on the other side of this coin, the hypnotic subject takes *overtly* the role of the obedient, super-compliant puppet; *covertly* he is not only sharing in the hypnotist's presumed omnipotence, but is pushing this in fantasy to the point of the hypnotist's having to abdicate completely [p. 98].

Here we have just the kind of emotional reciprocity that Gill would later be on the alert for in his work as an analyst, in which the interpretation of the transference always includes reference to the patient's plausible ideas about the analyst's countertransference response.

Toward the end of the book, Gill and Brenman discuss the reasons why many therapists often give up the use of hypnosis even as an adjunctive technique. Among the reasons they give is the growing awareness of the unconscious wish to assume the role of the omnipotent parent or, covertly and vicariously, of the helpless, regressed child. Whatever personal factors were involved, Gill left hypnosis behind both as a treatment technique and as an instrument for investigation of psychological phenomena. Instead of the unabashed exercise of psychological power that hypnosis epitomizes but which is more subtly represented in standard psychoanalytic technique, Gill eventually opted for a rigorous, critical understanding of interpersonal influence in the psychoanalytic situation as a means of liberating the patient from closed and repetitive patterns of interaction with others.

The Initial Psychiatric Interview

During his relatively short stay at Yale between 1950 and 1953, Gill collaborated with Newman and Redlich (1954) on *The Initial Interview in Psychiatric Practice*, a book that is remarkable for the extent to which it anticipates Gill's later perspective. In the first place, the book is based on three transcribed sessions, reflecting Gill's commitment to recording, which had already taken hold in the mid-1940s. In the second place, the book is a critique of the medical model as it is generally applied in psychiatric diagnostic interviewing—a critique that foreshadows Gill's (1976, 1977b) later repudiation of both biologistic psychoanalytic theorizing and medically tinged conceptualizations of psychoanalytic technique that emphasize the analyst's detachment rather than participation in the process.

The rejection of the medical model in this early work bears some special attention. Gill and his collaborators object to the prevalent practice of gathering information from the patient under various headings instead of following the patient in a relatively open-ended fashion. Of special interest, in view of what comes later, is the authors' rejection of history taking as the necessary way to arrive at a valid diagnosis. This position has continuity, of course, with Gill's later concern that analysts are often interested in genetic reconstruction at the expense of understanding the patient's experience of the relationship in the here and now.

There are, of course, important differences between Gill's later theory of technique and his approach to interviewing in 1954. Although some of these may be explained by the fact that the two types of clinical situations are not fully comparable, I think Gill's later position does entail principles that he believed can and should be extended to diagnostic interviewing. For Gill, what is of central importance diagnostically is the way in which a person relates in the here and now, including the patient's capacity to reflect upon the meaning of his or her immediate experience with the interviewer. Other considerations may also be important, but they are secondary. What we do not yet see in *The Initial Interview in Psychiatric Practice* is the full emergence of the focus on the relationship, including the technique of systematically searching for and interpreting disguised allusions to the transference, even at the beginning of the treatment (Gill and Muslin, 1977).

In *The Initial Interview in Psychiatric Practice* there are many examples of Gill's early conviction that the immediate process should take priority over collection of content. Concerning departures in interviewing from a "psychiatric copy of medical schedules" Gill and his collaborators (1954) wrote: "Probably the most important [departure] was the psychiatrists' realization of the significance of the patient-therapist relationship as the very framework within which the nature and meaning of the patient's productions must be understood" (p. 19).

Gill wrote in 1954 as though the mental status exam and other aspects of traditional, medically oriented interviewing were already passé, but what he had to say then is still germane considering contemporary zeal about ferretting out the biological factors in mental disorders. Foreshadowing his later sharp distinction between a psychological realm of discourse and a biological realm, Gill makes clear that the assessment he is talking about is one of psychological functioning, not of biological factors. This is not to say that the latter are not relevant to a complete understanding of the patient's functioning, but only that assessing psychological factors is something separate and apart, something requiring the adoption of an attitude that is not compatible with the type of diagnostic attitude associated with assessment of organic factors. As Gill, Newman, and Redlich (1954) put it: "In the psychiatric interview the interpersonal relationship is focal. The psychiatrist must deal adequately with this relationship to insure that the desired communication between patient and therapist shall take place. Should there be any indication of a somatic disorder, the patient must be further studied *by techniques which are not our concern here*" (p. 66; italics added).

One of the reasons these authors give for the persistence of the "old-fashioned mental status examination" is the psychological function it serves for the interviewer:

> The second reason for the "deaf and dumb" quality of the older examination lies in the psychiatrist's need to retain his equilibrium by demonstrating his superiority. The inquisitory technique is used, then, as an unconscious defense against the threatening content of the experience of his disturbed patient, and against an emotional relationship with the patient—particularly against the patient's emotional demands [p. 23].

Here, again, we find a foreshadowing of Gill's later emphasis on the inescapable fact that whatever an analyst's or therapist's behavior, it carries meaning that derives from his personal participation in the process. Gill might well have said the same later on about the function of silence and other allegedly neutral postures that an analyst may adopt. Similarly, Gill, Newman, and Redlich (1954) wrote of the inevitability of the reciprocal influence of patient and interviewer: "Reactions of both doctor and patient will of course change as each meets the reactions of the other in that progressive redefinition which is the essence of any developing relationship" (pp. 66–67).

As a final example of this early conviction, consider the following comment, which so clearly anticipates Gill's later emphasis on the here-and-now in psychoanalysis and his relative deemphasis of historical reconstruction if undertaken without reference to a reliving in the transference: "It has naturally occurred to us that we may be trying to push too far the idea of abandoning the collection of historical data in order to emphasize current interaction. But we are persuaded that doubts about our technique are caused by our inability more completely to divest ourselves of long-established and anxiety-reducing habits of professional practice" (Gill et al., 1954, p. 412).

It is also of interest that, of the various influences on the development of their own orientation, Gill and his coauthors consider Sullivan's to be the strongest, although they note that Sullivan does not go as far as they do in giving up adherence to a "relatively formal 'reconnaissance' and 'detailed inquiry'" (p. 62). Significantly, Gill later immersed himself in Sullivanian literature and wrote about the continuity of his own ideas and those of Sullivan as well as about important differences between them (Gill, 1983a).

There are many examples in the commentary on the transcribed sessions, the phonograph recordings of which were also published, in which the authors commend or criticize the interviewers depending on whether they followed the patients' leads or retreated defensively to some agenda of their own. Where the advocated technique and mode of listening depart from Gill's later view is in the failure systematically to interpret or even identify disguised allusions to the transference. I believe that, if Gill in the earlier period were to criticize the interviews and the authors' commentaries on them, he would point out that although much emphasis was apparently placed on the interaction, in practice, the approach failed to follow the patient's experience of the relationship in a systematic way, one that would require consistent attention to disguised allusions to the transference in the patient's associations (Gill, 1982, 1983a, 1984a; Gill and Hoffman, 1982a, b).

Psychoanalytic Technique

Probably the most carefully elaborated statement on psychoanalytic technique that Gill made while he was still immersed in psychoanalytic metapsychology and writing on hypnosis is found in "Psychoanalysis and Exploratory Psychotherapy" (Gill, 1954), published in an issue of the *Journal of the American Psychoanalytic Association* devoted entirely to papers on technique. It is useful and illuminating to compare Gill's views as represented in that paper with his later ideas (Gill, 1979, 1982, 1983a), keeping in mind always that Gill's point of view in 1954 is probably representative of much that is still in the mainstream of classical psychoanalytic thought. Gill (1984a) himself wrote a paper that undertakes such a comparative analysis.

Gill's definition of psychoanalytic technique in the 1954 paper is well known and often cited: "*Psychoanalysis is that technique which, employed by a neutral analyst, results in the development of a regressive transference neurosis and the ultimate resolution of this neurosis by techniques of interpretation alone*" (p. 775). The definition has three main elements, which Gill goes on to elaborate: the neutrality of the analyst, the necessity of regression, and the importance of relying on interpretation alone to resolve the transference neurosis.

Gill's (1984a) comparison of the classical position as he himself formulated it in 1954 and his revised view emphasizes the differences between the two. In the light of Gill's own emphasis on the contrast, a reader of the 1954 paper may be somewhat surprised at the points of continuity between the ideas Gill had then and those he developed subsequently. It is important to recognize, however, that although Gill may have sometimes underestimated the element of consistency in his ideas about technique and, perhaps even more so, the element of continuity in the kinds of issues that concerned him, the ways in which his ideas changed are very important and substantial. Even the apparent points of agreement pale when considered in their total context. The changes are associated with the paradigm shift noted earlier, and Gill was justified in regarding them as "radical."

One apparent point of agreement is the irrelevance of the arrangement—either the frequency of visits or the use of the couch—to the definition of the technique. On this matter, Gill could hardly be more emphatic in the 1980s than he was in 1954, when he labeled as "foolish" and "ridiculous" the tendency to regard such "outward trappings" as essential (pp. 774–775). This position has a very different meaning, however, in the context of Gill's later overall point of view than it had earlier. In 1954 these "trappings," although disdained as part of the definition of technique, were nevertheless consistent with the attempt to "enforce" a regression; an attempt that was a defining feature of psychoanalytic treatment (pp. 778–779). In 1984 these trappings lost this connection to the essence of the technique Gill advocated.

A second apparent point of agreement is that neutrality does not mean the absence of any emotional involvement on the part of the analyst. Gill already recognized in 1954 that the analyst was a participant in the process and not just an observer and that there was room in the psychoanalytic situation for the analyst to feel and even to show a range of emotional responses, including amusement, irritation, and sadness (p. 780). Moreover, then as later, what separated an analysis from psychotherapy was not the absence of any interpersonal influence or suggestion in the process, but the attempt in the long run to "resolve the suggestive influence of the therapist on the patient" by means of interpretation (p. 790).

In 1954, however, Gill also wrote: "The clearest transference manifestations are those which occur when the analyst's behavior is constant, since under these circumstances changing manifestations in the transference cannot be attributed to an external situation, to some changed factor in the interpersonal relationship, but the analysand must accept responsibility himself" (p. 781). Gill would never make such a statement in the later period since he then saw the analyst as implicated on a moment-to-moment basis in the nuances of the transference as they emerge. On the other hand, he would have agreed that the aim of analysis includes a heightened appreciation by patients of their share of the responsibility for the quality of the interaction as they experience it. The relationship between these points of agreement and disagreement might be clarified if we realize that what was a main point with regard to technique in 1954 becomes a qualification in 1984 and vice versa. Thus, for example, the 1954 position on neutrality might be paraphrased as follows: although there is always an element of suggestion in every analysis, *the analyst should try to maintain a relatively constant demeanor in order to be able to demonstrate to patients that the responsibility for their experience of the relationship lies primarily within themselves.*

The 1984 position (Gill, 1984a) would have the emphasis reversed, so that the attitude encouraged is quite different: although one of the goals of analysis is to enhance patients' appreciation of their responsibility for their experiences of themselves and others, and although it is important that the analyst avoid being so active or intrusive as to prevent this realization from emerging, *on a moment-to-moment basis, the analyst must pay attention to the ways in which he or she is contributing to the patient's experience and should include reference to these contributions, as they are plausibly construed by the patient, in his or her interpretations.*

In line with this important difference, Gill's main recommendation in 1954 to practitioners of "intensive psychotherapy" is that they be less directive, in order to bring the process closer to an optimal psychoanalytic one. His principal recommendation in 1984 to the same end is that they systematically analyze the transference—it being understood, of course, that analyzing the transference has a different meaning for Gill in 1984 than it had for him in 1954 and than it has for most classical analysts.[4]

The principal differences between Gill's position on technique in 1954 and his later one center on the following issues: (1) the type of influence that the analyst intentionally exercises, (2) the extent to which the transference itself is understood and interpreted as a plausible construction on the patient's part, and (3) the optimal frequency of transference interpretations.

With regard to the first issue, in 1954 Gill believed, following Macalpine (1950), that inducing a regressive transference neurosis was an essential feature of technique. As noted earlier, Gill subsequently abandoned this view. He ceased to consider the achievement of any particular regressive state, beyond what the patient brings to the analysis, necessary or desirable. The work is then regarded as no less analytic if the issues explored reflect high levels of ego functioning than if they are more overtly primitive, and there is no requirement that they become more primitive for the process to be called an analysis. Perhaps even more to the point is the emergence of firm opposition to manipulating patients in a manner that does not in itself become a subject of analytic investigation. Instead, the analyst is urged to openly encourage patients to explore their experience of the relationship, understanding that this encouragement may also have repercussions that require exploration.

---

[4] Gill (1991, 1994) proposed that the term "analytic therapy" be used to refer to the modality characterized by the application of psychoanalytic technique (i.e., analysis of transference in a perspectivist model) without the conventional arrangements (frequency, couch) of psychoanalysis proper. With rare exceptions he felt an effort should be made to analyze "suggestive" influence rather than making a commitment to noninterpretive interaction as the basis for therapeutic action.

Consistent with the creative, dialectical nature of Gill's thinking throughout his career, even with regard to the matter of regression, the 1954 discussion includes a foreshadowing of his later views. He argued then that theoretical advances in ego psychology lent greater weight to the importance of intrasystemic conflicts in the ego that achieve relative autonomy as opposed to the intersystemic id-ego conflicts from which they derived. He also reminds us that Freud (1926, p. 83) himself raised a question as to whether, in Gill's (1954) words, "after repression the original impulse necessarily persists in the unconscious" (p. 794). Gill suggests that the derivative conflicts may "exist in a form which allows a relatively firm resolution," particularly when psychotherapy takes on more of the character of psychoanalysis by being "more intensive and less directive." Moreover, he argues that "this may result in a quantitative shift which may not be so completely different from what often happens in psychoanalysis" (p. 793).

With regard to the second issue, the differences are both subtle and critical. It is clear that Gill recognized in 1954 that the general phenomenon of regression in analysis was not spontaneous but induced (e.g., pp. 778–779). The particular form that this regression took, however, was one that was relatively free of the analyst's influence, which Gill (1954) described as "a nonspecific, steady, unremitting regressive pressure" (p. 780). The analyst, as noted earlier, could put himself or herself in a position that would enable him or her to show the patient that the particulars of the transference were coming from the patient alone.

In contrast to this view, and in keeping with his later perspectivist orientation, Gill came to see the analyst as implicated in the transference in highly specific ways, since the transference is associated with continual plausible speculations on the patient's part about the analyst's inner state. Thus, the best transference interpretations generally refer to some way in which the analyst could plausibly be understood to have contributed to the patient's experience. To say this is not to abandon leverage for demonstrating the responsibility of patients for their own experience. Ultimately, the analysis leads to patients' heightened awareness of the repetitive patterns of interaction to which they are prone. The point is that they repeat patterns of interaction, and patients have reason to believe that the analyst's inner experience and outward behavior are colored by the pressure they exert to make the relationship repeat those patterns.

This shift is apt to be confused with the more common emphasis on the "real" influence of the analyst. Such emphasis is often presented as an alternative to the view that the analyst functions only as a screen for the transference and as a technical instrumentality. As noted earlier, Gill moved to a perspectivist view of reality, especially of emotionally significant interpersonal reality. From this point of view, the patient's ideas about the analyst are usually neither simply veridical nor simply groundless fantasy.[5] Gill's views are similar in some respects to those of Racker (1968), Levenson (1972), and Sandler (1976), among others. What these theorists—nominally, a Kleinian, a Sullivanian, and a Freudian—have in common is the idea of an inevitable degree of interlocking of transference and countertransference and a conviction that empathic transference interpretations must take this interplay into account (Hoffman, 1983).

The third difference noted in Gill's position on technique has to do with the frequency of transference interpretations that his later theory seems to encourage. Although Gill emphasized that considerations of tact and timing are exceedingly important, and although he recognized the importance of allowing the patient to have the initiative and to develop his or her own thoughts, the overall thrust of his position nevertheless encourages a generally more interactive stance, and certainly more frequent interpretations of allusions to the transference, than standard technique would recommend.

To some extent, this emphasis on regular interpretation follows from the fact that Gill was no longer interested in facilitating a mode of experiencing and communication that is remote from secondary process thinking. The conversation between analyst and patient is a special kind, to be sure, but there is no technical principle, such as the induction of regression, that is opposed on a moment-to-moment basis to the principle of analyzing the transference. In fact, instead of inducing regression by depriving the patient, Gill (1979, 1982) suggests that the transference should be "encouraged to expand" by continually explicating its immediate direct and indirect manifestations.

A second consideration that is consistent with more frequent interpretations is Gill's (1982) emphasis on the "ubiquity" of disguised allusions to the transference (pp. 69–79). Gill (p. 80) differs with the following statement by Freud (1913), especially with the first part, to which Freud gave special emphasis: "*So long as the patient's communications and ideas run on without obstruction, the theme of transference should be left untouched*. One must wait until the transference, which is the most delicate of all procedures, has become a resistance" (p. 139). Gill believed that Freud failed consistently to recognize resistance in indirect references to the transference. His review of Freud's ideas about transference (Gill, 1982, pp. 139–175) is thorough and illuminatmg, revealing Freud's tendency, despite some important statements to the contrary, to see the analysis of the neurosis as primary and to see the transference as an obstacle

[5] Since Gill's views were changing, some of his later writings show remnants of his earlier, more traditional stance that are inconsistent with his newer ideas. Thus, for example, in his monograph on technique, Gill (1982) sometimes divides the patient's experience into transferential and realistic components (e.g., pp. 94–96), although beginning with chapter 7, he adopts a more consistently perspectivist position.

that has to be dealt with only when it obstructs that analysis. Gill believed, instead, that the neurosis will find its way into the transference in one way or another, either in transference of wish or defense (p. 32), and that the transference can be usefully interpreted in a relatively molecular way throughout the analysis. Moreover, interpretation of transference per se is not seen as interfering with the therapeutic alliance (p. 84). On the contrary, tactful interpretation of transference from the first session on will promote the alliance[6] since it addresses issues that are troubling the patient in a very immediate sense but that the patient resists speaking of or thinking of explicitly for fear that they will not be accepted or understood. Instead of being concerned about managing his own behavior so as to promote a nonspecific regression on one hand, and a spontaneous specific transference on the other, Gill's attention as a clinician turns to identifying the various disguised expressions of transference, such as displacement and identification. Citing Lipton's (1977b) discussion, Gill (1982, p. 170) finds that familiarity with identification, which is less commonly recognized than displacement (or, I might add, projection) as a vehicle for indirect communication, greatly expands the range of associations in which it is compelling to infer that there is an implication for the transference.

Despite his encouragement to the analyst to regularly interpret disguised allusions to the transference, Gill certainly allows latitude for a wide range of frequency, depending on the patient, the type of material that is coming up, and the style of the analyst. It is a mistake to regard frequency of interpretation per se as the crux of the difference between Gill's position and the classical one. Indeed, it is quite compatible with Gill's ideas to be critical of overzealous interpretation of transference, a perversion to which Gill's theory of technique may be prone but which certainly is not required by it. More at the core of Gill's departure from the classical model are the changes associated with the first and second issues I have cited, namely, the opposition to deliberate manipulation and the understanding and interpretation of transference as a plausible construction, given the inevitability of the analyst's personal participation in the process. Gill (1984c) elaborated on this point in response to a collection of critiques of his position as he had presented it in his 1982 monograph.

All that I have said here pertains to what Gill (1979, 1982) calls "interpretation of resistance to the awareness of transference," as distinct from "interpretation of resistance to the resolution of transference." There is no question that Gill gives priority to the former as a matter of technique;

---

[6] Although Gill sometimes used the term alliance, he agreed with Lipton (1977a) that the concept is objectionable insofar as it denotes or connotes something that should be deliberately fostered with special techniques and that is uncontaminated by transference (see Gill, 1982, pp. 96–106; Reppen, 1982, pp. 173–174).

he feels that a good deal of resolution of transference will follow spontaneously from its explication in the here and now. The patient will come to recognize that, for example, he or she paid selective attention to the features of the analyst's behavior that he or she had previously disavowed entirely. Also, the patient will spontaneously recall experiences from childhood that will help to show that his or her perspective has particular historical origins. Gill (1982) is very concerned that genetic interpretations may be used as a flight from the here and now, but he also recognizes their importance and the importance of other kinds of interpretation for the resolution of the transference:

> It is important that the analyst not be tied to some rigid rule that he should make only transference interpretations. Not only can extra-transference interpretations be useful, but the spontaneity of the analyst's behavior is essential for the conduct of an analysis. If an extra-transference interpretation occurs to the analyst as a plausible clarification, he should make it. At the same time, he should be alert to its possible repercussions on the transference— but then he should be alert to the repercussions on the transference of a transference interpretation too.
>
> I conclude that while extra-transference interpretations play a role in analysis—and extra-transference clarifications certainly must—priority, in both time and importance, should go to transference interpretations. This principle may be more readily accepted if I emphasize that attention to resistance to the awareness of transference should come first and that, even though priority in interpretation designed to resolve the transference should go to interpretation within the analytic situation, working through requires extra-transference, transference, and genetic transference interpretations [pp. 125–126].

Gill speaks of the person paradigm or point of view, the interpersonal paradigm, and perspectivism almost interchangeably, because for him each implies the others. His more specific ideas about the analytic situation follow directly from these supraordinate concepts. In the old metapsychology, according to what Gill (1983b) calls the "energy discharge" point of view, the patient was encouraged to regress in order to arrive at the underlying infantile neurosis that would bear the stamp of the patient's bodily urges, relatively independent of environmental influences. In the old paradigm it was thought that "free association and regression will in time lead to the relatively direct expression of bodily urges little related to interpersonal interaction, whether with others in the past or with the therapist in the present" (p. 546). These urges are the decisive factors underlying the transference and the distortion of reality the transference entails. In other words, the emphasis on the past is linked with the idea of a somatic drive that precedes and determines interactions with others. But for Gill, there is nothing unearthed or reconstructed in psychoanalysis that antedates interactions. The present interaction, moreover, is the best place to look for the person's fixed ways of organizing interpersonal experience. Transference is redefined as a way of looking at things and as a way of being with other people—not a distorted way in any simple sense, but a rigid way that cuts off alternative potentials. The analyst interprets largely in the spirit of acknowledging the element of plausibility in the patient's perspective. There is no absolute reality to which the analyst has access but to which the patient is blind because of the transference. In fact, the patient's transference perspective may shed light on some aspect of the analyst's own participation (overt and covert) which the analyst resists. Neither participant has a corner on the truth, and yet they try to hammer out an understanding that makes sense to both of them and that has the feel of cogency. Even as they are doing so, the analyst must take the lead in turning a critical eye on what they have decided and how they have decided it. That is why historical exploration cannot get very far without being interrupted by a question as to its purpose right now. To raise this question does not preclude returning subsequently to reconstructive work.

This continual scrutiny of the relationship is, in the ideal, not an intellectual exercise, but rather a moving, new interpersonal experience that represents and promotes personal growth (Gill, 1982, pp. 118–120). The new experience associated with the analysis of the transference rests in part on the analyst's openness to the possibility that, wittingly or unwittingly, he or she has been the patient's accomplice in the perpetuation of the old, fixed patterns of interaction that the transference represents. At the very moment in which this openness is conveyed to the patient, the analyst stands a good chance of extricating himself or herself from the role of accomplice. Gill was fond of citing Strachey's (1934) and Loewald's (1960) classic papers on the therapeutic action of psychoanalysis in which both of them state that analysis cures because the analyst offers himself or herself not only as a technical instrumentality but as an object with whom the patient can have a new kind of experience. What Strachey and Loewald omit or underemphasize is the element of mutuality in the shaping of the transference and the countertransference on a moment-to-moment basis.

With psychoanalytic techique redefined in a manner that encourages more active engagement of the patient and that demands more systematic exploration of the patient's immediate experience of the interaction, the whole question of analyzability is thrown open. Gill's views on assessment of analyzability parallel those of Freud in calling for a "trial analysis" as the best way to begin. Gill did not have fixed ideas on who can benefit from a rigorous psychoanalytic approach based on standard types of classification. He felt that too many patients are written off as "unanalyzable" because they cannot adapt well to the couch and to a relatively silent and remote analyst who is systematically trying to induce a regression (Gill, 1984a). For Gill, this procedure is misguided, and a patient's refusal or inability to comply with it could be a sign of strength. Analyzability for Gill has to do with a patient's ability to engage in and reflect upon a relationship with an analyst who is emotionally available and who thinks of himself or herself as a co-participant in the process. Gill (1983a) mocks the standard view of analyzability, stating that "an analyzable patient is a patient with whom the analyst can maintain the illusion of neutrality" (p. 213). In fact, there may be relatively healthy patients with particular temperaments who cannot tolerate standard technique but who would respond well to Gill's approach. Similarly, there may be some very sick patients who are automatically written off because of their inability to adapt to the standard psychoanalytic situation but who may be able to respond relatively well to the more active focus on the here and now that Gill espoused.

Research in Psychoanalysis

As noted earlier, Gill was unwavering throughout his career about the necessity for systematic research on the psychoanalytic process, the third aspect of Gill's work that I will discuss here. He never accepted the common psychoanalytic view, which Freud himself promulgated, that the case study method, however much it has contributed to theory and practice, can obviate the need for a more rigorous application of scientific methods to the gathering and analysis of psychoanalytic data. To some, perhaps Gill's most important contribution to the development of psychoanalysis as a science was his pioneering effort to make the raw data of psychoanalysis available for study by independent observers through audiorecordings of psychotherapeutic and psychoanalytic sessions.[7] Inspired partly by Carl Rogers and others of the client-centered school, who made recording and research a central part of their practice from the start, Gill, along with a few others, began recording psychotherapy at the Menninger Clinic as early as the middle 1940s. The advent of tape recording greatly facilitated this effort. Over the years, Gill collected samples from each of a number of tape-recorded analyses, some conducted by himself and some by the relatively few other analysts who were willing to contribute.

Recording was instrumental in Gill's research on hypnosis during the

[7] Although I worked with him on the development of a coding scheme for the study of transcribed audio-recorded psychoanalytic sessions, I did not share Gill's great regard for systematic empirical research, as compared with carefully reported clinical experiences by individual practitioners, as a source of knowledge about the process.

1940s and 1950s, for example, in a study of spontaneous fluctuations in the depth of the hypnotic state during sessions of psychotherapy (Brenman, Gill, and Knight, 1962). In this study, ego functioning around the time of the fluctuation was assessed by having independent judges examine associations surrounding statements such as "I'm going deeper" or "I'm coming up lighter." The method itself provided a model that was later adapted by Luborsky (1967) in his studies of momentary forgetting in psychotherapy. The model also evolved into the broader "symptom context method" for investigating the appearance of physical and psychological symptoms during psychotherapy sessions (Luborsky and Auerbach, 1969).

In the 1960s, Gill and his collaborators wrote a landmark article on recording and psychoanalysis in which they took up and challenged many of the common sources of resistance to recording, some personal and some more clinical or theoretical. On the personal side, for example, there is fear of exposure and criticism. Gill recognized that for some patient-analyst pairs, recording may pose insurmountable difficulties (Reppen, 1982, p. 171). In general, however, he felt that the fear of exposure and criticism, both on an individual and an institutional level, must be overcome if analysis is to have any hope of growing or even surviving as a scientific discipline.

On the clinical side, objections to recording for research purposes include concern about compromising confidentiality as well as about introducing another purpose into the analytic situation that is extraneous to the analytic work itself and to the immediate interests of the patient. There is no question, of course, that patients will react in various ways to these circumstances. However, Gill (Gill et al., 1968; Reppen, 1982) argues, it does not follow that they preclude a successful analysis. Here Gill's point of view on technique dovetails with his attitude on recording. The transference does not develop in a vacuum. However the analytic situation is set up, its transference repercussions must be explored in the spirit of recognizing the element of plausibility in the patient's view of the situation. In the first place, the research situation is not so different from other analytic situations in which confidentiality is compromised or in which the analyst's self-interest is readily apparent. When, for example, an institute candidate sees a patient as part of training, confidentiality is not inviolate, and the patient has cause to feel used. These circumstances are generally understood to be important complications that need to be explored, but not of such a magnitude that they preclude a successful analysis. In the second place, even when the patient has reason to believe that confidentiality is strictly maintained, the situation is likely to have particular meanings that must be investigated. In what might be regarded by many as the optimal analytic setting, the promise of strict confidentiality, the strong recommendation that the frequency of sessions be four times per week or more, the use of the couch, the analyst's fee, and the analyst's silence are all very powerful stimuli, which the patient construes in plausible and yet also personally expressive and, in principle, analyzable ways (Gill, 1984a).[8]

Gill's theory of technique also became congenial to research on the psychoanalytic process in that it invites attention to each analytic hour as a unit that has a certain integrity of meaning. In the classical paradigm, in which the intent is to foster the unfolding of a regressive transference neurosis over a long period of time, it would be difficult to assess the quality of the analyst's technique as well as other variables because the context of each event is so temporally broad and so difficult to know and take into account. Although Gill was fully aware of the importance of context and knew that the analyst may be in a position to take it into account more than an external observer who has only a small sample of the data, Gill's molecular focus on the analysis of transference in the here and now lends itself to investigation of smaller and more manageable units of data. One of the fruits of Gill's commitment to systematic research was the development of a coding scheme (Gill and Hoffman, 1982b; Hoffman and Gill, 1988a, b), which permits classification of various kinds of patient communications and analyst interventions. The highlight of the scheme is the delineation of criteria for identifying disguised allusions to the transference in associations not manifestly about the transference. The research judge cannot claim that such an allusion has occurred without giving a specific basis for this inference. The basis may have the form of a previous statement by the patient that is explicitly about the relationship, or it may have the form of some readily recognizable event in the interaction about which neither of the participants has spoken. These criteria for coding allusions to the transference have clinical utility as well, because they set up at least partial guidelines to indicate when a transference interpretation might be called for and when it might not—guidelines that have been vague or lacking in clinical theory.[9]

---

[8] A factor that I believe Gill underestimated with respect to the effects of recording on the process is its potential to interfere with the analyst's personal spontaneity. The presence of the tape recorder may pull for greater than optimal self-conscious attention by the analyst to the therapeutic value of his actions, that is, to the methodical side of the dialectic between methodical and personally expressive participation (Hoffman, 1992a, 1994).

[9] In my view, Gill, in his enthusiasm for the analysis of the transference, may have been excessively impatient regarding the time it might take for certain transference-countertransference patterns to unfold and for the participants to work their way out of them. In the same vein, I do not believe he gave sufficient weight to the dialectical and paradoxical relationships between analyzed and unanalyzed interactions and between repetition and new experience (Hoffman, 1992a; 1994; Ghent, 1992; Pizer, 1992). To have given them greater weight might have promoted a sense that larger units of time were necessary to assess the quality of analytic work. I believe the impatience might also reflect an underestimation of the

Gill recognized that the development of this coding scheme was only a small first step toward a more comprehensive program of systematic research on the analytic process as he conceived of it. In the long run, Gill wanted to see variables defined and operationalized and methods developed so that it would be possible to study, on a molecular level, the differential effects of various types of intervention on the process and, on a molar level, the relative efficacy of one treatment approach or another.

Gill's commitment was not to research for the sake of research but to clinical research that deals with theoretically meaningful variables. It was a commitment to the scientific study of human intention and meaning, including the interpersonal conditions that promote change and growth. In this sense, psychoanalysis for Gill is a hermeneutic science, a contradiction in terms for some (Eagle, 1980; Blight, 1981), but for Gill a category that connotes the special combination of values he felt should characterize psychoanalysis as a discipline.

Conclusion

As we have seen, Gill's point of view changed radically over the years. His ideas continued to evolve. Any attempt to capture the thrust of his position at a given time is unlikely to do justice either to various important qualifications that he proposed later or to new ideas and revisions of theory that were still germinal in his thinking. For example, Gill (personal communication) in the 80s and 90s wrestled with several questions. Are there, after all, universal conflicts that play a role in every analysis, and, if so, what are they? Gill considered the conflict between attachment and autonomy as a primary issue of this kind. With regard to theory of technique, does the elimination of the principle of deliberately inducing a regression leave a gap that invites, instead of excessive restraint, overzealous interpretation of transference? What provision is there in the theory, formally speaking, to prevent the reductio ad absurdum that would have the analyst forever interpreting the transference repercussions of overzealous interpretation? Is it enough to emphasize the importance of common sense, tact, and timing, or to say that one does not interpret until one has a compelling sense of a latent transference meaning in the patient's associations? Or is it necessary to formulate another principle of technique to balance the principle of analysis of transference? Perhaps for Gill this principle would be supraordinate to the analysis of transference and would, in the most general terms, have to do with promoting a certain quality of

---

analyst's personal involvement and an ironically "classical" expectation regarding the ease with which the analyst could transcend it. In a relatively late paper, Gill and I (Hoffman and Gill, 1988a) reflected critically on signs of this attitude in our own coding scheme.

interpersonal experience.[10] This experience might be most powerfully served by the analysis of the transference but, presumably, could also be undermined by it at times. What this quality of experience would be, of course, needs to be spelled out. It would also have to be located in relation to other conceptualizations in the literature of the interpersonal experience in analysis, such as Gill's own concept of the new experience that accompanies the analysis of the transference, Zetzel's therapeutic alliance, Winnicott's holding environment, Kohut's self-selfobject tie, and Schafer's more generic atmosphere of safety.

Gill's intellectual style was to pursue steadfastly the logical implications of a particular line of thought without shrinking from their consequences for entrenched tradition. At the same time, in dialectical relationship with this tendency, his convictions about theory, research, and practice were united by his readiness to turn a critical eye on his own perspective and to consider other points of view. Thus, despite the vigor with which he advocated and defended his position, Gill also actively explored the points of convergence and divergence of his own views and those of Gedo (Gill, 1981), Melanie Klein (Gill, 1982, pp. 129–137; 1994), Kohut (Reppen, 1982, pp. 183–186; Gill, 1994), Sullivan (Gill, 1983a), and Langs (Gill, 1984b), among many others.[11] The very fact that he was actively engaged in dialogue with exponents of these diverse perspectives (as reflected in his publications, speaking engagements, and extensive correspondence) testifies to the bridge-building role that Gill occupied in the field. I believe that such a role was congenial to him because of his disdain for parochialism; he had a deep conviction that psychoanalysis would survive and grow only if exponents of diverse viewpoints engaged each other in an ongoing process of reciprocal, constructive criticism and ultimately submitted their differences to what Gill regarded as the arbitrating power of systematic clinical research.

References

Apfelbaum. B. (1966). On ego psychology: A critique of the structural approach to psychoanalytic theory. *Internat. J. Psycho-Anal.*, 47:451–475.

Basch, M. F. (1977), Developmental psychology and explanatory theory in psychoanalysis. *The Annual of Psychoanalysis*, 5:229–263. New York: International Universities Press.

---

[10] It was always a stretch for Gill to put noninterpretive interactions on a par with analysis of transference in terms of their mutative potential (see Mitchell's, in press, review of Gill's last book). In my view therapeutic action derives from the interplay of the two and from the resulting interpersonal experience as a whole (Hoffman, 1994).

[11] In his last book, Gill (1994) attempted to locate his point of view in relation to many perspectives in contemporary psychoanalysis.

Bateson, G. & Mead, M. (1942), Balinese character: A photographic analysis. *Special Publications NY Acad. Sci.*, 2.

Blight, J. G. (1981), Must psychoanalysis retreat to hermeneutics? Psychoanalytic theory in the light of Popper's evolutionary epistemology. *Psychoanal. Contemp. Thought*, 4:147–205.

Brenman, M., Gill, M. M. & Knight, R. P. (1952), Spontaneous fluctuations in depth of hypnosis and their implications for ego-function. *Internat. J. Psycho-Anal.*, 33:22–34.

Eagle, M. N. (1980), A critical examination of motivational explanation in psychoanalysis. *Psychoanal. Contemp. Thought*, 3:329–380.

——— (1981), Interests as object relations. *Psychoanal. Contemp. Thought*, 4:527–565.

Freud, S. (1913), On beginning the treatment. *Standard Edition*, 12:147–156. London: Hogarth Press, 1958.

——— (1923), The ego and the id. *Standard Edition*, 19:12–66. London: Hogarth Press, 1961.

——— (1926), Inhibitions, symptoms and anxiety. *Standard Edition*, 20:87–172. London: Hogarth Press, 1959.

Ghent, E. (1992), Paradox and process. *Psychoanal. Dial.*, 2:136–159.

Gill, M. M. (1954), Psychoanalysis and exploratory psychotherapy. *J. Amer. Psychoanal. Assn.*, 2:771–797.

———, ed. (1963), *Topography and Systems in Psychoanalytic Theory. Psychological Issues*, Monograph 10. New York: International Universities Press.

——— (1967), The primary process. In: *Motives and Thought*, ed. R. Holt. *Psychological Issues*, Monogr. 18/19. New York: International Universities Press, pp. 260–298.

——— (1976), Metapsychology is not psychology. In: *Psychology versus Metapsychology*, ed., M. M. Gill & P. S. Holzman. *Psychological Issues*, Monogr. 36. New York: International Universities Press, 71–105.

——— (1977a), Psychic energy reconsidered: Discussion. *J. Amer. Psychoanal. Assn.*, 25, 581–598.

——— (1977b), The two models of the mental health disciplines. *Bull. Menninger Clin.*, 41, 79–84.

——— (1978), Freud's concepts of unconsciousness and the unconscious. In: *The Unconscious, Vol. 1*, ed. A. S. Prangishvilli, A. E. Sherozia & F. V. Bassin. Tbilisi, USSR: Metsniereba.

——— (1979), The analysis of the transference. *J. Amer. Psychoanal. Assn.*, 27 (Suppl.):263–288.

——— (1981), The boundaries of psychoanalytic data and technique: A critique of Gedo's *Beyond Interpretation. Psychoanal. Inq.*, 1:205–232.

——— (1982), *Analysis of Transference, Vol. 1. Psychological Issues*, Monogr. 53. New York: International Universities Press.

——— (1983a), The interpersonal paradigm and the degree of the therapist's involvement. *Contemp. Psychoanal.*, 19:200–237.

——— (1983b), The point of view of psychoanalysis: Energy discharge or person. *Psychoanal. Contemp. Thought*, 6:523–551.

——— (1984a), Psychoanalysis and psychotherapy: A revision. *Internat. Rev. Psycho-Anal.*, 11:161–179.

——— (1984b), Robert Langs on technique: A critique. In: *Listening and Interpreting*, ed. J. Raney. New York: Aronson.

——— (1984c), Transference: A change in conception or only in emphasis? A response. *Psychonal. Inq.*, 4:489–523.

——— (1991), Indirect suggestion: A response to Oremland's *Interpretation and Interaction*. In: *Interpretation and Interaction* by J. Oremland. Hillsdale, NJ: The Analytic Press, pp. 137–163.

——— (1994), *Psychoanalysis in Transition*. Hillsdale, NJ: The Analytic Press.

——— & Brenman, M. (1959), *Hypnosis and Related States*. New York: International Universities Press.

——— & Hoffman, I. Z. (1982a), *Analysis of Transference, Vol. 2. Psychological Issues*, Monogr. 54. New York: International Universities Press.

——— & Hoffman, I. Z. (1982b), A method for studying the analysis of aspects of the patient's experience of the relationship in psychoanalysis and psychotherapy. *J. Amer. Psychoanal. Assn.*, 30:137–167.

——— & Klein. G. S. (1964), The structuring of drive and reality: David Rapaport's contributions to psychoanalysis and psychology. *Internat. J. Psycho-Anal.*, 45:483–498.

——— & Muslin, H. (1977), Early interpretation of transference. *J. Amer. Psychoanal. Assn.*, 24:779–794.

——— Newman, R. & Redlich, F. C. (1954), *The Initial Interview in Psychiatric Practice*. New York: International Universities Press.

——— Simon, J., Fink, G., Endicott, N. A. & Paul, I. H. (1968), Studies in audio-recorded psychoanalysis: 1. General considerations. *J. Amer. Psychoanal. Assn.*, 16:230–244.

Hoffman, I. Z. (1983), The patient as interpreter of the analyst's experience. *Contemp. Psychoanal.*, 19:389–422.

——— (1991), Discussion: Toward a social-constructivist view of the psychoanalytic situation. *Psychoanal. Dial.*, 1:74–105.

——— (1992a), Expressive participation and psychoanalytic discipline. *Contemp. Psychoanal.*, 28:1–15.

——— (1992b), Some practical implications of a social constructivist view of the psychoanalytic situation. *Psychoanal. Dial.*, 2:287–304.

——— (1992c), Reply to Orange. *Psychoanal. Dial.*, 2:567–570.

——— (1994), Dialectical thinking and therapeutic action in the psychoanalytic process. *Psychoanal. Quart.* 63:187–218.

——— & Gill M. M. (1988a), Critical reflections on a coding scheme. *Internat. J. Psycho-Anal.*, 69:55–64.

——— & ——— (1988b), A scheme for coding the patient's experience of the relationship with the therapist (PERT): Some applications, extensions, and comparisons. In: *Psychoanalytic Process Research Strategies*, ed. H. Dahl, H. Kächele & H. Thomä. New York: Springer-Verlag, pp. 67–98.

Holt, R. R. (1965), A review of some of Freud's biological assumptions and their influence on his theories. In: *Psychoanalysis and Current Biological Thought*, ed. N. S. Greenfield & W. C. Lewis. Madison: University of Wisconsin Press, pp. 93–124.

——— (1976), Drive or wish? A reconsideration of the psychoanalytic theory of motivation. In: *Psychology versus Metapsychology*, ed. M. M. Gill & P. S. Holzman. *Psychological Issues*, Monog. 36. New York: International Universities Press.

Klein, G. S. (1973), Two theories or one. *Bull. Menninger Clin.*, 37:102–132.

——— (1976), *Psychoanalytic Theory*. New York: International Universities Press.

Leary, T. & Gill, M. M. (1959), The dimensions and a measure of the process of psychotherapy: A system for the analysis of the content of clinical evaluations and patient-therapist verbalizations. In: *Research in Psychotherapy*, ed. E. A. Rubinstein & M. B. Parloff. Washington, DC: American Psychological Association.

Levenson, E. (1972), *The Fallacy of Understanding*. New York: Basic Books.

Lipton, S. D. (1977a), The advantages of Freud's technique as shown in his analysis of the Rat Man. *Internat. J. Psycho-Anal.*, 58:255–273.

——— (1977b), Clinical observations on resistance to the transference. *Internat. J. Psycho-Anal.*, 58:463–472.

Loewald, H. W. (1960), On the therapeutic action of psychoanalysis. *Internat. J. Psycho-Anal.*, 41:16–33.

Luborsky, L. (1967), Momentary forgetting during psychotherapy and psychoanalysis: A theory and research method. In: *Motives and Thought*, ed. R. R. Holt. *Psychological Issues*, Monogr. 18/19. New York: International Universities Press.

——— & Auerbach, A. H. (1969), The symptom-context method: Quantitative studies of symptom formation in psychotherapy. *J. Amer. Psychoanal. Assn.*, 17:68–99.

Macalpine, I. (1950), The development of the transference. *Psychoanal. Quart.*, 19:501–539.

Mitchell, S. A. (in press), Exits gracefully swinging: Review of *Psychoanalysis in Transition* by M. Gill. *Contemp. Psychol.*

Oremland, J. D. (1991), *Interpretation and Interaction*. Hillsdale, NJ: The Analytic Press.

Peterfreund, E. (1971), *Information, Systems, and Psychoanalysis. Psychological Issues*, Monogr. 25/26. New York: International Universities Press.

Pizer, S. A. (1992), The negotiation of paradox in the analytic process. *Psychoanal. Dial.*, 2:215–240.

Pribram, K. H. & Gill, M. M. (1976), *Freud's "Project" Reassessed*. New York: Basic Books.

Racker, H. (1968), *Transference and Countertransference*. New York: International Universities Press.

Rapaport, D. (1967), *The Collected Papers of David Rapaport*, ed. M. M. Gill. New York: Basic Books.

Rapaport, D. & Gill, M. M. (1959), The points of view and assumptions of metapsychology. *Internat. J. Psycho-Anal.*, 40:1–10.

Rapaport, D., Gill, M. M. & Schafer, R. (1945–46), *Diagnostic Psychological Testing* (2 vols.). Chicago: Year Book Publishers.

Rapaport, D., Gill, M. M. & Schafer, R. (1968), *Diagnostic Psychological Testing* (rev.), ed. R. Holt. New York: International Universities Press.

Reppen, J. (1982), Merton Gill: An interview. *Psychoanal. Rev.*, 69:167–190.

Ross, N. (1965), Review of *Topography and Systems in Psychoanalytic Theory* by M. M. Gill. *Internat. J. Psycho-Anal.*, 46:254–256.

Sandler, J. (1976), Countertransference and role-responsiveness. *Internat. Rev. Psycho-Anal.*, 3:43–47.

Schafer, R. (1976), *A New Language for Psychoanalysis*. New Haven, CT: Yale University Press.

Spence, D. P. (1964), *Review of Topography and Systems in Psychoanalytic Theory* by M. M. Gill. *J. Nerv. Ment. Dis.*, 15:401–403.

Strachey, J. (1934), The nature of the therapeutic action of psychoanalysis. *Internat. J. Psycho-Anal.*, 15:127–159.

chapter 4

Merton M. Gill: Publications and Awards

(1941), Malingering. *Bull. Menn. Clinic*, 5:157–166.

(1942), A case of amnesia and its bearing on the theory of memory (with D. Rapaport). *Character & Personal.*, II:166–172.

(1943), Comparison and clinical findings and psychological tests in three cases bearing upon military personnel selection (with R. P. Knight, M. Lozoff & D. Rapaport). *Bull. Menn. Clinic*, 7:114–128.

(1943), Functional disturbances of menstruation. *Bull. Menn. Clinic*, 7:6–14.

(1943), Treatment of a case of anxiety hysteria by an hypnotic technique employing psychoanalytic principles (with M. Brenman). *Bull. Menn. Clinic*, 7:163–171.

(1945), Hypnosis research project: First annual progress report (with M. Brenman). *Bull. Menn. Clinic*, 9:1–7.

(1945), *Diagnostic Psychological Testing*, Vol. I (with D. Rapaport & R. Schafer). Chicago: Yearbook Publishers.

(1946), *Diagnostic Psychological Testing*, Vol. II (with D. Rapaport & R. Schafer). Chicago: Yearbook Publishers.

(1946), Some recent observations on the use of hypnosis in psychotherapy (with M. Brenman). *Bull. Menn. Clinic*, 10:104–109.

(1946), Techniques of hypnoanalysis illustrated in a case report (with K. A. Menninger). *Bull. Menn. Clinic*, 10:110–126.

(1947), Problems in clinical research (with M. Brenman). *Amer. J. Orthopsychiat.*, 19:196–230.

(1947), *Hypnotherapy: A Review of the Literature* (with M. Brenman). The Menninger Monograph Series, No. 5. New York: International Universities Press.

(1948), Research in psychotherapy (with M. Brenman). *Amer. J. Orthopsychiat.*, 20:92–118.

(1948), Spontaneous regression on induction of hypnosis. *Bull. Menn. Clinic*, 12:41–48.

(1948), Alterations in the state of the ego in hypnosis (with M. Brenman & F. J. Hacker). *Bull. Menn. Clinic*, 12:41–48.

(1951), Ego psychology and psychotherapy. *Psychoanal. Quart.*, 20:62–71.

(1952), Spontaneous fluctuations in hypnosis (with M. Brenman & R. P. Knight). *Internal. J. Psycho-Anal.*, 33:22–34.
(1953), *A Planning Proposal for Research in emotional Growth and Mental Health*. New York: Social Science Research Council (privately circulated).
(1954), Psychoanalysis and exploratory psychotherapy. *J. Amer. Psychoanal. Assn.*, 2:771–797.
(1954), *The Initial Interview in Psychiatric Practice* (with R. Newman, F. C. Redlich & M. Sommers). New York: International Universities Press. (Published with phonograph records.)
(1959), The present state of psychoanalytic theory. *J. Abnorm. Soc. Psychol.*, 58:1–8.
(1959), *Hypnosis and Related States: Psychoanalytic Studies in Regression* (with M. Brenman). New York: International Universities Press.
(1959), The points of view and assumptions of metapsychology (with D. Rapaport). *Internat. J. Psycho-Anal.*, 40:1–10.
(1959), The dimensions and a measure of the process of psychotherapy: A system for the analysis of the content of clinical evaluations and patient-therapist verbalizations (with T. Leary). In: *Research in Psychotherapy*, ed. E. A. Rubinstein & M. B. Parloff. Washington, DC: American Psychological Association, pp. 62–95.
(1961), In Memoriam: David Rapaport. *J. Amer. Psychoanal. Assn.*, 9:755–759.
(1962), *Aportaciones a la Teoria y Tecnica Psicoanalitica* (with D. Rapaport). Mexico, DF: Editoria Pax, Libreria Carlos Cesarman, S.A.
(1963), *Topography and Systems in Psychoanalytic Theory*. Psychological Issues, III. New York: International Universities Press.
(1964), The structuring of drive and reality: David Rapaport's contributions to psychoanalysis and psychology (with G. S. Klein). *Internat. J. Psycho-Anal.*, 45:483–498.
(1967) (editor), *The Collected Papers of David Rapaport*. New York: Basic Books.
(1967) The primary process. In: *Motives and Thought*, ed. R. Holt. Psychological Issues, V. New York: International Universities Press. pp. 259–298.
(1968), Studies in audio-recorded psychoanalysis. 1. General considerations (with D. Simon, N. A. Endicott & I. H. Paul). *J. Amer. Psychoanal. Assn.*, 16:230–244.
(1968), *Diagnostic Psychological Testing* (with D. Rapaport & R. Schafer) (Revised edition, R. Holt, ed.). New York: International Universities Press.
(1969), Behavior therapy: Observations and reflections (with M. H. Kein, A. T. Dittman & M. B. Parloff). *J. Consult. & Clin. Psychol*, 3:259–266.
(1970), Studies in audio-recorded psychoanalysis. 2. The effect on the

analyst (with J. Simon, G. Fink, N. A. Endicott & I. H. Paul). *J. Amer. Psychoanal. Assn.*, 18:86–101.

(1972), Hypnosis as an altered and regressed state. *Internat. J. Clin. & Experiment. Hypnosis*, 20:224–237.

(1973), Introduction to George Klein's "Two theories or one?" *Bull. Menn. Clinic*, 37:99–101.

(1973), Analyzed and unanalyzed transference. *Internat. J. Psychiat.*, 11:328–335.

(1975), Book review of T. R. Sarbin & W. C. Coe, *Hypnosis: A Social Psychological Analysis of influence Communication*, 1972. *J. Nervous & Mental Dis.*, 160:58–61.

(1976), *Psychology Versus Metapsychology* (with P. S. Holzman, ed.). Psychological Issues, IX. New York: International Universities Press.

(1976), Metapsychology is not psychology. In: *Psychology Versus Metapsychology*. Psychological Issues. New York: International Universities Press, pp. 71–105.

(1976), *Freud's "Project" Reassessed* (with K. Pribram). New York: Basic Books.

(1976), Book review of C. A. Loew, H. Grayson & G. H. Loew, *Three Psychotherapies: A Clinical Comparison*, 1975. *Contemp. Psychol.*, 21:291–292.

(1976), Book review of D. J. Kiesler, *Process of Psychotherapy: Empirical Foundations and Systems of Analysis*, 1973. *Psychoanal. Quart.*, 45:323–324.

(1977), Early interpretation of transference (with H. Muslin). *J. Amer. Psychoanal. Assn.*, 24:779–794.

(1977), Psychic energy reconsidered: Discussion. *J. Amer. Psychoanal. Assn.*, 25:581–598.

(1977), Book review of *Psychotherapy and Multiple Personality: Selected Essays by Morton Prince*, ed. N. Hale, Jr. (Cambridge, MA, 1975). *Psychoanal. Quart.*, 46:700–701.

(1977), The two models of the mental health disciplines. *Bull. Menn. Clinic*, 41:79–84.

(1977), *El "Proyecto" de Freud* (with K. Pribam). Spanish translation of *Freud's "Project" Reassessed*. Buenos Aires: Ediciones Marymar.

(1978), Freud Neurologo (with K. Pribram). Italian translation of *Freud's "Project" Reassessed*. Torino, Italy: Boringhieri.

(1978), Metapsychology is irrelevant to psychoanalysis. In: *The Human Mind Revisited: Essays in Honor of Karl A. Menninger*, ed. S. Smith. New York: International Universities Press, pp. 349–368.

(1978), Transference in the Dora case (with H. Muslin). *J. Amer. Psychoanal. Assn.*, 26:311–330.

(1978), *Psychoanalytic Psychotherapy*. Tape recording published by Aronson, Northvale, NJ.

(1978), Freud's concepts of unconsciousness and the unconscious. In: *The Unconscious*, Vol. I, ed. A. Prangishvili, A. Sherozia & F. Bassin. Tbilisi, U.S.S.R.: Metsniereba Publishing, pp. 482–489.

(1978), Hypnosis as an altered and regressed state of consciousness. In: *The Unconscious*, Vol. II, ed. A. Prangishvili, A. Sherozia & F. Bassin. Tbilisi, U.S.S.R.: Metsniereba Publishing, pp. 152–161.

(1979), *Il Modello Topico Nella Teoria Psicoanalitica*. Italian translation of *Topography and Systems in Psychoanalytic Theory*. Torino, Italy: Boringhieri.

(1979), The analysis of the transference. *J. Amer. Psychoanal. Assn.*, 27 (supplement):263–288.

(1979), Book review of *The Evolution of Psychoanalytic Technique*, ed. M. S. Bergmann & F. R. Hartman, 1976. *Psychoanal. Quart.*, 48:506–507.

(1979), *O Projeto de Freud* (with K. Pribram). Portuguese translation of *Freud's "Project" Reassessed*. Sao Paolo: Editora Cultrix.

(1980), Reprint of Behavior therapy: Observations and reflections (with M. Klein, A. Dittman & M. Parloff) (1969). In: *The Interface Between the Psychodynamic and Behavioral Therapies*, ed. J. Marmor & S. Woods. New York: Plenum Medical Book, pp. 223–236.

(1980), A contribution to: Some views on effective principles of psychotherapy (with I. Hoffman). *Cognitive Therapy and Research* (Special Issue: Psychotherapy Process, ed. M. R. Goldfried), 4:271–306.

(1981), Book review of R. Langs, *The Therapeutic Environment*, 1979. *Contemp. Psychol.*, 26:36–37

(1981), Reprint of The analysis of the transference (1979). In: *Classics in Psychoanalytic Technique*, ed. R. Langs. New York: Aronson, pp. 69–82.

(1980–81), The analysis of transference: A critique of Fenichel's *Problems of Psychoanalytic Technique. Internat. J. Psychoanal. Psychother.*, 8:45–56.

(1981), Review of F. Sulloway, *Freud, Biologist of the Mind: Beyond the Psychoanalytic Legend. Psychoanal. Rev.*, 68:343–347.

(1981), El analisis de la transferencia. Translation of The analysis of the transference (1979). *Psicoanalisis*, 3:137–167.

(1981), The boundaries of psychoanalytic data and technique: A critique of Gedo's *Beyond Interpretation. Psychoanal. Inq.*, 1:205–232.

(1982), The analysis of the transference. In: *Curative Factors in Dynamic Psychotherapy*, ed. S. Slipp. New York: McGraw-Hill.

(1982), A method for studying the analysis of aspects of the patient's experience of the relationship in psychoanalysis and psychotherapy (with I. Hoffman). *J. Amer. Psychoanal. Assn.*, 30:137–168.

(1982), Reprint of "A contribution to: Some views on effective principles of psychotherapy" (with I. Hoffman) (1980). In: *Converging Themes in Psychotherapy*, ed. M. Goldfried. New York: Springer, pp. 155–190.

(1982), *Analysis of Transference: Vol. 1, Theory and Technique*. Psychological Issues 53. New York: International Universities Press.

(1982), *Analysis of Transference: Vol. 2, Studies of Nine Audio-recorded Psychoanalytic Sessions* (with I. Hoffman). Psychological Issues 54. New York: International Universities Press.

(1982), Merton Gill: An interview. *Psychoanal. Rev.*, 69:167–190.

(1982), On Sullivan, his life and work. *William Alanson White Newsletter* (Winter 1982–83), 17:6.

(1983), Review of J. Gedo's *Advances in Clinical Psychoanalysis* (New York, 1981). *Contemp. Psychol.*, 28:69–70.

(1983), The point of view of psychoanalysis: Energy discharge or person. *Psychoanal. & Contemp. Thought*, 6:523–552.

(1983), The interpersonal paradigm and the degree of the therapist's involvement. *Contemp. Psychoanal.*, 19:200–237.

(1983), Book review of *Psychoanalysis: Critical Explorations in Contemporary Theory and Practice*, ed. A. Jacobson & D. Parmelee. *Contemp. Psychol.*, 28:410.

(1983), Book review of H. Perry, *Psychiatrist of America: The Life of Harry Stack Sullivan. William Alanson White Newsletter*, 18:4–6.

(1984), Robert Langs on technique: A critique. In: *Listening and Interpreting. The Challenge of the Work of Robert Langs*, ed. J. Raney. New York: Aronson, pp. 395–413.

(1984), Book review of E. Peterfreund, *The Process of Psychoanalytic Therapy. Contemp. Psychol.*, 29:255–256.

(1984), Discussion of "Harry Stack Sullivan: The Web and the Spider." *Contemp. Psychoanal.*, 20:189–196.

(1984), Psychoanalysis and psychotherapy: A revision. *Internat. Rev. Psycho-Anal.*, 11:161–180.

(1984), Foreword to B. Barratt, *Psychic Reality and Psychoanalytic Knowing*. Hillsdale, NJ: Erlbaum, pp. vii–x.

(1984), Psychoanalytic, psychodynamic, cognitive behavior, and behavior therapies compared, a rejoinder to John M. Rhoads; and Differing views of transference: Commentary on John M. Rhoads. In: *Psychoanalytic Therapy and Behavior Therapy*, ed. H. Arkowitz & B. Messer. New York: Plenum, pp. 179–187, 193–194, 213–217.

(1984), Die Metapsychologie ist keine Psychologie. German translation of Metapsychology is not psychology (1976). *Psyche*, 38:961–991.

(1984), Foreword to H. Strupp & J. Binder, *Psychotherapy in a New Key*. New York: Basic Books.

(1984), Transference: A change in conception or only in emphasis? A response. *Psychoanal. Inq.*, 4:489–524.

(1985), A critique of Robert Langs' conceptions of transference, evidence by indirection, and the role of the frame. *The Yearbook of Psychoanalysis and Psychotherapy*, 1:177–187.

(1985), *Teoria e Technica dell'Analisi del Transfert*. Italian translation of *Analysis of Transference: Vol. 1, Theory and Technique* (1982). Rome: Casa Editrice Astrolobio.

(1985), The interactional aspect of transference: Range of application (participant in discussion and responses to introductory questions). In: *The Transference in Psychotherapy: Clinical Management*, ed. E. Schwaber. New York: International Universities Press, pp. 87–102, 121–137, 139–167.

(1985), Un nouveau regard sur la metapsychologie. *Rév. Fran. Psychanal.*, 49:1237–1252.

(1986), *Le "Projet de Psychologie Scientifique" de Freud: Un Nouveau Regard* (with K. Pribram). French translation of *Freud's "Project" Reassessed* (1976). Paris: Presses Universitaires de France.

(1986), Discussion of transference and counter-transference revisited by R. Chessick. *Dynam. Psychother.*, 4:31–33.

(1987), Le point de vac d'un psychanalyst americain sur la relation analytique et le transfert. In: *Hypnose et Psychanalyse*, ed. L. Chertok & M. Borch-Jacobsen. Paris: Dunod.

(1987), Discussion of M. Black, The analyst's stance: Transferential implications of technical orientation. *The Annual of Psychoanalysis*, 15:157–159.

(1987), Reprint of "The point of view of psychoanalysis." In: *Attachment and the Therapeutic Process: Essays in Honor of Otto Allen Will, Jr.*, ed. J. L. Sacksteder, D. P. Schwartz & Y. Akabane. Madison, CT: International Universities Press.

(1987), The analyst as participant. *Psychoanal. Inq.*, 7:249–260.

(1988), Converting psychotherapy into psychoanalysis. *Contemp. Psychoanal.*, 24:262–274.

(1988), Clinical reflections on a coding scheme (with I. Hoffman). *Internat. J. Psycho-Anal.*, 69:55–64.

(1988), Japanese translation of *Freud's "Project" Reassessed* (1976). Tokyo: Tuttle-Mori.

(1988), Book review of C. Bollas, *The Shadow of the Object: Psychoanalysis of the Unthought Known. Contemp. Psychol.*, 33:1095–1096.

(1988), A scheme for coding the patient's experience of the relationship with the therapist (PERT): Some applications, extensions and comparisons (with I. Hoffman). In: *Psychoanalytic Process Research Strategies*, ed. H. Dahl, H. Kaechele & H. Thomae. Berlin: Springer-Verlag, pp. 67–98.

(1989), Ego analysis and the relativity of defense: Technical implications of the structural theory (with B. Apfelbaum). *J. Amer. Psychoanal. Assn.*, 37:1071–1096.

(1989), Psicoanalisi e psicoterapia: Una revisione. Italian translation of Psychoanalysis and Psychotherapy: A revision (1984). In: *Psicologia*

Clinica, ed. F. del Corno & M. Lang Bianchi. Milano: Franco Angeli.

(1990), The analysis of the transference. In: *Essential Papers on Transference*, ed. A. Esman. New York: New York University Press.

(1991), Merton Gill speaks his mind. *Amer. Psychoanal.*, 25:17–21.

(1991), Indirect suggestion: A response to Oremland. *Interpretation and Interaction: Psychoanalysis or Psychotherapy*. Hillsdale, NJ: The Analytic Press.

(1991), Psychoanalysis and psychotherapy: An exchange with R. S. Wallerstein, in Letters to the Editors. *Internat. J. Psycho-Anal.*, 72:159–166.

(1992), Reprint of Merton Gill speaks his mind (1991). *Internat. J. Commun. Psychoanal. Psychother.*, 7:27–33.

(1992), Becoming a psychoanalyst. *Perspectives*: Newsletter of the Chicago Center for Psychoanalysis, 1: 1–4.

(1993), Interaction and interpretation: Commentary on Morris Eagle's "Enactment, transference, and symptomatic cure: A case history." *Psychoanal. Dial.*, 3:111–122.

(1993), One-person and two-person perspectives: Freud's "Observations on Transference Love." In: *On Freud 's Observations on Transference Love*, ed. E. Spector, C. Hagelin & P. Fonagy. New Haven, CT: Yale University Press, pp. 14–129.

(1993), Die analyse der Ubertragung. German translation of "The analysis of transference" (1979). *Forum Psychoanal.*, 9:46–61.

(1993), Review of E. Levenson, *The Purloined Self* (1991). *Internat. J. Psycho-Anal.*, 74:400–403.

(1994), Research in psychoanalysis. *Round Robin* (Newsletter of Section 1, Division 39 of American Psychoanalytic Association), 10:8–12.

(1994), Reprint of "The analysis of transference" (1979). In: *Essential Papers on Transference Analysis*, ed. C. Bauer. Northvale, NJ: J Aronson.

(1994), Letter to the editor regarding Levy and Inderbitzen on neutrality. *J. Amer. Psychoanal. Assn.*, 42:681–684.

(1994), Heinz Kohut's self psychology. In: *A Decade of Progress: Progress in Self Psychology, Vol. 10*, ed. A. Goldberg. Hillsdale, NJ: The Analytic Press, pp. 197–211.

(1994), Review essay on *Conflict and Compromise: Therapeutic Implications*, ed. S. Dowling. *Psychoanal. Quart.*, 63:756–778.

(1994), *Psychoanalysis in Transition: A Personal View*. Hillsdale, NJ: The Analytic Press.

(1995), Classical and relational psychoanalysis. *Psychoanal. Psychol.*, 12:89–108.

(1995), Psychoanalysis in transition: The current scene in psychoanalysis. In: *Confronting the Challenge to Psychoanalysis: Collected Papers from the 5th Annual Conference of the International Federation for Psychoanalytic Education*, pp. 7–18.

(1996), Discussion: Interaction III. *Psychoanal. Inq.*, 16:118–134.

Awards

Gill's outstanding contributions to psychoanalysis were recognized publicly by several organizations. Among the awards he received were:

Special Award of the Division of Psychoanalysis of the American Psychological Association (1991), the only nonpsychologist to receive this award

Heinz Hartmann Award of the New York Psychoanalytic Society (1992)

Hans Loewald Memorial Award of the International Federation for Psychoanalytic Education (1994)

Mary Singleton Sigourney Prize of the International Psychoanalytic Association (awarded shortly after his death)

PART IV

CURRENT CONTROVERSIES IN PSYCHOANALYSIS

Natural Science and the Hermeneutic Orientation: The Debate

Psychoanalysis as a One-Person and a Two-Person Psychology

Psychoanalysis and Psychotherapy: Critical Differences or Blurring of Boundaries?

Transference

Natural Science and the Hermeneutic Orientation: The Debate

Chapter 5

My Theoretical Differences with Merton Gill

Robert R. Holt

Editors' Introduction: *Holt captures an important ideal of Gill's: the latter's lifelong pursuit of an empirical approach to the study of human behavior. As a dedicated disciple, colleague, and friend of David Rapaport, Gill never retreated from his empirical orientation. He came to believe, however, a hermeneutic discipline more appropriately captured what he believed was central to analytic concerns, namely a systematic study of personal meanings.*

Holt continues his long-term argument with Gill about his hermeneutic position and puts into print for the first time a letter Gill wrote to Adolph Grunbaum after Gill's presentation of his ideas about psychoanalysis as a "hermeneutic science."

It is always at least a potential threat to a friendship when disagreements develop over issues both parties consider important. I even lost one good friend after writing what I thought was a respectful but critical review of a book. Merton Gill was far too large minded for that ever to have been a danger to our friendship. Nevertheless, now that he is gone, I had to overcome some reluctance to accept an invitation to contribute to this book, because I was so fond of him. Nothing I have to say diminishes my great respect for him as a person and as a lastingly important contributor to psychoanalysis.

I believe Merton[1] and I differed on theoretical matters in our latter years primarily because he was sold a bill of goods by other friends. All

[1] I refer to him by his first name because it is so natural and because it would feel awkward and stuffy to refer to such an informal person, who never stood on ceremony, as Dr. Gill.

of us faced some hard choices on the collapse of our hopes for a scientific psychoanalysis based on a clarified and reorganized metapsychology. Transparently, we shared that because of our common discipleship to David Rapaport. When his authoritative and persuasive voice no longer could call back any strays, we all began to leave his fold and found ourselves wandering without shepherd.

Merton was one of those who listened to the pipings of the hermeneuts, who offered a new authority and places in a warm manger with plenty of company, and more, though that would have been enough for him. Adopt hermeneutics, they urged, and you enter a promised land of a new, yet ancient, metatheory. Natural science was always a false ideal, they preached, for it is fundamentally hostile to the essential stuff of psychoanalysis: human meanings, longings, dreams, rationalizations, plans, and interpretations.

I was once drawn to hermeneutics, too, when I first learned that it was a discipline devoted to the study of interpretation. That was in the 1940s, when I was struggling to master the slippery art of interpreting TAT stories and needed all the help I could get. I naively turned to hermeneutics, hoping for well-thought-out rules to help discipline and limit the free wanderings of the interpretative imagination. But that was not at all the nature of this so-called discipline. At its heart was a repudiation of the idea there might be a correct interpretation of anything, replaced by a celebration of the fecundity of human intelligence in finding many kinds of meanings. True, there were guidelines to appropriateness: one should consider the context of a passage in the entire text, and the latter's place in a tradition. Some even endorsed what psychoanalysts loved to do—show the relevance of aspects of a text to the life and mental world of its author. Unfortunately, I had already been taught that and found nothing that would validate my dream of discovering a ready-made *science of interpretation*.

An attractive feature of hermeneutics is that it deals with meanings, in sharp contrast to the dry remoteness of metapsychology from the meaningful, even the clinical. I find it curious, in retrospect, that such careful scholars as Rapaport and Gill did not notice several key facts about metapsychology: that it was introduced offhandedly, almost as an aside in a paper concerned about something else (Freud, 1915); that Freud made very few attempts to carry out the announced program of systematically considering dynamic, economic, and topographic aspects of phenomena he wished to explain, indeed making little reference to metapsychology altogether in his subsequent works; and that he defined the three points of view so unclearly that there is to this day little consensus on just what is meant by them and by metapsychology (Holt, 1989). I'm afraid that Rapaport was so eager to convert psychoanalysis into a general psychology—which should be an explanatory scientific theory—that he seized the pretext of a programmatic statement on which Freud never carried through and tried to blow it up into a major aspect of the theory.

In his justification I believe that he saw correctly how much of the metapsychological apparatus was *implicit* in most of Freud's theorizing. Again, however, I marvel at the incongruity of Rapaport's expert knowledge of many sciences and his failure to see how anachronistic was Freud's conception of how to be scientific. For the founder of psychoanalysis, what was important was the persuasive language used, the number of modish bases touched in writing theory, and not at all how good the method was.

But, of course, it took me several decades of study to begin to see these weaknesses, and I wrote several papers (which I must now repudiate) while under the spell of Rapaport's ideal of a scientific psychoanalysis based on a clarified metapsychology. So I have no intention of criticizing Gill, who had been closer to Rapaport than anyone over a longer time, for his metapsychological writings of the 1950s and 1960s.

What I hope to do, instead, is to show how in turning away from the blind alley into which Rapaport had led all of us, his followers, Gill made a couple of relatively minor errors. First, based on the correct recognition that metapsychology had been an attempt to give psychoanalysis a basis in natural science, he concluded that not just this effort but *any* attempt to ground psychoanalysis in natural-scientific concepts and methods was mistaken. Assured by various hermeneutically intoxicated colleagues that natural science had no place for meanings, intentions, and other conscious phenomena, which were at the center of concern for hermeneutics, he took the turn into their camp.

Second, somehow he managed not to see clearly that his new friends did not share his continuing devotion to scientific method and the pursuit of truth. To his everlasting credit, Merton never wavered in his belief that there was a discoverable order in human affairs, and that psychoanalysis could become a *scientific* study of subjective phenomena as well as of behavior—the latter, moreover, viewed not as locomotion through space and time but as the meaningful pursuit of goals and purposes like the avoidance of pain and anxiety, the attainment of gratifications, and the pursuit of ideals.

At the Rapaport-Klein Study Group meetings in June 1983, he presented his conception of psychoanalysis as a hermeneutic science. Several persons, most notably Adolf Grünbaum (and including me), tried to explain that the very phrase was oxymoronic. After thinking about it for awhile and exchanging letters with Grünbaum, he sent the latter a notable letter on November, 29, 1983, in which he frankly admitted his error. He wrote, in part:

> In my ignorance, and I say that abashedly, I have been using the word "hermeneutic" to mean human sciences which deal with the dimension

> of meaning rather than employing the dimensions of space, energy, force and the like which to me are the dimensions of at least one batch of natural science. I learned, not only from you but from the very interesting book soon to appear by Barnaby Barratt that I am quite wrong about what people who call themselves hermeneuticists say. They are in fact anti-scientific and of course I am not. I am quite wrong therefore, to as you say, nail my flag to the hermeneutic mast but I will explain later how I got there. In any case I completely agree with you that the methods of science are the same for all science and that it is very misleading to imply that there is a kind of science which uses other methods. Sciences differ, therefore, in the material with which they deal not in their methods. . . .
>
> [You have said] psychoanalytic validation has problems of its own over and above the generic ones of the sciences. Why have those problems not been attacked? Why is research in the ordinary sense of scientific research in which the methodology of science is employed, in which data are collected, hypotheses erected, hypotheses examined in the light of the data of independent observers, and conclusions drawn according to the rules of logic or even statistics . . . so abysmally absent in psychoanalysis? I believe it was the effort to answer that question which led me astray in the various ways that I have confessed in this letter. I became convinced that the special problems of doing research in psychoanalysis must be responsible and that there therefore must be a different way of thinking about research in psychoanalysis. I became convinced that it is the reductionist flavor of psychoanalysis in terms of the alleged relationship between psychoanalytic metapsychology—which is in dimensions of force, energy, etc.—to clinical psychoanalysis—which is in the dimensions of meaning and reasons—which must be responsible. I vaguely heard that there was a different kind of world outlook that went by the name of hermeneutics that dealt with meaning and reasons, and, naively, without knowing that persons who actually labeled themselves hermeneuticists were in fact anti-scientific, I decided that there must be a hermeneutic science and that that's what psychoanalysis should be. I didn't have the slightest intention of removing psychoanalysis from the family of sciences. I therefore distinguished between natural science and hermeneutic science. You of course have shown me that that won't do. (So did Barratt.)

He was, of course, correct that there are other sciences besides the classical natural sciences of physics and chemistry, notably the social and behavioral sciences, which are directly concerned with various aspects of human meanings. He had majored in psychology as an undergraduate, had worked in close collaboration with psychologists from the beginning of his career (Rapaport and Brenman) to the end (Hoffman), and for many years was a member of the American Psychological Association. He once remarked to me that he felt more at home with psychologists than psychiatrists, even commenting something to the effect that we were the good guys of the mental-health field. He knew well enough that clinical and social psychologists worked scientifically with verbal texts, for example coding and scaling their meanings and doing statistical research with the resulting quantities. (See, for example, his paper with Timothy Leary, 1959; and his later work with Hoffman, 1982.) I am baffled by his failure to remember this other alternative to "natural science."

Sometime in the early 1980s, he apparently decided to stop writing about theory and metatheory and to concentrate his efforts for the rest of his career on psychoanalytic research. With Irwin Hoffman he developed a method of coding the many aspects of transference and applied it to the systematic study of this crucial aspect of psychoanalytic therapy. I think he made the right decision. In a way, however, it might have been neater if he had published his 1983 letter repudiating hermeneutics. The many colleagues who are still laboring under the illusion that that false prophecy is going to salvage psychoanalysis and make the difficult procedures of science unnecessary would not have been able to cite his papers from 1976 to 1983 as showing that he was one of them. But no one should be chided for avoiding a diet of crow.

When Merton sent me a copy of his letter to Grünbaum, he wrote, "I don't know why some people seem to read it as an abject surrender. Perhaps you can tell me. As for quoting from it, I would like to retain the privilege of reading and reacting to the quote before you publish it." As it happens, I did not have occasion to quote from it in his lifetime. Happily, Ilse Judas (his widow) has given permission for me to use it here.

An important theme in the letter is Gill's idea of a modest psychoanalysis, making a science out of its own data. Several implications of that theme can stand some discussion. First, he directs attention to psychoanalysts like Hartmann who have explicitly called for a general psychoanalytic psychology, which would borrow to some extent from other sciences, and be linked with them. Gill may be correct in his hypothesis that one reason these theorists have not done the research he felt was needed is their enchantment with the grandiose dream of such an overarching, integrative theory. That is, however, an empirical question, which can't easily be decided.

Third, I think he was quite correct in believing that the more we strive for a substitute for metapsychology of the kind Rubinstein (1997) advocated, the less the result resembles psychoanalysis. It seems both modest and reasonable to urge psychoanalysts to stick to what they know best and to try to do research on their own data.

The problem arises, however, when one proposes that somehow psychoanalysts have the right to create their own theory, a *theory* that does not need to be concerned with nonpsychoanalytic data or even data from outside the consulting room. Even that might be acceptable, if one did not claim that such a science can and indeed must explain its own phenomena in its own terms, without reference to concepts from other sciences. There is a hidden reductionism here, or the equivalent, the ultimately irrational claim that the freedom to create one's own distinctive science, based on data from the psychoanalytic clinical situation, implies that it is therefore explanatory. Rubinstein (1997) has most directly addressed this issue, showing how and why that hope is illusory.

Take Gill's somewhat unclear statement (in his letter of 11/29/1983), "If you mean that the topical distance means that we have to apply the methodology of science to understand how causality is operating and if that causality is the search for the chain of meanings which closes the gap in the topical distance, then I agree with you." He seems to say that we can establish causality by discovering a complete chain of meanings between an initiating event and a consequent. Freud and most psychoanalysts would surely have agreed. I believe, however, with Grünbaum, that it is a serious error. The very concept of rationalization is evidence that Freud himself did not always accept such a closed chain as satisfactory evidence of a causal explanation. Patients are very ingenious in inventing "chains of meanings" that purport to explain why they performed symptomatic actions for which the psychoanalyst prefers quite different explanations. Here is an example of the powerlessness of the hermeneutic approach: it provides no way to choose among equally plausible attempts of this kind. So, we have the familiar spectacle of the psychoanalytic meeting in which the presenter gives his interpretation of a patient's dream; various colleagues arise and present more or less ingenious alternatives; and the presiding officer declares, like the rat at the caucus race in *Alice in Wonderland*, that, thanks to overdetermination, "all have won and all must have prizes." Such are the dubious blessings of the relativism that lies at the murky heart of hermeneutic philosophy.

Is there, then, no way a modest, self-contained psychoanalysis can become a science? It will need a theory, and the obvious candidate is the existing clinical theory of psychoanalysis, as Klein (1976) urged. Aside from the many serious flaws of that theory, why should anyone accept the proposition that it is necessarily sufficient as a way of explaining the data of clinical psychoanalysis?

Recent advances in the pharmacological treatment of panic states, obsessive-compulsive disorder, and depression suggest that Freud may not have been far off the mark in feeling that psychoanalysis had a relatively short time to work with neurotic patients before chemical treatments preempted the therapeutic field. Just because a depressed mood and depressive ideation are subjective phenomena familiar in the psychoanalytic consulting room, does that mean they cannot have biochemical explanations?

Or, put another way, even if their meaningful *content* is indeed part of a gapless "chain of meanings," and even if it should prove possible to establish causality in some other way than merely demonstrating its completeness, how can one call the result scientific if it leaves out the biochemical and neurophysiological causes without which the depression would not have come to clinical attention? I have elaborated on these themes elsewhere (Holt, 1989).

Let me add a brief coda about Merton's last book. In it, he addressed the issues of what kind of science psychoanalysis is or should be and reverts to the notion of a hermeneutic science, apparently having forgotten his letter to Adolf and the reasons that convinced him then he was mistaken in hoping for such a synthesis.

With his characteristic modesty and lack of pretense, Merton began his final book (1994) with these disarming words: "Since I am not sophisticated in epistemology or philosophy, I believe it is important to state that I am using concepts like constructivism, hermeneutics, and objectivism . . . only in a global, connotative, more or less commonsensical way" (p. 1).

It seems churlish to object to such a frank statement, especially when one reflects that so many of our colleagues plunge into difficult philosophical waters as if they have had the requisite swimming lessons and flail about making much more splash than progress. Sadly, however, there isn't any easy analogue to wading here, and one easily gets in over one's head without realizing it. I am prepared to be told by those whose careers have been devoted to philosophical and methodological matters that the confidence with which I have written about the metaphysical foundations of psychoanalysis is exaggerated. So the following critical remarks are offered, not ex cathedra, but in hope of getting a fruitful dialogue going—alas, no longer with Gill himself, but with someone willing to develop his position.

He went on to identify constructivism with the unexceptionable "proposition that all human perception and thinking is a construction rather than a direct reflection of external reality." It might have been better had he said that constructivism begins with this empirical basis but then generalizes to less testable extensions such as those with which the paragraph ends: "Another familiar way of conveying the constructivist premise is to say that there are no facts as such. In a vivid metaphor, facts are soaked in theory. Science—obviously based on perception and thought—is constructivist. While this may appear more obviously true for the human sciences, it is true for the natural sciences, too" (p. 1).

Here, right away, is a misunderstanding, and a very common one in these days of deconstructionism, post-modernism, and other fashionable variants of relativism. The issues were nicely sharpened by the NYU physicist Sokal in his amusing spoof (1996) and were brought to a fine point by Steven Weinberg (1996) in a follow-up. *If* it were true that the laws of natural science "are relative to that [the human] perspective," then a harder form of constructivism would have to be espoused by all scientists.

It is not true, for two reasons: first, because autonomy does exist, and second, because much of scientific method is devoted to solving precisely this problem, of detaching facts and conclusions from wish, bias, subjective state, national or ethnic traditions and preconceptions, and so forth. It would not be easy for a constructivist to reject the slur that psychoanalysis is a Jewish science, just as Einstein's theories were alleged to have been. Gill had followed Rapaport and Hartmann in rejecting the "seething caldron" conception of naive id-psychology, but did not notice that claims of modern relativists about science, so neatly satirized by Sokal, amount to the same kind of refusal to admit any "ego autonomy." Weinberg's article (1996), and the ensuing discussion in the letter columns of the *New York Review of Books* (issue of October 3, 1996, pp. 54–56) are strongly recommended to anyone who finds my conclusion difficult to accept.

What is at issue here is mainly the metaphysical undergirding of psychoanalysis, even though Merton does not use the term *metaphysics* and discusses the competing paradigms occasionally as if they were metapsychology and a new, more clinical, and hermeneutic theory. But no one could be happier than me to see a discussion of the philosophical foundations of psychoanalysis, for I have felt lonely in recent years trying to persuade analysts to become aware of metaphysics and the fact that psychoanalysis, like any other science, has metaphysical foundations. Indeed, in my view, many of the troubles and confusions of Freud's theories stem from his various metaphysical commitments, of which he was largely unaware. But then the same is true of psychological theory at large.

Instead of what is implicitly a unitary "old paradigm," Freud's world hypothesis was a mixture of mostly mechanistic but to some extent animistic and pragmatist tenets, not only internally inconsistent but in several ways anachronistic. Freud's own era was a time when a genuinely new world hypothesis was being put together by the pragmatists, notably Peirce, Dewey, and James. Indeed, as I have argued in the last chapter of my recent book, Freud played an important part in paving the way for this new philosophical school by developing the case for psychological relativism. (I remind you here only of his 1917 paper, "A Difficulty in the Path of Psychoanalysis," in which he described three blows to man's narcissism but might just as well have called the target cognitive absolutism.)

In his 1994 book Merton did not make it as clear as would be desirable that the paradigmatic shift he wanted to promote meant first and foremost abandoning the old metaphysics and adopting a thorough-going and consistent pragmatism. He could then have shown how specific changes in theory and technique necessarily follow; but perhaps he feared that some of the audience would find a franker address to metaphysical issues intimidating or otherwise off-putting.

If he had taken that tack, he might have realized he should consider another alternative philosophical grounding for psychoanalysis, the even more recent world hypothesis of systems philosophy. As I have argued elsewhere, it has all of the advantages of pragmatism without a number of the latter's serious liabilities. Quite possibly it has its own disadvantages, of which I am not aware. I hope that Hoffman and others followers of Gill's will undertake a serious critique of systems philosophy from their own vantage point. Perhaps they can persuade me that it is a less satisfactory undergirding of psychoanalytic theory and practice than social constructivism.

What follows are what I consider to be the major deficiencies of Gill's and Hoffman's proposed "paradigm," using their term even though I prefer "metaphysics" or "world hypothesis." There is the matter of what they call objectivism, the assumptions that there *is* a real world and that we can make important progress toward knowing it. For the most part, they simplify their task by attacking objectivism in its least defensible form, naive realism: the notion that *I* can see what's true clearly enough, thank you, though less objective observers fall into various kinds of errors. The contemporary heirs of 19th-century mechanism, the modern materialists, long ago adopted a *critical* realism that cannot be dismissed so easily. No serious writer any longer asserts he or she has direct access to the truth or pretends that the world given us by sense perception is necessarily the true reality without any correction.

Merton recognized that science is defined by its method, but shrank from the task of specifying how a hermeneutic-scientific method would differ from ordinary scientific method. The latter has the central purpose of minimizing error and self-deception and helping us free ourselves from the limitations of particular contexts. Relativists earn their bread by tirelessly pointing out the ways in which our knowledge is determined by factors we don't want to be involved, ignoring the fact that scientific method is devoted precisely to discovering just such factors and ways of compensating for them.

A good example of relativism transcended in physics is the statement that water boils at 100°C. The statement is true only at sea level; as soon as atmospheric pressure lowers for any reason, the boiling point drops. Do we therefore invent a constructivist physics and declare that objective truth about the physical world is impossible? No, we learn to measure atmospheric pressure and plot the boiling point against it, discovering another law that helps us correct our first statement. Much of the progress of science consists in just such discoveries of limitations in what we thought we knew, followed by ways of approaching the elusive truth a bit closer. It is widely accepted that true, exact, and complete knowledge of reality is not an accomplished fact but an ideal which we can hope to approach only asymptotically.

I have been shown absolutely no reason why we cannot approach psychic reality in the same way. There is, in principle, one true story of how a patient developed his or her neurosis, albeit a complex and many-layered one (each layer containing a partial truth) that we cannot hope ever to reconstruct completely. Yes, all knowledge is constructed, but that does not make all constructions of equal value. Even those who assert the relativist position find it difficult to hold to it consistently, for to do so violates folk wisdom, the intuitive recognition that the world has a stubborn reality quite independent of our attempts to construct a picture of it. With his usual common sense, Gill (1994) explicitly adopts that view: "A construction is subject to the constraints of reality even if we cannot say what the reality really is" (p. 2).

So, if he did not want to carry constructivism to the point of becoming a new metaphysical foundation for psychoanalysis, just how far did he intend to go with it? The reader of his little book comes away uncertain, for Gill simply did not address the issue.

He turned, instead, to a reconsideration of hermeneutics. Now he backed away from his renunciation of 1983 on these grounds: the claim "that there can be no such thing as a hermeneutic science . . . seems to be based on the assumption that there can be a nonconstructivist science, that is, a science in which one can reach a positive, unequivocal, and certain knowledge of external reality" (1994, p. 2).

The nonconstructivist or "positivist" conception of science held up to scorn by the advocates of hermeneutics is evidently a straw man. The vast majority of contemporary scientists as well as philosophers of science believe in what may be called asymptotic realism: the position that science strives to construct an ever closer approximation to absolute truth about the universe, though it recognizes that we cannot ever be completely sure that the laws it discovers are free from error. And, though the point seems trivial, they are human constructs.

Nevertheless, in this book Gill continued to reject positivism, which "assumes facts that are in no way relative to the observer. [It assumes that] there is only one true answer." He then asked, "How can there be such a thing as science if there is no one true answer? . . . the contribution of the observer can never be reduced to zero." Again he failed to see that science is the effort to get as close as possible to zero, while conceding that we can never be sure we are there. Moreover, he left standing an apparent contradiction between his statement that "constructivism . . . allows for the validity of differing views of the same phenomenon" (p. 4) and his charge that "it is a reduction to an absurdity to argue . . . that one narrative is as good as any other or that narratives differ only in their aesthetic appeal. That kind of thinking is what I have referred to as radical constructivism" (p. 5f.).

In a sense I agree: that the conclusion is absurd, and that the procedure of getting to it is a kind of reduction, but it is a consequence of carrying through the logical implications of taking a thoroughgoing constructivism seriously. Some hermeneutically inclined psychoanalysts have been willing to face this implication. Gill hoped that by holding back from espousing a "radical" (i.e., complete and consistent) constructivism he could avoid biting that bullet. The price, however, is either inconsistency or vagueness about one's basic premises. Some of the time he seems to have fallen into inconsistency, but mostly I think that he simply avoided coming to grips with the hard questions, often by associatively turning to other aspects of a topic while leaving issues unresolved: "It is sometimes said—of course by those who consider that there *can* be a hermeneutic science—that the scientific method of a hermeneutic science is, or will be, different from the scientific method of the natural sciences. Just what these differences may be is a largely unexplored topic" (p. 7). A little further on he stated, "I shrink from the task of trying to define what the scientific method is and how it may be different in the natural and in the hermeneutic sciences.[2] Nevertheless, in the most general terms, the scientific method is the postulation of a hypothesis, the collection of data relating to that hypothesis, and the testing of that hypothesis in terms of the data according to a prescribed set of rules" (p. 8). In context, it is clear that for Gill, validation meant the testing of hypotheses, though he did not explicitly say so. Later on the same page, however, "I argue that all science, whether natural or hermeneutic, engages in validation only in the sense that the relationships between part and whole and whole and part are made more consistent and comprehensive" (p. 8).

Gill never made clear just what he meant by this kind of validation. If data and hypothesis are seen as parts of a whole, then one could say that empirically testing hypotheses fits this model, though that seems to me a strained and question-begging interpretation. Even so, I would not object strenuously as long as there were agreement that hypotheses need to be tested, and that mere clarification of meaning (another possible construction of those fine words about parts and wholes) is not given equal dignity. If Gill had unequivocally taken that position, however, I fear he would have lost the support of his hermeneutic friends.

Rather than continue to consider Gill's opinions—which is how he modestly describes them—point by point, noting my agreements (which are many) and my disagreements[3] (which point to problems Gill never solved), I wish to note only one more matter. In the sentence that follows his citing Rubinstein (1976) to back him up on a mind-body issue, he states his belief "that psychoanalysis can and should be a purely psychological dis-

---

[2] Who could blame him? So far as I know, no one else has made any real progress on this quixotic task.

[3] On the whole, I am in sympathy with the outlook of Gedo (1996) on these matters.

cipline" ((Gill, 1994, p. 9), ignoring Rubinstein's cogent demonstration that such a discipline cannot be explanatory. If it is reduced to being purely hermeneutic, concerned only with meanings and their interpretation, then psychoanalysis must give up any hopes of establishing causal connections between meanings, which leaves it a starveling "science," one that Freud would have repudiated instantly. Gone would be all the clinical theory's concern with etiology, for example. Construed as Gill would have it in this introductory chapter, psychoanalysis is perfectly correct in refusing to investigate the efficacy of its therapy; that falls outside the investigation of meanings and thus must be left to others, perhaps psychologists, who have a less restrictive definition of what are their proper data.

It pains me a little that we were never able to arrive at a final meeting of the minds on these largely metatheoretical issues. Mert loved a good theoretical discussion, and I always enjoyed hashing such things out with him, whether we ended up agreeing or not. At least, however, I have never seen any evidence that Merton Gill's shifting stand on them had any deleterious influence on his clinical work or his research.

References

Freud, S. (1915). The unconscious. *Standard Edition*, 14:166–215. London: Hogarth Press, 1957.

Freud, S. (1917). A difficulty in the path of psycho-analysis. *Standard Edition*, 17:137–144. London: Hogarth Press, 1955.

Gedo, J. E. (1996). Tribute to a serious man. *The Annual of Psychoanalysis*, 24:35–40. Hillsdale, NJ: The Analytic Press.

Gill, M. M. (1983). Unpublished letter to Adolf Grünbaum, November 29.

Gill, M. M. (1994). *Psychoanalysis in Transition*. Hillsdale, NJ: The Analytic Press.

Gill, M. M. & Hoffman, I. Z. (1982). A method for studying the analysis of aspects of the patient's experience of the relationship in psychoanalysis and psychotherapy. *J. Amer. Psychoanal. Assn.*, 30:137–168.

Gill, M. M. & Leary, T. (1959). The dimensions and a measure of the process of psychotherapy: A system for the analysis of the content of clinical evaluations and patient-therapist verbalizations. In *Research in Psychotherapy*, ed. E. A. Rubinstein & M. B. Parloff. Washington, DC: American Psychological Association, pp. 62–95.

Holt, R. R. (1989). *Freud Reappraised*. New York: Guilford.

Klein, G. S. (1976). *Psychoanalytic theory*. New York: International Universities Press.

Rubinstein, B. B. (1976). On the possibility of a strictly clinical psychoanalytic theory. In: *Psychology Versus Metapsychology*, ed. M. Gill & P. Holzman. *Psychological Issues*, Monogr. 36. New York: International Universities Press. (Paper is chapter 7 in Rubinstein [1997].)

Rubinstein, B. B. (1997). *Psychoanalysis and the Philosophy of Science*, ed. R. R. Holt. *Psychological Issues*, Monogr. 61/62. Madison, CT: International Universities Press.

Sokal, A. D. (1996). Transgressing the boundaries: Toward a transformative hermeneutics of quantum gravity. *Social Text,* Spring/Summer: 217–252.
Weinberg, S. (1996). Sokal's hoax. *New York Review of Books*, August 8, pp. 11–15.

Chapter 6

Reflections on Current Conceptions of Countertransference and Gill's Hermeneutic Construal of Psychoanalysis

Morris N. Eagle

Editors' Introduction: *Eagle raises a number of issues about Gill's views of transference and countertransference and wonders whether it is necessary to invoke the claims of a hermeneutic or social constructivist position to address these ideas. He also enters into the debate about the degree of the analyst's objectivity, a much-argued position in contemporary thinking. He is aware that the position the analyst maintains on issues of relative objectivity or subjectivity influences his or her stance with regard to theory and the theory of technique. Eagle poses the interesting question of the effectiveness of an exclusive focus on the transference, Gill's hallmark approach. Eagle spells out the pros and cons of such a restricted focus.*

Eagle also takes up the problem of Gill's hermeneutic approach to psychoanalysis. He believes that Gill rejected a scientific orientation because he equated it with Freud's metapsychological position of forces and energy, a view that Gill thought inappropriate for psychoanalytic inquiry and inconsistent with what he believed to be its legitimate domain. Like Holt, Eagle maintains that the scientific domain is not concerned with content but with "methods, procedures, and values," and that causal explanations are essential for psychoanalysis if it is to achieve the status of science.

Merton Gill had a remarkable career and showed an extraordinary flexibility in his thinking. When he became convinced that his earlier views were mistaken or needed revision, he had the courage to revise them, often in a radical way. As we can all attest, this is not an easy thing to do. Gill possessed an extraordinary degree of intellectual honesty and courage.

After devoting a good part of his early career to the systematization of psychoanalytic metapsychology, at a certain point in his professional life, he rejected much of this earlier work.

I will take up two broad issues with which Gill was concerned: first, the nature of transference and countertransference, and second, his constructivist stance and specific view that psychoanalysis is best understood as a hermeneutic discipline. I think of this chapter as a way of continuing my discussions and debates with Merton. I deeply regret that Merton is not around to disagree with me and correct me either in one of his lengthy, articulate letters or in his resonant, equally articulate voice. My discussion will not be limited to Gill's specific views, but will deal with the general topics and others' views on these topics.

Transference and Countertransference

In the spirit of Gill's critical thinking, I want to raise some questions regarding current views of countertransference and the relation between transference and countertransference. Wallerstein (1990) proposed that systematic attention to transference and resistance constitute an important aspect of the "common ground" of psychoanalytic technique, despite the differences in theory. Others (Gabbard, 1995) have suggested "that the notion that an analyst's countertransference can be a crucial source of information about the patient" (p. 475) constitutes another important common ground (see also Abend, 1989).

In considering the altered conception of countertransference, from "obstacle to analysis" to "an indispensable instrument" in which "the analysts' awareness of his response could give him vital clues as to what the patient was attempting to enact with him," Gill (1994) wrote: "A great danger, of course, is that the analyst, in regarding his feeling as necessarily "put into him" by the analysand, would fail to recognize the contribution from his own personality. This view is in a fact, a variant of the blank-screen conception of the analyst's role" (p. 102). Gill does not pursue this comment—although throughout his book he finds various ways of saying that both transference and countertransference are "based on the contributions of both participants to the here-and-now interaction as well as on their [i.e., analyst and analysand] respective past experiences" (p. 156). In this section of the chapter I want to pursue and elaborate on the "great danger" to which Gill referred.

In reacting against the classical, so-called one-person view of the analytic situation in which the analyst is viewed as a blank screen and presumably conceptualizing the therapeutic relationship more as an interactional two-person process, many contemporary psychoanalytic theorists have essentially produced a new and more subtle version of the blank-screen analyst and a new version of a one-person psychology, with the analyst, rather than the patient, now as the primary focus of attention. Much of this is expressed in discussions of new conceptions of countertransference and the relation between transference and countertransference. The basic assumption appears to be that the feelings, thoughts, fantasies, and the like that emerge in the analyst's consciousness are generally reliable and accurate indicators of the patient's unconscious feelings, thoughts, fantasies, and the like.

The assumption that the analyst's thoughts, feelings, fantasies, and the like serve as "an indispensable instrument" in gaining access to the patient's unconscious mental contents is stated in both a strong and weak version. As an early example of the former, Racker (1968), whose writings have exerted a strong influence on current conceptions of transference and countertransference, asserts with great confidence that "if the analyst is well identified with the patient and he has fewer repressions than the patient, then the thoughts and feelings which emerge in [the analyst] will be, precisely, those which did emerge in the patient, i.e., the repressed and the unconscious" (p. 17). At another point, and as an example of a weaker version of the same assumption, Racker writes, somewhat less absolutely and less unqualifiedly, that the countertransference "is, in great part, an emotional response to the transference, and as such *can* indicate to the analyst what occurs in the patient in his relation to the analyst" (p. 18, italics added). This second statement suggests that while the "analyst's emotional response to the transference" *can* indicate what occurs in the patient, it need not necessarily do so unerringly, invariably, and in a straightforward, simple way.

Some commentators adopt the weaker version I have described and are concerned with the abuses to which the strong version lends itself. For example, according to Spillius (1992), early on Melanie Klein was concerned that Heimann's (1950) conception of countertransference "might allow analysts to blame their patients for their own countertransference difficulties" (Gabbard, 1995, p. 476). And Spillius (1992) herself has cautioned that analysts may confuse their own feelings with those of the patient and therefore need to be constantly aware of this possibility. Spillius's caution echoes Sandler's (1987, 1993) similar caveat regarding the risk of assuming a one-to-one correspondence between the mental states of the analyst and the patient. As a final example of the abuses to which current conceptions of countertransference can be subject, McLaughlin (as cited in Gabbard, 1995) observed that in the concept of projective identification "the analyst is viewed as virtually empty and is simply a receptacle or container for what the patient is projecting" (p. 479). A good example of what McLaughlin is referring to is seen in Ponsi's (1997) description of projective identification as a phenomenon in which "the intrapsychic event originating in the patient gives rise to a corresponding modification of the analyst's mental attitude" (p. 247). Remarkably, there is no discussion of how an intrapsychic event originating in one person can give rise to a modification in another person's mental attitude; nothing is said about the mechanisms or processes that might be involved.

My impression is despite the cautions against confusing the analyst's feelings with those of the patient, the contemporary conception of and literature on countertransference heavily emphasizes that such reactions virtually unerringly reveal or point to the patient's mental contents. For example, in a recent paper, Levine (1997) writes that although the answer to the question of "whether or not *all* the thoughts, feelings, fantasies, acts, and impulses that arise within the analyst are attributable in some part to the interaction with the patient . . . may never be definitively settled, I . . . hope to demonstrate that there is a pragmatic value in assuming that even those thoughts and emotional experiences that clearly arise within the analyst from the analyst's own personal life and have seemingly little to do with the specific patient at hand—for example, when the analyst's personal life events intrude upon the hour to such an extent so as to encroach upon or even override his [or] her capacities to analyze effectively—can be presumed to have a patient-related component that contributes to their appearance in a given hour in a particular way" (p. 48). Levine's formulation, although weighted toward the "strong" side of the claims regarding countertransference, is nevertheless a nuanced and complex statement.

My strong impression is quite frequently cautions, caveats, and nuances are either ignored or given lip service, so countertransference, as well as projective identification, are understood in a way that suggests, in accord with Racker's (1968) strong version, that all an analyst (at least a well-analyzed analyst) need do to know the patient's repressed mental contents is to identify with the patient and, through an evenly hovering or suspended attention, permit thoughts and feelings to emerge in his or her consciousness. These thoughts and feelings will be *precisely* the unconscious thoughts and feelings that the patient has repressed. This suggests a view of the analyst's mind as a new kind of blank screen which will be filled with the patient's mental contents. In order for the analyst's thoughts and feelings to be precisely the patient's repressed, unconscious thoughts and feelings, it must be the case that the former has contributed nothing to the thoughts and feelings that enter his or her consciousness (or that such contributions could arise only from excess "repressions"). The analyst is, if not a blank screen, at least a mirror. And furthermore, like all good (i.e., accurate) mirrors, the analyst brings no prior images of his or her own. What other method guarantees such epistemological certainty or near certainty?

On the surface, the current view of countertransference appears to be an especially interactional and two-person perspective. As I have tried to show, however, in many respects, this is a new one-person perspective, the one person being the analyst. That is, the best way—for some perhaps the only way—of knowing the patient's unconscious inner world, particularly his or her transference reactions, is for the analyst to inspect his or her own thoughts and feelings.[1]

While I was working on this chapter, I attended a conference in which two separate case vignettes were presented by two female analysts who described an intense erotic transference of two male patients. In both cases the patients assumed their feelings were reciprocated by their analysts. Also in both cases, the analysts reported feelings of being imposed upon and intruded, with periodic intense feelings of hatred toward their patients. In discussing these cases, the discussant simply took it for granted that the analysts' countertransference feelings reflected the patients' unconscious sadism. (Both presenters disagreed with the discussant.) This seems to me a garden-variety example of current clinical reasoning.

I am not arguing against the weaker claim that one's associations, thoughts, and feelings,—often fleeting ones—*can*, under certain circumstances, provide important clues about the patient and, more to the point, about the interaction between patient and therapist. Rather, I am arguing against the stronger, uncritical, often implicit claim. This latter position is often encouraged by repeated references in the literature *only* to instances in which the therapist's thoughts and feelings turn out to be closely linked to the patient's unconscious mental contents. Very few, if any, examples are provided in which the therapist's reactions are *not* and instead constitute barriers to understanding what is going on in the patient. As Blum (1986) pointed out, although the "analyst's 'gut reactions' are often useful in terms of his understanding of the transference-countertransference field . . . these very reactions may also be an expression of countertransference" (p. 313). Here, Blum is using countertransference in the classical sense, that is, as a barrier to understanding and analytic work.

The preponderance in the literature of the stronger, unqualified claim tends to encourage its unthinking unacceptance, particularly among beginning therapists, and to discourage a critical examination.

Even when the therapist's thoughts and feelings *do* serve to reveal something of what is going on in the patient and in the patient-therapist interaction, they do not necessarily do so as a simple mirror. An informal mini-experiment I have been carrying out with one patient during the last few months illustrates this point. I wrote down on a pad a word or two of the basic theme(s) being presented by the patient; I put in parentheses the basic theme(s) of my interventions; and I place in brackets the basic theme(s) of my fleeting thoughts and feelings that have not yet been overtly expressed in an intervention. A recent session began with my patient

---

[1] Also see Kohut's (1984) characterization of psychoanalysis as a discipline in which one obtains data via vicarious introspection.

announcing enthusiastically that he and his fiancee had decided on a date for their wedding. My fleeting thought-feeling was "jealousy." Because of events in my own life, I felt a passing sense of envy in reaction to my patient's enthusiasm. A few minutes later my patient remarked, "You know, on the way here I had the thought that you might feel some jealousy about my getting married. " Of course, I was struck by the congruence between his comment and my earlier fleeting thought; even the same word "jealousy" was used. My patient, however, elaborated that he thought I might be jealous because I would no longer be able to control him, as he would now also be accountable to his wife. Thus, although the word "jealousy" was common to both my fleeting thought and his comment and although we were in the same general "ballpark" what he meant by "jealousy" and what I meant by it were somewhat different. In other words, although my countertransference reaction in some way reflected my patient's transference reaction, they were far from identical. Each of our reactions was 'filtered through' our own personal life experiences. Most important in the present context, had I assumed my jealousy was identical to his, I would have seriously distorted his meaning.

My impression is that when there is a degree of congruence between the therapist's countertransference reactions and the patient's transference reactions, it is more likely to be "in the same general ballpark" rather than an identity of thoughts and feelings. Talk about patients "putting" thoughts and feelings "into" the therapist or even inducing them is likely to be misleading to the extent that such talk ignores or minimizes the latter's idiosyncratic reactions and contributions.

Countertransference and Empathy

As noted by Levine (1997), in much of the contemporary literature, countertransference is indistinguishable from ordinary intuition and empathy. Such ordinary empathic understanding is ubiquitous and characterizes much human communication. However, in ordinary empathy, even when it is operating optimally, one experiences *something like* what the other is experiencing. Identification is always partial (otherwise it becomes merging, not identification), always includes one's own perspective, and therefore is always an approximation.

Furthermore, if one broadens the ordinary conception of empathy to include identification with another's unconscious defenses and unconscious mental contents, it is even less likely that thoughts and emotional reactions of the patient and analyst will be identical. Empathizing with someone's unconscious defenses and repressed mental contents is a far more complex process than empathizing with his or her conscious experiences. It is not clear what emotional reactions constitute empathy with someone's unconscious defenses or repressed wishes. Thus, in an extended conception of empathy, one's thoughts and feelings are likely to bear a complex and uncertain relation to what is going on in the patient (Eagle and Wolitzky, 1997).

Concordant and Complementary Identifications

Racker's (1968) distinction between concordant identification and complementary identification illustrates the complexity and confusion involved in the notion that the analyst's thought and feelings mirror the analysand's unconscious mental contents. According to Racker, in concordant identification the analyst identifies with the patient's ego and id, whereas in complementary identification the analyst identifies with the patient's internal objects. Dispensing with the theoretical terms ego, id, and internal objects, it is clear from Racker's writings that concordant identification is either identical or very close to the term empathy; and that complementary identification refers to the analyst's response in which he or she takes on the role "assigned" to him or her by the patient. An example provided by Racker (1968) is one in which the patient "projects his introjected father" (p. 137) on to the analyst and treats him or her as such. The analyst may then identify with the patient's introjected father and have feelings (e.g., anger, resentment) that are appropriate to the introjected father. If the analyst is not aware of what is going on, he or she may then *behave* like the introjected father and thus repeat an experience "that helped establish the patient's neurosis" (p. 138).

It is clear that Racker is describing a phenomenon that has been identified by others employing a variety of different terms. Sandler (1976) has used the term "role responsiveness" to refer to an interaction in which the analyst feels or responds in a way that is reciprocal (equivalent to Racker's "complementary") to the patient's role. Strupp and Binder (1984) have described the therapist's emotional response in terms of what the patient "pulls for." Finally, Holt (personal communication) has pointed out to me that Murray, the father of the Thematic Apperception Test (TAT), coined the term "recipathy" to refer to a feeling or response in Person A that is reciprocal or complementary to a feeling and accompanying behaviors in Person B and thus provides Person A a clue to what might be going on in Person B. Again, using a variant of Racker's example, the analyst's feeling of resentment may serve as a clue to a subtle attack on him or her launched by the patient.

Each of the foregoing writers employed a different term for a phenomenon in which the analyst's or therapist's feeling do not mirror the patient's feelings and mental states (i.e. , are not concordant with them), but are reciprocal or complementary to them. Thus, if I were to experience resentment in response to a patient's attacks and anger at me, I would not empathize with the anger, but am responding in a reciprocal or complementary way. If, however, I scrutinize the nature and source of my resentment, my response can serve as a clue to what is going on in the patient, namely, that he or she is angry and attacking me. My scrutiny of resentment can serve the aim of empathic understanding.

Terms such as "role responsiveness" and responding in terms of what the patient is "pulling for" do seem to capture the kind of interaction I have described above. It is not immediately apparent, however, in what way the analyst's experience of resentment constitutes an *identification* of any kind, concordant or complementary. What appears to lead Racker (1968) to understand this interaction as a complementary identification is his theoretical assumption that in the kind of interaction I have described, the analyst identifies "with the patient's internal objects, for example, the superego" (p. 134). Racker writes further: "The complementary identifications are produced by the fact that the patient treats the analyst as an internal (projected) object, and in consequence the analyst feels treated as such; that is, he identifies himself with this object" (p. 135). Thus, when the analyst responds with resentment to the patient's anger and attack, Racker assumes that the patient projects his internal object (i.e. , his introjected father) onto the analyst; in feeling resentment toward the patient and perhaps behaving in a resentful way, the analyst has identified with the patient's internal object and thus has experienced a complementary identification.

It seems to me that the concept of complementary identification does not shed much light on the phenomenon and, indeed, confuses matters. Racker himself noted that when the patient treats the analyst as his father (at whom he is presumably angry), the analyst "will feel treated badly—and he will react internally . . . in accordance with the treatment he receives" (p. 137). In Strupp and Binder's (1984) terms, the analyst will respond in accord with what the patient "pulls for." Why assume that the analyst's resentment constitutes an identification with the patient's internal object (introjected father)? Even if the patient's anger and attack is the product of unconsciously perceiving the analyst as his father, the analyst's experience of resentment is not sufficient grounds for assuming an identification with the patient's representation of his father.

People, including analysts, tend to feel resentment when treated badly. An analyst's resentment when attacked is an average, expectable response, not necessarily an identification with any aspect of the patient's internal life. This "average, expectable" response is what Strupp and Binder (1984) had in mind when they noted the therapist needs to be aware of what the patient "pulls for" in him or her. It also seems to have been implied in Sandler's (1976) concept of "reciprocal role relationship."

Awareness and scrutiny of one's resentment may lead to recognition of the patient's unconscious anger and attack, which may then lead to an empathic understanding of the nature of and reasons for the patient's anger. In other words, awareness of one's resentment may indirectly lead to a concordant identification with the patient's anger. Whereas the analyst's awareness of his or her resentment may eventuate in an increased empathic understanding of the patient's anger, it does not necessarily mean such resentment constitutes any kind of identification with the patient. Generally speaking, feelings of resentment, in response to being attacked, constitute *reactions to* such attack rather than identification with the attacker's internal object.

As Racker (1968), Strupp and Binder (1984), and Sandler (1987, 1993) all recognize, the therapeutic issue here is if the analyst actually *behaves* in an angry and resentful manner, that is, actually acts in accord with what the patient "pulls for," there is danger of retraumatization and the creation of the very condition that "helped establish the patient's neurosis" (Racker, 1968, p. 138). As the aforementioned commentators have agreed, after becoming aware of his or her feelings of resentment and what may have occasioned them, the analyst can interpret rather than react. As Racker (1968), Strupp and Binder (1984), and others note, interpretation is very different from the original pathogenic condition and constitutes a corrective emotional experience, or, a "rectification" (Racker, 1968, p. 138) rather than a retraumatization. Interpretation, rather than repetition, is the critical issue, quite independent of complementary identification.

There is an additional problem with the concept of complementary identification. According to Racker (1968), in a concordant identification the analyst identifies with the patient's ego or id, whereas in a complementary identification, the analyst identifies with the patient's internal objects, including the superego. This seems to be an arbitrary basis for the distinction between concordant and complementary identification. For, according to the Kleinian and object-relations theories (Fairbairn, 1952) from which the concept is derived, the internal object is as much an integral component of the personality as ego and id. (Indeed, for Fairbairn, the id is not included as personality component. For Freud [1921], the ego, no less than internal objects, is the product of identifications [pp. 108–109]) On what basis, then, does Racker make the distinction between concordant and complementary identifications? His implicit reasoning seems to be as follows: Because the ego and id are *inherent* components of the personality, the analyst's identification with the patient's ego and id is a concordant identification; because the patient's internal objects are introjected *external* (parental) figures, the analyst's identification with them is a complementary identification.

An identification with the patient's internal object, however, should be viewed as much a concordant identification as identification with the patient's ego or id. It is simply concordant with a different aspect of the personality. Thus, it is difficult to provide a clear or coherent meaning to the concept of complementary identification. There are only different concordant identifications or failures of identification.

One would think that for many patients superego aspects of the personality are experienced as more ego syntonic than repressed id impulses. For these patients, why would the analyst's identification with the patient's superego be any less a concordant identification than identification with the patient's id impulses?

I dwell on the concept of complementary identification, not only because the discussion of it raises important issues regarding patient-therapist interaction, but also because it is still another expression of the contemporary tendency to assume that virtually all of the analyst's emotional reactions are mirrors of some aspect of the patient's inner world. In the example I have been discussing, the analyst's resentment is taken to constitute an identification with the patient's internal object. Thus, once again, the analyst's emotional reactions are a sure-fire indication of the patient's inner world.

Projective Identification

Some of the issues I have been discussing are quite relevant to the currently popular concept of projective identification. One interpretation of this elusive concept (Ogden, 1982; Tansey and Burke, 1989) is that the patient projects an internal object, say an internal critic, onto the analyst; the patient then exerts interpersonal pressure on the analyst to feel and perhaps act critically. By virtue of feeling and behaving critically, the analyst introjects and identifies (introjective identification) with the patient's internal critic.[2] Projective identification is virtually identical to Racker's (1968) concept of "complementary identification" and is subject to the same criticism. If through interpersonal pressure the patient induces the analyst to feel critical and perhaps behave critically, it does not necessarily indicate the analyst has identified with the patient's internal object. Nor does it imply the patient projects onto the analyst. One needs good clinical evidence for the inference of projection.

The concept of interpersonal pressure is somewhat ambiguous insofar as it could mean either (1) the patient's behavior—for example, sullenness and sarcasm—simply *elicits* an average, respectable response, such as hostile and critical feelings in the analyst; or (2) the patient is consciously or unconsciously *motivated to induce* hostile and critical feelings in the analyst. The patient may be motivated to induce hostile feelings as a means of supporting a projection. Or the patient may be unconsciously

[2] A fourth component of projective identification is noted, namely, reinternalization. However, this is not relevant to the discussion.

motivated to induce hostile and critical feelings in the analyst in order to gratify an unconscious wish to be punished.

By invoking the concept of identification, either complementary or projective, the implicit claim is made that the analyst's emotional reactions are a *mirror* of some aspect of the patient's inner world, rather than are *elicited* by the patient. The former, as Gill recognized, is essentially a new version of the blank-screen analyst and one-person psychology, whereas the latter is a two-person psychology in which two people elicit reactions in each other.

Patient and analyst, each for different reasons, have, or should have, a great investment in understanding the nature and source of elicited reactions. It is too easy for the analyst to adopt a dogma or formula which dictates that reactions have been "put into" him or her and reflect identifications with the patient's internal object. Hence, I need not view my critical feelings as a reaction the patient has elicited in me (and try to understand what these feelings reveal about me).

The Weak Claim for Countertransference

My critique thus far has focused mainly on an extreme conception of the epistemological role of countertransference (and projective identification). What about the more moderate view that the analyst's countertransference *may* indicate what goes on in the patient? Gill (1994) observed that "the analyst's awareness of his response *could* give him vital clues as to what the patient was attempting to interact with him" (p. 102, emphasis added). In some of his writings, Racker (1968) recognized the analyst's emotional reactions are only fallible guides to the patient's psyche. Thus, he writes, "We can . . . use countertransference and, in particular, the complementary identifications . . . as a technical aid only if the identifications in question are true ones (and not projections of the analyst's own problems on to the analysand)" (p. 176). Here, Racker is suggesting the possibility that the analyst's experience of resentment (as an example from a large range of possibilities) may *not* be a reaction to the patient's anger and attack, but instead a projection, rationalization or other distortion.[3]

[3] Paradoxically, when the analyst's experience of resentment is based on a projection, it may be more similar to the patient's internal object (introjected father) than when the resentment is generated as a reaction to the patient's anger. It is more likely that the patient would have internalized an object or figure whose resentment were based on projections and who communicated resentment toward the patient with no apparent link to the patient's behavior than an object or figure who clearly responded with resentment to the patient's anger and attack. The latter is more easily managed in the world of external reality, whereas the former is the kind of traumatic situation that, according to at least Fairbairn's (1952) theory of internalization of objects, is dealt with by internalizing the object in order to better control a "bad" and unpredictable environment.

However, Racker says little regarding how one distinguishes between identifications that are "true ones" and those based upon "projections of the analyst's own problems" (p. 176), beyond noting that which identifications occur are a function of the analyst's own integration and his or her ability to "divide his ego into an irrational part that experiences and another rational part that observes the irrational part" (p. 176). (See Tansey and Burke [1989] for a more elaborate attempt to deal with this issue). I do not believe, however, that the issue here is true versus projected *identifications*. Rather, the issue is whether the analyst's experience of resentment is a reaction to the patient's actual anger and attack or whether it is the product of the analyst's own projections or some complex mixture of both. In short, the issue is the degree to which the analyst's experience of resentment serves as a reliable indicator of what is going on in the patient.

Gill speaks of the "analyst's *awareness* of his response," which emphasizes the importance of reflecting upon and scrutinizing one's responses to the patient. A number of observations are in order here. The purpose of such reflection and scrutiny is not entirely clear. Is it to 'capture' one's responses in order to employ them as a direct clue to what is going on in the patient? Or is it to understand the degree to which one's response *may or may not* indicate what is going on in the patient?

Although in both the "classicist" and the contemporary "totalistic" conceptions of countertransference (Kernberg, 1965), the importance of scrutinizing one's countertransference reactions is emphasized, there are differences in the rationale for such scrutiny. In the classical view, one is urged to scrutinize one's countertransference in order to remove the blind spots and barriers resulting from unresolved conflicts, anxieties, defenses, and the like that block one's understanding of the patient. In the contemporary view, one is also urged to scrutinize one's countertransference reactions, but here to understand what is going on in the patient's unconscious.

In both the classical and contemporary conceptions, countertransference is understood, in part, in terms of reactions elicited by the patient's transference. In the former, however, there is more awareness that what has been elicited is one's own responsibility and may reveal much about oneself. Most important, the relation between one's countertransference reactions—even if they are understood as reactions elicited by the patient's transference—and what is going on in the patient is complex and uncertain. How much one's countertransference reveals about what is going on in the patient may range from very little to a great deal. One cannot assume, as Racker (1968) and others seemed to, that the scrutiny of the countertransference constitutes a near-certain means of understanding another and somehow represents an epistemological holy grail.

In the current climate too much emphasis has been placed on automatic thoughts and feelings as an epistemological tool to understand another and too little emphasis has been put on one's cognitive apparatus and on rational and inferential processes. Even when one relies on identification and empathy to understand another's experience and inner world, one generally makes an active attempt to imagine what is going on in the other rather than simply allow thoughts and feelings to emerge passively. Racker (1968) did write about the importance of the analyst's active attempt to understand. However, he did not elaborate on the specific nature of the processes involved, nor did he comment on the relation between such active striving to understand and the evenly suspended attention the analyst is advised to maintain.

Further, although identification and empathy are often indispensable in understanding another, they have limits, particularly when the degree of difference between oneself and the other challenges one's capacity for identification. Then, the analyst's cognitive apparatus—which includes explicit and specific knowledge of the other, theoretical knowledge, explicit searches for patterns and cues, examination of evidence, and logical reasoning—may be able to provide what identification, empathy, and experience of passively emerging thoughts and feelings cannot.

I am reminded of Meehl's (1973) wonderful paper entitled, "Why I do not attend case conferences." He wrote: "The main reason I rarely show up at case conferences is easily stated: The intellectual level is so low that I find them boring, sometimes even offensive" (p. 227). He also describes "a sort of mush-headed approach which says that everybody in the room has something to contribute about anything . . ." (p. 228) and then notes that "in order to maintain the fiction that everybody's ideas are worthwhile, it is necessary to lower the standards for what is evidential" (p. 228). In line with this, he observes that "the ordinary rules of scientific inference and reliance upon general principles of human development . . . are somehow forgotten in a psychiatric case conference" (p. 229).

I have observed everything that Meehl describes, not only in psychiatric case conferences, but in many case conferences among psychologists and social workers, as well as in supervision. My experience has been that many students in training latch on to the latest fashion of countertransference and projective identification explanatory modes and take as their role models teachers and clinical supervisors who engage freely in, to borrow Meehl's term, "mush-headed" (p. 228) free-associative and uncritical thinking. I wince inwardly when a student's comments at a case conference begin with the words "I have a feeling that . . ." In reading this comment, Holt (1998, personal communication) wrote, "It reminds me strongly of my reaction, 40+ years ago, in diagnostic conferences, when colleagues would say, 'Don't ask me how I know this but . . .'"

I am also reminded of a recent experience I had with a supervisee. She had presented a case for which I was supervising her at a case conference and at the next supervision session informed me—for the first time—not only that she had been experiencing frequent headaches during the therapy sessions with this particular patient, but when she reported this at the case conference, she was informed by the participants her headaches were the result of "projective identification." After noting that the experience needed to be discussed further, I asked the student how she understood her headaches were due to projective identification. She replied the patient had "put the headaches into me." I asked her how. Her reply was, "through projective identification." When I asked what she meant by "projective identification," she stated it meant the patient had put something into her. I then suggested that the use of the term was preventing both of us from understanding what was going on in her and in her interaction with the patient that led to frequent headaches with this patient and not others.

I have read references to projective identification in the literature that are not essentially different from the preceding account. There is frequent talk of the patient "putting something into" the analyst without any seeming awareness of the need to at least try to specify the interpersonal processes (e.g., cues emitted by one person) involved—or without any seeming awareness that such ordinary, non-magical processes must exist. In some contexts talk about one person "putting something (e.g., thoughts and feelings) into" another might be considered delusional. Indeed, I recall a conference I attended in Italy in which the main theme of the paper was that projective identification was attributable to mental telepathy between patient and analyst.

I am not maintaining there are no actual phenomena that many people employing the term projective identification are trying to capture. But I am highlighting the muddle-headed nature of much discussion and thinking concerning projective identification and countertransference in contemporary psychoanalysis.

Gill's Hermeneutic Construal of Psychoanalysis

I turn now to another area with which Gill was directly concerned and which informed a good deal of his writings and formulations—namely, his hermeneutic constural of psychoanalysis.

Gill's disenchantment with metapsychology constituted the foundation for much of his thinking and writing during the latter part of his life. His basic objection to the metapsychological conception of the person as an object of natural science generated, or at least is logically linked to, Gill's constructivist and hermeneutic construal of psychoanalysis, his insistence that psychoanalysis is properly a two-person psychology, and his conception of transference and countertransference as interactional processes.

According to Gill (1994), because psychoanalysis "remains in the realm of wishes, aims, and feelings" (p. 146) and because Freud's (and all analysts') "influences about unconscious mentation were in the same language as his descriptions of conscious mentation, that is, the language of wishes, aims, and feelings," there is good reason to reject the "natural-science level of discourse for psychoanalysis" (p. 146) that is implied in the quasi-biological and physicalistic language employed in Freudian metapsychology. Gill proposed instead a hermeneutic and constructivist conception of psychoanalysis.

Throughout his writings, Gill made it clear that (1) what he means by the term "hermeneutic" is explanation or interpretation of any human behavior in terms of the agent's or person's aims, motives, and meaning, that is, psychic reality; and (2) he contrasts such explanation with a natural science or metapsychological form of explanation, which, he believes, employs the language and concepts of impersonal forces, energies, physiological and biological processes, and so on, and which concerns material or physical reality.

An example from his last work (1994) illustrates his understanding of hermeneutics: "What then is hermeneutics? It means interpretation . . . of human meanings . . . by human meaning I mean one that includes affective personal meaning, or, more generally, psychic reality in contrast to material reality" (pp. 2–3).[4] As a concrete example of a "hermeneutic meaning," Gill refers to "a patient's bitter tirade [that] may signify his denial that he is falling in love" (p. 4).

In an interview with Reppen (1982), Gill contrasted a hermeneutic approach with metapsychology, the latter defined as "the theory beyond psychology which explains psychology in another universe of meaning than that of a person's aims, whether as a biological organism, a neuropsychological entity, the natural-science dimensions of force and energy, or whatever" (p. 175). Later in the same interview, Gill states: "It is one thing to speak of a human being acting passionately, adaptively-realistically or self-assessingly, but it is another to speak of id, ego, and superego as agencies of a psychic apparatus. The first is to speak with hermeneutic and the second with natural-science implications" (p. 179).

It should be clear from the foregoing and other passages in Gill's writings that at the heart of his hermeneutic construal of psychoanalysis is his rejection of metapsychology, which he identifies with a natural-science mode of explanation employing biological and physiological concepts and the dimensions of force and energy. According to Gill (1994), although

---

[4] It is not clear why the personal meaning has to be affective. My account of my action in terms of my beliefs and goals or my understanding of a word, although not especially affective, is certainly a part of my psychic reality. In other definitions and discussions of what hermeneutic means, Gill does not include the affective as a criterion.

the biological may influence the wishes and aims we have, the business of psychoanalysis, and of psychology in general is to concern itself with wishes and aims and the meaning they have for the individual. In responding to my point (Eagle, 1984/1987) that biological structure partly determines the kinds of wishes, aims, and desires we are likely to have, Gill (1994) wrote: "Our biological structure, for example, is such that we all have sexual wishes, but the meaning sexuality has to each of us individually is in the psychological realm" (p. 145). Furthermore, Gill noted, Freud invited "rejection of the natural-science level of discourse . . . by noting that his inferences about unconscious mentation were in the same language as his descriptions of conscious mentation, i.e., the language of wishes, aims, and feelings" (pp. 145–146).

For Gill, the boundaries for psychoanalysis were clear: it deals with conscious and unconscious, particularly unconscious, personal aims, motives, desires, and meanings. In short, it deals with psychic reality. Whether this makes psychoanalysis a *hermeneutic* discipline is another matter. Gill used the term "hermeneutic" in a rather vague and idiosyncratic way, to refer to discourse and explanation in terms of the agent's personal aims, motives, desires, and meanings. If this is hermeneutic, then I suppose that when we speak in ordinary discourse—which is discourse in which we try to understand others in terms of their beliefs and desires—we are speaking hermeneutics, much like the character in Molière's *Le Bourgeois Gentilhomme* who did not know he had been speaking prose all his life. But let us not be distracted by terms. The important point is how one reacts to Gill's definition of psychoanalysis and its mode of explanation.

There are a number of points to be made regarding Gill's aforementioned arguments. Gill held a mistaken conception regarding the nature of natural science. What constitutes science is not marked by *content*, but its *methods, procedures, and values*. It is perfectly consistent to take the position that psychoanalysis should limit its accounts to the discourse of personal aims and motives and to simultaneously insist on the implementation of the methods of natural science, that is to say, concern itself with issues of reliability, validity, and what Meehl (1997) referred to in a recent article as "credentialled knowledge."

What gives a discipline a right to call itself a science or at least to earn status of a protoscience is its concern with such mundane issues as reliability, replicability, the public availability of data, accuracy of measurement, testability, refutability of hypotheses and theories, and so on. It is conceivable that one could develop a science or protoscience that dealt largely with personal aims, motives, desires, and meanings. In any case, one cannot rule out a priori the possibility of such a science. Such a science, if it dealt adequately with the methodological issues noted, would be a *natural* science, part of the family of natural sciences, which include the social and behavioral sciences like psychology, sociology, economics, and perhaps even history (Sulloway, 1996), not a special kind of hermeneutic science, whatever that is. After all, personal aims, motives, and such are as natural, as much part of the ontology of the world, as atoms and chemical reactions. Searle (1992) made this point with regard to consciousness, but it holds equally for desires, aims, motives, and meanings. Ironically, by maintaining natural science is limited to physical processes and phenomena, one somehow implies that aims, wishes, desires, mental processes, subjective experience, and consciousness itself are somehow not part of the natural world and require a nonnatural science or mode of explanation.

Of course, the *physical* sciences employ physical concepts and reference to physical processes. They deal with physical phenomena on a certain level. There is no mystery or deep philosophical issue here. It is obviously possible to do profound and creative scientific work on physical or physiological phenomena whatever one's philosophical commitments. Newton was a religious mystic, Eccles was a dualist, and so on. If one aspires to do scientific work on human aims, desires, motives, and meanings, one will need to confront complex issues of reliability and measurement, and one's specific concepts must be appropriate to the level of phenomena being studied. But it is the degree of adherence to certain methods, safeguards, procedures, and values—not the content of the concepts—that will determine the scientific status of the work.

If a so-called hermeneutic science is characterized by a different and distinctive set of methods and procedures, Gill did not make clear what they are. The closest he (1994) got to explicitly discussing this issue is a brief, unelaborated, and hopelessly vague reference to a hermeneutic circle "in which the whole determines the meaning of the parts and the parts determine the meaning of the whole" (p. 8).

One has the right to insist that any systematic approach to human behavior not resort to a reductionism which makes the very phenomena of interest—human aims, desires, motives, and meanings—disappear before one's eyes. However, as Rorty (1991) pointed out, "the irreducibility of the intentional" is not more "philosophically significant than the irreducibility of house descriptions to timber descriptions, or of animal descriptions to cell descriptions" (p. 4). The point here, one that Searle (1992) also made with regard to consciousness and social reality, is that human aims, houses, and animals are as much part of the world and have as much ontological dignity as physiological processes, pieces of timber, and cells. The latter are no more "real" than the former; they require different levels of description and constitute different levels of phenomena. Furthermore, one has a perfect right to focus one's interest and investigation on any level of description and any level of phenomena.

One also has the right to insist that in the systematic/scientific investigation of human aims, motives, or any other aspect of human behavior, the phenomena not be deformed by the methods by which they are studied. That is, one has the right to insist on the "ecological validity" of the research. Unfortunately, in the history of psychology, certain psychoanalytic concepts and phenomena have been trivialized and rendered unrecognizable by operationalizing them so that they are amenable to investigation in an experimental laboratory. This, it seems to me, is the sad truth about 50 or 60 years of attempts to demonstrate repression in the experimental laboratory (Holmes, 1990; Eagle, 1998, 2000). It is entirely possible that certain phenomena, including certain psychoanalytic phenomena, cannot be meaningfully studied in the experimental laboratory. But one must not make the mistake of equating scientific (or empirical) with experimental. There are also biological-physical phenomena that cannot be meaningfully studied in the experimental laboratory. That does not mean that they cannot be studied scientifically.

Gill's arguments also raise the issues of boundaries of a discipline and the depth and adequacy of explanation. Every discipline has the right to set its boundaries. Surely, in the clinical psychoanalytic situation, one is concerned largely with the patient's personal aims, wishes, meanings, and motives. Psychoanalysis, however, is not only a treatment, but also a *theory* of human behavior, personality development, and human nature. Freud believed that the major claim that psychoanalysis had on posterity lay, not in its accomplishments as a treatment, but in the insights provided by its theory. For Freud, the primary importance of even the data generated by the clinical psychoanalytic situation lay in what was revealed about how the mind works.

The question, then, is whether the terms, concept, and explanatory mode of psychoanalytic *theory* are, or should be, limited to the language of personal aims, wishes, meanings, and motives. If so limited, psychoanalysis becomes essentially a form of ordinary discourse. How adequate or complete is such a form of explanation?

Nature and Level of Explanation

I have been discussing human aims, motives, desires, and meanings as legitimate phenomena to be investigated, without reducing them to some other level of description or without deforming them. Here I deal with them not as phenomena to be investigated, but as *explanatory concepts*. In his book Gill (1994) took me to task for arguing that although accounting for behavior in terms of the agent's motives and aims constitutes a form of explanation, insofar as the motives and aims are themselves phenomena to be explained, such accounts cannot be complete and self-sufficient in themselves and need to be accounted for by deeper levels of explanation. I (1984/1987) go on to say that "while interpretive explanations in the clinical context may use the personal language of wishes, aims, and feelings, there is no good reason to expect that a theoretical explanation of these wishes, aims, etc. , needs to use the same language and the same kinds of concepts" (p. 152).

Gill's (1994) response was to ask, "What does he mean by deeper? He can only mean a biological substrate" (p. 145). He goes on to claim that "there *is* a good reason" (p. 145) to expect that a theoretical explanation of wishes, aims, and such will be limited to the very same language of wishes, aims, and such, and that reason "lies in the rejection of the natural-science level of discourse for psychoanalysis. Freud invited such rejection by noting that his inferences about unconscious mentation were in the same language as his descriptions of conscious mentation, that is, the language of wishes, aims, and feelings" (pp. 145–146).

Thus, Gill's position is quite clear. Psychoanalysis properly understood, either as a treatment or a theory, limits itself to explanatory accounts in terms of wishes, aims, and feelings, conscious and unconscious. Any departure from that mode of discourse or explanation, as, for example, in Freud's metapsychological writings, lands one in "a natural-science level of discourse" and, as such, is not a psychoanalytic account.

Perhaps "deeper" was not the best choice of words. But surely there are contexts, a systematic theory of human behavior, for example, in which an account of behavior in terms of the agent's aims and motives is neither a complete nor an adequate account. As Black (1967) put it in reaction to Louch's claim that explanation of human action needs to limit itself to the agent's reasons and motives:[5] "Surely, after having determined the reasons and motives for an action, an enquiring mind will want to press on to discover the provenance and etiology of those reasons and motives" (p. 656). If psychoanalytic theory is to be defined as a theory that concerns itself only with aims and motives, and does not press on to inquire about their provenance and etiology, it will be grossly limited as an adequate explanation of human behavior.

Contrary to Gill, it does not necessarily follow that if one does press on to determine the provenance and etiology of reasons and motives, one will automatically be dealing with a biological substrate. For example, one may acquire certain aims and motives based on childhood experiences that involve such processes as learning, identification, and modeling. Or, as is implied in Marxist theory, one may maintain that one's aims, motives, and other aspects of one's psychic reality are determined by one's class membership. Surely, a reasonable psychoanalytic theorist would not flinch from including in his or her explanatory account the tracing of the certain current aims and motives to childhood experiences and would not

---

[5] Indicating that such claims are not limited to the psychoanalytic context and to psychoanalytic theorists.

hesitate to invoke certain general psychological (and perhaps even biological, or at least, psychobiological) concepts and processes that are not themselves aims and motives. Such concepts and processes are already invoked in psychoanalytic theorizing, for example, affect regulation (Schore, 1994; Taylor, 1987) or self-defects (Kohut, 1984). Such concepts may involve or may be understood as causally generating aims and motives, but they are not themselves limited to aims and motives. Are they to be rejected as non-psychoanalytic because they cross over to "a natural-science level of discourse"?

Consider Bowlby's (1969, 1973, 1980, 1988a) attachment theory. According to Bowlby, there is much evidence that a wide range of species, including humans, are endowed with an innate attachment system, which is characterized by a particular behavioral repertoire (e.g., sucking, vocalizing, smiling, and soothability) and the "set goal" of seeking proximity to the caregiver. The attachment system is associated with certain proximal or personal aims and motives, such as looking to the attachment figure for "felt security" (Ainsworth and Marvin, 1995). It is also associated with certain unconscious strategies and defenses, such as "defensive exclusion" (Bowlby, 1988b) of attachment wishes and needs in order to avoid the pain of the caregiver's rejection and anger. An attachment instinctual system, including its embeddedness in ethological, transspecies observations and theory, provides a broader and, yes, deeper theoretical context in which to understand these aims, motives, and defensive strategies. Is one to say that psychoanalysis is concerned only with the aims and motives and cuts off all interest in the broader context? Is one to say that the former is hermeneutic and therefore within the province of psychoanalysis, and the latter is natural-science discourse and therefore outside the province? Knowledge and good theories do not work that way. They take one to as full and deep an evaluation of the phenomena as possible.[6]

As I have argued elsewhere (Eagle, 1980), although the specific content of Freudian metapsychology may have been grossly inadequate and more scientistic than scientific, Freud's conviction that an account in terms of the agent's aims and motives needed to be grounded in a broader theoretical conception of the nature of the mind and the nature of personality development was, I believe, correct. In accord with Black's (1967) comment noted earlier, Freud's enquiring mind was vitally and correctly concerned with attempting to determine the provenance and etiology of

[6] Holt (1998, personal communication) writes: "I don't see anything wrong with drawing the boundaries as Mert wanted to (there are plenty of precedents in other sciences), but *only on the condition* that one freely admit the necessity to draw on other disciplines to understand and explain our phenomena and problems. The trouble is that people who take the stance of drawing boundaries often proclaim the "right" of a science to explain its own data in its own terms, sometime even with the claim that it is reductionism not to concede that such explanations are sufficient."

the aims, reasons, and motives he had identified. In such an endeavor, it is very likely that one will be forced to go beyond a mode of explanation that is limited to aims and motives. The explanatory concepts that he developed in his metapsychology may not have been useful, but not because they ventured into a so-called natural science mode of discourse.

As discussed earlier, Gill (1994) maintained that Freud invited rejection "of the natural-science level of discourse for psychoanalysis . . . by noting that his influences about unconscious mentation were in the same language as his descriptions of conscious mentation, that is, the language of wishes, aims, and feeling" (pp. 145–146). There appears to be something of an inconsistency here insofar as Gill criticized Freud, not for rejecting, but for employing a natural science level of discourse in his metapsychology. There is no contradiction, however, if one assumes in the previous passage Gill referred to Freud's so-called clinical theory rather than his metapsychology (see Klein, 1976). In assuming, however, that the description of unconscious mentation in the language of wishes, aims, and feelings has the same conceptual status as descriptions of conscious mentation and is, so to speak, pure clinical theory devoid of metapsychology, Gill ignored the important work of Rubinstein (1997), who has shown that talk about unconscious wishes, aims, and feelings rests on metapsychological assumptions regarding the nature of the mind. Rubinstein has also shown that other formulations of the so-called clinical theory are logically linked to metapsychological assumptions. Rubinstein's work raises the question of whether it is possible to have a psychoanalytic theory of aims and motives without a whole set of metapsychological assumptions and thus casts doubt on the validity and viability of a clinical theory—metapsychology dichotomy. A discussion of this issue without reference to the work of Rubinstein is a seriously incomplete one.

Gill (along with many other analysts, including Freud) wrote about unconscious aims and motives as if they were simple, unproblematic concepts, similar to conscious aims and motives. Very serious thinkers, however, including Rubinstein (1997) and Searle (1992), found such a conception of unconscious mental processes as anything but simple and unproblematic. A discussion of the conceptual nature of unconscious aims and the kind of work such a concept is meant to do is beyond the scope of this chapter. My point here is that the use of the language of aims and motives for unconscious mentation, as is used for conscious mentations, is only the beginning, not the end, of a long and complex conceptual story.

Gill's Constructivism

Along with his hermeneutic construal of psychoanalysis, Gill was also very sympathetic to a general constructivist perspective. I do not wish to embark here on a thorough discussion of a constructivist construal of psychoanalysis. I do, however, want to make a few comments. First, it is important to note that since Kant any critical thinker was a constructivist of some sort, in the sense that the thinker recognized one's perception and understanding of reality are shaped and limited by one's a priori perceptual and cognitive categories. No one has direct and unmediated access to reality. The perceptual and cognitive categories that we (and other animals) have developed, however, have themselves been shaped by reality in the sense that they were selected out because of their fit or adaptation to environmental demands. In short, in order for survival to be possible, our constructions need to be constrained by reality and need to reflect or be faithful to central features of reality.

Whereas "post-Kantian commonsense constructivism" recognizes the constraints of reality on our constructions, radical constructivism either discounts or minimizes such constraints. Indeed, a truly radical constructivist would probably not accept as meaningful the idea of reality independent of one's constructions. In that sense, the broad philosophical issue is some form of realism versus anti-realism.

Gill (1994) disavowed radical constructivism when he stated: "I understand *radical* constructivism to mean questioning the certainty that there is any external reality at all or that one can know anything about external reality. I do not mean that kind of constructivism. . . . A construction is subject to the constraints of reality even if we cannot say what that reality really is" (p. 12). He also noted that because he is not "sophisticated in epistemology or philosophy," he is "using concepts like constructivism, hermeneutics, and objectivism . . . only in a global, connotative, more or less commonsensical way" (p. 1). There is little common sense, however, in equating constructivism with relativism, as Gill did or in the claim that "another familiar way of conveying the constructivist premise is to say that there are no facts as such. In a vivid metaphor, facts are soaked in theory" (p. 1).

I want to pursue some issues raised by Gill's constructivism and, in particular, his linking it to his conception of transference. Gill stated that his redefinition of transference requires or is derived from a "hermeneutic-constructivist-interactive model" of the analytic situation. However, it is far from clear that this is so. According to Gill, no analyst can be simply a blank screen, but is rather always emitting cues, that is, behaving in a particular way. Hence, the patient's transference reactions are never simply a distortion; rather, they constitute more or less plausible interpretations of cues emitted by the analyst.

I think that there are few analysts who would markedly disagree with Gill's general and valuable redefinition of transference. One question I raise, however, is whether the concept of constructivism (as well as hermeneutics) is really necessary or even especially relevant to this much more realistic and commonsensical view of transference. Does one really need a "hermeneutic-constructivist-interactive model" to support the conclusions that in any interaction between two people neither person can be a pure blank screen and each emits cues to which the other responds?

Other, less commonsensical issues that are raised by Gill's redefinition of transference merit discussion. Gill seems to have equated—I would say combined—the analyst as a blank screen with the analyst as an objective observer. Quite a while ago, Sullivan (1947, 1953) pointed out that the analyst is not simply a blank screen observer, but rather a *participant*-observer. Although the analyst is a participant rather than a blank screen, it does not mean he or she cannot also be as objective as possible. If one of the main tasks of the analyst is to *understand* the patient, what other kind of observer is one supposed to be? A subjective observer? What would that mean? Imposing one's subjective biases on one's understanding? There is a good deal of confusion regarding subjectivity and objectivity. Any personal understanding is subjective in the sense that it is personally experienced. But one can nevertheless strive for one's understanding to be as objective as possible, in the sense of accuracy. One might even argue, as Racker (1968) and others did, that one's subjective fleeting thoughts, feelings, and associations are an important means of gaining an objective or accurate understanding of the patient. What else could Racker mean when he says that one's countertransference reactions may serve as an important means of understanding the patient's inner world?

Gill here saw objective as cold and detached, not unbiased and accurate. Indeed, he seemed to have implicitly accepted the epistemological rationale for the blank screen stance, namely, one can be unbiased and accurate only by assuming a detached role, and being an interactive participant renders one unable to be unbiased and accurate. In many instances in life, one is an active participant and nevertheless reasonably unbiased and accurate, recognizing that accuracy and freedom from bias are never perfect.

Even if it were true, as Gill (1994) maintained, that "any perception or idea is from the particular perspective of the perceiver or thinker" (p. 1), it is possible, in varying degrees, to take account of or even overcome that perspective when evaluating a perception or idea. That is one aspect of reality testing, the observing function of the ego, and the capacity for self-reflection. As Piaget (1991) noted, in normal cognitive development, one becomes progressively less embedded in perceptual immediacy and an egocentric perspective and becomes increasingly capable of taking some distance from them. These ego functions do not operate perfectly, but they do operate.

At the core of a scientific outlook, properly understood in terms of its methods rather than contents, is a generally agreed upon set of procedures, values, and conventions intended to minimize the influence of personal bias, expectations, and history, not at the stage of conjecture and discovery but at the stage of evaluation and testing (Popper, 1962; Reichenbach, 1951).[7] As von Eckardt (1981) suggested, the appropriate scientific response to such phenomena as the influence of personal bias and expectations, the theory-saturated nature of data, and so on, is not to wallow in them and loudly proclaim their power at every turn, but to develop procedural safeguards, to the extent possible, that will minimize their influence. Contrary to frequent caricature, science does not deal with perfection and certainty, but with imperfection, uncertainty, and the "good enough."

Here is the heart of the disagreement I had with Gill about a hermeneutic and constructivist construal of psychoanalysis, particularly when contrasted with a natural science, objectivist, and so-called positivist view. A continuing preoccupation with the limitations of one's personal perspective and the degree to which these limitations supposedly result in the personal construction of reality and inevitably point to a radical constructivist view (or a deconstructionist or postmodern view or whatever) seems to constitute the kind of wallowing to which von Eckardt refers.

Of course, in the clinical psychoanalytic situation one cannot institute the kind of procedural safeguards built into a scientific experiment. One makes the best interpretations possible, likely as it is that interpretations reflect personal and theoretical biases. An analyst can attempt to be sensitive to evidence and scrutinize and reflect upon, not only countertransference reactions, but every aspect of understanding the patient. Closure and certainty are not possible nor perhaps desirable.

It is not necessary, however, to move to one extreme of concluding that each analyst constructs his or her patient, as if there were no "real" patient independent of the interpreting analyst, or the other extreme of assuming by virtue of identification and freely hovering attention the analyst's thoughts and feelings will automatically reflect the patient's unconscious. In the former position one despairs in the face of subjectivity and personal bias that color and limit the understanding of the patient; and in the latter position one reacts against the inevitable uncertainty and limitations of understanding by decreeing a new epistemological avenue to certainty. The positions are different sides of the same coin. In the former, because the analyst constructs the patient and because the resulting construction is saturated with the analyst's personal history and countertransference, the analyst is interacting with his or her own construction. In the latter, the analyst comes to understand the patient essentially through the thoughts and feelings that emerge in his or her own consciousness. Neither position grapples with the question of how, despite the fact that we participate in constructing the world, we manage to avoid solipsism and form a good-enough conception of the world and of others.

---

[7] After writing this, I read Holt's chapter, which makes precisely the same point I make here.

Let me turn now to other issues raised by Gill's conception of the transference. Gill (1994) wrote that the patient's transference reactions constitute a "*plausible* experience of the [therapeutic] relationship" (p. 155, emphasis added). Gill (1982) also wrote that "if the analyst recognizes that the patient is attempting to be as rational as he can with what he has to work with, he is respecting the patient's sanity. If, on the contrary, he focuses on the patient's experience of the relationship without looking for something real that the patient may be responding to, he implies that the patient is manufacturing his experience out of whole cloth" (p. 117).

Gill's (1982) technical suggestion to always "take into account the manner in which the analyst's behavior becomes the point of departure for the patient's transference elaborations" (p. 3) makes very good sense and, indeed, is more respectful of the patient than the reflexive assumption that the patient is distorting. One cannot, however, decide *a priori* to what degree a patient's transference reactions and elaborations are plausible or represent a distortion or contain features of both. I think one must distinguish between, on one hand, a respectful attitude toward the patient in which one always tries to understand the patient's transference reactions as a plausible interpretation of one's own behavior and, on the other hand, a priori insistence that the transference reactions are always, in fact, plausible.

I suspect that Gill's across the board emphasis on the patient's plausible interpretation and his reluctance to view any transference reactions as distortions were motivated, not only by the importance of a respectful attitude toward the patient, but also by his epistemological constructivism. That is, in a thoroughgoing constructivist position, virtually any interpretation possesses plausibility. The analyst is reluctant to view any interpretation as a distortion, insofar as it implies that the analyst makes a judgment as to what is the reality and what is a distortion. I do not see why an analyst cannot both judge that a particular reaction constitutes a distortion and, in a respectful manner, bring it up for patient and analyst to examine.[8]

I do not agree with the claim that the patient's transference reactions always constitute plausible interpretations of the analyst's cues. A recent session comes to mind in which the patient's perceptions represented obvious distortions. During the discussion of sensitive material which, in the

---

[8] It does not seem to be accurate to say that the traditional, blank-screen conception of the analyst that emphasizes the patient's transference constitutes a distortion. For it is not always clear how one would distort a blank screen. Indeed, one might say that, given the blank-screen role of the analyst, there are a wide range of transference interpretations that are plausible, just as with Rorschach ink blots there are a wide range of plausible responses. It seems more accurate to say that according to the traditional view, the patient *projects* onto the blank screen.

past, was associated with the patient's expectation of his father's disapproval and criticism, the patient thought I had "grimaced" when I was simply listening to him with my usual interested expression. In that same session, he heard "perhaps" as "penalty." I do not believe that either reaction entailed a plausible interpretation of cues I emitted. Indeed, both reactions involved some degree of distortion. Distortion does not depend upon the assumption that the analyst is a blank screen. One can, of course, argue I unwittingly emitted cues that could be plausibly interpreted as a grimace and, in some subtle and unconscious manner, I conveyed a punitive attitude which, therefore, rendered plausible the patient's mishearing of "perhaps" as "penalty." If one insists on making this sort of blanket argument in every case where a relatively clear-cut distortion takes place, then it becomes totally circular, irrefutable, and simply a matter of faith.

In a face-to-face session with another patient, I noticed a sudden change of facial expression, a short interval of absorbed silence, and a change of topic. I asked the patient what was going on and she burst out crying. She then told me that I had momentarily and slightly looked away—which I had done—and that this meant to her I was bored. She therefore changed the topic to something I might find more interesting. What made her cry, she told me, was her recognition of the degree to which she had catered to other people's interests, in particular her father and men she dated. Much more went on, but the point is that my patient's interpretation of my action was certainly plausible. That in itself, however, tells little about her. More idiosyncratic and more important are her strong affective reactions to my looking away.

Is it plausible to feel boring and uninteresting and feel the need to, in her words, "bend [herself] out of shape" when I momentarily looked away? Somehow, the issue of plausibility versus distortion fades away in importance. What takes its place in importance is her particular plausible interpretation, the intensity of her affective reactions, and her personal associations to the whole experience.

Analysis of the Transference

Along with many others, Gill (1982, 1994) believed that analysis of the transference is at the heart of the therapeutic process and that extra-transference interpretations are of limited therapeutic value. There has been much debate around this issue; what is remarkable is that, as far as I know, no one in psychoanalytic literature, including Gill, has addressed whether any reliable, empirical evidence suggests that systematic analysis of the transference leads to better therapeutic outcome. Rather, the debate is carried on with repeated assertions and repeated references to various authorities. Although Gill (1982) recognized that "analysis maybe perverted to an end rather than a means" (p. 126), he does not adequately address the issue of whether analysis of the transference is an end in itself or a means to an end, namely, positive therapeutic outcome.

The only legitimate reason for analyzing the patient's transference reactions is that they are presumably relevant to the patient's inner life and general pattern of behavior, not simply inside, but also *outside the treatment situation*. If the patient's transference is based largely on the analyst's truly idiosyncratic behavior and reaction to the patient, then the patient's transference, whether plausible or not, may be, in large part, an *iatrogenic* phenomenon, perhaps unique to the particular interaction. Indeed, implicit in Gill's criticism of the blank screen conception of the analyst is that an excessively silent, unresponsive, and detached analyst may elicit iatrogenic reactions. His critique has been especially cogent because of the irony that the very rationale for the blank-screen stance—to minimize the analyst's influence and allow the "pure" transference to emerge—may be undermined by the analyst's blank screen behavior. Behaviors other than blank-screen silence and detachment, like excessive or hostile involvement, may also elicit iatrogenic transference phenomena, however. At least in part, the phenomena are not especially characteristic and revealing of the patient's object relational pattern. Whether plausible or not, if the patient's transference reactions do not tell something vital about his or her inner world and general pattern of behavior outside the treatment situation, what is the point of analyzing the transference or even carrying out treatment?

I do not think that Gill would have objected to these observations and questions. I raise them because he did not. I also raise them because they speak to the limits of such rhetoric as constructing the patient, jointly developing (i.e., patient and therapist) "aesthetic fictions" (Geha, 1984; see Eagle, 1984, for a critique of Geha), and forging a new narrative without raising serious questions about the entire therapeutic enterprise. After all, the therapeutic enterprise, including the therapeutic interaction, is a means to certain ends outside the therapeutic situation, not an end in itself.

These ends include the discovery of important core features of a patient's personality and psychic life. Two points here are noteworthy: (1) the purpose of analyzing the transference is to discover these core features that transcend the therapeutic situation, and (2) the patient, including his or her history, conflicts, wishes, desires, and anxieties is an independent reality against which the analyst's hypotheses, narratives, and constructions are to be judged—just as the categories through which we experience physical reality are to be judged against the degree to which they are faithful to an independently existing external reality. It is possible that multiple sets of categories can be faithful to reality in somewhat different ways or can capture different aspects of a complex reality. This does not also preclude the possibility, however, that sets of categories should be rejected because they violate core features of reality. It is not sufficient to simply say that—as Gill did—all categories, hypotheses, or theories are from a particular perspective. Of course they are. But what it means to reflect on one's hypotheses and to evaluate theories is to attempt to transcend a particular perspective and subject them to a broader perspective in which evidence, competing accounts, and so forth are taken into account. Most patients are interested in learning some important truths about themselves, as well as, obviously, overcoming suffering and distress, rather than creating "aesthetic fictions" (Geha, 1984) and persuasive and serviceable narratives (e.g., Spence, 1982; Schafer, 1992) that bear little relationship to the core features of who they are.

Gill (1982) draws an analogy between, on one hand, day residue and dream wish and, on the other hand, the analyst's behavior and the transference. That is, just as the latent dream wish is expressed in the dream through the point of departure of day residue, the patient expresses his or her transference reactions through the point of departure of the analyst's behavior. If this analogy is valid, it suggests that just as the unconscious wish is a core, stable feature of the dreamer's psychic life, similarly the patient's transference is a core, stable, and transsituational phenomenon. Hence, analogous to the day residue, the analyst's behavior is merely a convenient "trigger" for the expression of the transference. Gill's analogy narrows the gap between the blank screen and his conception of the transference. That is, in both cases, the analyst's behavior is a trigger or a convenient scaffold on which to hang the core of transference. The analogy suggests that although the patient's reactions and interpretations may be plausible, the plausibility essentially serves as an excuse for the transference.

The importance, then, of viewing the patient's transference as a plausible interpretation of the analyst's behavior rather than as a distortion is largely a means to show greater respect for the patient and a technical stance to facilitate the patient's readiness to examine his or her transference reactions. If the plausibility of the patient's interpretations and reactions is no more than the equivalent of a day residue, than it does not really determine the shape of the core transference. It merely facilitates a particular entry to and version of that transference. If, however, the patient's transference reactions and interpretations do vary with the analyst's behavior, then we are back again to the question of the extent to which the transference is an iatrogenic phenomenon, as well as to other questions which cannot be pursued here, such as the role of countertransference in the classical sense of the term and the dangers of retraumatization.

One final issue with regard to Gill's (1982) conception of the therapeutic role of analysis of the transference is noteworthy. He stated that "however expertly one analyzes the transference, the effects of an analysis will still, to a certain extent, depend on the gratification of the unanalyzed and persisting transference. . . . One can only hope to make the outcome as dependent as possible on the analysis of the transference, with the inevitably accompanying new experience, and as independent as possible of persisting transference" (pp. 119–120). Gill attributed *all* of the therapeutic value of treatment to "the analysis of the transference [and] the accompanying new experience" (p. 119). Whatever new "corrective emotional experience" the patient has is linked entirely to the analysis of the transference. There is no room for any, so to speak, psychoanalytically legitimate therapeutic benefit outside of the analysis of the transference. Such benefits are attributed to 'the gratification of the unanalyzed and persisting transference" (p. 119). As noted, one can only hope that the latter are kept to a minimum. Thus, according to Gill, any therapeutic experience that is not linked to interpretation of the transference is due to "the gratification of the unanalyzed and persisting transference" and is to be avoided or minimized.

Gill's stance strikes me as rather dogmatic—ironic, for someone whose redefinition of the transference was partly motivated by a reaction against previous dogma. No good evidence suggests that only analysis of the transference is linked to a positive therapeutic outcome or that a positive outcome related to other interventions and experiences is any less desirable or durable. Also, there is some evidence that what Weiss and Sampson and the Mt. Zion Research Therapy Group (1986) refered to as "test-passing"—without interpretation of any kind, including analysis of the transference—is followed by positive changes at least within the treatment situation.

The issue I am debating with Gill here is a familiar one. In commenting on a case study I published (Eagle, 1993) in which a patient's persistent symptom dramatically disappeared following a particular enactment between the patient and myself, Gill (1993) raised the issue of the enactment remaining uninterpreted and suggested that the patient's transference reaction should have been interpreted. I intuitively believed then, as I do now, that certain patient-therapist interactions retain greater therapeutic power when, at least during a particular period in the treatment, they are left uninterpreted. I cannot prove this, but I base my belief, not only on my dramatic experience with a particular patient, but also on my belief that the foundation for legitimate benefits of treatment is not limited to one factor and one kind of intervention, namely, analysis of transference.

When I presented the foregoing case many years ago at a number of psychoanalytic institutes, one of the frequent reactions I encountered was that I was describing a "transference cure." In effect, Gill would have viewed a transference cure as any change that cannot be attributed to the analysis of the transference, but that is attributable, according to Gill (1982), to "gratification of the unanalyzed and persisting transference"

(p. 119). I am not at all sure one can easily and reliably distinguish a so-called transference cure from a bona-fide, nontransference, psychoanalytic cure (particularly because any kind of cure is not that easy to come by). I cannot prove this, but I strongly suspect that any kind of significant and lasting therapeutic change is attributable to a set of complex, interacting factors, including the simple fact that a good therapist "naturally" reacts to the patient in a way that differs from what the patient has consciously and unconsciously come to expect. Therapeutic change cannot be attributable to any single factor, including analysis of the transference.

Vision of Psychoanalysis

During the last part of his very productive career, Gill focused mainly on the clinical situation, and it is here that he made his greatest recent contributions—his writings on transference and analysis of transference. He was interested in that aspect of psychoanalytic theory that deals with the clinical situation and with the data and phenomena generated by the clinical situation. In contrast to his earlier writings, he had little to say regarding psychoanalytic theory as a theory of mental functioning, personality development, psychopathology, and human nature. Indeed, he seemed to eschew any broader references and claims of psychoanalytic theory. Perhaps that was due to his disillusionment with psychoanalytic metapsychology, his rejection of what he took to be the mode and methods of the "natural sciences," and his turn to hermeneutics and constructivism. In contrast to some other contemporary literature in psychoanalysis, Gill's writings contained virtually no references to work in such other areas as infant research, infant-mother interaction, attachment research and theory, cognitive psychology, and affect regulation, which have had a strong influence on contemporary psychoanalytic theory.

I view psychoanalysis as a theory of human behavior that, while focusing on unconscious wishes, aims, and motives, includes reference to a broad range of phenomena and processes and is open to influence in relevant findings from other disciplines. Kitcher (1992) presented a convincing case that Freudian psychoanalytic theory is essentially an interdisciplinary theory that is based, not only on the data generated by the clinical psychoanalytic situation, but also on the absorption of relevant findings and concepts from other areas. I believe this continues to be the case, and I also believe that in its interdisciplinary nature and openness to other disciplines lie the best hope for continuing vitality.

Finally, I want to underscore that I earnestly wish Merton were around to carry on the debate. I have been critical of many of Merton's ideas in this chapter, but it is a criticality with enormous respect for the man's thinking and role in psychoanalysis and with enormous affection for the man. I think that Merton would have enjoyed this chapter, would have enjoyed the opportunity to point out my errors, and would have enjoyed acknowledging the legitimacy of some of my arguments and criticisms.

References

Abend, S. M. (1989). Countertransference and technique. *Psychoanal. Quart.*, 48:374–395.

Ainsworth, M. D. S. & Marvin, R. S. (1995). On the shaping of attachment theory and research: An interview with Mary D. S. Ainsworth (Fall 1994). *Monogr. Soc. Res. Child Development*, 60:3–21.

Black, M. (1967). Review of A. R. Louch's "Explanation of Human Action." *Amer. J. Psychol.*, 80:655–656.

Blum, H. P. (1986). Countertransference and the theory of technique: Discussion. *J. Amer. Psychoanal. Assn.*, 34:309–328.

Bowlby, J. (1969). *Attachment and Loss, Vol. 1*. New York: Basic Books.

Bowlby, J. (1973). *Attachment and Loss, Vol. 2*. New York: Basic Books.

Bowlby, J. (1980). *Attachment and Loss, Vol 3*. New York: Basic Books.

Bowlby, J. (1988a). *A Secure Base*. New York: Basic Books.

Bowlby, J. (1988b). Defensive processes in response to stressful separation in early life. In: *The Child in His Family, Vol. 8*, ed. A. E. James & C. Chiland. New York: John Wiley & Sons, pp. 23–30.

Eagle, M. N. (1980). A critical examination of motivational explanation in psychoanalysis. *Psychoanal. Contemp. Thought*, 3:329–380.

Eagle, M. N. (1984). Geha's vision of psychoanalysis as fiction. *Internat. Forum Psychoanal.*, 1:141–162.

Eagle, M. N. (1984/1987). *Recent Developments in Psychoanalysis*. Cambridge, MA: Harvard University Press.

Eagle, M. N. (1993). Enactments, transference, and symptomatic cure: A case history. *Psychoanal. Dial.*, 3:93–110.

Eagle, M. N. (1998). Freud's legacy: Defenses, somatic symptoms and neurophysiology. In: *Freud and the Neurosciences*, ed. G. Guttman & I. Stolz-Strasser. Vienna: Verlag der Osterreichischen Akademie der Wissenschaften/ Austrian Academy of Sciences Press, pp. 87–101.

Eagle, M. N. (2000). Repression (Parts I & II). *Psychoanal. Rev.*, 87 (Nos. 1 & 2):1–38; 161–187.

Eagle, M. N. & Wolitzky, D. L. (1997). Empathy: A psychoanalytic perspective. In: *Empathy Reconsidered*, ed. A. Bohart & L. Greenberg. Washington, DC: APA Books.

Fairbairn, W. R. D. (1952). *Psychoanalytic Studies of the Personality*. London: Tavistock.

Freud, S. (1921). Group psychology and the analysis of the ego. *Standard Edition*, 18:67–143. London: Hogarth Press, 1955.

Gabbard, G. O. (1995). Countertransference: The emerging common ground. *Internat. J. Psycho-Anal.*, 76:475–485.

Geha, R. E. (1984). On psychoanalytic history and the "real" story of fictitious lives. *Internat. Forum Psychoanal.*, 1:221–291.

Gill, M. M. (1982). *Analysis of Transference, Vol. 1*. New York: International Universities Press.

Gill, M. M. (1993). Interaction and interpretation: Commentary on Morris Eagle's "Enactment, transference, and symptomatic cure: A case history." *Psychoanal. Dial.*, 3:111–121.
Gill, M. M. (1994). *Psychoanalysis in Transition*. Hillsdale, NJ: The Analytic Press.
Heimann, P. (1950). On counter-transference. *Internat. J. Psychoanal.*, 31:81–84.
Holmes, D. S. (1990). The evidence for repression: An examination of sixty years of research. In: *Repression and Dissociation*, ed. J. L. Singer. Chicago: University of Chicago Press, pp. 85–102.
Kernberg, O. (1965). Notes on countertransference. *J. Amer. Psychoanal. Assn.*, 13:38–56.
Klein, G. S. (1976). Two theories or one? In: *Psychology versus Metapsychology: Psychoanalytic Essays in Memory of George S. Klein*, ed. M. M. Gill & P. S. Holtzman. New York: International Universities Press.
Kitcher, P. (1992). *Freud's Dream*. Cambridge, MA: MIT Press.
Kohut, H. (1984). *How Does Analysis Cure?* ed. A. Goldberg & P. Stepansky. Chicago: University of Chicago Press.
Levine, W. B. (1997). The capacity for countertransference. *Psychoanal. Inq.*, 17:44–68.
Meehl, P. E. (1973). *Psychodiagnosis*. Minneapolis: University of Minnesota Press, pp. 225–302.
Meehl, P. E. (1997). Credentialed persons, credentialed knowledge. *Clin. Psychol.: Science & Practice*, 4:91–98.
Ogden, T. (1982). *Projective Identification and Therapeutic Technique*. Northvale, NJ: Aronson.
Piaget, J. (1991). Advances in child and adolscent psychology. In: *Learning to Think*, ed. P. Light & S. Sheldon. London: Routledge, pp. 5–15.
Ponsi, M. (1997). Interaction and transference. *Internat. J. Psychoanal.*, 78:243–264.
Popper, K. R. (1962). *Conjectures and Refutations*. New York: Harper Torchbooks, 1968.
Racker, H. (1968). *Transference and Countertransference*. Madison, CT: International Universities Press.
Reichenbach, H. (1951). *The Rise of Scientific Philosophy*. Berkeley: University of California Press.
Reppen, J. (1982). Merton Gill: An interview. *Psychoanal. Rev.*, 69:167–190.
Rorty, R. (1991). *Essays on Heidegger and Others*. New York: Cambridge University Press.
Rubinstein, B. (1997). Collected papers. In: *Psychoanalysis and the Philosophy of Science*, ed. R. R. Holt. *Psychological Issues*, Monogr. 62/63. Madison, CT: International Universities Press, pp. 415–465.
Sandler, J. (1976). Countertransference and role-responsiveness. *Internat. Rev. Psycho-Anal.*, 3:43–47.
Sandler, J. (1987). The concept of projective identification. *Bull. Anna Freud Centre*, 10:33–49.
Sandler, J. (1993). On communication from patient to analyst: Not everything is projective identification. *Internat. J. Psychoanal.*, 74:1097–1107.
Schafer, R. (1992). *Retelling a Life*. New York: Basic Books.
Schore, A. N. (1994). *Affect Regulation and the Origin of the Self*. Hillsdale, NJ: Lawrence Erlbaum Associates.

Searle, J. R. (1992). *The Rediscovery of Mind.* Cambridge, MA: MIT Press.
Spence, D. P. (1982). *Narrative Truth and Historical Truth.* New York: Norton.
Spillius, E. B. (1992). Clinical Experiences of Projective Identification. In: *Clinical Lectures on Klein and Bion,* ed. R. Anderson. London: Tavistock/Routledge, pp. 59–73.
Strupp, H. H. & Binder, J. L. (1984). *Psychotherapy in a New Key.* New York: Basic Books.
Sullivan, H. S. (1947). *Conceptions of Modern Psychiatry.* New York: Norton.
Sullivan, H. S. (1953). *The Interpersonal Theory of Psychiatry.* New York: Norton.
Sulloway, F. J. (1996). *Born to Rebel.* New York: Pantheon Books.
Tansey, M. J. & Burke, W. F. (1989). *Understanding Countertransference.* Hillsdale, NJ: The Analytic Press.
Taylor, G. (1987) *Psychosomatic Medicine and Contemporary Psychoanalysis.* Madison, CT: International Universities Press.
von Eckardt, B. (1981). An evaluation of the scientific status of psychoanalysis. *J. Philosophy,* 78:570–572.
Wallerstein, R. (1990). Psychoanalysis: The common ground. *Internat. J. Psychoanal.,* 71:3–19.
Weiss, J., Sampson, H. & the Mt. Zion Psychotherapy Research Group (1986). *The Psychoanalytic Process.* New York: Guilford Press.

Chapter 7

Are Minds Objects or Dramas?

Lawrence Friedman

Editors' Introduction: *Both Friedman and Gill are struggling with similar epistomological isssues but conclude with different emphases. Gill wanted psychoanalysis to bridge both science and hermeneutics. Gill recognized that in endorsing a hermeneutic orientation for psychoanalysis, he acknowledged a perspectival orientation for the clinician thereby recognizing the subjectivity of the analyst.*

Friedman agrees that when Freud abandoned his search for repressed memories and substituted the utilization of "broad expressive procedures," he relinquished an objective, natural science quest and simultaneously opened the floodgates to a variety of underlying philosophical stances that challenged the idea of objectivity in the analytic interaction. Nonetheless, he sees Gill's position as flawed in that it abandons the concept of objectivity. Friedman believes objectivity is still an important goal for the individual patient.

Friedman reconceptualized his understanding of perspectives and its relationship to mental events and thereby challenges Gill's position on perspectivalism. He grants the importance of acknowledging perspectivalism in the psychoanalytic encounter and situates it from a particular vantage point that obviates the need for contrasting objectivity and subjectivity in the analytic dyad, a position that clashes with Gill's insistence on the mutual subjectivity inherent in the analytic interaction.

Perspectives from Friedman's vantage point "are the way that we feel out the objective reality of personhood, as well as its human environment." He maintains that when the analyst's focus is on the patient's fantasy perspectives of the analyst as well as on the relationship, that is, the domain of transference, it offers the patient the best opportunity to explore self-understanding. Self-understanding is an attempt on the patient's part to obtain a more objective perspective on his or her mind.

Friedman accepts the existence of patients' perspectives, biases, and unconscious motives, yet believes that if there is "a capacity and an inclination" in patients, they can advance in the direction of achieving "autonomy and self mastery." Patients can learn to understand their various motives and defenses as characteristic of the way their minds function, which can lead to increasing progress in their becoming more "abstract and disinterested" about understanding the nature of their minds.

The protopsychoanalysis described in "Studies on Hysteria" (Breuer and Freud, 1895) was an effort to retrieve eidetic memories along with their affects. When that procedure gave way to psychoanalysis proper, analysts found themselves faced with an acute epistemological crisis: they had to find an object to replace memories, a new object that psychoanalytic inquiry could reach for. It was not easy to point to an objective prize in this new, nondirective, broadly expressive procedure.

In a sense, Freud's "Papers on Technique" is a hunt for a new object to replace eidetic memory. In "Remembering, Repeating and Working Through" (1914), Freud devoted very intense and sometimes tortured thought to the problem. He tried to retain memory as the sought-after object by defining memory-retrieval in terms of other, less concrete and object-like goals, such as the removal of repressions and the elimination of resistance. In effect, he "commissioned" *behavior* as an honorary memory (or procedural memory, in modern parlance). He could have said "We no longer look *just* for memories, but *also* for repetitive behavior." He chose not to. He said repetitive behavior is *the way* patients remember. Thus, although the behavior in question was rapidly taking on the boundless meaning of a transfer of all the "nonserviceable" traits of a personality (1914), psychoanalysis would still have a specific object to look for at least in name.

The task of finding objects in the analytic process is no easier at the turn of this century than it was at the turn of the last. Contemporary analysts are uneasy about all definitiveness—definitiveness of descriptions, definiteness of roles, givenness of the patient's mind. None of these has the tidy outline that memories were once thought to possess. (Some of the despair about definiteness is expressed in animadversions on "positivism.")

Merton Gill led the way in challenging objective units and definitions in psychoanalysis. He spoke for those who criticize the old interpretive confidence that ignored the enormous leeway we have (and therefore the potential arbitrariness we risk) in describing any objective phenomenon. In particular, Gill summarized the late realization that, as a result of Freud's initial abandonment of abreactive memory conjuring, analysts are left to inscribe figures in a phenomenologically amorphous and fluctuant field.

For decades, analysts had been aware of the complexity of the treatment scene (as at the Marienbad Conference in 1962), but that was less disturbing to earlier analysts because they were more confident of their technique. These days, however, when settled questions of technique have been thrown wide open for passionate debate, analysts are more handicapped by the lack of any simple object of search, around which the rest of the confusion might be organized. The dizzying complexity of the field is no longer a merely intriguing topic; it is now a matter of urgent, practical concern. Analysts ask themselves how they can possibly direct their attention and their participation in such an indefinite morass. (See Friedman, in press.) An analyst who is not sure what surrounds him, what he is moving toward, and what he is trying to grasp will also wonder what professional role and tactical posture makes sense.

Merton Gill devoted the later part of his life to a search for the right posture. I do not think he found the right one, but it is to his credit that he did not compromise himself by settling into a well-worked-out false posture. For Gill, the essential duty of an analyst is to allow no feature of the scene to be taken for granted, and the (post-)modern challenge fits well with that obligation. But Gill was not simply a critic; he was also an inquirer and a confronter, and he thought it just as important for the analyst to refuse to be intimidated in his views, as it was for him to allow them to be challenged.

Gill, therefore, was anything but a harmonizing peacemaker with his patients (or, I need hardly remind the reader, with his colleagues). Even in abstract theory his conception of "plausibility" put a limit to the range of acceptable alternative views of the relationship. But it was hard for many who sympathized with Gill's attitude of self-scrutiny to find a cognitive foothold. His approach seemed to yield only shifting views of the patient and the patient's shifting views of themselves, with nothing left over that could be an object of inquiry. Having cursed "positivism," it may seem that an analyst is left with just views and more views as far as the eye can see. There being no object of inquiry in sight, it is difficult to find anything else for treatment to do but pool views together in the vague hope that an alchemical transformation will benefit the patient, perhaps by precipitating a new meaning with an unspecifiably beneficial effect. In practice, Gill was more definite than that, but he did not identify the source of his definiteness.

If we look closely at the distressing vagueness of the clinical field, we see that the essential problem is the difference between—more specifically, the heteronomy of—dramas and objects. Analysts have become self-critically aware that, instead of physics-like propositions, their judgements often amount to an evocation of dramatic human views of a patient whose own mind is also filled with dramatic views. It just isn't clear how dramatic views can be said to be descriptive of objects, or how dramatic perspectives can pretend to be objective judgements, much less how one's dramatic views of oneself can constitute an object like a mind.

Once descriptions of mind are identified with perspectives, it is but a short step to the relativistic notion that mind is nothing *but* perspectives—perspectives on the world and on oneself. The absence of anything but perspectives in this account makes the goal of objectivity seem obsolete, the thrust of treatment obscure, and (therefore) the analyst's role and rules quite random. Previously envisioned pretensions to neutrality, abstinence, and objectivity are hard to justify in an exchange of perspectives. It is hard to find anything but enactment in a process of mutually evoked, perspectival attitudes. At this point, therefore, few tasks are as urgent as a reconsideration of the relationship between perspectives on people, on one hand, and the cognition of mental objects, on the other. If we could restore the balance between personal dramas and mental objects, the nature of the therapeutic interaction might become clearer.

I suggest we think of momentary fantasies and perspectives (which I picture on a continuum) as surveillance actions: exploratory manipulations of both the outer and inner world. They explore opportunities in the world at the same time as they explore one's wishes and nature. They canvass a genuine mental object, whose enduring facets allow us to repeatedly re-evoke "the same" momentary fantasy or perspective, or take a new view of oneself. After all, what other tools do we have for exploring our objective personhood? We cannot touch or rotate our mind, or chip it with a chisel. We cannot place under a microscope the meaning we have had or could potentially have to others, or they to us. Perspectives, I suggest, are the way that we feel out the objective reality of personhood, as well as its human environment. Competing treatment projects can be understood as different strategies for improving that on-going perspectival exploration of our mental object. The analyst's "subjectivity" is not to be contrasted with objectivity, since it is the same sort of "feeling out" that is required of every mental object; "subjectivity," as a *contrast* to objectivity is just the failure to accurately factor our particular perspectival attitude into our judgement.

I write of "perspectives," and, later, "attitudes," as the "handling" of a mental object, but I do not offer these terms and phrases as new or revelatory. They are obviously not new. ("Perspectivism" has a whole school named after it.) They introduce no special insights. I am merely sketching an image for the analyst's use rather than a theory. I am not even sure how philosophically coherent my conception is. I offer it as a suggestion for others to try, although for simplicity's sake, I will describe it more confidently.

Perspectives in Analytic Theory

Well before Freud revised the seduction theory he recognized that an etiological agent alone does not explain an illness; one must also point to an afflicted system—a system with lawfully describable processes. Without an organ to infect, a tuberculosis bacillus is a paper tiger. To characterize a *system* for trauma to affect, Freud very early postulated, for example, an organic tendency to repeat. In other words, Freud knew from the start that meanings alone don't decide things; it's the human way of handling meanings, that is, the regularity of interconnection among meanings, that determines outcome. Right from the beginning, Freud's wider ambition had always been at work, using etiology to probe for mental *mechanisms*.

The abandonment of the seduction theory was simply an occasion to move on to a general theory of mind. It enabled Freud to deal with finer details than taxonomy, to describe individual nuances beyond nosology, and to plot universal mechanisms of mind. What boosted the theory to a new power was its capacity to handle the *interconnectedness* of meanings (for instance, the meaning of family relationships as it bears on the meaning of one's wishes), rather than the mere *cooccurence* of meanings (such as the correlation of a "germ"—an experience of seduction—with a symptom, such as paralysis).

Thus, the abandonment of the seduction theory and the emphasis on psychic reality was first and foremost an acknowledgement of the complex interconnectedness of personal meanings.

In other words, the abandonment of the seduction theory was part of a general movement away from picturing the mind as made of units. As theory moved away from bits and pieces, practical wisdom joined in and dictated a corresponding change in treatment strategy. Treatment that had formerly been a hunt for atoms of experience (traumatic memories), evolved into a watchful waiting for random clues, and was finally transformed into a project of detecting idiosyncratic perspectives with cross-currents of purpose (fantasies and resistance).

In several places Freud came close to explicitly describing a transition from hard items to vaguer relationships of meaning. In his Postscript to the case of Dora, he (1895) lamented that "combatting" transference is "by far the hardest part of the whole task. It is easy to learn how to interpret dreams, to extract from the patient's associations his unconscious thoughts and memories, and to practice similar explanatory arts: for these the patient himself will always provide the text. Transference is the one thing the presence of which has to be detected almost without assistance and with only the slightest clues to go upon, while at the same time the risk of making arbitrary inferences has to be avoided" (p. 116). Here Freud acknowledges the difficulty of making authoritative pronouncements about an ambiguous continuum when compared to the easier task of translating an already worded, and therefore segmented, subject like dream symbols. Also relevant is Freud's (1914) confession that "we must still be grateful to the old hypnotic technique for having brought before us single psychical processes of analysis in an isolated or schematic form. Only this could have given us the courage ourselves to create more complicated situations in the analytic treament and to keep them clear before us" (p. 148). I take that to mean that he would not have had the courage to designate items that the patient's conscious or dreaming attention hadn't already selected from the flow as individual, circumscribed objects.

In effect, when treatment moves from the retrieval of hypnotic, traumatic memories to psychoanalysis proper, what the historian sees is the shift from uncovering easily demarcated items to the evocation of influential perspectives. The transference is the archetypical set of such perspectives within the treatment domain: the analyst is admonished to sustain these transference perspectives, not only to milk them for information (as memory equivalents), but also for use as perceptual grids, that is, as ways of seeing the analyst and the relationship that make treatment personally meaningful to the patient and (in the case of the "unobjectionable positive transference") desirable to him.

Freud wrote that psychoanalytic treatment aims to transform these passionate, perceptual grids into memories. That is inexact, of course. A transference does not actually become a memory. In effect, those biased perceptual grids were to be *subsumed* under more comprehensive perspectives, which include perspectives on the pastness of infantile dangers. It stands to reason that such a corrective assimilation to a larger perspective can happen only to a perspective that is currently active and salient. (That, I believe, is the meaning of Freud's admonition [1912, p. 108] that "it is impossible to destroy anyone *in absentia* or *in effigie.*")

Taking place before our eyes as we progress through Freud's "Papers on Technique" is the discovery that transference perspectives are not just obstacles, nor indeed just valuable sources of information, but are a means by which patients actively explore themselves as they explore their opportunities with the analyst. Patients acquire a palette of perspectives as they struggle with an analyst who is not neatly grasped in the original perspective but also does not place himself outside it, requiring the patient to develop other and larger perspectives and a more multifaceted view of the analyst and of himself.

Then there is the matter of resistance analysis. Freud (1914) said that in working through, the patient becomes familiar with (the sources of) the labeled resistances by continuing to work despite them. What that means phenomenologically is that the patient gives a new, focused attention to his reluctances and thus arrives at a sensory appreciation of the antianalytic values/interests he is protecting. This is, of course, a definition of treatment as a demonstration of conflict. But we should note that it is an experiential demonstration: the patient is encouraged to *feel* the impulse tugging at his sleeve as he works; he must respect what it is costing him (in terms of his wishes) to cooperate with the analyst. Why should we expect that to be helpful? Presumably because he will now have a *perspective* on himself (an actual sighting) that subsumes the reality of both the wish to be analyzed and the wish not to be "analyzed." Freud here reminded analysts that merely *describing* the resistance accomplishes only a limited task: it acts to focus the patient's attention, but that is not enough. Something more than a description will ultimately be needed. I believe he meant that what is needed is a perspective. (Thereafter analysts reminded themselves that "intellectual understanding" isn't sufficient.)

"Perspective" is a good word not only for what the patient achieves, but also for what the analyst communicates. In the protopsychoanalytic treatments that preceded psychoanalysis proper, the therapist's interventions were essentially reminders of a preexisting memory. Later, in psychoanalysis proper, an intervention was often an effort to *orient* a patient in a way that would give him a glimpse of his purposes. Most generally, psychoanalytic interpretations in later practice suggest a useful perspective that the patient can take on his life.

Fantasy as Perspective

It may seem strange that I use the word "perspective" to refer to both (transference) fantasy and (self-)perception. Outside of Kleinian circles fantasy is often regarded as the polar opposite of normal perception. I must digress momentarily and describe the historic continuum that embraces them both.

In this chapter I dodge the onerous task of inventorying the myriad meanings of the word "fantasy" and use it in its broadest possible sense. That may open me to the charge of comingling flat-out fantastic distortions with accurate, though highly charged, perceptions. But the relationship between prejudicial forms and veridical information has never been clearly worked out in psychoanalytic theory. For instance, unconscious fantasy, despite its subjection to primary process, is sometimes thought of as so closely related in form to consciousness as to be exactly translatable into words (for example, by the interpreting psychoanalyst). In this scenario we might almost forget the primacy of primary process and picture the unconscious as translating conscious thoughts, word-for-word, into primary process "language," which it is then the analyst's job to reverse. Even Freud's speculation that some fantasies are atavistic memories, utterly unrelated to individual experiences, placed them on a *formal* par with organized perception. That is not surprising, considering that, even in dreams, there is a limit to how different primary process can be from secondary process if it is to be interpretable. I therefore choose transference as an example of the interweaving of fantasy and reality, even though (or just because) it does not exhibit the stark opposition of pure prejudice versus veridical perception that beguiles us in clinical examples of unconscious fantasy.

The historic transition from isolated memories to a continuum of meaning was greatly facilitated by the concept of unconscious fantasy. But fantasy has played a double role in psychoanalytic theory. It began as one of the items in the mind, on a par with a memory (e.g., the fantasy of infantile seduction in its simplest formulation). Later, fantasy helped to blend memories and current perceptions (as in the fantasy nature of the transference). More recently, fantasies may be thought of as organizers of experience (e.g., the mind as a set of narratives).

One can see such a dialectic already in Freud's early writing (e.g., 1912). In early psychoanalytic theory a fantasy was an atavistic route leading away from healthy openness, inward toward a particular, old relationship. It was portrayed as a slippery slope on which a frustrated adult wish can slide back into a fixated, infantile attachment. But fantasy also accounted for a *constant* infusion of old, familiar patterns *into* contemporary events—a general expression of the conservative "spin" of the repetition compulsion (or attraction of the unconscious), which causes us to assimilate new experience to old. Thus, fantasy might be thought of either as an occasional, sick sacrifice of the contemporary world to an impoverished fixation on the parents, or else as the way we normally export meaning into the world. It is the difference between fantasy as an apparition and fantasy as tinted vision.

The young analytic theory commemorated each of these significances of fantasy in turn, as both Freud and Ferenczi wrestled with its double direction. Freud (Breuer and Freud, 1895) was initially inclined to view transference as an unintended mistaking of the present for the past. Even in 1912, he wanted to envision transference as stealing the patient's affection from the real world, by safeguarding her infantile attachments. (That is why he found Jung's term "introversion" appealing.) Freud obviously preferred to see transference that way because it simplified the rationale of treatment (and thus made resistance a more clear-cut concept). For that reason, when transference passion loudly declared otherwise and unmistakably seized the analyst himself, Freud continued to insist that its centrifugal force was a clever ruse to throw the analyst off the track and protect its real, centripetal intent. But Freud also had to acknowledge the transformative, contemporary aspect of transference (1915). So, without disowning its withholding significance, he declared that archaic psychic reality was not just a retained, infantile, masturbatory reverie, but a transformative effort to obtain satisfaction in the present—albeit one of limited flexibility.

In this formulation, Freud agreed with Ferenczi (1909), who had described neurotics as *overly* involved with the world, and tending to personalize neutral situations. (Ferenczi was probably thinking of neurotic hypersensitivity, self-consciousness, phobias, and the like.) Ferenczi emphasized the seeking aspect, rather than the concealing aspect of transference. To explain how it can be that fixation paradoxically causes too great an openness to the world, Ferenczi proposed that unrealistic aims leave the neurotic with an eternally hungry libido, ready to draw the objective world into his subjective framework—a process Ferenczi called "introjection" (in startling contrast to Jung's and Freud's preference for the term, "introversion").

One continues to see this dialectic of past and present in the contrast between particular fantasies (dramas about the past) and fantasy-drenched perception (proclivities for construing the present).

The Mind Must Be More Than Perspectives

The idea that perception is drenched in fantasy has encouraged many later psychoanalysts to describe the mind entirely in terms of fantasy or narrative or perspective. That would require fantasy to be (1) a phenomenal experience, (2) an underlying substance, and (3) a mechanism of transformation, all rolled into one. But fantasy (or narrative) cannot refer to both the momentary phenomena and the process of mind on one, uniform level of discourse. The mind cannot just be fantasies.

Moreover, even if we were not obliged to account for the regularities of transformation, we still could not picture the mind as a collection of fantasy perspectives (or versions or narratives) *about* oneself, because that would leave unanswerable what the self is that they are perspectives on. A facile relativism makes it impossible to say what it is that renders my view *relative* to me rather than just *belonging* to me. We would not be able to say what makes the converging views of different observers cousins rather than just different, unrelated mental events. We would not be able to say how my perspective at one time bears on the same thing as my "changed" perspective at another time: why aren't they just two, random states of mind?

Perspectives are relative to an observer when, and only when, other perspectives might be directed from different positions onto a *common* object. (A Kantian formula *defines* an object as the lawful relationship between appearances.)

When discussing vision, for instance, nobody would dream of *denying* that the terms, relativity and perspective, get their meaning from a common reality. But when we talk of perspectives on the mind, it is easy to let perspectives "lose" their objects, because of the mind's continous reflexiveness. Because we are always viewing ourselves in the process of viewing, our interest in what we initially have in mind can be quickly replaced by our interest in the act of attending to it. The perspective then constitutes a new object of our attention, and that, in turn, can then be replaced by a view of the view, and so forth. In the end, the infinite regress may fool us into thinking that we never did have any *thing* in mind, but only perspectives all along. The continuous blurring of mental states into each other from moment to moment makes it even harder to resist the illusion that everything is perspective; harder, still, to claim anything substantial for mind. We have abstracted from each level in our self-awareness, and made an object out of each awareness, and ended up supposing that with so many objects, there is no underlying object at all. Of the mind, as of Los Angeles, it is said that "there is no there, there." (See Ryle, 1949, p. 34.)

But if we resist that optical illusion and recognize that the mind is a determinate (though changing) something, we face a difficult task: we must describe the relationship between introspective perspectives and what it is that they are perspectives *on*, and that is a lot easier to do with vision than with mind.[1]

That is very much our concern when it comes to interpretation. Like all communications, psychoanalytic interventions are efforts by one person to direct the attention of another. That may be done by sharing a perspective, but we are obliged by the reasons given to say how perspectives scan a mental fact, or, in other words, how the analyst's direction of attention helps to acquaint a patient with a truth about himself.

Admittedly, that is not as easy with mental objects as it is, for instance, with visual objects. When it comes to visual perspectives, the repeated action of looking at the way we look is a process of successive abstraction that starts from proprioception and retinal mapping and culminates in a book-knowledge of geometry. The "human" equivalent is far more complicated. For one thing, the process never reaches a final abstraction, since we continue to be concerned with individuals. We may suppose that the abstraction of features from mental life continuously emerges out of vague, global, hedonically tinged attitudes which gradually shape up into more focused, and therefore more abstract, partly verbalizable form. The major difference between physical perspectives and human perspectives is that the latter have an intrinsically dramatic, moral, happy–unhappy aspect, to be discussed in a later section of this chapter.

---

[1] The fact that a mind falls apart when deprived of minimal social sustenance no more proves that the mind is composed of interpersonal perspectives, than the fact of a body's burning in fire proves that there never was a body but only physical interaction with a cooler environment. The interrelatedness of elements of the world is important, but it does not prevent us from considering the separate things in the world.

Perspectives as Explorations of an Object

I think the function of perspectives is usefully illustrated in Piaget's work. Even though recent research suggests that infants have more direct ways of knowing about minds than he supposed, it seems to me that Piaget's (1962) general principles stand us in good stead long after the particulars of his developmental theory have been challenged. According to the broadest Piagetian paradigm, people learn about objects by integrating the ways they operate on them. Piagetian realisticness is the achievement of equilibrium among the various ways of handling the world.

Piaget (1976) suggested that efforts to coordinate actions result in an increasingly refined schema of both the object acted on and the actor's efforts. In discussing the construction of a continuous "will," he implied that a person or a self is located in the persistence and consistency noted in "experiments" with momentary desires (Piaget, 1967). I have elsewhere suggested that patients form a clearer view of themselves by "operating" on the freely manipulable therapist (Friedman, 1988). I now suggest that they "operate" on *themselves* as they view themselves in different ways with different attitudinal perspectives (whether presented by the analyst or by themselves). Patients may learn about themselves both by coordinating more and more perspectives (or fantasies) on themselves and by accumulating more detailed experience of the motives behind their preferred perspectives.

In a similar fashion, Vygotsky (1978) appreciates children's imaginative play as leading to cognitive refinement. Play actions *elucidate* the child's wishes and the roles he is interested in. In play the child explores himself as an intentional agent. When imagined in his play-self, his wish no longer blends imperceptibly into the rest of life's events and actions. (See Wilson and Weinstein [1996] for a suggestion of how a process of teaching *toward* the "Zone of Proximal Development" can be found in psychoanalytic treatment.) The psychoanalytic perspectives offered to a patient may work the same way, supplemented by the patient's read-out from his own handling of the analyst.

Human Perspectives Are Oriented by Attitudes

A large body of literature now describes the interpersonal manipulation involved in simple speech and its dependence on context even just to convey a straightforward proposition. A powerful, modern tradition deals with the nonpropositional use of speech, that is, language as a way of affecting someone in order to bring about certain results. (See Shapiro, 1999.) One thinks of studies by Morris (1946) on pragmatics, a revival of interest in rhetoric (Burke, 1950; Goffman, 1969), studies of metaphor and the expressive "construction" of the universe (Pepper, 1942; Goodman, 1978; Lakoff and Johnson, 1980), and of the social world (Berger and Luckmann, 1966). Studies of speech acts (in contrast to pure language) have flourished in Oxford (Austin, 1962; Grice, 1989). A fruitful examination of narrative strategies has been undertaken by White (1973), and Bruner (1990). (Wittgenstein 1958, inspired some of this, but he was addressing more fundamental problems.) This work tends to undermine the idea that interpretations, for example, can capture, transmit, and be decoded as personally unjudged, detached, unequivocal assertions of fact. The new studies discourage the older, idealized, psychoanalytic hope of devising interpretations by which the analyst's gloved hand, so to speak, reaches over, replaces a brick that has dropped out of the patient's edifice, and withdraws, leaving no fingerprints.

But, after all, psychoanalysts do not need outside experts to inform them of what they see all the time, namely, that their comments are never received by their patients as disembodied descriptions, floating to them from a data base, but always as a reaction of the man or woman in the room with them, who sees them in a certain way and wants to move them in a certain direction (as Raphling [1995] has pointed out). Patients receive comments that way because that is the way everybody understands everybody else. (See Friedman, 1988.)

At first glance, it might seem that the analyst's attitudinal bias compromises his usefulness, and it is true that if his vision were entirely attitudinal and not balanced by a mechanistic theory of the mind, his activity would not be psychoanalytic (though it might be quite helpful in an ordinary way). But it would be a mistake to assume that attitudes are simply distortions. There is no other way to take a perspective on a person (as opposed to a mental apparatus) than through attitudes. We can describe human bodies in physical terms, and we can even describe persons in terms that are almost physical—what I call a "physical-ish" description—as when we say, "I have a bad memory" or "you get angry easily." But when we use those physical-ish descriptions in *communication* with ourselves or each other, they are even more saturated by their context than other utterances; their meaning becomes entwined with the interpersonal motivation for speaking. If a male analyst were to start a session by observing to his female patient, "you have a sunny disposition," it would not at all be heard as a physical-ish description.

Unlike the geometric readings of visual perspectives, human perspectives on human beings (including the self) tend to be intrinsically dramatic and moralistic. (See Ricoeur, 1984, p. 59.) Human perspectives are defined by attitudes, rather than by the spatial location of the viewer. In those terms, Schafer (1983) has provided a comprehensive account of the function of dramatic perspectives in psychoanalytic practice. Even our own fantasies include a self-evaluating commentary of some sort or other. Just as a physical perspective can be thought of as a cone of vision looking out on a widening scene, a personal perspective may be thought of as widening out around and about the object to include a dramatic tableau.

The patient's perspectives on himself, no less than his analyst's comments, are defined by attitudes, each with wishful, fearful, and evaluative angles to it. Much of our imagination of ourselves amounts to an assemblage of arguments, civil or bitter, mumbling or vociferous. Psychoanalysis acknowledges this in the concept of unconscious fantasy. (For the intrinsically moralistic, rhetorical form of accounts of human beings, see Burke [1950], White [1973], Ricoeur [1984], Schafer [1983], and Spence [1982]. For the dialogic nature of thought and speech, see Vygotsky [1978], and Bakhtin [1981], and Freudian theory of the superego.) As Waelder (1934) implied, there are always interests at stake in our view of reality. Indeed, it is just because people's sense of themselves is already a kind of argument that the analyst has leverage to change it: When the secret argument publicly draws the analyst into it, it reveals the rhetoric that had been defining the patient's sense of himself and his world, and the patient can then explore alternatives.

But these alternative attitudes bear on a self and a world that are already present and waiting for the patient to regard. My suggestion is that we think of a patient as cornering his reality by operating on himself with his attitudes. He experiences himself in various agonistic dramas, until those attitudes triangulate a center with a felt coherence, that is, a coherence that makes sense of all its many manifestations. Many types of dreams show this kind of exploration, both of one's self and one's intimates.

When a person exercises an apt variety of attitudes on himself (dramatic visualization, moralizing, ironic redefinition, and the like), he is "handling" the facts of his nature, much as he might in a darkened room grope out the nature of a nearby object. The analyst's relative evasiveness and detachment act as a clutch to disengage the patient from a restricted exploration and allow the object (the patient's reality) to rotate freely before his gaze. The characteristic detachment-in-closeness in psychoanalytic treatment would also provide the as-if quality described by Vygotsky (1978, pp. 99–101) that emboldens aims and objectives in childrens' play.

How Can Attitudinal Perspectives Be Objective?

Just as a variety of perspectives best defines a physical object, so, I assume, a variety of attitudes will better triangulate the facts of a person than just a few.[2] But I am also assuming that these attitudes that are triangulated

---

[2] See Mary Main's (1995) adult attachment interviews. In Main's studies, the ability of a mother to provide secure attachment for her child can be predicted

on oneself are warranted; in other words, they are more like a visual perspective than like an imaginative construction. Well or badly, these perspectives find a target. Insofar as they take narrative form they may be somewhat conventional, but the person they explore has a shape of his own, which, though it *includes* his preference for certain perspectives, is not limited to those preferred perspectives.

People do not create themselves by perspectives. Individuals have a nature, a constitution, a temperament, a personality, strengths, and weaknesses. It is true that a person's stock of fantasies is part of his definition, but that is because it gathers reflective perspectives on his essential self. (He can fantasize *about* his fantasies and make up dramas about his fantasies as figures in his mind.) A person will not become less cowardly simply by thinking himself so, but he might see cowardice, instead, as misperception, and, by highlighting courage he hadn't seen, that might make him more essentially confident.

Thus, even if perspectives do not create a self, people seem to be able to change in some ways when they examine their nature; otherwise, analytic treatment would be a false promise. When we challenge patients' perspectives they are forced to focus them more persuasively, and in the process, they discover and elaborate features of themselves that had been glossed over (see Margolis, 1987).

But a more useful criterion of accuracy in a perspective is the degree to which it takes in its own motivation. Even though a person is not made up entirely out of his perspectives, nevertheless his choice of perspective on himself is a manifestation of the same self he is viewing: perspectives are always enabled and motivated by a mental state; the motives for seeing oneself one way or another are properties of a real object (the mind). When I reflect on myself, I see more or less of what in me makes me look in that fashion. When the sweep of a perspective does not include its cause we talk about self-deception. If a patient visualizes himself as helpless in order to placate his analyst (or to galvanize the analyst into action), he is, to be sure, seeing a truth about himself, but his perspective will corner less truth than if it had also surveyed the full, active agency that authored it, that is, his manipulative intent. (See Freud's [1912] first definition of "working through" referred to previously.) If a patient cannot constantly abstract to a larger perspective that takes in the motives of his more immediate perspectives, he will, to that extent, fail to "feel out" the object that constitutes his person. He is like a surveyor who can see what lies before him, but does not know where he is standing to view it. The reader will say, "But there is a limit to our ability to be 'one up' on ourselves." (Gödel's Theorem will be invoked). That is true. (It is one justification for Brenner's [1994] dismissal of the ego-concept.)

---

from the complexity and integration in her account of her own experience of her parents, irrespective of the quality of the described relationship.

What would a perspective look like that was *most* consistent with its own motivation? At the extreme (and in the ideal) it would be motivated by a pure wish to know the truth, and it would be characterized by a *lack* of attitude—or, if you like, an attitude of disinterested objectivity. I have argued that this is an impossibility. We cannot view anybody that way, least of all ourselves. We can picture a mind in that fashion, but not a person. We always have some interests and some motives at work. But if there is both a capacity and an inclination to achieve autonomy and self mastery, perspectives can progress in that *direction*, becoming more abstract and disinterested, accurately reflecting in their form the real confidence and courage of the mind that made them.

Human Perspectives Are Oriented by Attitudes

Gray's (1994) teaching is a good place to see how far we can go to strain personal attitudes out of analytic interventions. Gray alerts patients to moments when they are obviously using a motivated perception of the analyst as a disciplinarian or a bribed protector, in order to regulate their expression of impulse, especially aggression. During treatment, patients learn to pick out these inhibitory (or seductive) maneuvers from the smooth functioning of their customary equilibrium, and they learn to make their impulse and their worry into objects of attention. Patients are encouraged to tear themselves away from their ordinary equilibrium and see their mind almost as though it were a balancing *mechanism*. In this way, patients objectivize their strategies, and they ultimately see their concerns as features of their mind's operation. As much as possible, Gray avoids reflecting dramatic, moral, and elaborately descriptive attitudes toward his patient, so as not to encourage reciprocal views of himself that are shaped by transference wishes; instead he encourages perspectives motivated by desire for autonomy. The kind of perspective that he encourages comes as close to "physicalish" objectivity as is possible.

But, as noted, nobody develops a purely theoretical sense of himself. It is not difficult to imagine "human" attitudes that characterize even the perspectives that Gray has generated. To begin with, a patient will have some individualized "take" on Gray's conspicuous refusal to court a customary attitude from his patient. Then the patient may come to recognize himself as an artist of pleasurably aggressive fantasies where previously he had sensed himself to be dangerous, devious, and insecure. With his new freedom, Gray's patient might romantically view himself as an amused sojourner in an overly compulsive society. He might see himself as braver than he thought he was; he would have to see himself as more honest than usual. Of course, on top of these especially Graysian attitudes, he might experience all the usual psychoanalytic attitudes: his life as a tragicomedy, himself an apt student of his analyst, and so forth. (We may assume that all these perspectives on himself are simultaneously perspectives on other persons, so that the patient will see more opportunities for satisfaction in his family and associates, if only in being freer around them.)

But the austere autonomy fostered by Gray's technique is not the only sort of motivation that can lead to abstraction. Any effort to *solve a problem*—for example, to solve a frustrating transference temptation—can reconfigure the field of action in a way that highlights new aspects. (The best illustration I know is French's [1958] sequence of increasingly daring dreams stimulated by transference temptations, and testifying to a gradually widening "integrative field.") For that reason, the analyst's refusal of social responsiveness can be expected to inspire an abstractive tendency in his patient.

What Is Common to the Gamut of Therapeutic Influences?

It is very hard for the modern analyst to ignore the multiplicity of forces at work in treatment. That is a source of more uneasiness than is usually acknowledged. When it is acknowledged, analysts sometimes feel they must give up their old theories of therapeutic action. But if we could legitimately describe treatment as the generation of attitudinal perspectives, we would no longer feel as miscellaneous in our work. Relationship factors and cognitive factors, specific and nonspecific influences would no longer seem so heterogenous, and insofar as heterogeneity makes us feel unprofessional, that would be welcome. (There are, of course, other reasons to worry about noninterpretive forces). If we think of situation, behavior, and interventions as all lying on a continuum of perspectival messages we might worry less about what has gone into a happy outcome of treatment. At one end of the continuum would be inadvertent, undefinable attitudes, including those that are communicated by the relationship structures built up between analyst and patient; at the other end would be the sharply defined and focused attitudes known as interpretations. All attitudes toward the patient are interpretations and all interpretations express attitudes.

Within this continuum, how would we describe the uniqueness of *analytic* interpretations? Psychoanalytic interpretations (1) are explicit, or, rather, as explicit as an attitude *can* be, and (2) wear their source on their sleeve, so they do not covertly smuggle perspectives as powerfully as do insidious attitudes. (Incidentally, it would be easy to imagine different schools of interpretation inspiring similar perspectives in a patient.) We would expect that the most useful perspectives in treatment would be those that explore areas of conflict and dysphoria, because a person in trouble is already in the market for additional attitudinal perspectives, and because a felt problem guarantees that an answering perspective will register as definitive (a good, Piagetian maxim, as well as good common sense).

To repeat, the analytic element in all these influences would be their *abstractive* tendency. The technical challenge would be to maximize the abstractive outcome, and that has always been the classic objective of analytic treatment.

Treatment as Abstraction and Object-Making

The act of abstracting from undiscriminated reality locates *objects* of attention. When all the many, competing, explicit and implicit theories of therapeutic action are surveyed, they are seen to refer in one way or another to an induced objectification of mind and its components. Sterba (1934) explicitly encouraged his patient to look at himself from the outside as the analyst does, abstracting his inner procedures from his overall negotiations with the analyst and thus objectifying his mind. Kris (1956) wrote that, "Self-observation, as autonomous function, tinged as it may be by both self-critical and self-loving components, is essentially characterized by its detachment, or, as one might say, by the individual's ability to achieve objectivity in his perceptions about himself (p. 267)." Kleinians (e. g., Caper, 1996) hope patients will disembed aspects of their mind from their representation of the analyst-parent, and thus distinguish their minds objectively from a perceived, interactive world. Strachey (1934, 1937) wanted the patient to identify with partial aspects of the analyst, to objectify his principles, rather than react to him as a person, and by that feat of abstraction to see himself more objectively. For Loewald (1960), analysis teaches patients how to recognize unformed potential as a source of more articulated definition: in other words, to recognize themselves as objects, with endless, unprobed possibilities. Kohut not only described maturation as a progressive abstraction of selfobject values (1977), but explicitly described analysis as a movement toward the objectification of one's self-experience (1984, p. 184ff). Gray (1994) makes an object of the mind and of the analytic process, encouraging the patient to view his relationship with the analyst objectively and deal with wishes as mental objects that he is free to examine and to play with. Schafer (1983) and Arlow (1969) lift out story-lines for the patient to look at objectively. Gill (1973, 1988) insisted that no feature of the analytic interaction should remain a part of the background, none spared the objectifying glare of a searching, many-sided, analytic examination. Fonagy (1991) proposes to teach patients to become aware of their minds as objects. In all of these divergent approaches, the patient is encouraged to move apart from himself in some way and experience himself objectively (which does not mean unfeelingly). It is the most prevalent image of the action of treatment. (I must acknowledge that it is not the only image. Two others are: the growth model, as found in Ferenczi and Rank [1925] and the disruption image, as in Brenner [1976]).

It is useful to look at those actions of a therapist (not just a psychoanalyst) that may inspire a patient's abstraction even though they are not, themselves, abstract statements. The simple repetition of a word taken from the patient's last comment, by detaching one element from the patient's flow of speech, may also detach one attitude from a conflicted amalgam. It may detach a more basic truth from its concealing trappings (Shapiro, 1989). Furthermore, it may detach the patient momentarily from the appeal he is making to the therapist. Even the mere presence of a central organizing principle around which the analyst's interventions cluster might subliminally give the patient a sense of unfulfilled potential (Loewald, 1960). All of these patient reactions would be acts of abstraction—abstraction prompted by the impact of the therapist's attitude or perspective, rather than by his propositional utterances.

An abstractive (self-objectivizing) attitude is fostered in patients by many aspects of the analyst's behavior. In general, the analyst's nonaffirmation of the patient's immediate sense of himself and evident appreciation of a deeper potential, shake the patient out of his taken-for-granted immersion in immediate experience and encourage him to abstract his wishes and assumptions. The result is a slightly more objectivized view of himself in action. Analysts also have other, more particular, attitudes that treat the patient *as though* he were a this or a that, and these have a similar abstracting, objectivizing tendency (Loewald, 1960; Friedman, 1988).

The Analyst's Subjectivity and Objectivity

In the previous section, I have argued that if the mind is an object, then a view of it will be a perspective on such an object. (That fits well with recent child studies showing that a child learns that he has a mind partly from his mother's perspectives on it.) I have sketched a range of perspectives, extending from limited views, at one extreme (which, by their nature, are less defined and less differentiated into thoughts, feelings, and perceptions) to coordinated perspectives at the other end that "feel out" the full roundedness of the object (which may be a feeling, the mind as a whole, or even, a collection of dramatic configurations). And I have referred to a variety of ways of communicating a perspective, ranging from declarative sentences to personal reactions, each with its own mixture of abstractions of quality.

I believe these considerations suggest a reformulation of the problem currently discussed as "the analyst's subjectivity." In ordinary language "subjective" and "objective" refer to the degree to which feelings are ingredient in a perception. But the type of data should not be confused with the way of handling them. (This point has been cogently argued by

Gabbard [1997], and Smith [1999].) Whether or not our feelings are involved, our attention always acts to abstract significance from a field. Attention singles out features of a something whether the something is our own response or a thing outside us that we are responding to. If we are being what is ordinarily called "objective," we might, for example, attend to stylistic aspects of a painting; if we are being what is ordinarily called "subjective," we might attend to aspects of our pleasure in the painting. In either case we can be more or less objective, in the strict sense.

When I say that a feature is abstracted from the unmarked flow of experience, I am referring to the way features are lifted out and given a detached prominence. Obviously, that sort of detachment does not mean "drained of feeling." Indeed, feeling is usually *heightened* when particular aspects of our perception are abstracted from their embeddedness in on-going experience. (That is one function of art.) I could have avoided this misunderstanding by referring, instead, to "symbolizing," which is the modern way of discussing the issue. The term, symbolization, has the virtue of suggesting an artist rather than a dull professor. The trouble is that it is all too easy to think of "symbols" as a clever code that allows us to "manipulate" the world or "communicate" with others. It is my impression (especially since philosophy's "linguistic turn") that the word, "symbol," distracts attention from the truly monumental *action* that the symbol crowns, which is the mental act of framing an aspect of an object of attention. Every degree of abstraction in the way one focuses attention is a step toward object-seeking. When I reflect on—or even become explicitly aware of—a feeling or an anxiety, I have seen it as an object. I can subsequently attribute that, in turn, to another object (e.g., myself, my mind, a fantasy), as one of its aspects. The more perspectives I have of something, and the more abstracted from its background (or symbolically worked over) it is, the more objective I am being. (In certain of its meanings, the unconscious is that part of experience that is not objective. See Freud's reference to words as the realm of relations.) Whatever hasn't been very much "handled" in this way is more or less imperceptibly blended in experience, and simply colors mental states and perception. That is as true of outside perception as of introspection. As I develop a sense of somebody's personhood I make a genuine object of him, as can be seen by the way he behaves in my dreams. (The more-and-less of this can be illustrated by Mary Main's [1995] Adult Attachment Interview.)

What, then, is "the analyst's subjectivity?" If it refers to what is going on inside him, then "the analyst's subjectivity" is on a par with the analyst's "biologicity." It is not by itself a problem or a limitation. It is the statement of a simple fact of his constitution. We all have a subjectivity. On top of that, we all have an objectivity since we are explicitly aware of various separated things. The analyst's objectivity is just as much a part of him as his subjectivity. Of course, neither "the analyst's subjectivity" nor "the analyst's objectivity" connotes "the analyst's accuracy."

Accuracy seems to be what the current debate is about, which is clearly a violent reaction to the naive certainty that firmed the hand of some earlier psychoanalysts. Thus, the practical question is really how accurate the analyst's objective judgements can be, both those bearing on his own subjectivity and on the patient's state. The concern has to do not with subjectivity but with judgement, specifically the inaccuracy of judgements about oneself and others. (Kant demonstrated that judgement is intrinsically tied to the notion of an object.) Moreover, the concern is not just about any inaccuracy (though philosophically considered, every inaccuracy might be said to arise from some unobjectivized "subjectivity") but specifically the analyst's failure to factor his own perspective bias into his objective judgement of his patient. Quite simply, "the subjectivity of the analyst" often means that when the analyst thinks he is being "objective" about his patient, his judgement is false because he hasn't been sufficiently "objective" about himself. Many theorists these days add that such is always bound to be the case because it is impossible to be objective about oneself and therefore about another.

One salutary effect of this nihilistic belief is to reduce an arrogance by which practitioners are inclined to (understandably) defend themselves while working in a vague domain. But we should also be grateful to the current skeptical critique for a larger service: Even if knowledge of others requires us to objectivize both our own perceptions and feelings, it is nevertheless true that objectivizing is always a matter of more-and-less (in psychoanalysis, as in all knowledge). In particular, the objectivizing of dramatically construed figures tends to be more limited than, for instance, the objectivizing of someone as a biological organism. A perspective on a biological organism implicitly calls for an unlimited number of companion perspectives, and that is not true of a dramatic construal. To be sure, good literature portrays a multidimensional scene, but even at its best, artistic perspectives must be finally limited to achieve a desired effect. Because we tend to view human life and action in a dramatic fashion, the perspectives we take on patients will also be at best only relatively free of that sort of bias, determined by the observer's life, by that part of his theory that spells out typical life dramas, and by his fantasies. In both the analyst's descriptions and the patient's introspection, there is always a characterized *person* who is being revealed. It is the purpose of the analyst's causal theory to interfere with this ordinary, characterizing human reaction, but causal theory can only interfere and never replace the human "take" on the patient and his situation.

The Analyst's Omnipresent Attitudes

Those who say that the analyst's subjectivity is ineradicable call our attention to the fact that what we radiate to a patient is just one or another perspective on their mind, their feelings, and so forth. In other words, to the extent that we are dealing with a person and not just a mind, we treat patients with perspective "takes" that are more and less embedded in figures of our own imagining. Because our vision of patients is personal (as it would not be, for example, of laboratory subjects), I think it is appropriate to call even our most austere professional actions "attitudes." This is without prejudice to the greater objectivity that some attitudes have in comparison with others by virtue of either (1) being more compatible with a greater number of other dimensions, or (2) being more weighted by a physicalish view of the patient's mind, as provided by the analyst's theory.

Although the analyst attempts to distract himself by his physicalish, causal theory, and succeeds more than his patient wishes, he is, nevertheless, always partly swayed by the personal, dramatic figure who is his companion for the hour. Therefore, patients correctly see us as reacting in attitudinal ways; that is, they see that a meaning in themselves has induced a certain reactive attitude in us. ("His attitude to me is such that my behavior has evoked this perspective in him.") Theorists who emphasize the limits of neutrality help us monitor events realistically, for if we think that the patient is reacting to disembodied information rather than to a human attitude we will be deceived about what happens next. What happens next will often depend on how the patient sees himself being fitted into the analyst's dramatic visualization which carries ethical connotations. That is true even when the dramatic message is very subtle. Patients vary, from time to time and among themselves, in how much they scan for the dramatic, ethical tinge in the analyst's viewpoint. Analysts have always wished patients to (partially) ignore the valuational implications of the analyst's view. (That is why Raphling [1995] had to remind analysts that they are always importing it.) But no matter how simply factual it may be, at the baseline, the analyst's communication always includes his *tendency* as a treater.

But it would be going too far to say that there is no significant difference in kind between various attitudes that the analyst may take. In fact, we are daily aware of the difference between, for example, esthetic and ethical attitudes, angry and admiring attitudes, scientific and impassioned attitudes, and so forth. We are routinely aware that some persons (especially those close to us) arouse a great variety of attitudes, while upon others (for example, hated political figures) we train a narrow, stereotyped perspective. In talking to patients we favor an attitude in which components have been abstracted and framed by reflection. That is what we call objective thinking.

Again, those more objective attitudes carry no guarantee that we are even roughly accurate; it is the *type* and not the accuracy that renders a perspective "objective." A more objective attitude is one that fits most easily with the largest number of other attitudes, a principle that the reader can confirm by turning his eye to a piece of furniture in the room. (With neither inanimate objects nor persons is it coherence per se that makes the perspectives useful; what makes the perspectives useful is the way they triangulate an object with expectable properties.)

The ultimate contextual embeddeness of everybody's individual experiences, however, is not the only issue. These days, emphasis on the analyst's subjectivity is blurred with two other issues. One is the postmodern denial that there is any object of knowledge to be objective about. The other arises from the novelty and fluidity of relationships, the analytic relationship included.

I believe that the postmodern critique should be detached from discussions of the analyst's subjectivity. Subjectivity and objectivity have meaning only within a world of objects. The origin and merit of "antiessentialist" theories require a different discussion—a discussion of logical rather than psychological problems.

A more relevant challenge is the second. It is argued that the patient's state is partly or wholly determined by the way the analyst reacts (the state is said to be "coconstructed") and so it cannot be the focus of the analyst's objective scrutiny. This view has the merit of highlighting the fluctuating nature of experience, and its continuous modification in self- and other-reflection. It must be remembered, however, that continuous reshuffling is not unique to an analytic relationship or, indeed, to interpersonal events in general. Even an isolated mind is continuously reflecting on itself, which means that it makes an object of itself and its manifestations. The human fate is to objectify oneself, but also to keep re-doing it. We continuously turn our scrutiny onto our own objectifications. (The development of this quality, as well as its variability, is the subject of recent child studies, see Fonagy [1995].) It could be said that a person is always coconstructing *himself*, were it not that this scants the great number of "collaborators" involved in internal review. The fact that we keep revising our perspectives does not mean that we have not focused, abstracted, selected, set against a background, and so forth. In the relationship of patient with analyst, both parties are continuously objectivizing each other's minds and feelings, then reacting to those perceptions, and doing it ever again. Part of the objective scene is the mutual impact that each is having on the other; it is an empirical (not a methodological) question how much of a patient's mentation endures throughout this slippery process as a characteristic of his mind, and how much of it is a novel emergence due to the momentary interaction. The analyst must scrutinize the interaction to make that judgement. There is no guarantee that he will judge accurately, but he cannot fail to judge, for people always monitor their interaction to determine what effect they are having on what preexisting state of their partner. In all cases, there is an "it" that the judgement bears on, and this is readily apparent in every analyst's report, irrespective of his philosophical embroidery. In fact, there may be many "its." The "it" may be what Ogden (1994) calls "the analytic third," the cooperative creation Winnicott describes, or a cocreated relationship, but an "it" is always there.

In a cocreated relationship, the parties mutually create a determinate relationship, and then explore it by means of their individual cognitive and behavioral perspectival manipulations; the manipulations then subtly change the relationship, and so on. At each moment, patient and analyst build and then modify a structure with real possibilities that objectively inhere within it. The structure of the relationship is a kind of grammar that acquires meaning in each of the participant's minds, some of it shared (through biological and social community) and some of it idiosyncratic. An anthropologist would make an "etic" analysis of the shifting structure, and an "emic" analysis of its shifting, shared meaning (Hymes, 1964). Each person's individual meanings affect the objective structure, of course, and thus affect the partner's sense of the relationship, but meanings do that through actions, usually subtle, and the ultimate meaning finally resides within each meaning-maker, either the individuals involved, or the inquiring onlooker, who might, for example, examine what is common in the ideas of both individuals. The observer of a psychoanalysis might conclude that the common ideas given to the common structure is that of physician caring for a patient, or, perhaps, is analogous to parents caring for children. Or, giving up on those comparisons, an observer might settle for a "thick description" of what is going on, a la Geertz (1983), hoping to give the uniqueness of the analytic structure some coherent familiarity. Durkheim's (1895) "social fact" is the unspoken unity which all these meanings reveal. The structure that is built, with all of its potential meanings, is an objective fact. The shared and unshared, conscious and unconscious meanings given to it by participants are perspectives on it, or attitudes toward it, and analysts would wish that those perspectives would include the sort that a relatively disinterested observer could take.

If "coconstruction" is more than a synonym for interaction, it risks presuming telepathy. Analysts have customarily worked to demonstrate that the relationship in which the patient feels himself situated is not cocreated. Analytic technique is an attempt to prevent a comfortably coconstructed mini-society from establishing itself, even while coconstructions (enactments) keep rising over the horizon. The hope is that the patient will abstract his own constructing perspectives away from the co-constructed event. (For this to be accomplished, it is not necessary that the patient believe the analyst to be a blank screen.) The process is parallel to what has been called the development of metacognition.

As mentioned, an abstractive (self-objectivizing) attitude is fostered in patients by many general aspects of the analyst's behavior besides his specific interpretations. In general, the analyst's nonaffirmation of the patient's immediate sense of himself, together with his evident appreciation of a deeper potential, tends to dislodge the patient from the taken-for-granted texture of the immediate experience and edges him toward abstracting from his wishes and assumptions into a slightly more objectivized view of himself in action. Other, more particular, but still subtle attitudes that treat the patient *as though* he were a this or a that have a similar abstracting, objectivizing tendency (Loewald, 1960; Friedman, 1988).

References

Arlow, J. (1969). Unconscious fantasy and disturbance of conscious experience. *Psychoanal. Quart.*, 38:1–27.

Austin, J. L. (1962). *How to Do Things with Words*. Cambridge. MA: Harvard University Press.

Bakhtin, M. M. (1981). Discourse in the novel. In *The Dialogic Imagination*, ed. M. Holquist. Austin: University of Texas Press, pp. 259–422.

Berger, P. & Luckmann, T. (1966). *The Social Construction of Reality*. Garden City, NY: Doubleday.

Brenner, C. (1976). *Psychoanalytic Technique and Psychic Conflict*. New York: International Universities Press.

Brenner, C. (1994). The mind as conflict and compromise formation. *J. Clin. Psychoanal.*, 3:473–488.

Bruner, J. (1990). *Acts of Meaning*. Cambridge, MA: Harvard University Press.

Burke, K. (1950). *A Rhetoric of Motives*. Berkeley: University of California Press.

Caper, R. (1996). Play, experimentation and creativity. *Internat. J. Psycho-Anal.*, 77:859–869.

Durkheim, E. (1895). *The Rules of Sociological Method*, tr. S. A. Solvay & J. H. Mueller. Chicago: University of Chicago Press, 1938.

Ferenczi, S. (1909). Introjection and transference. In: *Sex and Psycho-Analysis*, trans. E. Jones. London: Badger, 1916, pp. 35–93.

Ferenczi, S. & Rank, O. (1925). *The Development of Psycho-Analysis*, tr. C. Newton. New York: Nervous and Mental Diseases Publications.

Fonagy, P. (1991). Thinking about thinking: Some clinical and theoretical considerations in the treatment of a borderline patient. *Internat. J. Psycho-Anal.*, 72:1–18.

Fonagy, P., Steele, M., Steele, H., Leigh, T., Kennedy, R., Mattoon, G. & Target, M. (1995). Attachment, the reflective self, and borderline states: The predictive specificity of the adult attachment interview and pathological emotional development. In: *Attachment Theory,* ed. S. Goldberg, R. Muir & J. Kerr. Hillsdale, NJ: The Analytic Press, pp. 233–278.

French, T. (1958). *The Integration of Behavior, Vol 3*. Chicago: University of Chicago Press.

Freud, S. (1895). Studies on hysteria. *Standard Edition*, 2. London: Hogarth Press, 1955.

Freud, S. (1912). The dynamics of transference. *Standard Edition*, 12:97–108. London: Hogarth Press, 1958.

Freud, S. (1914). Remembering, repeating and working-through. *Standard Edition*, 12:147–156. London: Hogarth Press, 1958.

Freud, S. (1915). Observations on transference-love. *Standard Edition*, 12:159–171. London: Hogarth Press, 1958.

Friedman, L. (1988). *The Anatomy of Psychotherapy*. Hillsdale, NJ: The Analytic Press.

Friedman, L. (in press). The mapmaker's dilemma. *J. Amer. Psychoanal. Assn.*

Gabbard, G. (1997). A reconsideration of objectivity in the analyst. *Internat. J. Psycho-Anal.*, 78:15–26.

Geertz, C. (1983). *Local Knowledge*. New York: Basic Books.

Gill, M. M. (1973). Interaction and interpretation: Commentary on Morris Eagle's "Enactments, transference, and symptomatic cure." *Psychoanal. Dial.*, 3:111–122.

Gill, M. M. (1988). Converting psychotherapy into psychoanalysis. *Contemp. Psychoanal.*, 24:262–274.

Goffman, E. (1969). *Frame Analysis*. Boston: Northeastern University Press.

Goodman, N. (1978). *Ways of Worldmaking*. Indianapolis, IN: Hackett.

Gray, P. (1994). *The Ego and Analysis of Defence*. Northvale, NJ: Aronson.

Grice, P. (1989). *Studies in the Way of Words*. Cambridge, MA: Harvard University Press.

Hymes, D. (1964). *Language in Culture and Society*. NY: Harper & Row.

Kohut, H. (1977). *The Restoration of the Self*. New York: International Universities Press.

Kohut, H. (1984). *How Does Analysis Cure?* ed. A Goldberg & P. Stepansky. Chicago: University of Chicago Press.

Kris, E. (1956). On some vicissitudes of insight in psycho-analysis. *Internat. J. Psycho-Anal.*, 37:445–455.

Lakoff, G. & Johnson, M. (1980). *Metaphors We Live By*. Chicago: University of Chicago Press.

Loewald, H. (1960). On the therapeutic action of psycho-analysis. *Internat. J. Psycho-Anal.*, 41: 16–33.

Main, M. (1995). Recent studies in attachment. In: *Attachment Theory,* ed. S. Goldberg, J. Muir & J. Kerr. Hillsdale, NJ: The Analytic Press.

Margolis, H. (1987). *Patterns, Thinking, and Cognition*. Chicago: University of Chicago Press.

Morris, C. (1946). *Signs, Language and Behavior*. New York: Prentice-Hall.

Ogden, T. H. (1994). The analytic third: Working with intersubjective clinical facts. *Internat. J. Psychoanal.*, 75:3–19.

Pepper, C. S. (1942). *World Hypotheses*. Berkeley: University of California Press.

Piaget, J. (1962). *Play, Dreams and Imitation in Childhood*, tr. C. Cattegno & F. M. Hedyson. New York: W. W. Norton.

Piaget, J. (1967). *Six Psychological Studies*. New York: Random House.

Piaget, J. (1970). *Structuralism*. New York: Basic Books.

Piaget, J. (1976). *The Grasp of Consciousness: Action and Concept in the Young Child*, tr. S. Wedgewood. Cambridge: Harvard University Press.

Raphling, D. (1995). Interpretation and expectation: The anxiety of influence. *J. Amer. Psychoanal. Assn.*, 43:95–111.

Ricoeur, P. (1984). *Time and Narrative, Vol. 1*. Chicago: University of Chicago Press.

Ryle, G. (1949). *The Concept of Mind*. New York: Barnes & Noble.

Schafer, R. (1983). *The Analytic Attitude*. New York: Basic Books.

Shapiro, D. (1989). *Psychotherapy of Neurotic Character*. New York: Basic Books.

Shapiro, T. (1999). From Monologue to Dialogue: A Transition in Psychoanalytic Practice. The A. A. Brill Lecture. New York Psychoanalytic Society, November 30.

Smith, H. F. (1999). Subjectivity and objectivity in analytic listening. *J. Amer. Psychoanal. Assn.*, 47:465–484.

Spence, D. P. (1982). *Narrative Truth and Historical Truth: Meaning and Interpretation in Psychoanalysis*. New York: W. W. Norton.

Sterba, R. (1934). The fate of the ego in analytic therapy. *Internat. J. Psycho-Anal.*, 15:117–126.

Strachey, J. (1934). The nature of the therapeutic action of psycho-analysis. *Internat. J. Psycho-Anal.*, 15:127–159.

Strachey, J. (1937). Symposium on the therapeutic results of psycho-analysis. *Internat. J. Psycho-Anal.*, 18:139–145.

Vygotsky, L. S. (1978). *Mind and Society*, ed. M. Cole & V. John-Steiner. Cambridge, MA: Harvard University Press.

Waelder, R. (1934). The problem of freedom in psychoanalysis, and the problem of reality testing. In: *Psychoanalysis: Observation, Theory, Application*, ed. S. Guttman. New York: International Universities Press, 1976, pp. 101–120.

White, H. (1973). *Metahistory*. Baltimore, MD: Johns Hopkins University Press.

Wilson, A. & Weinstein, L. (1996). The transference and the zone of proximal development. *J. Amer. Psychoanal. Assn.*, 44:167–200.

Wittgenstein, L. (1958). *Philosophical Investigations*, ed. G. E. M. Anscombe. New York: Macmillan.

Psychoanalysis as a One-Person and a Two-Person Psychology

Chapter 8

The One-Person–Two-Person Controversy: A View from the Future

Theodore J. Jacobs

Editors' Introduction: *Many of Jacobs's ideas are in agreement with those of Gill on the nature of the therapeutic action of psychoanalysis. Thus, like Gill, Jacobs discusses what he believes is the inevitability of a two-person perspective. He suggests that the power of a long, engaged interactive experience inevitably promotes reciprocal influences and transforms both participants, with, of course, the analysand showing the greater impact of change. Like many contemporary theoreticians addressing countertransference experiences, Jacobs describes the unavoidable unconscious affect that the analysand's psychic communications stir in the analyst, with the possibility that the analyst will unconsciously rework aspects of his or her own conflictual issues. Thus, he challenges those analysts who maintain a view of their objectivity in their interactions. (For contrasting positions, see Eagle, Friedman, Holt, and Kernberg in this book.)*

Through the use of a clinical example, Jacobs demonstrates how his patient illuminated a countertransference reaction. He describes the intermingling of the analyst's psychic inhibitions and his analysand's own conflicts thereby potentiating an impasse. Such deadlocks are circumvented by the analyst's pursuit of the patient's view. This view of the mutual shaping of the transference-countertransference interaction is what Gill was highlighting.

Jacobs's position, however, is different from Gill's and especially Hoffman's constructivist view which Gill adopted on at least the following isssue. From within Gill's framework, the use of a two-person perspective promotes the idea that both patient and analyst are guided by unconscious and conscious perspectival positions which constantly shape and influence each's understanding of the discourse. Meanings are always

> *being constructed and superseded by new understanding. Thus, the analyst is not in a unique position to understand that no enactment is taking place. Jacobs believes that enactments are not on-going and inadvertent. He believes that enactments occur when the analyst is unaware of his own conflicts. Thus, from Jacob's perspective, the analysis may proceed apace until something in the patient's dynamics reverberates within the psychic life of the analyst. If the analyst does not recognize the critical and reciprocal unconscious interplay, a stalemate results. From Gill's outlook such a position minimized the constant presence of unconscious resistances within the analyst as well as within the patient. It reduces, as well, the recognition of the inherent ambiguity of communications, thereby constraining what an analyst can understand about the dyadic interaction.*

My paper begins with a conversation which, though imaginary, might well take place in the future. The time is the last decade of the 21st century. Two historians of psychoanalysis are talking in the large office they share. Each is named Peter and each is descended from distinguished psychoanalytic forebears. The first chap, Peter Gay IV, is in a state of excitement to which more than a dash of incredulity has been added.

"This is amazing, Pete," he says to his colleague, Peter Loewenberg V. "You'll never guess what I found in this stack of old programs from meetings of the American Psychoanalytic Association."

"Well, let's see. From the tone of your voice, it has to be something that has knocked your space socks off. A reference to Jung, maybe, or a mention of Harry Stack Sullivan."

"Nothing that far out. Or, I should say, far out in a different way. Take a look at the panels they held at the end of the last century. At one meeting there actually was a panel with the title, 'What Do We Mean by a One-Person or a Two-Person Psychology?' Can you imagine that? Would you believe that at that time, less than a hundred years ago, these characters were still fussing over the one-person–two-person psychology issue?"

"You're joking? After the Renik revolution?"

"Apparently so. I guess it was a rule in those days never to decide anything. Never come to a conclusion. And, especially important, never agree on anything having to do with the analytic process."

"But in this case, what was there to disagree about? By then the evidence was in. I didn't think at that time you could still find an analyst who believed analysis is a one-person psychology, not even among the diehards at the old-line institutes."

"It seems there were some holdouts among the classicists. That is particularly interesting since Freud (1912) himself had such a keen appreciation of the fact that unconscious messages are regularly transmitted between patient and analyst. His use of the famous telephone metaphor shows clearly that he recognized that unconscious communication in analysis is a two-way street."

"Yes. And what about his views on countertransference? Anyone who says no analysis can proceed farther than the countertransference permits is making a pretty profound statement about the potential impact on the patient of the analyst's unconsciously transmitted conflicts. From early on, he recognized that transferences operating in two directions are central to all that happens in the analytic encounter."

"Yes, and just think of all the subsequent work that expanded and elaborated Freud's early insights in this area. By the year 2000, not only had intersubjectivists like Stolorow and analysts in the British school been writing about the two-person psychology idea for years, but a number of classically trained analysts like Poland (1988), Schwaber (1983), Boesky (1990), Renik (1992), McLaughlin (1981), and others had utilized clinical material to demonstrate the interplay between the psychologies of patient and analyst and their effect on the analytic process. So what more was there to say on the matter? Why in the devil did they schedule panels on nonissues?"

"Beats me. But from going over old programs, I've discovered that analysts in those days liked to hear the same issues debated year after year. In this case, though, the panel may have needed to cover old ground in order to help their colleagues assimilate a perspective that, for many of them, was quite different from what they'd been taught."

"That's possible, but I suspect that something else was going on here. If you look closely at the title of the panel that I mentioned, you get the idea that they weren't so much debating the issue as trying to clarify what people *meant* by these terms."

"What the terms meant? I wasn't aware there was any confusion about that."

"But there was. In the 1990s factionalism had developed even between those who endorsed the basic idea of a two-person psychology, not to mention those who opposed it. Jacobs (1991) and Hoffman (1991), for instance, could speak about a two-person psychology and about the impact of patient and analyst on each other and be thinking about such transactions very differently. In fact, they had quite different views of the analytic process and of the way in which the interactions of patient and analyst are best understood and utilized. As far as I can tell from Hoffman's writings, for instance, he believed that analysis is something that is created or constructed between two people. There is no one-person psychology. It is always a matter of two minds at work building something together. Jacobs had a different view. I have some notes from that panel and I gather from what he said then that he thought that analysis was a one-person *and* a two-person psychology."

"That sounds like him. As lucid as a block of granite. In fact, trying to figure out what Jacobs said must have been a little like trying to puzzle out a verbal crosstic."

Here the record breaks off, leaving me concerned that as a result, I may come across to the reader about as plainly as Casey Stengel quoting scripture. So for the sake of clarity and to avoid being labeled in the future as an analyst who expressed himself in Stengelese, I will explain how I view the one-person–two-person issue and what I have in mind when I say, for me, analysis is inevitably both a one-person and a two-person psychology.

Let's go back to the beginning. Although, as we know, the psychoanalytic relationship is a unique one, it nevertheless shares with other human relationships certain common features. Among these are the inevitable influences on one another that two individuals have when placed in close proximity for lengthy periods of time, one person revealing his innermost self, the other being an empathic listener. Communicating through multiple channels—word and deed, posture and gesture, tone, phrasing, and affect—these individuals send messages to one another that stir memories, stimulate fantasies, and arouse strong and often conflictual feelings. By means of projective and introjective mechanisms and through unconscious processes of identification, as well as through insight and the reworking of old conflicts, each partner in analysis is affected, each is altered. Of course, it is the patient who undergoes most change. It is he or she who is the focus of the work and is chief beneficiary of the insights gained and the conflicts worked through. But unless the analyst is affectively removed and is operating in an insular and detached way, he or she, too, is altered. The inevitable arousal of strong countertransference feelings, and the reactivation of old issues and old conflicts contained within them, provides a fresh opportunity for their confrontation and mastery. By immersing himself in the inner world of his patients, the analyst engages himself, comes in touch once again with bits and pieces of his own history, and in a silent, often unconscious way, continues the process of working through. If the analyst remains untouched by his patient and unaffected by their work together, one might well question what kind of analytic engagement has taken place.

Although the idea that unconscious communication between the minds of patient and analyst is an integral part of analytic work, a notion articulated by Freud and almost as old as analysis itself, it was not until about 15 years ago that the issue came to the fore in America as one that deserved serious investigation. Since that time, a number of colleagues have explored this phenomenon, identified the often subtle ways in which unconscious transmissions take place in analysis, and assessed their impact on the analytic process. In the vanguard of this effort have been Schwaber (1983), McLaughlin (1981), and Poland (1988), who, along with the other colleagues mentioned by our future historians, have demonstrated clinically how the metacommunications, or unconsciously transmitted messages that flow beneath the surface of analytic dialogue, affect not only the transference-countertransference interactions and the emerging material, but the course and outcome of the analytic work.

Although, to many of us, this work seems convincing and supports the early findings of Gill (1982) that clearly demonstrated that patients' associations are regularly influenced by, and contain concealed references to, their perceptions of the analyst, still some distinguished colleagues oppose this view. They maintain that in a well-conducted analysis, with a well-trained and well-analyzed analyst, the analyst's subjective experiences will have little, if any, influence on the analytic material or on the ongoing analytic work. These colleagues also hold fast both to the idea of the objective analyst whose mind operates essentially as a recording and decoding instrument, and to a view of analysis as a one-person psychology. For them, it is the patient's psychology that is—and should be—the prime, if not the sole, focus of the analyst's attention. Apart from obvious countertransference responses, which clearly require correction, the analyst's psychology makes no significant contribution to the patients' associations, which arrive quite exclusively from inner conflict.

While all of us have seen patients whose associations seem to derive almost entirely from this source—patients who are so preoccupied with their own struggles that the analyst's subjective responses seem to have little impact on the material—in my experience such individuals are exceptions to a general rule. But it is not entirely clear that they *are* exceptions. Their apparent failure to register the analyst's subjectivity may, in fact, not constitute a true absence, not a true nonregistration, but a defensive need to deny and ward off certain communications from the analyst and perceived aspects of his psychology.

In most patients, however, it is not difficult to detect the influence on their thoughts and fantasies of their perceptions of the analyst and of the unconscious communications that pass between them. I will illustrate this phenomenon with several clinical vignettes.

Some years ago, I was working with a young comedian whose keenness of perception and ability to pick up subtle communications from others contributed to his gift as a comic. At one point in our sessions, feeling frustrated when I did not offer an opinion on a dispute he had with his manager, Mr. K turned around on the couch, looked back at me, and said reassuringly, "You don't really have to worry. Daddy is not looking over your shoulder. Just this once you can let go and say what you really think."

This comment, really an interpretation, had a profound effect on me. Resonating in my thoughts and dreams, it stirred deep feelings within me and served as a catalyst to self examination and to reflection on my way of working with this patient. An unusually perceptive individual who had an uncanny ability to pick up unconscious cues transmitted by others, he perceived that in working with him I was under constraint. It was as if someone were watching me, looking over my shoulder and, out of anxiety that I would be criticized for deviating from accepted technique, I self-consciously hewed a proper analytic line.

In fact, there was truth in this observation. Mr. K's comment brought home to me something I also sensed in myself, but had not focused on: my behavior with him was more restrained, more formal, and more measured than was usual for me. It was not that I was a silent or removed analyst. With this patient that would have been quite impossible. But quite deliberately I tried to adhere to the time-honored principles of neutrality, anonymity, and measured abstinence. I kept distance not because I disliked Mr. K. Quite the opposite. I enjoyed being with him, admired his gifts, and found myself tempted to slip into the role of appreciative audience for the on-the-couch performances that characterized his style. It was, in fact, partly because I enjoyed and liked him so much that I held back, quite aware that he was using his talent as a resistance and was seeking, defensively, to use humor and "schtick" to divert us from the task at hand.

As I listened to Mr. K, I was, in fact, aware of "Daddy" looking over my shoulder in the form of supervisors, teachers, and analysts, all authority figures urging me to hold the line and maintain a proper and neutral analytic stance, voices that reinforced my own natural work inclinations. Moreover, at that time, I was presenting this case to a seminar on technique in which a mentor, a renowned classical analyst, participated. Often during sessions with Mr. K, I was cognizant of this senior colleague metaphorically looking over my shoulder, ready to censure me should I depart from correct and quite traditional analytic technique.

There were other personal factors, too, that influenced my responses to Mr. K. As a boy, I often experienced fear of my father who, not infrequently, lost his temper in ways that I found quite threatening. Much of my behavior—especially my interactions with my mother—was influenced by thoughts of him and how he might respond to what I was doing or not doing. In a sense, then, he was always looking over my shoulder, as later I experienced my teachers and supervisors to be doing. My anxiety about displeasing and possibly alienating these authorities, which clearly had oedipal roots, was augmented by my own concealed aggression toward them and by a wish to rebel against their authority.

These conflicts were at the root of certain inhibitions in myself which, in part, I experienced as coming from restraints placed on me by these vigilant authorities. Thus, for me, the idea of daddy watching over my shoulder was powerful and condensed a variety of elements: thoughts, fantasies, projections, reactivated anxieties, and memories of actual experiences. My work with Mr. K had brought out and magnified these aspects of my psychology and somehow, through style and manner, I had communicated them to him. With his sensitivity, my patient had picked them up and, in his usual satiric and gently mocking way with underlying seriousness, he had interpreted my difficulties to me.

On his side, Mr. K's response to my way of working also evoked strong memories and resonated with certain important experiences of his own. His mother, who was raised, and remained, strongly influenced by a strict, puritanical father, was herself something of a martinet. She demanded total obedience from her son. Chafing under his yoke, the boy often thought if only his mother could shed the influence of her father, who seemed omnipresent, she might become the relaxed and loving parent he craved.

Thus, Mr. K's perception of me as too tight, too controlled in my interactions with him resonated with memories of his mother and evoked strong feelings in him. But, like me, Mr. K also concealed from himself certain character traits—like a certain stubbornness and rigidity of his own—that developed as an identification with his mother. These he experienced as coming quite exclusively from me.

Both of us, then, brought to the treatment our own inner world of memories, fantasies, and defenses, some of which we projected onto the other. In the crucible of the treatment situation, these worlds fused and mixed, forming transference-countertransference interactions that were the product both of our histories and of our current responses to one another. It was through tuning in on my own rather constricted way of working with K, an insight he helped me attain, that I could begin to explore not only the personal roots of the restrictions in myself affecting the treatment, but also a certain quality in K that contributed to my reactions. This was a hidden aggression, a subtly conveyed hostility representing an unconscious identification with his severe mother. It was through accessing my own responses to this trait of K's that I could, through interpretation, help him come in touch with this warded-off, though covertly expressed and highly significant, aspect of his character.

In another clinical situation it was not only the interplay of transferences that proved important, but also the reawakening of memories in patient and analyst that interacted in ways that affected the course and outcome of the treatment.

Some years ago, after I had finished my residency and had just entered practice, I received a most welcome phone call. A highly respected and much admired teacher of mine was on the line.

"I've got a great case for you," he exclaimed in his typical enthusiastic, high-energy manner. "Just up your alley. A remarkable lady; a poet, teacher, scholar, and wit. I've spent two delightful hours in consultation with her. She's fascinating, has neurotic hangups, and was in a bad treatment that ended abruptly. She's ready for something good this time around. I've told her all about you and she's anxious to meet you and to get started. She can't pay a whole lot, but listen, this is a terrific case. I'd take her myself if I had time."

"Well okay, I'd be interested. You say she's neurotic? What problems is she having?

"Depression mostly. There's a lot of repressed anger and some self-destructive fantasies, but nothing unworkable. I have no doubt you can help her. In fact, you two should get on famously."

You can imagine the excitement I felt when I hung up. I had gotten a great referral and a vote of confidence from a highly valued teacher. I was walking on air and was looking forward with high expectation to meeting this remarkable woman; a patient who, incidentally, would constitute the first bona fide neurotic case in my fledgling practice. My fantasies about the patient were further aroused by my speaking to her on the phone. She had an attractive voice, soft and resonant, and was clearly a cultured and intelligent person. I had visions of a young Mary McCarthy, or, if it were true that she suffered from longstanding depression, a Virginia Wolff-type whose tragic fate I could prevent by means of my effective, deeply empathic treatment.

The patient I encountered in the waiting room resembled neither of these literary ladies. Sighting the large and imposing figure perusing my bookshelf with what I took to be an expression of amused disdain, I had to fight off the flood of memories of disappointing blind dates. The patient turned, looked at me quizzically, and waited for me to speak. I imagined the disappointment was mutual. Trying to compose myself, I smiled and looked as welcoming as I could.

"Ms. S, I'm Dr. Jacobs," I said pleasantly. Apparently my bright tone did not conceal my true feelings.

"Who did you expect," she asked, "Catherine Deneuve?"

Not being a foreign-film buff at the time, I had only the vaguest idea of whom she meant, but I covered up my ignorance.

"Actually, Dr. Y told me a good deal about you," I put in quickly. "Won't you come in?

Slowly and quite reluctantly, she entered the office and sat on the edge of the patient's chair, looking distinctly unhappy.

"I thought you'd be a good deal older," she remarked, "not someone just out of school."

"You had some idea of me in mind then," I replied, trying, as I had been taught, to explore the inner world of fantasy.

"Actually, I did," Ms. S said. "I imagined, since you were recommended by Dr. Y, you might look like one of Freud's younger colleagues, perhaps Rank or Abraham."

I knew then that I was in big trouble. This lady knew more about Freud's inner circle than I did. Although I had heard the names of these early analysts, at that point, I knew very little about them. In fact, on that score they were pretty much in the same boat as Catherine Deneuve.

I looked at this new patient sitting across from me and I felt tense and anxious. What was I to do with this formidable Freudian scholar who promised to be a lot more, as well as less, than I bargained for? Ms. S stared back at me as though I still had a face full of acne. I imagined that she was thinking of me as the analytic equivalent of Andy Hardy or Henry Aldrich, a disconcertingly pubescent therapist.

Clearly, Ms. S and I were unhappy with each other. Although there was a good deal more to it, initially my disappointment had to do with the disparity between the patient whom I expected and the patient who arrived in my office. Ms. S was not the ideal patient of my imagination, and it took some time for me to sort out the personal elements concerning my wish for a particular kind of woman in my life, which had suffused my initial perceptions of her. Ms. S's disappointment, I came to understand, was connected with certain experiences both of the recent and more remote past. Although for quite some time she said nothing about it, the combination and sequence of recent events in Ms. S's life, including the abrupt ending of her prior therapy, the consultation with Dr. Y, and the referral to me, stirred up a host of memories that colored her initial responses to me and nearly capsized the treatment.

Ms. S was the daughter of a ne'er-do-well father, a compulsive gambler, who abandoned the family when the patient was 18 months old. Being married and supporting a child, he decided, was not for him. Although there were occasional post cards from places like Las Vegas and Tahoe, Ms. S saw her father only once more. A brief visit was arranged when she was eight years old. In her mother's eyes the father was a pariah, the devil incarnate, who had wreaked havoc on the family. Ms. S was not to think about him or even to mention his name.

Under these circumstances, the girl did as she was told. She suppressed all thoughts about her father, including the wish that he return one day, and instead turned for love and support to her stepfather, a clever, outgoing, successful businessman. Although he possessed much in the way of charm and charisma, the stepfather was actually a vain, self-involved individual who avoided intimacy and related to Ms. S in a cool, arms-length manner. Not understanding his need to maintain distance, she experienced his behavior as a painful rejection.

The one male with whom she had close ties, and highly ambivalent ones at that, was a brother four years younger than herself. The project of her mother's second marriage, this boy was the golden child, the son who carried the hopes of the family. He was designated to become a shining star, perhaps a noted physician or scientist, while Ms. S was regarded as a nice but undistinguished girl from whom little could be expected. D, the brother, was sent to a prestigious prep school and an Ivy League college, while Ms. S went to the local high school and a nearby branch of the State University.

In childhood, and for years thereafter, Ms. S was consumed by feelings of resentment toward, and envy of, her brother. There was little she did in life that she did not compare with his achievements. Listening to her, one had the impression she was obsessed by such comparisons.

From the first session, it became clear that a brother transference would be a central feature of the treatment. What I did not realize then was that the sister-brother scenario that was to unfold was a multifaceted one involving not only aspects of Ms. S's history, but of mine as well.

Ms. S's therapist had decided to retire from practice on rather short notice. For Ms. S, his abrupt departure had stirred memories of her father's sudden abandonment, and she handled the current loss as she did the earlier one, by suppressing her loving feelings and focusing on the negative ones. Her therapist was dull, predictable, and not very intelligent, she claimed. She had learned little from him and was not sorry to see him go. The deep attachment that she had to this man, an attachment that surfaced only gradually in treatment, was denied and initially was not available in consciousness.

To Dr. Y, my old teacher, Ms. S reacted as she did to her stepfather. She viewed him as the same kind of man: successful, personable, and outwardly friendly, but ultimately rejecting. She felt hurt and put down when he sent her away. In typical fashion, however, she kept those feelings to herself.

In Ms. S's mind I was immediately linked with her younger brother, the golden boy who was Dr. Y's protégé and his favorite son. I was the privileged one who, given every advantage, had become a doctor and believed myself superior to her. From the opening gun she wanted to show me up, defeat me, and thereby prove she was not only my equal, but, in fact, had more ability and a keener intelligence than I. At the same time, she experienced guilt over these feelings and was plagued by the idea that in our relationship her rightful place was to remain behind me and in my shadow.

From the first, then, emotionally laden memories and predetermined patterns of responses triggered by the ending of Ms. S's treatment, the consultation with Dr. Y, and his referral of her to me dominated her thinking, led her to be wary of me, and made anything more than superficial collaboration difficult to achieve. But she was not the only one who was influenced by such forces. I, too, was under the sway of certain memories, expectations, and pre-set ideas.

To begin with, my reaction to Dr. Y, the referring analyst, was complicated. As I mentioned, I had always admired him for his charisma, his wide-ranging knowledge, and his remarkable energy. In that respect, he was quite unlike my own father who, often depressed, lacked this vibrant quality. For me, Dr. Y became the father I had always wanted but did not have. I wished, therefore, to please him, to do well with the patient he had sent me, and to prove that I was worthy of his respect. On the other hand, I found myself angry with Dr. Y for what I regarded as a misrepresentation of Ms. S. He had, I thought, sold this patient to me and was not entirely honest in doing so. As it happened, my father was also in sales and, when the spirit moved him, he could be an effective salesman. On more than one occasion, he broke promises to take me places; after a while, I became suspect of his promises.

Dr. Y's behavior in promising, but not delivering, the wonderful case he described must have played into memories of this aspect of my father's behavior and caused me to react, as I had done in childhood, with resentment and a wish to strike back at the man who had deceived me. In this situation, that meant an unconscious wish on my part not to please Dr. Y and not to do what he wanted. Since, clearly, his wish was for me to do a sterling job in treating Ms. S, the mix of reactions I had toward Dr. Y complicated the response I had to the patient and affected the development of my collaboration with her. How often does it happen that our initial reactions to patients, and perhaps even our more enduring ones, are colored by our relationship with the referring source? This factor, I believe, can exert an important influence on the beginning phase and, indeed, on the entire course of treatment.

It happened, too, that just as Ms. S. was an older sister to a younger brother, I am a younger brother who has an older sister. As was true in Ms. S's family, the boys in our family were given certain advantage. Like D, I went to a private school and an Ivy League college, while my sister attended local schools. As was true in Ms. S's situation, more was expected of me and my brother than of my sister. Thus, Ms. S's history reverberated in important ways with my own and stirred reactions in me that I had kept at bay for some time.

As a result of old feelings of guilt newly aroused from the outset of treatment, I found myself in quite total sympathy with my patient's view of her own life. She had gotten a raw deal, she believed, and her resentment and rage were fully justified. She was the victim of discrimination, her life was decisively affected by this fact, and her present unhappiness was directly traceable to this state of affairs. She sought, and was entitled to, reparations.

While, of course, there was much truth in this view, it did not represent the whole story. A great many other factors, including the way Ms. S reacted to her own wishes and fantasies, clearly played important roles in her difficulties. Under the sway of unconscious guilt feelings aroused by Ms. S's story and a rapidly developing transference to her as my older sister, I initially identified so closely (and defensively, I suspect) with her position that it was difficult for me to assume a sufficiently objective stance in my work with her.

At the same time, I found myself responding to my patient's competitive remarks, especially to her put-downs, with a wish to join the fray and defeat her. Whenever my sister competed with me, my tendency was to assert myself, win the competition, and maintain the natural order of things; that is, with me, the first-born son, as the cock of the walk. It took some errors in Ms. S's case, including falling into a couple of unproductive skirmishes with her, for me to get a handle on the problem and recognize how easily I could slip into enactments related to an old scenario.

One might say that this was an extraordinary situation; rare parallels existed in the life circumstances of patient and analyst. This coincidence put a particular spin on treatment, stimulating transferences in both of us that were unusually rapid and intense.

It is also true, however, that this case is not quite as unique as it may seem. Parallels in the lives of patient and analyst, especially in the sharing of certain psychological experiences, are not so rare. In my work, at least, I find much in the inner worlds of my patients that resonates meaningfully with what I have known and experienced. Sometimes in our ways of thinking and responding, rather than in actual experiences, significant sharing occurs. Unless our self-scanning efforts pick up these less obvious similarities between ourselves and our patients, they may lead to bits and pieces of acting out based on unconscious identifications. Often, such behavior occurs early in treatment before we can develop a fuller understanding of our patients' psychology and the way in which it resonates with our own. While sometimes the analyst's actions being in tune with particular wishes or needs of the patient have the effect of strengthening the alliance and promoting the development of genuine collaboration. Other times, they unwittingly undermine the possibilities for such rapport. In the case of Ms. S, if earlier on I had been aware of the long-forgotten piece of my history that was enacted with her, perhaps I would have avoided the problems caused both by my initial disappointment in Ms. S and, later, my putting too much weight on the realities of her early life and, especially, on the childhood inequities. While, assuredly, these were important in her development, equally important were her longstanding rivalrous and hostile fantasies and guilt feelings that she harbored for so long a time.

Colleagues like Robert Stolorow, who represent the intersubjective point of view, emphasize that in analysis two personalities, two worlds, two life stories inevitably collide and affect each other. In this, I believe, they are correct. In a truly engaged analysis, how could it be otherwise? In his book *Self Inquiry*, Gardner (1983), a classically trained Freudian analyst not part of the intersubjective school, clearly demonstrated the analyst with motivation and talent to explore his own inner experiences while analyzing will discover in himself memories that, resonating with those of the patient, will connect with and illuminate the patient's associations. He, of course, will also discover experiences that are very different from those of the patient. Those differences, too, are useful as points of dysjunction that help the analyst maintain a therapeutic distance; that is, sufficient distance and perspective to analyze rather than be caught up in an unconscious identification with his patient. In both instances, however, it is the collision of two individuals, two lives, two inner worlds, that stimulates the memories and fantasies in both that provide the raw material for effective analytic work.

This interaction of two lives is a viewpoint that some colleagues trained in the classical tradition have difficulty accepting. They see the intersubjective dimension of analysis much as they saw the interpersonal school 30 years ago; that is, as a superficial approach that avoids infantile sexuality and the drives and seeks to cure, as Ferenczi (1919) did, not through insight, but by providing a substitute healing relationship for the inadequate ones of early childhood.

Such a view—I heard it expressed recently by a distinguished colleague—demonstrates how very hard it is for us to give up long-held attitudes, those to which we are tied by bonds of loyalty to past teachers and mentors. Modern ideas about interaction and communication between patient and analyst, in fact, share little with Ferenczi's formulations. Rarely in the current literature on intersubjectivity and the dyadic aspects of the analytic situation do we encounter the naive belief, held by Ferenczi, that neuroses can be effectively treated by means of a compensatory relationship. Rather, the complex transference-countertransference interactions that develop between patient and analyst, including the covert communications that pass between them and the subjective experiences of the analyst, are used as data that help uncover and elucidate the inner world of the patient. At times only such material provides insights into that world.

An example I have cited elsewhere (Jacobs, 1991) illustrates how subtle communications transmitted between patient and analyst, as well as enduring identifications enacted in treatment, can affect the course of analysis. In this case, it was the decision to terminate—which to me seems particularly subject to enactments of unconscious motives—that was affected by what was transpiring between Mr. G and myself.

For eight years, analytic work with this patient, an anxious and quite obsessional man, had proceeded extremely slowly. On one occasion I had the image of two alligators attempting to swim through molasses. Small gains were evident from year to year until, in the ninth year of treatment, progress stopped—or seemed to. For weeks on end, we covered the same ground without anything new. After a time, the patient brought up the idea of ending, which surprised me because he never initiated anything, especially the ending of relationships. Termination seemed reasonable, however, in light of what was happening, and I very nearly agreed to setting a termination date. On the face of it, it would have been quite a reasonable decision.

But something did not seem quite right. As I later learned, Mr. G had picked up my feelings of frustration and the fact that I had begun to withdraw emotionally from him. Very sensitive to slights and rejections, he had launched a preemptory strike by proposing to end.

What was transpiring between us was of the greatest importance. Our interaction contained a good deal of my patient's neurosis—and a good deal of mine. Dealing with these feelings opened up a new pathway for us. Meaningful work could be done, not only on this issue, but on the source of the stalemate, which was also related to Mr. G's tenacious defenses against his growing wish for my love, and my reaction to his keeping me at so great a distance. We continued treatment for two more years and these turned out to be the two most productive years of the analysis.

Of particular interest in this case is that, unknown to me, my behavior was influenced by something my analyst had said some years before. At that time, long after my analysis had ended, he was the discussant at a case conference involving a lengthy, but stalemated, analysis.

"If you have not broken through after nine years of treatment," I recall him saying, "perhaps you should acknowledge that further progress is unlikely."

It was in the ninth year of the analysis that I found my doubts about the treatment increasing. For reasons not clear to me then, I experienced more frustration and became less hopeful about the outcome. No doubt this attitude, communicated to my patient and leading to emotional withdrawal on my part, was largely responsible for his wish to end the analysis. My recollection of the conference involving my former analyst, which arose suddenly one day as we were discussing termination, was a clue to important transactions that were taking place between Mr. G and myself. I realized my identification with my analyst carried within it a longstanding wish for his love and approval. It was just this kind of yearning, increased by my subtle withdrawal from him, that my patient was protecting himself against through the use of rigid defenses, defenses that I found off-putting and which I responded to by pulling back.

As important as the interplay between patient and analyst is, however, it is neither sufficient nor accurate to say the analytic process can be defined in terms of interaction or that the heart of the process lies in the illumination of interaction. There is no question this aspect of analysis deserves our most careful attention. In fact, progress in our field in the last decade or so has come in no small measure from our greater understanding of the often indirect and subtle way in which the transactions between patients and analysts are communicated. But to make the interplay between patient and analyst the central focus of analysis and material derived from this source the prime data to understand our patients is to overlook two points. First, such interactions often serve the purpose of resistance on both sides of the couch. Second, in any case, our aim is—or should be—to employ interactions not as ends in themselves, but as a means of accessing and exploring the patient's unconscious conflicts and fantasies.

It is also true, as Hoffman (1991) and others have said, that much is forged, much is created in analysis. Our insights and interpretations are, in a very real sense, creations. To understand our patients' communications, we subject them to complex mental processes within ourselves, which involve thoughts, fantasies, memories, intuition, logic, and the integration of these diverse elements. The end product, insight, is thus a compromise formation in that it unconsciously draws on and combines these elements, fusing them into an interpretation that can be conveyed to the patient.

Our interpretations, however, are not facts in the sense of scientific truths, but our best guesses. What they guess at, and thereby seek to illuminate, however, are truths of another kind—psychological truths buried in our patients' psyches.

Some colleagues today claim there is no such thing as psychological truth. They do not believe that our patients carry within them longstanding preset fantasies and conflicts. Or, if they allow that these exist, they maintain the fantasies and conflicts can neither be recovered in analysis nor their meanings to the patient understood. For them, truth, insofar as one can speak of it as a psychological concept, is created by the joint efforts of patients and analysts. The same with meaning: it is created, not discovered.

To me, this view fails to account for the fact that identifiable conflicts and fantasies have existed within our patients since earliest childhood; because these longstanding conflicts have caused much suffering they have sought our help. Patients harbor fantasies and beliefs that constitute their psychological truths, originally developed independent of us, these key ideas which motivate behavior can nevertheless be understood, in part, through the vicissitudes of the transference-countertransference relationship.

It is true, patient and analyst forge understandings to which both can subscribe. These insights, or best guesses, are not ends, the ultimate way of understanding the patient's inner life, but searchlights that seek out and illuminate childhood fantasies and beliefs that lie at the root of our patients' conflicts. Sometimes, with the help of such illuminations, these conflicts become clearly visible. Other times, we can obtain only a glimpse of them. They continue, however, to exist as powerful forces in our patients' lives, and a central part of our work is to cast as much light as we can on them.

While it is undoubtedly true that two lives, two histories, two worlds inevitably mix and fuse in analytic work, each influencing the other, it is also true that the aim of this process is the in-depth understanding of only one mind, that of the patient. In the process of analyzing, of course, aspects of the analyst's psychology surface and can be usefully understood, but his mind is not the subject of the analysis. Nor can self-scrutiny on the part of the analyst, no matter how rigorously applied, provide a deep analytic experience. That experience belongs—and quite properly so—solely to the patient. It is his or her mind, his or her inner world, that is the territory we need to map and explore. In doing so, we use ourselves and our analytic instruments as valuable tools to assist in our exploration. From that perspective, analysis always involves two psychologies. That goes with the territory. But in the end, it is only one psychology, that of the patient, that is—or can be—thoroughly illuminated. From the point of view of the aims and goals of our work we can speak of psychoanalysis as a method whose essence is the exploration and understanding of the psychology of just one individual, the patient.

What I believe we have, then, in analytic work is both a two-person *and* a one-person psychology, the one used to illuminate the other. I believe our problem in resolving this issue lies not in genuine confusion over whether analysis is a one-person or a two-person psychology, but in our struggle with the kind of ghosts my comedian patient perceived in his analyst, the ghosts of former teachers, supervisors, analysts, and, in fact, Freud himself who command our loyalties and our adherence to their views. Whether we find ourselves pulled to adopt the traditional stance they advocated or impelled to react against it, the influence of these ghosts lives within all of us, blinding us to certain evident facts and causing us to make artificial and divisive choices between views of the analytic process that are not in opposition.

On the contrary, one-person and two-person psychology are parts of the truth, parts of a whole that, unfortunately, has become divided and fragmented by our need to see matters in accordance with our preset conceptions. If this is true, our task is clear; we need to look within ourselves, seek out the ghosts that haunt us, and use our insights and our powers of self-reflection to dispel them. Only then will we obtain the clear-sighted vision needed to develop an accurate and integrated view of the analytic process.

References

Boesky, D. (1990). The psychoanalytic process and its components. *Psychoanal. Quart.*, 59:550–584.

Ferenczi, S. (1919). On the technique of psychoanalysis. In: *Further Contributions to the Theory and Technique of Psychoanalysis*. London: Hogarth Press, 1950.

Freud, S. (1912). Recommendations to physicians practicing psycho-analysis. *Standard Edition*, 12:111–120. London: Hogarth Press, 1958.

Gardner, R. (1983). *Self Inquiry*. Hillsdale, NJ: The Analytic Press.

Gill, M. M. (1982). *Analysis of Transference, Vol. I.* New York: International Universities Press.

Hoffman, I. Z. (1991). Discussion: Toward a social constructivist view of the psychoanalytic situation. *Psychoanal. Dial.*, 1:74–105.

Jacobs, T. (1991). *The Use of the Self*. Madison, CT: International Universities Press.

McLaughlin, J. (1981). Transference, psychic reality and countertransference. *Psychoanal. Quart.*, 50:639–664.

Poland, W. (1988). Insight and the analytic dyad. *Psychoanal. Quart.*, 57:244–271.

Renik, O. (1993). Countertransference enactment and the psychoanalytic process. In: *Psychic Structure and Psychic Change*, ed. M. J. Horowitz, O. F. Kernberg & E. M. Weinshel, Madison, CT: International Universities Press.

Schwaber, E. (1983). Psychoanalytic listening and psychic reality. *Internat. Rev. Psycho-Anal.*, 10:379–392.

Chapter 9

Arithmetic of a One- and Two-Person Psychology: Merton M. Gill, an Essay

Doris K. Silverman

Editors' Introduction: *Silverman highlights the tension in Gill's thinking as he integrates a one- and two-person psychology position. Gill's enduring belief in unconscious fantasy as a powerful organizer of meaning for the individual led to his insistence on maintaining a one-person psychology orientation in addition to his advocacy of a two-person psychology position inherent in his social constructivist orientation. Silverman spells out Gill's stress on innate "drives" as having developmental priority over social interactions, and she raises the theoretical problems these pose for Gill's social constructivist point of view. These problems notwithstand, Gill's call for an alteration of the traditional understanding of the analytic interaction was consistent with a social constructivist outlook. Gill relentlessly argued with "establishment" analysts about the necessity to relinquish conventional notions about technique. His views about the reciprocal influence and mutual shaping of the transference and countertransference led him to his two-person psychology orientation.*

Although I believe that psychoanalysis never achieved the scientific status that Kuhn (1962) suggested warrants the label of a paradigm, I nonetheless use the concept of paradigm and paradigm shift in a broad sense. I wish to encompass changes in clinical technique and a change in a philosophical outlook, both of which have increasingly garnered attention in the psychoanalytic community. To the extent that we are willing to loosely use the term paradigm change in psychoanalysis, Merton Gill was in the forefront of this shift at least in these two arenas. As I hope to demonstrate, I think his underlying assumptions are less clear, at times even inconsistent; however, Gill would have been the first to acknowledge that he had not tackled the philosophical issues in any systematic way.

He believed (Gill, 1994b) that the philosophical orientation for psychoanalysis should be social constructivism, and because psychoanalysis addresses a discourse of personal meanings, it is a hermeneutic science. Very little of his intellectual energies addressed these philosophical issues. I certainly understand his reluctance. To step into the complex philosophical hermeneutic literature—a literature, by the way, in which I am a novice—is to confront embattled positions, arguments of differences, and the insistence on the part of many hermeneuticists of the importance of logical discourse, reasoned argument, and the aesthetics of meaningful, coherent, and persuasive treatises (e.g., Habermas, as discussed by Bernstein, 1983; McGowan, 1991, and especially Norris, 1990; Gadamer, 1975). For a discussion of current philosophical views in psychoanalysis, their complex and subtle different nuances, and their influence on the clinical process, see Silverman (1999, 2000).

There is, of course, the other side, more dominated by Jacques Derrida's (1982; also Norris, 1990) deconstructionist position or what some think of as a postmodern viewpoint. It is an outlook that at times challenges the use of rational criteria, reasoned argument, truth claims, and standards of validity. Philosophers such as Richard Rorty (1989, 1991, 1993) may belong here, as well may the early Frankfurt school, the social philosopher Michel Foucault (1977), and, in the literary arena, the critic Stanley Fish (1989). For Derrida, the leading deconstructionist, all texts are contextualized, with meaning indeterminate in any given case. There is always infinite "free play" (quoted in Norris, 1990, p. 38), an open-ended contextualized account, which Derrida calls "unlimited semiosis" (p. 58). Clearly this is not the position toward which Gill inclined. He was too much of a reasoned empiricist. His last book (Gill, 1994), for example, raises questions concerning issues that have been asserted and assumed as gospel in our field. He challenged many of these positions, offered his own counter-arguments, and in the end insisted, in effect, that it is an empirical question.

I believe there is much that Gill (1982) valued in traditional psychoanalysis. However, he saw serious limitations in its practice. His focus was on the transference–countertransference experience and his view that these were coconstructed. That is, he maintained that the dyad was unique. Each participant brought to the therapeutic experience a complex cultural, sociohistorical, conscious, and unconscious personal context. These characteristic factors for each participant interacted in ways unique to this couple. The need to bridge communication between the two forged an intersubjective field, co-created by both participants. (With the use of the term *intersubjectivity*, I am stressing a shift from the patient as subject and the analyst as object—the latter as an independent, autonomous, external observer—to the concept of two interacting subjectivities.)

Gill (1992, 1993, 1994b) agreed with the idea of two subjectivities, believing that each of the participants were shaped and shaping each other's psyche in this setting. He referred to this interaction as a *two-person psychology*, and he maintained as well that there was simultaneously a *one-person psychology*. By the latter he meant the private psychic life of an individual, fashioned by significant external factors that were internalized, and that these factors interacted with endogenous drives and thereby organized psychic life. (It is a difficult balancing act when you are describing and developing one aspect of a one- and two-person dialectic. When focusing on one perspective, there is a temporary obliteration of the other.)

Gill's (1987, 1994a, 1994b) insistence on a one-person psychology permitted the retention of the concept of unconscious fantasy: a private, intrapsychic experience that the patient brought to the potential intersubjective field. Gill's position on unconscious fantasy was that it was not a discovery, something innate waiting to emerge, but rather a construction. Nonetheless, I believe he did not abandon the original idea of "the innate" or the idea that fantasy could be rediscovered. This is reflected in his view that innate drives have developmental priority over the social interaction in the infant. The innate drives were, as Gill (1982) wrote, the "biological givens, in their psychological representation [which] enter into development as independent factors. . ." (p. 41). Although he indicated that these biological givens interact with the environment, the privileging of these innate, independent factors divides the mind from its social context and biases his theoretical ideas in the direction of a one-person psychology.

Advocating a view of development as intersubjective, Gill favored a major shift away from Freud's and Rapaport's views about the contributions to conflict, neither accepting Freud's (1905) complemental series, nor what he called Rapaport's, (1951) additive position (Gill, 1994b). Nonetheless, a commitment to the concept of the priority of the innate drives more readily lends itself to the greater shaping influence of unconscious fantasies that are derivatives of drives. It leads more systematically to a particular view of the patient's mind as more autonomous and that the patient's unconscious fantasies shape perceptions. Such a vantage point is more consistent with Brenner's (1976) position, for example, when he offered that the real aspects of the analyst are "a stimulus to the patient's mental activity like any other" (p. 126). For Brenner the focus is on the mind of the patient. This then permits Brenner to think that the specific personality characteristics and behavior of the analyst are grist for the patient's unconscious fantasies, fueled by the patient's drive mill. Challenging such a view, Gill did not believe in the spontaneous unfolding of the analytic process characteristic of a one-person psychology; nonetheless, he insisted that the same major problems of the patient will be exposed by any competent analyst (Gill, 1994, p. 149). This position seems close to denying his own two-person psychology by positing a significantly greater role to the unfolding of endogenously organized experience governing the process than he has spelled out in his clinical work.

The tenor of his writings, especially in his final book (Gill, 1994b), is consistent with what I have been describing. He offered the idea that drives organize fantasy meanings and that these meanings retain their original compelling power. Therefore it is not clear whether this aspect of his theory is really a one- and two-person psychology, the only perspective he thought tenable. However, if his point of view reflected a two-person psychology, Gill would have needed to elaborate on ways unconscious fantasy would emerge as a unique construction cocreated by this dyad. Further, the coloration and flowering of the fantasy in the analytic setting would need to be somewhat differently shaded by the analyst's contributions than in any other dyadic setting. One might consider as well that the analytic duo might lend itself to the emergence of certain unconscious fantasies and not others. It would be reasonable to argue from a two-person psychology construction that either for the patient or for the analyst or together, particular theory-organized or unconscious conflictual ideas (or both) would be foreclosed, whereas others might be encouraged. Such considerations, I suggest, are more consistent with an intersubjective position.

However, as I have indicated, Gill's one- and two-person psychology at times seems to rest more in the one-person psychology camp, at least when he was presenting his integrative theoretical ideas in contrast to his clinical technique. Thus I believe there is some tension in bridging his theory and clinical process. I have addressed this in some detail because many relationalists have taken up his banner and energetically wave it, believing that Gill's position reflected greater intersubjectivity than I think is inherent in his theoretical position.

On the other hand, his clinical objective is more consistent with his two-person psychology and the more typical relational position. Whereas his secondary view of treatment is the emphasis on the patient's psychopathology, Gill's (1983, 1987, 1992, 1994b) overriding clinical considerations shift from a traditional Freudian one that focuses on the workings of the patient's more endogenously organized mind, to his announced goal of understanding the nature of the patient's relationships, starting with the analytic one. This has led many Freudians to assume that Gill had given up the exploration of unconscious fantasy and opted for what many traditionalists consider a more superficial interpersonal analysis. (See, for example, the special section in *Psychoanalytic Psychology*; Sugarman and Wilson, 1995). They consider it superficial in that it deals with the actual relationship between the patient and the therapist and treatment that is typically associated with the interpersonalist position.

Whereas I think this is often a caricature of the interpersonalist position, I think Gill (1983, 1994b) also lumped together the interpersonal and the relational perspective too readily. (Because the differences between these two orientations are not my focus in this essay, I shall only comment that I believe there are distinguishing theoretical features and clinical emphases of each perspective and that their linkage obscures these.)

I wish to discuss the concept of unconscious fantasy further because I am aware that it is around this issue that clinicians experience an important divide. It is a central pursuit in traditional analysis, and classical analysts maintain it is downgraded by those who emphasize the relevance of a two-person psychology and pursue its implications in the clinical interaction.

There are, no doubt, differences among clinicians in the frequency of interventions they permit themselves (i.e., seeing where the patient's mind goes spontaneously vs. intervening), traditionalists being less inclined to intervene. One cannot have it both ways. In the noninterventionist camp, the idea is that the unencumbered flow of associations are likely to offer unconscious fantasy derivatives. For Gill (1994b) though, the interruptions were clinically relevant and were consistent with his two-person psychology orientation. In the traditional position the encouragement of free associations, so the theory goes, offered the opportunity for a more regressive primary-process domination of the patient's productions. This was an untenable position for Gill (1994b), who insisted on compromise formation in mental life, that is, that defense and resistance are a continuing accompaniment of the free association process. In addition, he thought that associations are chronically influenced by the analyst, who was a constant even if only a background part of the patient's productions. Thus, for Gill, unless the analyst pointed to the defensive components, including the transference, there would be no deepening of the analytic process, including the emergence of unconscious fantasies.

When evaluating a focus on either unconscious fantasies or on the interactive process, traditionalists—who may be guided in their thinking by a dichotomization—value the former and often describe the latter as typically stressing manifest content and a superficial interpersonal orientation. Setting aside the denigrations, traditional analysts have no real grounds for insisting that an intersubjectively organized view precludes a concept of a private conscious and unconscious self. Such a view is not necessarily an outgrowth of the hermeneutic position. Gadamer (1975), for example, emphasized the goal of increasing self-knowledge, although he recognized its interactive, contextual, and historical nature. Neither do traditionalists have any basis for arguing that unconscious fantasy is unretrievable via a transference focus that is understood as intersubjectively organized and is clinically pursued. That is an empirical question.

On a number of occasions, Gill (1992, 1994b) described how his own personal analyses led to reconsiderations of transference and, by extension, countertransference. It is in the transference domain that he offered "a radically new perspective." Thus, Gill's emphasis on the pursuit of the transference and the therapist's acknowledgment of the plausible aspects of the patient's experience and perceptions shifts the nature of the encounter for both participants. His vantage point challenged the hierarchical nature of the analytic dyad. Although he acknowledged that most analysts have abandoned the myth of the neutral analyst, he explicitly maintained that the analysand knows considerably more about the analyst than is recognized and that such knowledge shapes transference. While trying to maintain even relative neutrality, he would offer Freud's words that, "our secrets ooze out of every pore" (Gill, 1994b, p. 71). Therefore, in acknowledging the patient's plausible views, the tacit assumption is that it is not exclusively the analyst who knows about material reality. Furthermore, his vantage point challenges the idea that it is only the analyst who understands unconscious psychic reality for both the patient and the analyst. Gill addressed the prejudgments, prejudices, and limitations along with the recognized facilitating and healing aspect the analyst brings to the experience.

By highlighting the patient's plausible views of the transference, Gill extended and ultimately influenced novel conceptions about countertransference. A continuum of positions now exists among contemporary Freudians, and tradition-challenging ideas are under consideration by those utilizing a two-person psychology framework.

A blank-screen model has been abandoned in principle by most Freudian analysts, and the history of the concept of countertransference, like transference, has altered from viewing it as a resistance to acknowledging it as a potential facilitator of the analytic work. However, there remains considerable prohibition against self-revelation, countertransference actions, and enactments. The more traditional view holds that the patient's transferences readily stir the analyst's own conflictual issues and a countertransferential reaction occurs, which is a unidirectional, one-person psychology point of view. In addition, the analyst maintains relative neutrality by simultaneously attending to his or her psychic reverberations, and in this manner analysts catch countertransference reactions and thereby eliminate actions. For some contemporary Freudians there is greater acceptance of the analyst's contribution—limited, however, by certain constraints. This is reflected in the concept of *enactment*. Here is Chused's (1991, p. 629) definition: "Enactments occur when an attempt to actualize a transference fantasy elicits a countertransference reaction." Although she talks about "symbolic interactions between analyst and patient which have unconscious meanings to both" (Chused, 1991 p. 615), the thrust of her ideas remains more unidirectional: the patient initiates transference pulls to fulfill fantasy wishes to which the analyst unintentionally responds. Sandler's (1976) idea of role responsiveness which preceded the concept of enactment is similar. He too acknowledges the inevitability of the analyst's response to the patient's needs and that actions on the analyst's part are unavoidable. Thus, a shift has taken place from the initial view of countertransference as maladaptive, to recognizing it but reducing it to a zero effect, then to acknowledging its value in highlighting patients' neurotic transference wishes and to the more contemporary idea of the inevitability of the analyst's enactment. However, Gill (1992, 1994b) did not believe that even the more modern views of countertransference fully engaged the actualities of the analytic two-person psychology experience. His interest in Racker's ideas more closely supported his paradigm and it seems to me readily lends itself to viewing enactments as co-constructed.

Racker (1968) maintained that the analyst was not a dispassionate, objective listener decoding derivatives but was one who also struggled with internally generated, powerful peremptory wishes, anxieties, guilt, and defensive, resistant reactions, as well as induced ones. Freudians such as Bird (1972) also prepared the way for a potentially more interactive view. He described the powerful emotional immersion of both participants when a meaningful analytic experience is in progress, even suggesting that "the analyst's own transference involvement is necessary" (p. 235). In a more current article, Boesky (1990) offered these complementary ideas: "transference as resistance in any specific case is unique and would never and could never have developed in the identical manner, form, or sequence with any other analyst and that the manifest form of the resistance is . . . unconsciously negotiated by both patient and analyst." Thus "there can be no treatment conducted by an analyst without counterresistance or countertransference" (Boesky 1990, pp. 572–573). These ideas propose that both analyst and patient experience potent transferences that involve enactments.

Such considerations suggest that enactments are not only inevitable, but a constant accompaniment of the treatment. As an analyst becomes consciously aware of an enactment and attempts to derail it, it may unconsciously invoke an alternative enactment. However, even this point of view would be an insufficient conceptualization for Gill, because of the unidirectional one-person psychology orientation it implies. Here I quote Gill (1994): "A truly interactive concept is one in which both parties are contributing to the interaction, not one in which one party is merely responding to the other" (p. 103). Thus, transferences and countertransferences are bidirectional and cocreated. The danger of such a point of view is that we may be in an infinite regress and feel that we are frequently in the dark about our own and our patient's motivations. However, conceding the inevitability of multiple enactments can inform our work. Useful as well is the acknowledgment of the sometimes slow, confusing, and evolutionary nature of advancing knowledge. In addition, I offer the views of the philosopher Bernstein (1983), who, in talking about the scientific endeavor, argued that in the pursuit of science our future views may reflect modifications of the "standards, reasons and practices" (p. 69) we associate with our discipline. "Such a modified view of scientific standards should not lead to skepticism, but to the acceptance of human fallibility and the limitations of human rationality" (p. 69).

In the uneasy struggle to integrate one- and two-person psychologies, positions are frequent biased in one or the other direction, and I have tried to demonstrate this aspect in Gill's thinking. However, I suggest that such biases are inevitable as we are in the formative stages of a new paradigm. In addition, there is no experimental data to solidify either position. Some of the difficulty in this current controversy, as I read the literature, is suggested by each side arguing that the other misunderstands their views. What is required is extensive clinical documentation. We need to establish whether there are significant differences between a one and one- and two-person perspective. If so, can the clinical implications be demonstrated, and, finally, will such distinctions offer outcome differences? Gill would undoubtedly concur with the need for such documentation. He was a passionate promoter of clinical research. With his death, we will miss his powerful voice and compelling advocacy as well as much more.

Acknowledgment

This article was first presented at a memorial meeting for Merton M. Gill that took place at the Rapaport–Klein Study Group meeting held at Austen Riggs, June 1995. Merton Gill was a valued and esteemed member of the group.

References

Bernstein, R. J. (1983). *Beyond Objectivism and Relativism.* Philadelphia: University of Pennsylvania.

Bird, B. (1972). Note on transference: Universal phenomenon and hardest part of analysis. *J. Amer. Psychoanal. Assn.*, 20:267–301.

Boesky, D. (1990). The psychoanalytic process and its components. *Psychoanal. Quart.*, 59:550–584.

Brenner, C. (1976). *Psychoanalytic Technique and Psychic Conflict.* New York: International Universities Press.

Chused, J. F. (1991). The evocative power of enactments. *J. Amer. Psychoanal. Assn.*, 39:615–640.

Derrida, J. (1982). *Margins of Philosophy*, trans. Alan Bass. Chicago: University of Chicago Press.

Fish, S. (1989). *Doing What Comes Naturally.* Oxford, UK: Clarendon Press.

Foucault, M. (1977). *Language, Counter-Memory, Practice*, ed. & trans. D. F. Bouchard & S. Simon. Ithaca: Cornell University Press.

Freud, S. (1905). Three essays on the theory of sexuality. *Standard Edition*, 7:130–243. London: Hogarth Press, 1953.

Gadamer, H.-G. (1975). *Truth and Method*. New York: Seabury.

Gill, M. M. (1982). *Analysis of Transference: Vol. 1*. New York: International Universities Press.

Gill, M. M. (1983). The interpersonal paradigm and the degree of the therapist's involvement. *Contemp. Psychoanal.*, 19:200–237.

Gill, M. M. (1987). The analyst as participant. *Psychoanal. Inq.*, 7:249–260.

Gill, M. M. (1992). *Current Trends in Psychoanalysis*. Heinz Hartmann Award Lecture delivered at the New York Psychoanalytic Institute, November.

Gill, M. M. (1993). Interaction and interpretation. *Psychoanal. Dial.*, 2:111–122.

Gill, M. M. (1994a). Heinz Kohut's self psychology. In: *A Decade of Progress: Progress in Self Psychology, Vol. 10*, ed. A Goldberg. Hillsdale, NJ: The Analytic Press, pp. 97–211.

Gill, M. M. (1994b). *Psychoanalysis in Transition*. Hillsdale, NJ: The Analytic Press.

Kuhn, T. S. (1970). *The Structure of Scientific Revolutions*. Chicago: University of Chicago Press, 1972.

McGowan, J. (1991). *Postmodernism and Its Critics*. Ithaca, NY: Cornell University Press.

Norris, C. (1990). *What's Wrong with Postmodernism*. Baltimore, MD: Johns Hopkins University Press.

Racker, H. (1968). *Transference and Countertransference*. New York: International Universities Press.

Rapaport, D. (1951). *Organization and Pathology of Thought*. New York: International Universities Press.

Rorty, R. (1989). *Contingency, Irony, and Solidarity*. Cambridge, UK: Cambridge University Press.

Rorty, R. (1991). *Objectivity, Relativism, and Truth, Vol. 1*. Cambridge, UK: Cambridge University Press.

Rorty, R. (1993). Centers of moral gravity. *Psychoanal. Dial.*, 3:21–28.

Sandler, J. (1976). Countertransference and role responsiveness. *Internat. Rev. Psychoanal.*, 3:43–47.

Silverman, D. K. (1999). Bridging natural science and hermeneutics: An oxymoron or a conjunction? Commentary on paper by Maurice Cortina. *Psychoanal. Dial.*, 9:597–608.

Silverman, D. K. (2000). An interrogation of the relational turn: A discussion with Stephen Mitchell. *Psychoanal. Psychol.*, 17:146–152.

Sugarman, A. & Wilson, A., eds. (1995). Contemporary structural psychoanalysis and relational psychoanalysis [Special section]. *Psychoanal. Psychol.*, 12:1–114.

Psychoanalysis and Psychotherapy: Critical Differences or Blurring of Boundaries?

Chapter 10

Merton Gill, Psychotherapy, and Psychoanalysis: A Personal Dialogue

Robert S. Wallerstein

Editors' Introduction: *Wallerstein and Gill have been at the forefront in considering the conceptual and technical distinctions that can be made in the spectrum of therapeutic modalities, in particular the similarities and differences between psychoanalysis, psychoanalytic psychotherapy, and other psychotherapies. There has been much controversy and debate as to whether the distinctions among these modalities should be sharpened or blurred.*

In this chapter, Wallerstein traces the evolution of Gill's views on these issues, and then focuses primarily on areas of agreement and disagreement with Gill, as expressed primarily in a 1991 published exchange of letters (Gill and Wallerstein, 1991). According to Wallerstein, Gill, though he denied it, did assimilate "expressive psychotherapy to psychoanalysis" by claiming that the analysis of the transference could be accomplished under less than optimal extrinsic conditions (e.g., with lesser frequency of sessions). At the same time, Wallerstein clearly agrees with Gill that all varieties of psychotherapy, including psychoanalysis, are by their very nature interactional and that, contrary to Gill's (1994) impression of his views, he believes "that there is an inevitable (and inherent, not accidental or contaminating) interpenetration of what had once been considered mainly psychotherapeutic components or modes into every psychoanalysis—and, incidentally, vice versa—and that this has made the once very distinct conceptual differentiations between the two modalities of psychoanalysis and psychoanalytic psychotherapy much more ambiguous in both theory and practice than they were in earlier years felt to be." Nonetheless, contrary to Gill, Wallerstein finds it useful to try to maintain technical and conceptual distinctions between the two modalities.

Reprinted by permission from the *Journal of the American Psychoanalytic Association* (1997, Volume 45, Part I, pp. 233–256).

References

Gill, M. M. (1994), *Psychoanalysis in Transition*. Hillsdale, NJ: The Analytic Press.

Gill, M. M. & Wallerstein, R. S. (1991), An exchange of letters to the editor. *Internat. J. Psycho-Anal.*, 72:159–166.

Merton Gill occupied a unique place in my intellectual and emotional scheme of things, as close friend and colleague, as scientific ideal and moral gadfly, and as research mentor and supporter, although—despite mutual wishes that would have had it otherwise—we never worked collaboratively in the same setting. I first met Merton in the early 1950s—now more than four decades ago—a time when I, at the very start of my career as a psychotherapy researcher, was fashioning, together with some colleagues, what would evolve into the Psychotherapy Research Project of the Menninger Foundation, an ambitious thirty-year study of the processes and outcomes of both psychoanalysis and the psychoanalytic psychotherapies. At the time, we were applying to the Foundations' Fund for Research in Psychiatry for our first extramural funding.

Merton, whom I knew then only through his early writings on the nature of psychoanalysis and psychotherapy and on their relation (writings that had played a seminal role in the conceptual organization of our project), came as one of the Fund's site visitors. At our first meeting he was his characteristically incisive and lucid self, probing (often uncomfortably so) and at times acerbic, but at the same time always curiously respectful. After the visit none of us could be sure of Merton's take on the project, but in due course we were awarded the grant, which helped launch our project on its long-term career. And it was in that project that my own lifelong preoccupation began with these same issues of the psychoanalytic psychotherapies vis-à-vis their psychoanalytic parentage, issues that had already so engaged Merton's interest and to which his early contributions in 1951 and 1954 had already given an almost defining cast.

Over the next four decades, Merton and I, though we were engaged in a variety of other theoretical and technical concerns, each maintained an abiding interest in these issues, which have been a major preoccupation, both conceptually and technically, for the entire field of American psychoanalysis for half a century now, and yet remains today a still unsettled and ambiguous range of issues, theoretically and clinically, as will become clear enough over the course of this essay. My format in this tribute to Merton will be a close focus, via extensive quotation, on the development and evolution of Merton's thinking in this area over that time span, which will highlight his central role both in defining, in the earlier period, the emerging dimensions of these conceptualizations, and in formulating, in the later one, the sharp revisions arrived at by a significant portion of the field. My own views, both agreement and disagreement, will emerge via my organization of Merton's thinking and my responses to it, which include, in the early nineties, a published exchange of four letters seeking to clarify our respective understandings (Gill and Wallerstein, 1991). Hence the subtitle of my essay, "A Personal Dialogue."

Two comments are in order before we begin. First, a good number of analysts besides Merton Gill, most notably Robert Knight, Edward Bibring, Leo Rangell, Leo Stone, and Anna Freud, played major roles in formulating the consensus that emerged in American psychoanalysis during the late forties and early fifties regarding what constitutes psychoanalysis proper, what constitutes the range of psychoanalytic psychotherapies, and how their relationship is to be understood. The reaching of this consensus, crystallized in the contributions of these and other authors to a series of panels in the early fifties, and published together in one issue of the *Journal of the American Psychoanalytic Association*, is a story I have recounted at length elsewhere (Wallerstein 1989, 1995b). Here I will trace only Merton's role in these developments, and while this risks exaggerating his place in the overall picture, it is no exaggeration to place him only after Knight, who in the late forties first framed the conceptions denoting psychoanalytic psychotherapy as *psychoanalytic* but nonetheless distinct from psychoanalysis proper, and who, within the demarcated range of the psychoanalytic psychotherapies, first formulated authoritatively the proposed fundamental distinction between expressive and supportive therapeutic approaches. With the single exception of Knight, Merton Gill played a larger role than anyone else in delineating the similarities and differences between psychoanalysis and the derived psychoanalytic psychotherapies.

My second comment is to point out that I have long felt—though Merton never agreed, and indeed this was the focus of our 1991 exchange—that over the years Merton's evolving views on psychotherapy vis-à-vis psychoanalysis underwent a radical shift. To my mind, by the late seventies he had reversed himself almost totally, yet curiously his early and late views have been (and remain) almost equally influential. But that has also been a feature of Merton's influence on our field.

This is a paradox I noted in a 1984 appraisal of Merton's 1982 monograph *Analysis of Transference*. I began with an admiring paragraph locating him, and his influence in American psychoanalysis—in my view—as follows: "It has been Merton Gill's fate to be an acknowledged leader in (American) psychoanalysis almost from the beginning of his career. An uncommon percentage of his writings have been almost instantly—and justly—hailed for their critical influence at particular points in the history of analysis in America, in relation both to psychoanalytic clinical practice (and its relation to the derivative dynamic psychotherapies) and to psychoanalytic theory formulation (in the ascendency and then the decline of ego psychology—the apotheosis of metapsychology)" (Wallerstein, 1984, p. 325). I then went on to cite a succession of Merton's contributions which I felt substantiated this assertion, ending the paragraph with this final sentence: "Curiously, the signal influence of each of these successive landmark contributions has endured despite Gill's own subsequent turning away from and even disavowing positions that he had so persuasively earlier espoused" (p. 326). Merton did indeed acknowledge these profound changes of mind readily in regard to first his impassioned espousal and later his equally passionate repudiation of the ego psychological metapsychology paradigm, saying once to me, regarding his influential 1963 monograph *Topography and Systems in Psychoanalytic Theory*, that he disavowed every word in it and wished he had never written it. He by no means acknowledged, however, what I felt to be an equally great turnabout in his views on the nature of the psychoanalytic therapeutic enterprise—but that is part of the unfolding story to which I now turn.

Gill's Early Views

Gill's first article on this subject, published in 1951, came in the wake of Knight's seminal formulations published in the 1940s. Gill began with a revision, in the light of those formulations, of Freud's definition of psychoanalysis as stated in a well-known passage in "On the History of the Psychoanalytic Movement" (1914). There Freud had stated, of "the facts of transference and resistance," that "any line of investigation which recognizes these two facts and takes them as the starting-point of its work has a right to call itself psycho-analysis even though it arrives at results other than my own. But anyone who takes up other sides of the problem while avoiding these two hypotheses will hardly escape a charge of misappropriation of property by attempted impersonation, if he persists in calling himself a psycho-analyst" (p. 16). Gill's modification was as follows: "In point of fact the designation 'psychoanalysis' is reserved for that technique which *analyzes* transference and resistance. Psychoanalytic therapy is any procedure which *recognizes* transference and resistance and rationally utilizes this recognition in the therapy, though this may be done in many different ways, and part or all of the transference and resistance may not be analyzed" (1951, p. 62).

It is these "many different ways," in which "part or all of the transference and resistance may not be analyzed," which represent the various distinctions made among the expressive and supportive modes delineated originally by Knight. Gill stated these differences in terms of goals and strategies. Of the first he said, "In psychoanalysis the goal is relatively clear: a progressive analysis from the surface to the depth; analysis of the defenses and the motives for defense; the development and analysis of the transference neurosis; a resolution of symptoms, and as complete a 'structural' alteration of the neurotic aspects of the personality as possible. In psychotherapy the goal may be anything from as quick relief of a symptom as possible, with the restoration of the previous integrative capacity of the ego, through a whole range of more ambitious goals *up to* analysis, the most ambitious of all. *The choice of therapy may be divided into that which determines the minimum necessary to restore the ego to functioning, and that which strives for the maximum change that is possible*" (p. 63; emphasis added).

In terms of strategy, Gill said, "The gross major decision is whether the defenses of the ego are to be *strengthened* or *broken through* as a preliminary toward a reintegration of the ego. . . . The decision to strengthen the defenses is made in cases in which this is *all that is necessary*, or in those in which this is *all that is safely possible* (p. 63; emphasis added). At the other end of the spectrum, "Analysis then is clearly the procedure for a *middle range* in which the ego is sufficiently damaged that extensive repair is necessary, but sufficiently strong to withstand pressure" (pp. 63–64; emphasis added). And then determinedly at the end, in connection with the question of the inevitability and necessity of the transference neurosis and Freud's famous statement that an enemy cannot be slain in effigy, Gill stated, "Psychotherapy must determine how thoroughgoing an alteration in personality can be achieved by only partial development of the transference neurosis" (p. 70). Of course, Gill also made room for common enough admixtures of technique: "While the two poles of either strengthening the defenses, or of analyzing them as first steps toward reintegrating the damaged ego, stand as the gross opposites of two theoretical modes of approach, the psychotherapy of any specific case will show intricate admixtures of both" (p. 65).

And finally, in this rather brief paper, Gill added to the sophistication of the conceptualization of supportive techniques through his elaboration of three different ways of "strengthening the defenses": "A first principle, then, for techniques of strengthening defenses is to encourage, praise, or in general to give narcissistic support for those ego activities in which defense is combined with adaptive gratifications [e.g., compulsive hard work], and to discourage by subtle or direct techniques those activities which are maladaptive gratifications, whether or not they are combined with defense" (p. 66). "A second principle . . . is that one must take great care not to unwittingly attack an important defense [e.g., the denial of dependency longings]" (p. 66). The third "way in which the theory of strengthening the defenses may be formulated is the one proposed by Glover. He suggests that artificial neuroses may be set up which offer a partial discharge for derivatives of instinct. . . . For the theory of the results achieved by such a technique Fenichel suggests that 'by this partial discharge the instinct becomes relatively weaker and the work of defense against the remainder becomes easier.' The defense may then be said to have been relatively strengthened" (pp. 66–67). This 1951 delineation of the modi operandi of three specific supportive techniques was the first such psychoanalytic conceptualization. The simplistic assumption prevailing to that point had been that support meant no more than varieties of reassurance, encouragement, etc.—this despite the clear knowledge that simple reassurance is often not at all reassuring.

Gill's next paper on the subject is his best known, a contribution to the debates published in *JAPA* in 1954. The impetus for this concentrated outpouring of articles on a single theme was severalfold. An important aspect was the intense ferment stirred up within psychoanalysis by the bold technical proposals of Alexander and his coworkers, proposals that met a wide range of reaction, from great enthusiasm for having pointed the way to more effective and speedier psychoanalytic treatment, to severe dismay that the dilution of proper psychoanalysis into an amorphous psychotherapy, all the more dangerous because it masqueraded as real analysis and so could hoodwink the uninformed, was under way, perhaps irreversibly. The latter development was regarded as the logical but extremely unhappy outcome of the growing closeness in America between psychoanalysis and psychiatry. Alexander himself participated in two of the panels, as did Frieda Fromm-Reichmann and Edith Weigert, who held similar if not identical positions. At the same time, a substantial portion of the presentations of those with opposite views (Gill, Rangell, Stone) was devoted to a rebuttal of the Alexander innovations, as no longer psychoanalytic (though possibly effectively psychotherapeutic), and to a redefining of Alexander's concept of the corrective emotional experience to bring it more into line with properly psychoanalytic precepts.

An even more encompassing impetus to the publications of 1954 was the growing controversy over how the similarities and differences between psychoanalysis and psychotherapy were to be understood. Here the central confrontation occurred between two major viewpoints on the most appropriate way to conceptualize the relationship between dynamic psychotherapy and psychoanalysis proper. Basically, the issue lay between the position advanced by Alexander, Fromm-Reichmann, and their colleagues (but altogether a distinct minority), who saw the historical trend as *blurring*, if not ultimately altogether obliterating, the technical distinctions between dynamic psychotherapy and psychoanalysis, and the viewpoint espoused by the great majority of analysts, for whom Bibring, Gill, Rangell, and Stone served as major spokesmen. The latter conceived the scientific problem to be the clarification and *sharpening* (and thereby the preservation) of the conceptual and operational distinctions between the two. It was these diametrically opposed views that clashed at the panels published in 1954. And of all the contributions to those debates, it was Merton Gill's that emerged as the most incisive, the one that most clearly defined the dimensions of the emerging majority consensus on the relation of psychotherapy to psychoanalysis—that of an established *diversity* of goals and techniques (the spectrum of psychoanalytically based psychotherapies, ranging from the most supportive to the most expressive, psychoanalysis itself) within a *unity* of theory (that of psychoanalysis). He thereby ushered in an era of consensus that lasted for approximately twenty years, though with increasing strain over that time span.

It must be remembered that Gill's response to Alexander's technical innovations, particularly the concept of the corrective emotional experience, was written from the ego psychological standpoint of the 1950s, considerably before the evolution of his own later thinking in terms of an interactive "two-body psychology" wherein the transference was reconceptualized as a plausible construction by the patient of the ongoing analytic interaction. This caveat in mind, let us see how the Merton Gill of 1954 tackled the conceptual issue:

> there is little doubt that Alexander is correct in stating that by overt behavior toward the patient one can more quickly get him to change some aspects of his behavior. But what is the meaning of such a change? It is an adaptation to this particular interpersonal relationship—as it exists between patient and analyst. But this is not the goal of analysis. The goal of analysis is an intrapsychic modification in the patient, so that for example his dependent behavior is given up not because he has learned that if he acts too dependent he will be punished by a loss of therapy hours, but because despite the invitation to regress and the maintenance of the frequency of his hours he has come to feel and understand his dependency in such a way that he no longer needs it or wants it—and that this is a conclusion valid not simply for this particular interpersonal relationship but has more general applicability, in short has the status of an intrapsychic change [p. 781].

Though Gill did not state it explicitly, his conclusion was clear: Alexander's innovations had taken him beyond the realm of proper analysis. Despite his claim that they were merely part of a more effective analysis, one better geared to the needs and requirements of his patients, they were to Gill's mind a variety of psychoanalytically oriented psychotherapy. Though granting that such a therapy could well be appropriate, depending on the clinical circumstances, Gill deemed it important to maintain the distinction. Gill ended his discussion of the issue by redefining what he considered a *true* corrective emotional experience: "Certainly to meet the patient's transference behavior with neutrality *is* to give him a corrective emotional experience without the risks attendant on taking a role opposite to that which he expects, as Alexander suggests" (p. 782).

But the larger part of Gill's essay was focused on the central issue of the overall similarities and differences between psychoanalysis and the derived psychoanalytic psychotherapies, all from the perspective of conceptual clarification and a sharpening of distinctions. Gill began by offering a definition of psychoanalysis, the parent therapy, a succinct statement that came to enjoy very wide currency: "Psychoanalysis is that technique which, employed by a neutral analyst, results in the development of a regressive transference neurosis and the ultimate resolution of this neurosis by techniques of interpretation alone" (p. 775). He went on for several pages to explicate each phrase of this sentence in extended detail.

Clearly, this definition circumscribes psychoanalysis far more precisely than did Freud's definition of 1914, which stated simply that any therapy that *recognizes* the two facts of transference and resistance and takes them as the *starting point* of its work can call itself psychoanalysis. It is also consistent with Gill's earlier modification (1951, p. 62) of Freud's definition whereby Gill drew a distinction between psychoanalysis (which *analyzes* transference and resistance) and psychoanalytic psychotherapy (which *recognizes* transference and resistance and rationally utilizes this recognition in the therapy), though that might be done "in many different ways."

In the 1951 paper, Gill (following Knight) had already made the point that the "gross major decision is whether the defenses of the ego are to be strengthened or broken through as a preliminary toward a reintegration of the ego" (p. 63). In 1954 he elaborated on this idea. "Methods of psychotherapy . . . ," he wrote, "are primarily supportive or primarily exploratory, with all grades in between. . . . Exploratory psychotherapy may be brief or it may be long, even longer than the usual psychoanalysis" (p. 772). He focused in the later paper on this exploratory (or expressive) psychotherapy as an entity on the spectrum of therapies "in between" supportive therapy and analysis proper.

This spectrum he arrayed as follows. A primarily supportive therapy is the preferred mode for patients too ill for analysis (or for the expressive therapies). These are patients whose egos are not strong enough to withstand pressure, whose failed psychic equilibrium is to be restored via that "strengthening of defenses," to be carried out through a variety of supportive techniques spelled out by Gill, Knight, and others. "A major contraindication" to expressive therapies with such patients "is the presence of severe regressive factors or the danger that such may develop. The instances of rather sudden onset of psychosis shortly after beginning psychoanalysis are to be attributed to the regressive pressure of the technique *per se* in a precariously balanced personality" (p. 780). A primarily expressive therapy is the preferred mode for patients whose illnesses are less severe—circumscribed neurotic problems, acute reactive disorders—or who need help negotiating transitional life states. Their egos, not unduly deformed, can tolerate efforts at "analyzing the defenses" to the extent necessary, via established methods of interpretation leading to insight. These are patients on the other side, neurotically ill but "too well" for psychoanalysis, in the sense that they neither require nor warrant a treatment so ambitious and far-reaching.

This way of conceptualizing the spectrum of therapeutic modes and their differential indications puts expressive psychotherapy exactly in that "intermediate" position—certainly as regards technique—between supportive therapy and psychoanalysis. Two quotations from the 1954 paper indicate the delicate balancing Gill had in mind. "In contrast to our analyst . . . ," he wrote, "the psychotherapist is willing to permit many transference manifestations to remain unresolved on the one hand and on the other to behave in ways which would make it more difficult to resolve if he were to attempt it" (p. 784). But he also believed that "we have failed to carry over into our psychotherapy enough of the nondirective spirit of our analyses" (p. 786). "My stress on this point," he added, "arises from my feeling that discussion of therapeutic results in psychoanalysis and psychotherapy too often views them as polar opposites, with psychoanalysis regarded as producing structural changes, and psychotherapy as unable to produce any significant intrapsychic change, but only altering techniques of adjustment through transference effects and shifts in defensive techniques" (p. 787). By way of further explication, he raised the question "whether there is not more to be said on results and mechanisms in prolonged psychotherapy with more ambitious goals by a relatively inactive therapist and in intensive [expressive] psychotherapy" (p. 789).

In this connection, Gill made the statement, surprising for the time, that after all, psychoanalysis was not such a totally definitive therapeutic reconstruction as its theory—as then understood—perhaps promised. "It is generally," he wrote, "the more experienced analysts who are not so optimistic about the sweeping character changes often hoped for from psychoanalysis. And there is no doubt that we can still recognize our friends and colleagues, even after they have been analyzed. In *Analysis Terminable and Interminable*, Freud quotes wryly the observation that 'Every advance is only half as great as it looks at first'" (pp. 786–787). Given this, Gill could more readily see the similarities and closenesses (in goals, methods, and results, though with real differences) between psychoanalysis and the expressive psychotherapy that he now called an "intermediate type of psychotherapy":

> What we might call more intermediate types of psychotherapy are relatively recent. This is the psychotherapy done by people analytically oriented or trained whose goals are intermediate between rapid symptom resolution [i.e., supportive psychotherapy] and character change [i.e., psychoanalysis], where techniques are in a sense intermediate—for example, relative neutrality and inactivity; transference dealt with,

> though not a full regressive transference neurosis; interpretation the principal vehicle of therapist behavior—and, I suggest, where results are likewise intermediate [p. 789].

By this, he wrote, "I wish not to be misunderstood. I am not suggesting that psychotherapy can do what psychoanalysis can do; but I am suggesting that a description of the results of intensive psychotherapy may be not merely in terms of shifts of defense but also in terms of other intra-ego alterations" (p. 793). This theme he emphasized again in his final summarizing statement: "I have tried to say that techniques and results in psychoanalysis and intensive, relatively non-directive psychotherapy are not the polar opposites which they are often declared to be, and that a more positive and detailed description of changes both in psychoanalysis and in psychotherapy which will take account of our newer formulations in ego psychology and include descriptions in terms of intrapsychic alterations and techniques of adaptation, will help to make this clear" (pp. 795–796). But, of course, Gill's balancing caveat, already quoted, is apposite here, that "the psychotherapist is willing to permit many transference manifestations to remain unresolved . . . and . . . to behave in ways which would make it more difficult to resolve if he were to attempt it" (p. 784).

All of this adds up to the statement that in contrast to the maximalist goals of psychoanalysis in terms of fundamental conflict resolution and character reorganization, the goals in the other psychotherapies range from the most minimal to the increasingly more ambitious, with no agreement as to how asymptotically close to those of psychoanalysis they can reach in the different kinds of patients treated psychotherapeutically. In 1954, Gill put it similarly to the way he had in 1951:

> The goals of psychotherapy extend over a very wide range. To take first the goals of psychotherapy with a relatively strong ego. The goal may be the resolution of a crisis, assistance through a troubled period, or symptom amelioration. . . . But goals may range up to more ambitious aims in cases where there is no pressing problem, but where psychoanalysis is impossible or not used for external reasons . . . goals are much more ambitious than in palliative psychotherapy, and . . . more important results are achieved than I believe is often admitted [p. 785].

Here is the full exposition of Merton Gill's perspectives in the 1950s, upon psychoanalysis and the dynamic psychotherapies and the clear distinctions posited between them, even while acknowledging all the areas of relatedness and of overlap. However old-fashioned or even rigidly mechanical these early views of Gill may seem when placed against the more complexly interactive and fluid relational conceptions and two-body perspectives of today, it should be remembered that they prevailed as accepted doctrine on these issues, despite their gradual erosion, well into the 1970s, and that in somewhat muted form they undergird much of the thinking and teaching on psychotherapy vis-à-vis psychoanalysis even today, and that Merton Gill more than any other individual was their architect.

The 1979 Revision

Gill had not revisited this specific subject for a quarter century, when in 1979 the Southern Region Psychoanalytic Societies sponsored a symposium in Atlanta to which three of the central protagonists in the 1954 debates—Gill, Rangell, and Stone—were invited to update their views in the light of all the changes that had occurred within psychoanalysis in the intervening period. Many of these changes bore clearly on issues of psychotherapy vis-à-vis psychoanalysis and called out for expression at some point in the evolving discourse around these issues. I refer here to such trends as (1) the delineation of the therapeutic or working alliance as distinct from the transference evolution, with a postulated interactive relationship between the two; (2) a growing focus on the affectively charged therapeutic relationship as a coequal and interactive determinant (together with veridical interpretation leading to working through and insight) in bringing about therapeutic change; (3) a growing shift from a "one-body" to a "two-body" psychology, with an increased focus on an interactional, interpersonal, and subjectivist paradigm explanatory of the transference-countertransference interplay within the analytic situation; (4) the increasing acknowledgment and acceptance of theoretical diversity or pluralism within organized psychoanalysis worldwide, a situation in which the question inevitably arises of where the boundaries between psychoanalysis and the derived psychotherapies can properly be drawn, and in which one person's psychoanalysis can readily become another's psychotherapy; and (5) the new diagnostic and therapeutic conceptualizations being advanced in regard to the widening scope of patients appearing in psychoanalytic consulting rooms (i.e., the borderline personality organizations and the narcissistic personality disorders), the conceptual and technical considerations being proposed for their therapy, and the extent to which these should be considered still psychoanalytic or clearly psychotherapeutic.

Gill, Rangell, and Stone had essentially been in full agreement during the debates of the early fifties; they had been representatives of the "classical" position, then the majority view, that posited a continuous spectrum of psychotherapies—one marked, however, by an articulated and distinctive crystallization of differentiated therapeutic modalities along its length. These ran from psychoanalysis through expressive psychotherapy (the "intermediate therapy") to supportive psychotherapy, each with its specific and differentiated applicability to a particular nosological segment (reasonably coherent) of patients specifically amenable to it. It is this appearance at the Atlanta panel of three contributors who, a quarter of a century earlier, had spoken with so united a voice, that rendered all the more impressive the significant divergence of views—on precisely the same questions and issues—that marked their discourse in 1979.

Of the three, I believe, the one whose views had shifted most radically was Merton Gill (though he did not agree with this assessment). Gill, following upon Knight, had been clearest in the early fifties in his distinct delineation of psychoanalysis, expressive therapy, and supportive therapy, each with distinctive characteristics, different techniques, and different goals, and each differentially indicated for a different segment of the psychopathological spectrum. The very radical shift that I detect in his views has followed—to my mind—as a direct consequence of his preoccupation over this same period with his evolving conception of the overriding primacy of the interpretation of the transference as *the* criterion of psychoanalysis and of what is psychoanalytic. These newer views on the nature and place of transference interpretation include a distinction between resistance to the awareness of transference and to its resolution; an insistence on the earliest possible interpretation of the transference, including a searching out of all possible implicit transference allusions and making them explicit from the very start of the treatment; a focus on the here and now as against the genetic thrust in the transference interpretation; and the need to elaborate all the implications of the two-person as against the one-person view of the two participants' contributions to the transference. All of this was presented in detail by Gill in a succession of publications (1979, 1982, 1984; Gill and Hoffman, 1982; Gill and Muslin, 1976) and is discussed by me elsewhere (Wallerstein 1984). Here I will pursue only the implications of these views for my present theme—Gill's now very significantly altered ideas on the nature and relationship of psychoanalysis and psychotherapy. These implications he made specific in his contribution to the 1979 symposium, published in a revised version in 1984 as "Psychoanalysis and Psychotherapy: A Revision."

Gill developed these new views with his customary logical precision, summarizing his 1954 paper in a single sentence: its thrust "was to insist on the difference [between psychoanalysis and psychotherapy] and at the same time to recognize that the two are on a continuum" (Gill, 1984, p. 162). He then reviewed both the "intrinsic criteria" by which analysis is customarily defined—"the centrality of the analysis of transference, a neutral analyst, the induction of a regressive transference neurosis and the resolution of that neurosis by techniques of interpretation alone, or at least mainly by interpretation" (p. 161)—all strikingly consistent with his 1954 definition, and the commonly recognized "external criteria" or markers—"frequent sessions, the couch, a relatively well integrated patient, that is, one who is considered analyzable, and a fully trained psychoanalyst" (p. 161). It was then that he came to his taking-off point: "The question of the relationship between psychoanalysis and psychotherapy is even more important in practice today than it was in 1954 because of the practical difficulties in maintaining the ordinarily accepted extrinsic criteria of analysis. . . . The question becomes: How widely can the range of extrinsic criteria be expanded before the analyst must decide for psychotherapy rather than psychoanalysis?" (p. 162).

After reviewing the sociocultural and economic difficulties that analysts face today in maintaining the external criteria of psychoanalysis, Gill went on: "The changes I will propose are more radical than a simple extension of the recommendation I made in 1954 that we carry more of the nondirective spirit of psychoanalysis into our psychotherapies" (p. 163). Rather, "I will argue that with the definition of analytic technique at which I will finally arrive, it should be taught to all psychotherapists and that how well it will be employed will depend on their training and natural talent for the work" (p. 163). And, "I mean that analytic technique as I will define it should be employed as much as possible even if the patient comes less frequently than is usual in psychoanalysis, uses the chair rather than the couch, is not necessarily committed to a treatment of relatively long duration, is sicker than the usually considered analyzable patient and even if the therapist is relatively inexperienced. In other words, I will recommend that we sharply narrow the indications for psychoanalytic psychotherapy and primarily practice psychoanalysis as I shall define it instead" (p. 163). What we see here, of course, is a proposal to assimilate to psychoanalysis what Gill in 1954 had taken such pains to demarcate as the related but nonetheless distinct arena of expressive psychotherapy—that "intermediate form of therapy"—or, in other words, to now blur, perhaps obliterate altogether, the differences he had once felt it so vital to maintain. To me, this is in effect a revival of the position, held by Alexander and his followers, that Gill had once led the effort (largely successful) to reject.

Gill clearly acknowledged the basis for these radically altered views: "The recommendation I am proposing is an outgrowth of my changed views on transference and its analysis . . ." (p. 164). He then went on for ten pages, reviewing his newer views on the overriding primacy in psychoanalytic work of transference interpretations in the here and now and ending with a summarizing statement: "My reconceptualization of these intrinsic criteria of analysis, namely transference and its analysis, the neutral analyst, the regressive transference neurosis, free association, and the role of experience in addition to interpretation lead me to the conclusion that the centrality of the analysis of transference, as I have defined transference . . . is alone the distinguishing characteristic of analytic technique. . . . it is the distinguishing feature of psychoanalysis. It is what distinguishes it from psychotherapy. It remains for me to try to show that it can be maintained *even in an expanded range of external criteria*" (p. 172; emphasis added). "My changed conceptions of the intrinsic criteria of analysis, some beginning efforts to apply them, and experience in teaching them to therapists of varied experience [have] led me to believe that the attempt to use analytic technique in this broader range of circumstances is justified" (p. 173).

Gill then went on to develop his idea that even a necessary frequency or use of the couch may be dispensable in proper psychoanalytic work—depending on the patient and, implicitly, the patient-analyst dyad:

> While the couch is ordinarily considered to be conducive to regression, it may enable an isolation from the relationship which has a contrary effect. No universal meaning of any aspect of the analytic setting may be taken for granted. It follows that no universal prescription can be given for this or that type of case. One may generalize that analytic work goes better with healthier patients lying down and sicker patients sitting up and with frequent sessions for both kinds of patients but a particular patient may not conform to the rule. The meaning of the setting must be analyzed in each instance. Nor is degree of pathology the only variable which determines a patient's response to the analysis of transference. Apart from pathology, some take to it like a duck to water and can work despite infrequent sessions, while others never seem to find it congenial [p. 174].

Gill, then, dealt specifically with the impact of each of the usual external parameters of the psychoanalytic situation. As for frequency, "It would seem obvious that one can accomplish more with greater frequency simply because there is more time to work. But if greater frequency is frightening to a particular patient, frequent sessions may impede the work despite interpretation. One cannot simply assume that more is better. The optimal frequency may differ from patient to patient. We must not confuse optimal frequency with obligatory ritualized frequency" (p. 174). As for the couch, "The argument that psychoanalytic technique cannot be used in the face-to-face position because of the reality cues afforded the patient is a variant of the mistaken idea that it is the external stimulus rather than the patient's interpretation of that stimulus that matters. Discussions of this issue seem to gravitate to quantitative terms as though there are fewer stimuli if the patient cannot see the analyst. It may be that the patient facing the analyst is exposed to a wider range of stimuli but the patient's response is to the quality not the quantity of stimuli" (p. 175). As for the experience of the therapist, "Therapists use the technique to whatever degree their skill and comfort in exposing the transferential experience of the relationship permits" (p. 175). Finally, as for the relatively long duration and open-endedness of analytic work, "I do not know the lower limit in duration for the use of the technique I advocate, but I have used it successfully in once-a-week therapy preset to last no longer than nine months" (p. 175).

Gill declared that central to the views he was challenging was an

> implicit assumption about the psychoanalytic process which I would like to question. It is that analysis is a kind of all-or-none proposition, yielding its positive results only if carried through to the end. It is this belief which may sustain patient and analyst through long periods of apparent stagnation and stalemate, but this belief is often a vain illusion. Freud compared interrupting an analysis to the interruption of a surgical operation. I suggest, on the contrary, that in the changed way of conducting it which I am proposing, analysis may be a process with progressively cumulative benefits, interruptable at various points without necessary loss of what has been gained [p. 176].

Surely this characterization of the prevailing view of psychoanalysis as an all-or-nothing endeavor is something of a straw man, since analysis can assuredly rest or stop at all stages of incompleteness, quite aside from the understanding that in theory analysis is never completed in any but an asymptotic sense. None of this, however—and this is my point—is the same as assimilating every expressive-interpretive psychotherapy to psychoanalysis, as Gill has here proposed we do, his only stipulation being that the therapeutic thrust be focused unswervingly on interpretation of the transferences (implicit as well as explicit) in the here and now.

In this entire uncompromising statement of his radically altered perspective on the relation of dynamic psychotherapy to psychoanalysis, Gill made only one concession to the generally prevailing views he was challenging. At the very beginning of his article he had written, "Although I will propose that psychoanalysis . . . as I define it is applicable across the whole range of psychopathology, my convictions are strongest for its application to patients ordinarily considered analyzable for whom issues of time and money preclude the usual setting of analysis" (p. 161).

Where, then, would all this leave the issue of psychotherapy vis-à-vis psychoanalysis? Gill posed the question this way: "Should the use of the technique I describe in less than the optimal setting for an analysis still be called psychoanalysis?" (p. 176). He obviously felt that the answer to this query was yes, though he did say that "other things being equal, obviously an analysis conducted at lesser frequency cannot accomplish what otherwise could be" and that "there ought to be different names for an analysis carried through as fully as it could be and one which is partial and incomplete" (p. 176). The only alteration of name that he proposed, however, was of "psychoanalytic psychotherapy," which he now said "should be reserved for a technique which *does not* deal with the transference in the way I have suggested is the essential criterion of analytic technique" (p. 176; emphasis added). In other words, "psychoanalytic psychotherapy" should be the designation for that therapeutic approach that is not psychoanalysis (i.e., that does not systematically interpret transference). That is what Knight originally, and Gill after him, called in the 1940s and 1950s psychoanalytically oriented supportive psychotherapy. And, in what can be considered a further retrograde step, there is more than a passing allusion to the idea that this psychotherapy that is not psychoanalysis rests fundamentally on "witting and unwitting suggestion" (p. 177)—a return to what I have elsewhere called the first era in the developmental history of dynamic psychotherapy in relation to psychoanalysis, the era of the simple assumption of Freud (and of Jones and Glover) that the sole operative mechanism in all therapy other than "strict and untendentious psycho-analysis" is basically hypnosis or suggestion.

A 1991 Exchange of Views

I have presented these perspectives on Gill's early and late views within the context of an historical overview of the relation of psychotherapy to psychoanalysis that I published in 1989 and subsequently expanded in my book on that topic (1995b). Merton, in a letter to the editor of the journal in which my article appeared, took serious exception to my representation of his views. That initiated our public dialogue on our differing assessments of his new position, a dialogue we had already been privately engaged in over a considerable length of time.

Gill's letter (Gill and Wallerstein 1991) began with the statement that my assessment of his views in my 1989 article, "however well intentioned, is a serious misrepresentation" (p. 159); he asked, a bit further on, "How can as thoughtful, conscientious, and well-versed a man as Wallerstein go so far astray?" (p. 159). My seeming misunderstanding became clearest to Gill when I compared his revised views to Alexander's. He then granted that indeed there was a similarity to Alexander, in that both of them espoused a two-person view of the analytic situation, but insisted that there was also a significant difference, in that Alexander advocated the manipulation of the interaction (the corrective emotional experience), while he, Gill, advocated interpreting the interaction as fully as possible. He then said that I had presented neither the similarity nor the difference correctly. The reason he gave for this putative misunderstanding was his feeling that I did not really appreciate the analytic situation to be interpersonal and interactional, despite the fact that I might say I do. From there he went on to say that my view of the analytic situation remained essentially within the framework of a one-body psychology, and that though I might regard psychotherapy as interactional, I did not view psychoanalysis as such, however beset it might be by unavoidable countertransferences and "infiltrations." This meant, according to Gill, that I regarded "interaction in analysis as advertent and inadvertent infiltration, not as part and parcel of the situation" (p. 159).

Asked by the editor to respond to Gill's letter, I began my response (Gill and Wallerstein, 1991) with the statement, "Despite the strenuous efforts that both Merton Gill and I characteristically make towards the utmost of clarity in the presentations of our views and despite the mutual goodwill and serious intention that we bring to understanding the nature of our agreements and our disagreements, it seems that we each feel that the other seriously misunderstands and misrepresents his viewpoint. Let me explain" (p. 161). I then said that I agreed fully with Gill's description of both the similarity and the very significant difference between his position and that of Alexander; where the latter would manipulate the interpersonal interaction in analysis, Gill would interpret it. However, in my linking of Gill's current views with Alexander's, I had been referring neither to the particular similarity nor to the particular difference that Gill described in his letter. I was referring rather to the efforts of Alexander in the fifties and of Gill in 1979 (completely contra to Gill in the fifties) to array both expressive (or exploratory) psychotherapy and psychoanalysis proper along a continuum in which differences are merely quantitative and all distinctions based on the usual criteria for psychoanalysis are declared not critical. Alexander had in fact called for the "unification" of psychoanalysis and dynamic psychotherapy (see Wallerstein, 1989, p. 569), a position Gill had strongly opposed in 1954 but now, in a complete reversal of his earlier view, espoused a quarter century later. Gill's letter had clearly not convinced me that I had misread him. When I called his position *on this issue* a return to the position of Alexander, which in 1954 Gill had led the effort to counter, I had in no way tried to equate Gill's views with Alexander's on any other salient matter. Nor, incidentally, did I see any contradiction between this assessment of Gill's position (and Alexander's)—as blurring if not completely obliterating any distinction between expressive psychotherapy and psychoanalysis—and my other assessment that on the issue of the nature of supportive psychotherapy Gill had reverted to the early position of Freud (and of Jones and Glover), viewing it essentially as nothing more than simple suggestion.

I also addressed Gill's claim that I viewed psychotherapy as interactional but still adhered to a one-person view of transference that would render psychoanalysis itself noninteractional. My counterclaim was that I considered both modalities interactional and that that was not where I located their essential difference. Rather, to quote my letter,

> My view is that I see psychoanalysis simply as the therapy that rests centrally (though not exclusively) on . . . the effort to systematically analyze, in so far as one can, including analyzing the psychoanalytic interaction and all the suggestive elements that enter into it. I see psychoanalytic psychotherapy (varyingly supportive and expressive) as resting partly, where possible, on an interpretive-analytic base, but also, in varying degrees, depending on the characteristics and needs of the particular patient, on many other kinds of (supportive) technical interventions—which I have adumbrated and illustrated at great length in my book, *Forty-Two Lives in Treatment* (1986) [p. 163].

That is, I view both psychoanalysis and analytic psychotherapy as interactional; I see the difference in the comprehensiveness of the effort to analyze (i.e., interpret) the interactions and in the elaboration of a wide array of kinds of interaction (called in my book *supportive interventions*), rather than subsuming them all under the single rubric of suggestion.

When Merton received my response to his letter, he wrote to the editor—and to me—asking the special dispensation that he be allowed to respond to my response, with the understanding that I would in turn be able to respond to that; at that point the exchange would come to a close, with no further effort on his side, and the four letters would then be published. This was agreed to. Gill began his second, briefer letter with the statement that the first exchange had indeed clarified where we agreed and disagreed. He further expressed his satisfaction that I did adhere to "the centrality of the interpersonal aspect of the psychoanalytic situation" (p. 164). He also acknowledged that he was using the term *suggestion* far more broadly than I, meaning by it "*any* interpersonal influence whether direct or indirect" (p. 164; emphasis added). Where he correctly thought we disagreed was in his feeling that he was sharpening the distinction between psychoanalysis and all other psychotherapy by insisting that it is always possible to readily and simply distinguish psychoanalysis and psychotherapy, as follows: "If the therapist is attempting to deal with the analysis of the transference as completely and thoroughly as he can, the therapy is analysis. If he is not it is psychotherapy" (p. 164). He said my confusion in this matter lay in the idea that his "belief that psychoanalytic technique can be done at a lesser frequency and sitting up" necessarily allied him with Alexander. "I have attempted," he said, "to clarify that these are extrinsic, not intrinsic criteria, and I have insisted that analysis must be defined in terms of its intrinsic criteria" (p. 165).

My equally brief response to this last letter agreed that indeed much had been clarified about our respective views. After indicating the areas in which we were in full accord, on the centrality of the interpersonal aspects of the psychoanalytic situation, and on the fact that I never intended to impute to him Alexander's conception of the corrective emotional experience, I then stated the two main issues on which we agreed that we disagreed. The first was my feeling that he had indeed returned to Alexander's earlier efforts to assimilate expressive psychotherapy to psychoanalysis: "The nub of our difference is Gill's current belief that any therapy that tries to analyze the transference as completely as possible is psychoanalysis, no matter what the conditions or dimensions of the treatment (what he calls 'extrinsic criteria'). I believe that it can only be analysis if the conditions of treatment are such as to properly facilitate and enable a psychoanalytic process to unfold. . . . Otherwise it is an expressive psychoanalytic psychotherapy in which transferences can indeed be analyzed to the extent possible under less-than-optimal conditions" (pp. 165–166). My other disagreement was with Gill's predilection for using the term *suggestion* more broadly than I considered useful. I felt that this return to the usage of Freud conflates varieties of distinctive interventions under one general rubric that diffuses out specific meanings and differentiated understandings (as well as guides to interventions).

After these 1991 letters our subsequent and aborted exchange is doubtless anticlimactic. It came in connection with a request from *JAPA* that I review Gill's capstone book, *Psychoanalysis in Transition: A Personal View* (1994). Overall, I wrote an appreciative review (Wallerstein, 1995a) elaborating why I was calling it "a 'must read' for seasoned analysts and neophytes alike, indeed for anyone concerned to be *au courant* with the status of American analysis and Merton Gill . . ."; but I also stated that "yet, as is usually the case when Gill is concerned, I must enter my caveats" (p. 598). I went on to state where I felt that once again—not surprisingly, in the selfsame area of the nature of psychotherapy vis-à-vis psychoanalysis—Gill in expounding his own viewpoint misunderstood or misrepresented mine.

In chapter 5 of this final book, "Psychoanalysis and Psychotherapy," Gill declared that the Psychotherapy Research Project that I headed at the Menninger Foundation (my final clinical accounting was reported in *Forty-Two Lives in Treatment*) buttressed his position that the erstwhile ideal of psychoanalysis as a therapy is unattainable and that interactive elements enter necessarily into every analysis. But he then went on to claim that I had not given up the ideal in principle but had concluded only that it was unattainable in practice and that analysis therefore often "necessitated the introduction of interactive *contaminants* into the analytic situation" (Gill, 1994, p. 62). Though Gill stated explicitly that contaminants was his word, not mine, he went on to argue the difference between his position and mine on the basis of my viewing interactive components of the analytic process only as necessary contaminants (no longer identifying this as his word) rather than as inherent, ubiquitous, and vital to the full understanding of the process.

While Gill and I do have significant differences on these issues—witness our 1991 exchange—I disagree with their characterization in Gill's final book. Rather, I see as a major thrust of the Menninger project and of *Forty-Two Lives in Treatment* the demonstration that there is an inevitable (and inherent, not accidental or contaminating) interpenetration of what had once been considered mainly psychotherapeutic components or modes into *every* psychoanalysis—and, incidentally, vice versa—and that this has made the once very distinct conceptual differentiations between the two modalities of psychoanalysis and psychoanalytic psychotherapy much more ambiguous in both theory and practice than they were in earlier years felt to be. On this issue I consider myself fully in accord with Gill's position; I too view psychoanalysis as both a one- and a two-person situation, accepting all the implications of that position, including the fact that every analysis is inherently both interactive and interpretive.

My actual differences with Gill on these issues, while substantial, are quite other. The main ones are two. (1) For all the greater overlap consensually acknowledged today (as compared to the 1950s) between psychotherapy and psychoanalysis—I have called this their mutual infiltration or interpenetration—there are still to me, and I think to most of those involved with these issues, though clearly not to those adhering to Gill's views, conceptual and technical distinctions between the two modalities that I feel important to retain in the interest of clarity and precision in our work with patients. (2) Corollary to this, since neither psychoanalysis nor psychotherapy exists anywhere in its pure form, since interpenetrating elements are always present (necessarily so if the interests of patients are to be served), it follows that the interactions inherent in analysis are not always interpreted, don't always need to be, and in fact should not always be. It is a special sadness to me that I was informed of Merton Gill's death the very day I was finishing my review of his final work; my effort might have led to yet another friendly but critical exchange of views, as again we would try to clarify precisely how we understood each other, and where we agreed and disagreed.

Conclusion

I have devoted this essay to such a detailed exegesis of Merton Gill's always formative impact on our continually evolving conceptions of the nature of psychoanalysis and the psychoanalytic psychotherapies, and of their ever altering relation to each other, because clearly it has been such a central concern of his as well as of mine, but also and most importantly, of our whole discipline as a purposeful clinical healing endeavor. If in the 1950s it seemed that a majority consensus was being formed regarding a definition of psychoanalysis and the range of psychoanalytically based psychotherapies, as well as an understanding of their similarities and differences, together with a promise of ever increasing clarification and specification as theory advanced and clinical experience accumulated, this was as much as any single person's the doing of Merton Gill. And if in more recent decades this convergence of psychoanalytic perspectives has progressively unraveled, and the once seemingly crystal clear conceptual boundaries and relatednesses have become less clear, more problematic, replaced now by a range of reconceptualizations responsive to the varying tenets of a psychoanalytic world now more relational, constructivist, and pluralistic, then it can be said of Merton Gill that he has been a leading influence in staking out one of the significant contending positions on these issues, though it is not mine. But whatever our differing individual takes on these issues, we can all agree that Merton Gill's influence is writ large and will endure.

References

Freud, S. (1914). On the history of the psycho-analytic movement. *Standard Edition*, 14:1–66. London: Hogarth Press, 1957.

Gill, M. M. (1951). Ego psychology and psychotherapy. *Psychoanal. Quart.*, 20:62–71.

Gill, M. M. (1954). Psychoanalysis and exploratory psychotherapy. *J. Amer. Psychoanal. Assn.*, 2:771–797.

Gill, M. M. (1963). *Topography and Systems in Psychoanalytic Theory. Psychological Issues*, Monog. 10. New York: International Universities Press.

Gill, M. M. (1979). The analysis of the transference. *J. Amer. Psychoanal. Assn.*, 27(Suppl.):263–288.

Gill, M. M. (1982). *Analysis of Transference: Vol. I.*, Monogr. 53. New York: International University Press.

Gill, M. M. (1984). Psychoanalysis and psychotherapy: A revision. *Internat. Rev. Psycho-Anal.*, 11:161–179.

Gill, M. M. (1994). *Psychoanalysis in Transition*. Hillsdale, NJ: The Analytic Press.

Gill, M. M. & Hoffman, I. Z. (1982). *Analysis of Transference: Vol. 2. Psychological Issues*, Monog. 54. New York: International Universities Press.

Gill, M. M. & Muslin, H. I. (1976). Early interpretation of transference. *J. Amer. Psychoanal. Assn.*, 24:779–794.

Gill, M. M. & Wallerstein, R. S. (1991). An exchange of letters to the editor. *Internat. J. Psycho-Anal.*, 72:159–166.

Wallerstein, R. S. (1984). The analysis of transference: A matter of emphasis or of theory reformulation? *Psychoanal. Inq.*, 4:325–354.

Wallerstein, R. S. (1986). *Forty-Two Lives in Treatment*. New York: Guilford Press.

Wallerstein, R. S. (1989). Psychoanalysis and psychotherapy: An historical perspective. *Internat. J. Psycho-Anal.*, 70:563–591.

Wallerstein, R. S. (1995a). Review of Merton Gill's *Psychoanalysis in Transition: A Personal View. J. Amer. Psychoanal. Assn.*, 43:595–600.

Wallerstein, R. S. (1995b). *The "Talking Cures."* New Haven, CT: Yale University Press.

Chapter 11

A Psychoanalysis on the Chair and a Psychotherapy on the Couch: Implications of Gill's Redefinition of the Differences Between Psychoanalysis and Psychotherapy

Paolo Migone

Editors' Introduction: *In contrast to his earlier position in which he delineated the specific criteria that distinguished psychotherapy from psychoanalysis, Gill revised his judgment on this issue. He spelled out what he saw as extrinsic criteria (such as number of sessions, use of the couch, and constancy of the setting) as distinct from intrinsic criteria (analysis of transference and resistance). It is the emphasis on the latter that constitutes a psychoanalytic process for Gill.*

Migone uses a clinical example to demonstrate the problematic effect of focusing on extrinsic criteria as a definition of psychoanalysis. He argues that when extrinsic criteria are thought of as a priori designations—a right or wrong way to engage in a psychoanalytic process—their particular meanings might be insufficiently explored or as Migone suggests, "it becomes uninterpretable."

Migone takes up a number of relevant issues that Gill found challenging, including the disturbing tendency toward manipulation on the analyst's part. Gill was convinced that conventional aspects of the analytic setting (the analyst's silence, anonymity, use of the couch, and other aspects of extrinsic criteria), which were thought to facilitate transference regression, were never sufficiently recognized and discussed (Macalpine, 1950).

Migone also struggles to address the difficult question of why Gill, so late in his life, began to contest the classical view of technique. Migone regards his open-ended questioning as consistent with Gill's unwillingness to foreclose debate with final answers.

References

Macalpine, I. (1950). The development of the transference. *Psychoanal. Quart.*, 19:501–539.

Merton Gill was able to clarify the differences between psychoanalysis and psychotherapy in an unprecedented way, resolving the many incoherences that characterized discussions on this topic for decades (for an overview of some of these discussions spanning more than two decades, see Wallerstein, 1969, 1989). Gill was not interested in this investigation *per se*, but as part of a major endeavor he pursued in the last part of his life, namely a redefinition of psychoanalysis and of one of its central tenets, the analysis of transference. With the intellectual honesty he was known for, he revised his own classical and oft-quoted positions put forth in the 1950s (Gill, 1954) and gave psychoanalysis an enlarged and more coherent meaning, utilizing only strict "intrinsic" criteria (i.e., the analysis of transference or, as I will discuss later, better put, the "analysis of the relationship"). Psychoanalysis, so defined, becomes applicable to a wide range of clinical situations, from individual intensive therapy to the treatment of the most severe diagnoses in diverse psychiatric settings. In a way, he fully implemented what Freud (1933) meant when he said that psychoanalysis is not like a pair of spectacles that can put on and taken off (p. 153). In fact, "Freud practiced only analysis, whatever the circumstances" (Gill, 1984, p. 175; see Lipton, 1977, 1979, 1983).

Gill's coherent radicalization of the identity of psychoanalysis implied the possibility of broadening its "extrinsic" criteria, since these were no longer relevant for the identity of the method. (By extrinsic criteria Gill meant what Leo Stone [1954, p. 570] called "formal" factors, i.e., the couch, a high frequency of session per week, and so forth.) As a consequence, the definition of psychotherapy was restricted almost to the point of its disappearance: according to Gill's (1984) revision, psychotherapy proper is a therapeutic practice where the therapist, purposely, decides not to share with the patient any knowledge he may have about him and of the possible meanings of their relationship, not because of some defenses on his part (in which case there would be no theoratical reason why these defenses shouldn't be open to being worked through and hopefully overcome). In other words, all that is left for psychotherapy is a method in which one has no interest in the patient learning about himself. Needless to say, it is hard to imagine today such a practice and its rationale. Hypnosis could be an example, even if expert dynamic hypnotists, after

The author thanks Robert R. Holt and Morris N. Eagle for having read the manuscript and given some suggestions.

having modified specific symptoms, explain to the patient every detail of the therapeutic process and analyze the repercussions of the suggestive intervention on the transference (incidentally, Gill, with Margaret Brenman, studied "hypnoanalysis" [Gill and Brenman, 1959]).

Before entering into a more detailed discussion of Gill's contributions and analyzing the far-reaching implications of his theoretical revision, I will present a clinical vignette of a patient I followed some years ago (Migone, 1991, pp. 54–55; 1995, pp. 88–89). At that time I discussed this clinical material at length with Merton. I find this clinical vignette useful because—amusingly, in a way—it turns upside down the traditional way of seeing the differences between psychoanalysis and psychotherapy (Gill, 1984). At the same time it illustrates the risk of many orthodox psychoanalyses, where the analyst may perform a manipulative psychotherapy. That is, as Gill showed very well, he may allow part of the clinical material to escape from interpretive work if he believes in the universality and givenness of the classical psychoanalytic situation. The clinical details of this case should be used as an occasion to examine the theoretical implications of Gill's definition of psychoanalysis.

> A 31-year-old female patient was in a three-times-a-week therapy *vis-à-vis*. During a difficult phase of the treatment, she began to show various manifestations of what is usually called negative transference (such as aggressive feelings, fears of not being understood, and threats of interrupting treatment). Among other things, she said she could not tolerate the eye-to-eye contact with me. She would have preferred the couch which could have allowed her to feel more "contained," "protected," "relaxed," and to express more easily her inner feelings.
>
> The following information is relevant to a fuller understanding of this material. The patient's parents, who never married, had stopped seeing each other right before the patient's birth; the father, who had strongly tried to convince the mother to have an abortion, refused to give the child legal recognition. Because of a series of arguments not well understood by the patient, the mother's contacts with the father stopped completely. The father, a physician, came from a much higher social class than the mother, and was living in the same town. At times, they would meet in the street, and always they would pretend not to know each other. The patient's feelings were characterized by strong aggression, mixed with fear, affection, and feelings of inferiority and shame caused by the ambivalent fantasy that her father, for some reason, had done "the right thing" in abandoning her and in behaving in such a cruel way. Obviously, the patient could have taken the initiative to talk with the father, but she had not out of fear of exploding with anger. Furthermore, if she had approached the father she could have betrayed her loyalty to the mother, with whom she was still living and to whom

she was strongly attached. The mother, for her own reasons, had been unable to resolve her problems with the father, and out of pride she was hoping he would make the first step. Needless to say, this situation was an unresolved mourning process for the patient, having contributed, for example, to a strong inhibition regarding having a family and a child (despite the many opportunities she had had in her life). She also exhibited little assertiveness in her career and a strong inferiority complex (such as feelings of being a "second class citizen," of not deserving the same rights as everybody else).

The pattern was also well expressed in the transference in the form of a devaluation of me and actually of herself too. By not using the couch I was not doing a real psychoanalysis, but a psychotherapy, and I was not a member of the "official" psychoanalytic association that would have been the only one that could have legitimated her (the patient was a therapist as well). But I was also well aware that in her ambivalence she had chosen me as a therapist because, in a way, I was an ally. In her eyes I was not recognized (as an analyst I was born, so to speak, "out of wedlock").

Her emotional difficulty with eye-to-eye contact was possibly also related to her difficulty in experiencing and expressing the painful and ambivalent feelings toward her father. (It may be relevant to note, as often mentioned by the patient, that, like her father, I was a male physician from a higher social class.) Her request for the couch could have repeated the lack of relationship with the father, and if I had agreed, maybe unconsciously I could have given the image of a father who does not want to deal with the very emotions she wanted to avoid. We can further hypothesize that I could have been trapped by the patient's transference. That is, she could have unconsciously succeeded in evoking in me her transference's "role responsiveness" (Sandler, 1976).

But I do not want to discuss further these hypotheses, because, whether they are correct or not, they are easily understandable by any expert therapist, and are not the subject of this discussion. For the sake of the theoretical discussion I invite the reader to assume the correctness of the aforementioned psychodynamic hypotheses. What I will discuss here is the role of the elements of the setting in the inner logic of psychoanalytic interpretation. Fortunately, in this case the interpretive working through, centered upon the unconscious meaning of her request for the couch, succeeded in overcoming the patient's difficulties and in helping her to remember and work through a series of memories and painful feelings, both about herself and the father. So the therapy proceeded in a positive way. But let's assume that my interpretive efforts had not succeeded, that is, the patient had felt unable to tolerate the face-to-face interaction and had threatened to interrupt treatment if I did not accept her request. What would have been the right thing to do at that point? I ask this question here only as a theoretical exercise, assuming the correctness of my analysis on the genesis of the patient's resistance.

Because of the patient's "ego weakness," I might have introduced what Eissler (1953) called a "parameter" in this "psychoanalysis on the chair," temporarily performing a "psychotherapy on the couch" in order to continue the analytic work, up to the point when it became possible to return to the "basic model technique" of this analysis (i.e., the use of the chair). Thus, paradoxically, psychoanalysis would have been on the chair and psychotherapy on the couch, because the interpretive work would not have been sufficient to overcome her resistance.

This clinical vignette clearly exemplifies the implications of Gill's (1982, 1983, 1984, 1991, 1994 chapter 5) redefinition of psychoanalysis. In Gill's view, psychoanalysis is simply a continuous attempt on the part of the therapist (and hopefully also of the patient unless he is temporarily incapacitated by his defenses) at exploring and analyzing the various meanings of the relationship. I say "analysis of the relationship" and not "analysis of transference" (even as these terms are used interchangeably) because Gill gave a different meaning to the traditional concept of transference. According to his "relativistic," "perspectivistic," or "socio-constructivistic" paradigm (Hoffman, 1991, 1998), the analyst has no right to define what is transference (what is distorted from a supposedly non-distorted or realistic relationship), since "distortions" are part and parcel of any ways of perceiving reality. Actually, we should not use such terms as distortions or manipulations in the first place (hence the quotation marks), since it might imply we believe in the opposite, that is, that it is possible to eliminate distortions and perceive an uncontaminated or "true" reality.

In analysis there are only various types of realities, various ways of perceiving and feeling, and these can be discussed freely until a consensus can be reached on a shared reality that seems to us more "realistic." Although our perception is subject to the constraints of reality, "we cannot say what the reality really is" (Gill, 1994, p. 2; see also Freud, 1940, p. 196). There is no single definitive or ultimate way of understanding reality, because analysis is an endless process. (In this sense Gill is close to the hermeneutic positions, but only in this sense, because he disagreed in other respects. I will not discuss here Gill's views on hermeneutics.) The perception of the analyst (or, for that matter, the patient) at any one time, T_1, is considered as *the reality*. If later, at time T_2, the perspective changes, he may label as *transference* the perception he had at T_1; in turn, the perception at T_2 could eventually be seen as transference once later interpreted, and so on.

In this Socratic, hermeneutic dialogue, the therapist has no right to think he is more knowledgeable than the patient. He is simply trying to do his job, and the patient hopefully benefits from the therapist's help. If the patient believes, however, that the therapist, simply because of his role, must necessarily know the "truth" better than himself, this could be a matter for analysis and may be a transferential reaction. (Similarly, the analyst's belief that he knows more than the patient could be a countertransferential reaction.) The fact that one of the two asks for the other's help and pays him a fee (we should not forget, however, that also some therapists "need" their patients and depend on them) is an asymmetry that marks the entire meaning of the interaction, with obvious suggestive implications. This asymmetry can be discussed by both partners, and in theory, when it is sufficiently analysed and resolved, the therapy may end. Indeed, the patient's request for treatment itself, when appropriately analyzed, could be seen as his "symptom," and in such a case should be interpreted and worked through.

In a traditional way of conceiving the ground rules of analysis—as for example in Eissler's (1953) classical concept of "basic model technique"—the couch, a high weekly frequency of the sessions, a form of silence, anonymity, neutrality, and so on, were seen as instrumental to the emergence of the transference. To the extent that we accept these traditional ground rules as psychoanalysis (and also, to the extent that these or other rules are officially adopted as technical standards by international psychoanalytic organizations), it is assumed they bear universal meanings and are relevant to the identity of psychoanalysis. Gill clearly implied that this very assumption is in itself, so to speak, antipsychoanalytic. No wonder that Gill, although much respected for his theoretical contributions, was never the best candidate for a career in the psychoanalytic establishment. If we believe the traditional ground rules have always a given meaning for the patient, we block the interpretive process; we cannot proceed further in the understanding of the patient's inner reality. Some classical analysts, for example, see the couch as an instrument for inducing an openness toward the investigation of the patient's unconscious; this meaning, however right or wrong it may be, is taken as an a priori. In Codignola's (1977) terms, it belongs to the realm of the "true" and not of the "false," that is, it becomes uninterpretable (see Migone, 1987).

The clinical vignette presented earlier is an example of how the couch could have a very different meaning. The same applies of course to other elements of the setting, like the frequency of sessions. A patient might feel unbearably invaded by frequent sessions (see Gill, 1994, p. 66), and in this case only a lesser frequency could establish an analytic situation. As Gill often said, some patients fear the couch, while others cannot resist jumping defensively onto it, avoiding eye contact with the analyst. Obviously it is great mistake to interpret only the former behavior as a resistance.

Gill's (1984, pp. 168–169) critique of Macalpine's (1950) concept of "infantile setting" (i.e., a setting of stable and secure elements that may induce a form of regression, transference, or both) was particularly acute. This setting is supposed to induce infantile strivings to be analyzed later. But, Gill argues, if we are looking for a "pure" transference uncontaminated by current reality, why in the first place do we need to provoke it or create it by a suggestive or manipulative attitude aimed at inducing an infantile reaction? This is not a transference, then, but an appropriate regressive reaction to an infantile setting. It is an iatrogenic symptom. This form of psychoanalysis is, *pace* the "orthodox" analyst, a manipulative psychotherapy, conceptually similar to hypnosis.

Macalpine's conception, in my opinion, refers to the widespread and commonsensical idea that, in order to better see and analyze the transference, it could be useful to "maximize" it with an appropriate setting or attitude. Gill did not specifically oppose attempts at maximizing the transference, he simply implied that it is a mistake to believe any given attempt at maximization (e.g., the classical ground rules, or, for that matter, also a nonclassical setting) favors the emergence of *the* transference (as a pure repetition of the past). Every therapist's behavior evokes a response, because it is "interpreted" in light of the patient's transference. This has been well understood also by Weiss, Sampson, and their colleagues of the San Francisco Psychotherapy Research Group (Weiss, Sampson & the Mount Zion Psychotherapy Research Group, 1986; Weiss, 1993) who have often argued—supported by research data—the therapeutic environment is never neutral. It is always interpreted by the patient in light of his pathogenic beliefs (i.e., of his transference); in some cases even an unorthodox analytic attitude could be very well suited for identifying and changing a specific pathogenic belief.

One may ask: what is the appropriate setting to evoke the "real" transference, and what are the ideal ground rules for analytic treatment? There is no way to evoke a pure transference, if one means a set of patient's reactions that are uninfluenced by the therapist's cues or behaviors. Every patient's behavior includes a mixture of responses to the therapist's current attitude and material from the past. We can only realize that and accept it as a welcome opportunity. One of our aims, for example, is to observe rigidities in the transferential patterns we evoke, and investigate why different responses are not preferred by the patient. This kind of questioning is highly personal; it varies from analyst to analyst, and this is one of the reasons why every analysis is different. It is only by being aware of our influence on the patient that we can begin to analyze it, and to try to understand the idiosyncratic ways with which the patient responds. The question, then, is not why the patient *distorts*, but why he distorts or reacts in one way and not another.

Gill gave the best definition of "analytic neutrality" I ever heard. He said an analyst is neutral when he strongly believes that he can never be neutral, that is, when he is aware he knows only minimally the infinite ways in which he influences the patient. Only in this way does the analyst have some chance, so to speak, to begin to be somehow "neutral."

That's why a "classical analysis" could be also a perfect analysis, insofar as the analyst were aware of his infantile contribution to the transference (if this were the case). There is no difference, in principle, between a classical and a nonclassical analysis, both have manipulative aspects. What we could call an "adult setting" exerts a suggestion to behave in an adult way. But why should we induce an adult or an infantile transferential reaction from our patient? Gill (and, to some extent, Leo Stone [1961, p. 15]) questioned the need to induce further regression beside the regression already part of the patient's psychopathology. In my opinion, however, the important factor is the rationale for a given rule, the way we explain it to the patient, and especially the way we explain it to ourselves. It is important to know, for example, if a given setting is employed for self-defensive reasons or to help the patient. We cannot know, especially at the beginning of an analysis, what is the best setting for a patient. Actually, it would be antipsychoanalytic to know it; it would mean one had an a priori idea of the "ideal transference." Only during the unfolding of an analysis may we construct some meanings of the setting for both partners. Probably the best explanation for the use of a classical setting is simply admitting to the patient that this is how we learned it from our teachers, analysts, and supervisors; we are used to this way, or, simply, we like it this way and we feel comfortable with it. But we should be open to discussing and analyzing it with the patient, in order to discover further meanings or other possible unconscious and possibly countertransferential explanations. Freud (who, in this respect, was never a Freudian) gave us an admirable example—not only of honesty but also of theoretical consistency—when he justified his use of the couch simply by saying he could not bear to be gazed at for eight hours a day (Freud, 1913). Other therapists may like to look patients in the eyes, both for defensive and nondefensive reasons. Hoffman (1994, p. 200), Gill's closest associate, once honestly admitted to one of his supervisory patients who questioned the four-session-a-week frequency that this was what he had to do in order to graduate from psychoanalytic school—hardly a psychoanalytic reason, some might say, but an explanation consistent with theory.

In what follows I will trace a critical history of terminological issues regarding the difference between psychoanalysis and psychotherapy in theory and technique. My aim is to complement Gill's (1984) theoretical revision and his discussion of terminology, which reveals important theoretical problems.

Terminological Issues as a Reflection of the Consistency of the Relationship Between Theory and Technique: A Historical Review

Terminological inconsistencies may express a lack of clarity concerning the relationship between theory and technique. One of the most common terms in our field, "psychoanalytic psychotherapy," is a pivotal example. Because Freud (1915), right or wrong, said severe pathologies were not treatable with psychoanalysis because the patients were not able to develop a transference, gradually the term psychoanalytic psychotherapy was used for those treatments that were somehow derived from psychoanalysis and employed for these more severe cases. This, however, is only one meaning of the term. Many therapists today treat classical neurotic patients—and not psychotics—with psychoanalytic psychotherapy, by which they usually mean a modification of the traditional analytic technique; that is, a nonclassical method. The rationale for this modification is not justified by external factors such as severe pathology, but is based on an internal reason (i.e., internal to the theory). Undoubtedly there is a need for discussion and clarification on this issue, and Gill's theoretical research went in this direction.

In order to improve our understanding of the term psychoanalytic psychotherapy, it is useful to return to the original meaning of the term psychoanalysis. To Freud (1923a) it meant three things: a research method, a therapeutic technique, and a psychological theory. But we should not forget—and this is an important point—that, according to Freud, psychoanalysis rested *simultaneously* on these three levels; they could not be separated from each other. Consistent, then, with Freud's conception, if psychoanalysis is a general theory that can be applied in various clinical situations, we could legitimately talk about "brief psychoanalysis," "psychoanalysis without the couch," "group psychoanalysis," "psychoanalysis once a week," "psychoanalysis to the psychoses," and so on. But if we fragment the triad Freud postulated, and if by psychoanalysis we mean only a *technique* (i.e., the classical tradition), we are forced to call psychoanalytic *psychotherapy* a technique that, although maintaining psychoanalysis as a general theory, implies some modification such as once a week sessions or the face-to-face setting. One may object that Freud (1923a), in his oft-quoted triadic definition, said that psychoanalysis is also a *techinque*, but we should not forget that eight years earlier he had espoused explicitly an enlarged definition of technique, tied only to intrinsic criteria. Anyone who recognizes transference and resistance is a psychoanalyst, Freud said, even if he comes to conclusions other than his own (Freud, 1914).

A complication comes from the fact that, according to a certain classical conception (the one expressed, among others, by Macalpine, 1950), there is a strict link between analytic method and analytic setting, one influencing the other. Some formal aspects of the setting (the couch, frequent sessions, some constancy of the environment, etc.) are just those that characterize an "infantile setting," which produces regressive phenomena such as the "transference neurosis." They are considered indispensable to the analytic process because they are the very phenomena to be interpreted and worked through during the course of analysis.

We are confronted then with two theoretical positions. According to one, a given setting (the classical one) is the only and necessary condition that allows the analytic process to emerge and grow; the development of transference, as such, would not appear in therapies that are different from classical psychoanalysis. According to the second position, the transference is not exclusive or unique to psychoanalysis, but a natural phenomenon that appears in various human conditions—interpersonal relations, love relations, and so on. In analysis it is simply "analyzed," that is, put under our professional attention.

According to how we define psychoanalysis we can speak about psychoanalytic *psychotherapies* or *psychoanalyses*—different technical *types of psychoanalysis* (time-limited, with groups, with psychotics, etc.). This latter term means the application of a general theory to different situations according to the field of intervention (institutions, groups, emergencies, etc.), the type of patients (more or less severe diagnoses), and our goals (more or less deep therapeutic changes).

In the history of the psychoanalytic movement there has been no unanimous definition, or position statement, on the term psychoanalysis. On one hand, as Sandler (1982) noted, in some case the best that we could do was to say, tautologically, that "psychoanalysis is what is practiced by psychoanalysts" (p. 44), and, circularly, that "psychoanalysts" are those who practice "psychoanalysis." Often, only members of the International Psychoanalytic Association or other private associations are considered to be psychoanalysts. This definition, of course, is not only illegal—motivated by monopolistic reasons, as was successfully argued by a recent legal suit—but also dangerous because, by defining psychoanalysis by institutional affiliation, one puts into serious danger the discipline's scientific status. On the other hand, the common trend within the psychoanalytic movement to separate theory from technique (and hence to fragment Freud's triad) unfortunately favors the use of the term psychoanalysis only for a given technique, namely the classical one.

An interesting phenomenon has resulted. For the founder of psychoanalysis, theory and technique were interdependent. Later, because of the trend of defining psychoanalysis mostly as a professional practice codified by a series of behavioral rules, theory and technique have become progressively split, undermining the scientific status of the discipline. For example, when Freud was convinced of the theory that the cure occurred through the recovery of repressed memories, he did not hesitate to manipulate his patients to help them to remember, by puting pressure on their foreheads, exhorting them, hypnotizing them, and so on. Later, when he realized that the memory reached through hypnosis was not curative in itself, but the curative factor was the emotional experience in overcoming the resistances to remembering, Freud coherently changed technique and employed free associations, thus creating psychoanalysis and paving the way to what later, with an emphasis on the analysis of defenses, transformed psychoanalysis into ego psychology.

But throughout this century, psychoanalytic theory has undergone various modifications in some of its basic assumptions, up to the point where today it is not only fragmented into multiple schools, but also shaken by an epistemological crisis (i.e., the crisis of the concept of "true interpretation" and what it can mean for the entire theoretical edifice). As a consequence, classical technique became more and more a ritualized activity, void of its original meanings, transmitted by the various generations of analysts almost in a sacred way (Cremerius, 1984, 1986, 1987, 1989; Fossi, 1984, 1989; Kernberg, 1986, 1996; Holt, 1989, 1990). Poignant, in this regard, is Grünbaum's (1984) critique of the technique of hermeneutic analysts as inconsistent. They continue to employ free associations, forgetting that this method was originally developed by Freud in order to "discover" something, to reconstruct a missing link in the patient, and not in order to "construct" a new meaning or to have a dialogue to make up a story. For that purpose a normal dialogue without free associations (and, for that matter, without the couch) would be much more appropriate.

The motivations behind the growing identification of psychoanalysis with simply a technique now seem clearer: given the crisis and the fragmentation of the theory, the natural tendency was to find "common ground" in the technique. In addition, technique was more objectifiable, more concrete, and more functional for the pressing needs of a well-organized, international, professional group.

The gap between theory and technique manifested itself very soon in the history of the psychoanalytic movement. Already in the 1920s Freud himself was a dissident towards the Institutes of London and Berlin that had become more and more orthodox (Cremerius, 1982). In the following decades this situation grew to the point where it was possible to see, within the technical level, the use of concepts (such as anonymity, abstinence, free associations) detached from the theoretical context in which they had been formulated, as if they could legitimize themselves autonomously. Technique was monstrously raised to the rank of theory. There were no more precise theoretical principles, but only behavioral rules that had to be followed within an established setting, as they had been taught by supervisors and training analysts, who in turn had learned them from the previous generation. It is not a coincidence, as Galli (1986, 1988a, 1990) often noticed, that gradually some previously strong concepts of the psychoanalytic method (such as insight or interpretation) began to be deemphasized, while other concepts, previously peripheral to the method and close to the technical pole (such as setting or therapeutic environment) were emphasized.

The problem grew as more therapists began experimentally altering the psychoanalytic method with patients who were not classical neurotics. One of the pioneers who tried psychoanalysis with previously excluded patients was Sullivan, who worked with psychotics. His did not talk about psychoanalysis but about psychotherapy (if not *tout court* psychiatry—see, for example, the titles of all Sullivan's books and of many of his articles). The same occurred for brief therapies, which were called "psychoanalytically oriented" or "short-term dynamic psychotherapies" and not "brief psychoanalyses" (for a detailed critique of the radical theory of short-term dynamic psychotherapy, see Migone, 1985, 1995 chapter 3). Likewise, for group therapies there was a trend not to talk about "group psychoanalysis." In some instances, when psychoanalytic institutions were confronted with proposals to found associations for group psychoanalysis, they imposed their veto on the usage of the name psychoanalysis, but suggested simply group psychotherapy or group-analysis (see Galli, 1989, p. 216). We could go on with such examples. Curiously, however, this problem did not arise when psychoanalysis was proposed for children. The term "child psychoanalysis" was used, and not "child psychotherapy." This seems paradoxical, considering the great differences between the technique for adults and that for children, in which, for example, play technique modifies radically the classical rules. No doubt the authoritative presence of Freud's daughter in this field had some influence. We should, however, consider a sociological hypothesis, that it was little danger to the identity of the discipline to keep the term psychoanalysis for patients of a different age range where the competition with other therapies was less important, while for adult therapies the problem of the threat to identity (especially at the market level) was higher.

Parallel to the "widening scope" (Leo Stone, 1954) of psychoanalysis, the studies on ego psychology (Hartmann, 1937, 1964; Hartmann, Kris, and Loewenstein, 1964) developed, whose beginnings can be traced, even before Anna Freud's (1936) contribution on defenses, to Freud's (1923b) introduction of the structural theory, the tripartite model of ego/id/superego that marked the long transformation of psychoanalysis from id psychology to ego psychology (according to some contemporary authors, today we might be in the phase of Self Psychology). According to the conception of id psychology (a term that is incorrect because the concept of id belongs to the structural theory, being inseparable from the concept of ego), the therapeutic work consisted essentially in rendering conscious the unconscious, while with the introduction of the structural model naturally concepts such as ego, defenses, adaptation, and development gained more importance. This new approach necessarily implied a different psychoanalytic technique, in which a modification of the classical technique was legitimized. One no longer selected patients to suit the technique, but it was the technique that had to be selected to suit the patient. The patient, not the technique, was the independent variable.

The literature on the ego, defenses, and developmental point of view formed the conceptual basis of what later became the debate on psychoanalytic psychotherapy and on the differences between psychoanalysis and psychotherapy, that is, on the possibility of changing the standard technique according to the patient's ego structure. This point is important; we need only consider that within psychoanalytic schools outside of Ego Psychology, such as the Kleinian school, the standard technique is employed with every patient, even severely disturbed psychotics. There has never been any room in the Kleinian literature for the debate on psychotherapy. It is for this reason that Gill, in his characteristically provocative way, used to say that clinically he felt close to the Kleinians.

Conclusions

With his detailed theoretical revision, Gill was able to show that the traditional difference between classical psychoanalysis and psychoanalytic psychotherapy had little meaning. Of course, a once a week therapy can be a different experience from a four times a week therapy, but it is also true that a four times a week therapy of one patient can be very different from a four times a week therapy of another patient, and that a once a week therapy can be different from a four times a week therapy for reasons that are the opposite from what one may believe. The crucial factor is how the patient experiences the frequency of sessions.

The seeds of this conceptualization were already present in the development of Ego Psychology, a school in which Gill participated actively for awhile. When another conceptualization of the psychic apparatus and of the concept of defense was put at the center, naturally the theoretical difference between the two modalities collapsed. In other words, psychoanalysis and psychotherapy, from the theoretical point of view, gradually began to overlap already back in the 1930s and 1940s, and the discussion about their difference continued for many years probably because of the reasons discussed above. As far as terminology is concerned, Gill (1984, p. 175) tentatively chose to call—in my opinion reductively—his revised technique "psychoanalytic therapy," in order to differentiate it from the traditional usage of the term psychoanalysis, which so often, unfortunately, is linked with extrinsic criteria such as four or five weekly sessions and the use of the couch. A definition based only on extrinsic criteria is a poor definition because it doesn't shed light on the essence of the analytic process, which could be present in once a week therapies and, for that matter, could be absent in an "orthodox" psychoanalysis.

In his latest revision Gill espoused a relational or "socio-constructivistic" paradigm (Hoffman, 1991, 1998) of the analytic situation, and this new perspective is what allowed him to put forth his critique of the theory of technique. Still, a problem seems to me not yet resolved: why was Gill able to come to these theoretical conclusions only so late in his life, in the late 1970s and early 1980s? The bulk of the theoretical advances to which Gill alluded had already been made by the analysts of the interpersonal tradition early in the century, even starting in the 1920s. His adoption of a relational paradigm added his lucid, detailed theorizing to the pioneering intuitions of Sullivan, Fromm-Reichmann, and other interpersonal analysts. They had anticipated the same ideas and had believed in a total overlapping not only between psychoanalysis and psychotherapy, but also between psychoanalysis and psychiatry itself. Why did Gill, like many others of his colleagues in the course of this century, remain for so many years loyal to the classical tradition, unable to see its limits?

For a long time I did not succeed in finding a convincing answer. It seemed to me reductionistic to point to fear of going against authority, threat to professional identity, or the enormous economic advantages of a profession rigidly characterized by standards such as four sessions per week. Even if these factors have played a role for some analysts, surely many American psychoanalytic theorists did not make their living solely on their professional practice and had enough independence not to submit to overt or subtle pressures of organized psychoanalysis. Further, Gill was never afraid to expose his ideas and to change them if necessary. It is worthwhile to note that both in the USA and in Europe many analysts who at the political level had espoused progressive or radical positions remained conservative at the theoretical level, thus showing some form of cultural submission. Also, personal life circumstances (such as Gill's analysis with Samuel Lipton) could have had an influence. Further, the delay could have been related to the well-known isolation of psychoanalysis from the advances of other disciplines, especially philosophy of science and neurobiology. Only in recent years, psychoanalysis has been trying to fill the gap and to update itself in various areas of the discipline. But these reasons seem insufficient. How, then, can we explain the delay that still persists in wide sectors of the psychoanalytic movement?

I was finally able to ask Merton directly. The reason he made his theoretical revision so late, he told me, probably was what he called the "objectifying" culture, the "one-person psychology" derived from an outdated (and, in my opinion, misunderstood) medical model that so strongly influenced American psychoanalysis and made it very difficult for many analysts of his generation to make such a theoretical revision.

Although I find this explanation interesting, I still feel this enigma is not totally resolved. Maybe one day historians or sociologists of science will shed more light on this question. In the meantime, I think we could leave this problem open to further analysis. Such critical analysis and uncertainty toward the "truth" probably would have pleased Merton.

References

Codignola, E. (1977). *Il vero e il falso. Saggio sulla struttura logica della interpretazione psicoanalitica*. Turin, Italy: Boringhieri. English translation: The true and the false. Essay on the logical structure of psychoanalytic interpretation. In: *The Yearbook of Psychoanalysis and Psychotherapy, Vol. 2*, ed. R. Langs. New York: Gardner Press, 1987, pp. 339–377.

Cremerius, J. (1982). The significance of dissidents for psychoanalysis. *Psyche*, 36:481–514.

Cremerius, J. (1984). The psychoanalytic rule of abstinence: From rule-bound to operational application. *Psyche*, 38:669–800.

Cremerius, J. (1986). Staying on track: The psychoanalytic movement and the distress of the psychoanalytic institution. *Psyche*, 40:1063–1091.

Cremerius, J. (1987). When we as psychoanalysts organize psychoanalytic education, then we must organize it psychoanalytically! *Psyche*, 41:1067–1096.

Cremerius, J. (1989). Analisi didattica e potere. La trasformazione di un metodo di insegnamento: Apprendimento in strumento di potere della psicoanalisi istituzionalizzata (Training analysis and power: the transformation of a teaching method into a power instrument of institutionalized psychoanalysis). *Psicoterapia e scienze umane*, 23(3):4–27.

Eissler, K. R. (1953). The effect of the structure of the ego on psychoanalytic technique. *J. Amer. Psychoanal. Assn.*, 1:104–143. Internet edition: http://www.psychomedia.it/pm/modther/probpsiter/eiss53-2.htm.

Fossi, G. (1984). *Le teorie psicoanalitiche*. Padua: Piccin.

Fossi, G. (1989). New prospects in the relationship between psychoanalytic theory and technique. *Internat. Rev. Psycho-Anal.*, 16:397–412.

Freud, A. (1936). *The Ego and the Mechanisms of Defense*. New York: International Universities Press, 1946.

Freud, S. (1913). On beginning the treatment (Further recommendations on the technique of psychoanalysis). *Standard Edition*, 12:123–144. London: Hogarth Press, 1959.

Freud, S. (1914). On the history of the psycho-analytic movement. *Standard Edition*, 14:7–66. London: Hogarth Press, 1957.

Freud, S. (1915). Papers on metapsychology. *Standard Edition*, 14:117–258. London: Hogarth Press, 1957.

Freud, S. (1923a). Two encyclopedia articles. *Standard Edition*, 18:235–254. London: Hogarth Press, 1955.

Freud, S. (1923b). The ego and the id. *Standard Edition*, 19:12–66. London: Hogarth Press, 1961.

Freud, S. (1933). New introductory lectures on psychoanalysis. *Standard Edition*, 22:5–182. London: Hogarth Press, 1964.

Freud, S. (1940). An outline of psycho-analysis. *Standard Edition*, 23:144–507. London: Hogarth Press, 1964.

Galli, P. F. (1986). Poscritto. *Psicoterapia e scienze umane*, 20(3):369–378.

Galli, P. F. (1988a). Le ragioni della clinica. *Psicoterapia e scienze umane*, 22(3):3–8.

Galli, P. F. (1988b). Teoria clinica e pratica psicoterapeutica tra dogmi e stereotopie/Clinical theory and psychotherapeutic practice between dogmas and stereotypes. *Per la salute mentale/For Mental Health*, 2(2/3):113–119.

Galli, P. F. (1989). Continuità e mutamenti nella cultura psichiatrica italiana. Il ruolo delle riviste scientifiche. In: *I Fattori di Cambiamento in Terapia. Riviste a Confronto*, ed. G. Di Marco. Chieti: Métis, 1990, pp. 213–220.

Galli, P. F. (1990). "Psychoanalysis as the story of a crisis." Paper read at the *Rapaport-Klein Study Group* Annual Meeting, Austen Riggs Center, Stockbridge, MA, June 10. (Published version: Crisis of psychoanalysis? From the scientistic solution to the semantic perspective. *Ital. J. Psychiat. & Behavioral Sci.*, 1994, IV, 1:23–28; German version: Die Psychoanalysen und die Krise der Psychoanalyse. In: *Entfernte Wahreit*; ed. M. Kuster. Tübingen: Diskord, 1992, pp. 146–165; Italian version: Le psicoanalisi e la crisi della psicoanalisi. *Ricerche di Psicologia*, 1990, 14[4]:39–58.)

Gill, M. M. (1954). Psychoanalysis and exploratory psychotherapy. *J. Amer. Psychoanal. Assn.*, 2:771–797.

Gill, M. M. (1982). *The Analysis of Transference, Vol. 1. Theory and Technique*. New York: International Universities Press.

Gill, M. M. (1983). The interpersonal paradigm and the degree of the therapist's involvement. *Contemp. Psychoanal.*, 19:202–237.

Gill, M. M. (1984). Psychoanalysis and psychotherapy: A revision. *Internat. Rev. Psycho-Anal.*, 11:161–179. Internet edition: http://www.publinet.it/pol/ital/10Gil-aI.htm.

Gill, M. M. (1991). Indirect suggestion: A response to Oremland's *Interpretation and Interaction*. In: *Interpretation and Interaction: Psychoanalysis or Psychotherapy?* by J. D. Oremland. Hillsdale, NJ: The Analytic Press, 1991, pp. 137–163.

Gill, M. M. (1994). *Psychoanalysis in Transition*. Hillsdale, NJ: The Analytic Press.

Gill, M. M. & Brenman, M. (1959). *Hypnosis and Related States*. New York: International Universities Press.

Grünbaum, A. (1984). *The Foundations of Psychoanalysis*. Berkeley, CA: University of California Press.

Hartmann, H. (1937). Ich-psychologie und anpassungsproblem. *Internat. Zeitschr. für Psychoanalyse*, 1939, 24:62–135. (Engl. trans.: *Ego Psychology and the Problem of Adaptation*. New York: International Universities Press, 1958.)

Hartmann, H. (1964). *Essays on Ego Psychology*. New York: International Universities Press.

Hartmann, H., Kris, E. & Loewenstein, R. (1964). *Papers on Psychoanalytic Psychology*. New York: International Universities Press.

Hoffman, I. Z. (1991). Discussion: Towards a social-constructivistic view of the psychoanalytic situation. *Psychoanal. Dial.*, 1:74–105.

Hoffman, I. Z. (1994). Dialectical thinking and therapeutic action in the psychoanalytic process. *Psychoanal. Quart.*, 63:187–218.

Hoffman, I. Z. (1998). *Ritual and Spontaneity in the Psychoanalytic Process: A Dialectical-Constructivist View*. Hillsdale, NJ: The Analytic Press.

Holt, R. R. (1989). *Freud Reappraised.* New York: Guilford.
Holt, R. R. (1990). Una perestroika per la psicoanalisi: Crisi e rinnovamento. *Psicoterapia e scienze umane,* 24:37–65.
Kernberg, O. F. (1986). Institutional problems of psychoanalytic education. *J. Amer. Psychoanal. Assn.,* 4:799–834.
Kernberg, O. F. (1996). Thirty methods to destroy the creativity of psychoanalytic candidates. *Internat. J. Psycho-Anal.* 77, 5:1031–1040. Internet edition: http://www.psychomedia.it/pm/modther/probpsiter/kernberg-2.htm.
Lipton, S. (1977). The advantages of Freud's technique as shown in his analysis of the Rat Man. *Internat. J. Psycho-Anal.,* 58:255–274.
Lipton, S. (1979). An addendum to "The advantages of Freud's technique as shown in his analysis of the rat man." *Internat. J. Psycho-Anal.,* 60:215–216.
Lipton, S. (1983). A critique of so-called standard psychoanalytic technique. *Contemp. Psychoanal.,* 19:35.
Macalpine, I. (1950). The development of transference. *Psychoanal. Quart.,* 19:501–539.
Migone, P. (1985). Short-term dynamic psychotherapy from a psychoanalytic viewpoint. *Psychoanal. Rev.,* 72, 4:615–634.
Migone, P. (1987). Introduction to Enzo Codignola's *The True and the False. Essay on the Logical Structure of Psychoanalytic Interpretation.* In: *The Yearbook of Psychoanalysis and Psychotherapy, Vol.* 2, ed. R. Langs. New York: Gardner Press, 1987, pp. 326–339.
Migone, P. (1991). La differenza tra psicoanalisi e psicoterapia: Panorama storico del dibattito e recente posizione di Merton Gill. *Psicoterapia e scienze umane,* 26:35–65.
Migone, P. (1995). *Terapia psicoanalitica.* Milan: Franco Angeli.
Sandler, J. (1976). Countertransference and role responsiveness. *Internat. Rev. Psycho-Anal.,* 3:43–47.
Sandler, J. (1982). The training analyst's dilemma. In: *Psychotherapy: Impact on Psychoanalytic Training,* ed. E. Joseph & R. Wallerstein. New York: International Universities Press, 1982, pp. 39–47.
Stone, L. (1954). The widening scope of indications for psychoanalysis. *J. Amer. Psychoanal. Assn.,* 2:567–594.
Stone, L. (1961). *The Psychoanalytic Situation.* New York: International Universities Press.
Wallerstein, R. S. (1969). Introduction to panel on psychoanalysis and psychotherapy. *Internat. J. Psycho-Anal.,* 50:117–126.
Wallerstein, R. S. (1989). Psychoanalysis and psychotherapy: An historical perspective. *Internat. J. Psycho-Anal.,* 70:563–591.
Weiss, J. (1993). *How Psychotherapy Works.* New York: Guilford.
Weiss, J., Sampson, H. & the Mount Zion Psychotherapy Research Group (1986). *The Psychoanalytic Process.* New York: Guilford.

Chapter 12

Psychotherapy as Applied Psychoanalysis: Further Arguments Vis-à-Vis Merton Gill

John E. Gedo

Editors' Introduction: *Gedo challenges Gill's overriding emphasis on transference interpretation on the grounds that such an exclusive focus limits one's understanding of psychopathology to the verbal stage and more likely to the oedipal period. He argues that difficulties emanating from the preverbal period are not properly dealt with by searching after meaning. Rather, the patient requires reeducation, the "repair of an apraxia" (p. 243).*

More generally, Gedo raises the challenging point that transference interpretation with patients who show indications of serious developmental arrests are of questionable value, if not detrimental. He questions whether addressing psychological meanings of any kind will help patients with significant ego deficits and claims that Gill was operating on the incorrect assumption that "all human behavior is wish-fulfilling" (p. 243). In contrast, Gedo believes that "mental contents are epiphenomenal; I believe every form of psychopathology to be the consequence of some form of relative failure in processing information." (Gedo, 1995). He sees the value of transference interpretation as limited to the restoration of an adequate therapeutic alliance in the context of which the focus is on teaching the patient skills "essential for tension regulation, affective control, the setting of emotional priorities, reality testing, and the like" (p. 244).

Gedo's argument poses a serious challenge to the use of one standard technique for all patients and to a primary focus on transference interpretation. We believe that Gedo is correct in claiming that Gill viewed his approach as the treatment of choice for virtually all patients. Whether Gill would have argued his approach should not be used with patients with significant ego deficits or developmental arrests is not clear. One would think Gill would have included among the selection criteria for psychoanalysis (as he defined it [Gill, 1984]) that the patient should have some capacity for self-reflection and an ability to process verbal meanings on a symbolic level. It seems that Gill would have to have conceded psychotherapy might be the treatment of choice for the archaic pathology Gedo describes.

References

Gedo, J. (1995). Working through as metaphor and as a modality of treatment. *J. Amer. Psychoanal. Assn.*, 43:339–356.

Gill, M. M. (1984). Psychoanalysis and psychotherapy: A revision. *Internat. Rev. Psychoanal.*, 11:161–179.

Psychoanalysis Versus the Psychotherapies

The application of psychoanalytic theories and clinical skills to the psychological treatment of various pathologies through nonanalytic methods was already predicted—and sanctioned—by Freud (1919) at the end of the First World War. The experience of a number of analysts in military psychiatry (Abraham et al., 1919) undoubtedly contributed to his conviction; similar activities by noted colleagues (including Gill's mentors, the Menningers) during the Second World War ushered in the acceptance of psychoanalytic psychotherapy by American society (later, by much of the Western world).

Initially, the development of psychotherapies derived from psychoanalysis was largely fueled by the wish to make the potential benefits of psychological treatment more widely available. This desideratum led to clinical trials, notably at the Chicago Institute for Psychoanalysis, intended to test whether psychoanalytic results could be achieved on the basis of treatment schedules of just one or two sessions per week (Alexander and French, 1946; Deutsch, 1949; Alexander, 1956). These proposals created a storm of controversy because some of their advocates seemed to claim that the outcomes of their experiments were superior to those of analyses conducted in the traditional manner. (Hence, when Alexander hypothesized that the curative factor of his treatment was a "corrective emotional experience," this notion was widely condemned because it was rightly understood as an alternative to existing theories about the mode of action of psychoanalysis proper.)

The second major component in the expansion of psychoanalytic therapies was the effort to use them with patients who required hospitalization, including even schizophrenics (see Fromm-Reichmann, 1957). This was the most optimistic manifestation of a movement (one that is by no means spent) to broaden the scope of psychoanalysis as treatment, to use a phrase coined by Stone (1954). It soon became clear that, in many of these cases of severely impaired people, technical modifications of standard psychoanalysis were unavoidable. As a result, two incompatible traditions of psychoanalytic therapy developed side-by-side: on one hand, therapies that differed from psychoanalysis only in terms of a reduced frequency of sessions, on the other hand, those in which the technique itself was modified but the schedule of visits was not necessarily reduced.

When I began to work as an analyst more than 40 years ago, the conventional wisdom still held that psychoanalysis proper was to be recommended for people who met rather stringent criteria of analyzability. Analytic "therapy" was regarded as the treatment of choice for patients whose psychological resources seemed insufficient for analysis—in the conceptual vocabulary then employed, this lack was formulated as "ego weakness" or "ego deficit." Such problems could be dealt with through a "therapeutic" relationship (see Grinker et al., 1961) or, in selected cases, through a "preparation for analysis" (Rappaport, 1960) wherein the patient's ego functions could be strengthened (mostly through identification with the therapist's adaptive tools).

In that golden era of American psychoanalysis, one seldom had to compromise by agreeing to a less than optimal treatment plan for *financial* reasons—the occasional person without insurance coverage who might use psychoanalysis could easily be referred for low-cost care at the clinics run by analytic institutes. Hence there was no temptation to *try* for analytic results if it was impossible to set up the conditions required to produce a psychoanalytic situation (Stone, 1965). Occasionally, a patient whose analyzability one underestimated would spontaneously transform the treatment into a quasi-analytic enterprise; such experiences taught many of us that, in certain rare instances, analytic results could indeed be obtained without using the couch, at a reduced frequency of sessions, or both. In many of these cases, it was possible gradually to bring the external criteria of the treatment into conformity with the usual analytic standards. (Hence I believe that it is certainly feasible to transform some psychotherapies into analyses.)

A generation ago, the greatest uncertainty about psychoanalytic psychotherapy concerned those patients who were then considered unanalyzable (for example, those who were deemed too "narcissistic" to develop the usual libidinal transferences) but not so impaired as to eliminate all hope of remediation. With patients in this heterogeneous category, many analytically oriented therapists tried various ways to compromise between analytic goals and nonanalytic procedures. (For one attempt to suggest some rational criteria for therapies within this gray zone, see Gedo, 1964, 1966,1967.)

In the interval, the therapeutic scene in America has utterly changed: many technical proposals have been made that have widened rational criteria of analyzability (such as Kohut, 1971; Gedo, 1979), but for the vast majority of prospective patients market forces have undermined the feasibility of affordable psychoanalytic care. As a result, the "treatment of choice" is nowadays seldom selected; even fully trained analysts seem ready to compromise on some less expensive alternative—treatments of shorter duration and lesser frequency of visits than psychoanalysis proper. The unstated premise behind such treatment plans appears to be the unlikely contention that in potentially analyzable patients face-to-face therapies on a weekly or twice-a-week schedule (often without invoking the "basic rule" of free association) will more often produce those conditions usually called an "analytic process" than they formerly did with individuals who were thought to be more impaired.

These unfavorable social conditions have reinforced a persistent current of opinion within psychoanalysis that has regarded psychotherapies that come as close as possible to the model of "classical" psychoanalysis as the best available. Of course, the same conditions have facilitated the emergence of an analytically based "brief therapy" movement, marked by some degree of overoptimism, but otherwise a creditable response to current needs (Gustafson, 1986). Perhaps the most eloquent spokesman for the view that the best of psychotherapeutic tools is transference interpretation has been Gill, who reiterated this claim in his last book, *Psychoanalysis in Transition*. In this connection, it must be noted that Gill (1982; Gill and Hoffman, 1983) was also committed to the unsubstantiated belief that transference interpretation is *the* crucial curative instrument of psychoanalysis proper.

I share the widespread opinion that the manner in which one deals with transference is one crucial aspect of any treatment enterprise, for uninterpreted transferences invariably come to interfere with the progress of treatment. Concerning the psychotherapies, perhaps the best statement of such a view was that of Tarachow (1963), whose sharp differentiation of analytic therapy from psychoanalysis proper forms the antithesis of Gill's position. In Tarachow's schema, analysis may be conceptually differentiated from other forms of psychological treatment on the basis that in analysis transferences are allowed to attain maximal intensity because they are *not* interpreted until they do impede the therapeutic process, that is, until they become "resistances." (Gill's espousal of *early* transference interpretation in psychoanalysis proper marked a considerable departure from previously accepted technical prescriptions!) Thus, Tarachow defined "analytic therapy" not by means of external criteria but on the basis of the technical strategy of keeping transferences to a minimum through early (genetic) interpretation.

I have no doubt that in this controversy most analytic therapists presently side with Gill. Moreover, this preference transcends ideological differences—for example, within self psychology, Basch (1988) adopted a position analogous to that of Gill within ego psychology. I also have some empirical evidence for this judgment. To cite only one of these observations, for some years I served on a committee that passed on the applications of prospective nonmedical candidates for training under the auspices of the American Psychoanalytic Association; in the process, I read scores of their case reports. Both the great majority of applicants and of the analysts on the committee endorsed Gill's view on this matter.

The Lesson of Outcome Studies in Psychoanalysis

In retrospect, it seems paradoxical that the ideal of eliminating most distinctions between analytic therapies and psychoanalysis proper should in recent years have gained adherents, for the past generation has seen the publication of convincing evidence that the classical technique of psychoanalysis (that is, almost exclusive reliance on transference interpretation) is effective in relatively few cases. In other words, as long as we adhered to a single technical prescription, the stringent criteria of analyzability we were taught prior to 1960 were in fact appropriate. Several well-designed follow-up studies (Firestein, 1978; Schlessinger and Robbins, 1983; Wallerstein, 1986) have demonstrated that the resolution of intrapsychic conflicts through interpretation of a transference neurosis is seldom sufficient to produce a satisfactory adaptive outcome.

The Topeka research reported by Wallerstein (1986) covers the widest range of psychopathology, including several case histories of persons treated with psychoanalysis on the basis of "heroic indications"—that is, because it was thought only a maximal effort had any chance of ameliorating their condition. Many of these patients were periodically hospitalized. The results of these analyses were uniformly disappointing and occasionally disastrous—so much so that Wallerstein (1986) concluded that such analytic attempts are actually *contraindicated*.

The remainder of Wallerstein's sample is similar to those of the other studies cited (or, for that matter, to the patient population I encountered in my own practice [Gedo, 1991, chapter 10]). In all three analytic centers—the New York, Chicago, and Topeka Institutes—the analytic model followed when these treatments were performed was unequivocally classical. The follow-up interviews are reported in sufficient detail to permit the reader to make an independent assessment of the outcomes. (For my own view of the results of the cases from New York, see Gedo [1980].) Suffice it to say here that these results were everywhere disappointing, a conclusion explicitly stated both by Schlessinger and Robbins and by

Wallerstein. (Firestein made no overt attempt to evaluate the outcomes he described.) Schlessinger and Robbins (1983) attribute these poor results to the analysts' exclusive focus on oedipal transferences and their neglect of the derivatives of earlier developmental vicissitudes. In my judgment, their conclusion applies equally well to the outcomes reported in the New York and Topeka studies.

Limited improvements did, however, take place in all three groups of analysands. These changes consisted of two distinct clusters: on one hand, the mastery of certain sexual and competitive conflicts often led to some amelioration of functions in love and at work; on the other hand, there were nonspecific external gains as a result of the relative calm produced by being in treatment—these advantageous changes were often consolidated and became permanent. (Wallerstein pointed out, however, that such improvements could have been achieved without the commitment of time and resources entailed in an analytic effort.) Despite such positive changes, in most cases the analysands' major difficulties (for instance, character problems, depression, perversions, and addictions) continued to haunt them.

Lest we give in to the temptation to shrug off these sobering data because the analyses in these studies were conducted by candidates or other inexperienced persons, we should also recall that Erle (1979; Erle and Goldberg, 1984) has shown that there are no significant differences in outcome between analyses conducted by candidates (at the New York Institute) and those performed by a national selection of well-reputed analysts. The other major finding of Erle's research was that, in order to bring analyses to a mutually agreed upon termination, in more than a third of the cases, significant departures from "classical" technique had to be instituted in both groups. One can only wonder how often analysts who were less firmly wedded to a single technical prescription than those surveyed in the follow-up studies would have used "parameters" and how greater flexibility of that kind might have changed the outcomes of these analyses.

Psychoanalysis "Beyond Interpretation"

It was Eissler (1953) who first articulated the need for variations in analytic technique (what he called parameters) whenever the patient's ego resources make it impossible to promote the analytic process through interpretations alone. As the work described in Erle's reports illustrates, Eissler's plea for flexibility was accepted with extreme reluctance, as if resort to a parameter were a confession of the analyst's lack of skill with a purely interpretive technique. This reluctance was demonstrated when Kohut's (1971) suggestion that idealizing transferences should not be met with early interpretation (although in Tarachow's terms, Kohut's recommendation is the most appropriate of *analytic* responses) was widely judged to be advice to overindulge in (presumably needless) parametric adventurism.

Some 25 years ago, partly impelled by a wish to provide a rational classification of parametric (i.e., noninterpretive) interventions, I introduced a hierarchical developmental viewpoint to the psychoanalytic model of mental functions (Gedo and Goldberg, 1973). (Readers interested in the evolution of the model over the past 25 years should consult Gedo, 1991, chapter 3.) Perhaps the simplest way to explain the principles of such an epigenetic schema is to emphasize that it parallels the hierarchical organization of the central nervous system. Psychological development is portrayed as a succession of five phases because these reflect the sequential reorganization of brain functioning in the course of childhood: from a mode essentially lacking in cortical control (I), to one in which (in right-handed persons) the right cerebral hemisphere is predominant (II), to another (III) in which the left hemisphere gains dominance, to the establishment of well-balanced bicamerality (IV), and the subordination of the entire system to the highest (prefrontal) centers (V). In accord with the principle of epigenesis, the capacity to function in accord with earlier modes is not lost as later ones become available, and the organism may revert to their use whenever that is advantageous for immediate adaptation.

Each mode of neural (and therefore psychic) organization, I through V, has its characteristic pathology. As Freud (1926) already demonstrated, the inability to resolve intrapsychic conflict because of unmanageable anxiety is the typical problem of the oedipal period (which corresponds to mode IV in the hierarchical model). In such conditions, the indispensable first step in treatment is interpretation of the conflicting motivations involved. In the more archaic modes that precede the establishment of full bicamerality, there are few intrapsychic conflicts (although interpersonal ones are abundant). This is not the place to review the full complexity of the problems typical for the more archaic modes of organization and of the therapeutic measures appropriate for their remediation (for fuller accounts, see Gedo and Goldberg, 1973; Gedo 1979, 1988; Gedo and Gehrie, 1993); I shall merely illustrate this principle through the example of mode III.

Kohut (1971) brought to our attention a set of archaic transferences (the he initially called "narcissistic") of preoedipal origin. These primitive mental dispositions are characterized by the persistence of illusions, either about oneself or parental figures, or both. Typically, these are not defended against through repression but by means of disavowal. In the split-off section of mentation—which represents the input of the right cerebral hemisphere (see Levin, 1991)—reality testing is severely deficient, and these conditions generally persist even if they have been brought into consciousness. To produce adaptive changes, the illusions must gradually be relinquished through after-education in reality testing—the process Goldberg and I called "optimal disillusionment."

The hierarchical developmental model was well received, but its necessary concomitant, that successive phases of development are subject both to different principles of behavior regulation and distinct pathologies—and consequently call for distinctive therapeutic modalities—has met with considerable skepticism, not least from Gill (1981).

I infer that Gill could not accept a theory of technique that goes beyond the use of interpretation because he rightly understood that such a proposal is based on rejection of the longstanding theoretical assumption that psychopathology is the consequence of the vicissitudes of mental contents—as he put it in his last book (1994), that psychoanalysis is exclusively a matter of dealing with "human meanings." If we accepted Gill's premise, resort to a parameter would indeed be an irrational surrender to irrationality (or, if you will, a reprehensible inability to come up with the *correct* interpretation). Yet we have wide consensus on the fact that, beyond insight into the meanings of mental contents, adaptive change is contingent on processes that have been designated as "working through" (Freud, 1914. For the operational meaning of this metaphor, see Gedo, 1995); there is also agreement on the idea that these processes must alter the ways in which the mental contents in question are handled—cognitive and affective changes made possible by actual modifications of the neural substrate. From this vantage point, the *meanings* of mental contents are epiphenomenal. The actual work of analysis consists in preventing regression to primitive modes of organization or, in cases where development has been arrested, in promoting new learning (modifications of brain functions) to process information more effectively—such as improved reality testing. I prefer to call such a remedial procedure the repair of an apraxia (Gedo, 1988).

Paradoxically, Gill (1981) opposed purposeful departures from an interpretive technique despite his keen awareness of the inevitability and frequency of noninterpretive interventions on the part of the analyst. Under the impact of constructivism, Gill (1994) eventually softened his opposition to goal-directed noninterpretive activities, but he never abandoned his commitment to the view that prelinguistic or protolinguistic phenomena in psychoanalysis are only significant in terms of their subjective meanings to the analysand at the time of their occurrence. Thus, Gill conceived of psychoanalysis as a hermeneutic discipline and felt free to finesse the inconvenient problem of devising a valid metapsychology.

As I (Gedo, 1981) once wrote, "Gill finds it implausible to distinguish between [the] realm of subjectivity Freud included within the sway of the pleasure principle and a nonexperiential realm, involving organismic needs, [the] realm beyond the pleasure principle" (p. 302). In other words, Gill admitted defeat in matters that are derivatives of the preverbal periods of development and justified this policy by postulating, arbitrarily, that *all* human behavior is wish-fulfilling. Contrary to his view, I believe that early biological experiences, such as patterns of affectivity, which (from our customary psychological perspective) are, when repeated, passively endured, affect later behavior because they are *automatically* repeated in an active mode.

Yet the fundamental difference between Gill's therapeutics and my own goes even deeper: his focus on meanings gives mental contents and their elucidation priority of place. In contrast, I view mental contents as epiphenomenal because I believe every form of psychopathology to be the consequence of some form of relative failure in processing information (Gedo, 1995). From a slightly different viewpoint, this means that every form of psychological treatment depends for its success on its ability to enhance the procedural skills of patients in thought processing. One example of mastering a psychological apraxia is the repair of an alexithymia (Krystal, 1988). This is what Freud (1933) presumably meant by writing that treatment must accomplish that "where id was, there shall ego be."

The classical technique of psychoanalysis improves adaptation not because it illuminates certain specific matters dealt with in the interpretations. As Gardner (1983) was the first to conceive, analysis is successful if the analysand acquires the capacity to interpret his or her own mental contents. This is another way of stating that the occurrence of mental conflicts is endless. From a neurophysiological viewpoint, we may see conflict as the inevitable concomitant of the bicamerality of the human brain (Levin, 1991, chapter 2). Conflict per se is not pathological. It is the inability to resolve conflicts whenever the person regresses to function in a less mature mode wherein the free flow of information among various modules of the central nervous system is interrupted because of anxiety, that constitutes neurosis. Psychoanalysis ideally facilitates the resolution of conflicts by training patients to process information more reliably through novel skills such as free association, evenly hovering attention, mastery of affect intolerance, and so on. In this sense, any failure to resolve a conflict betrays the presence of a psychological deficit—a failure to transcend the conditions of mode IV.

In a sequence of works over the past generation, I have tried to spell out various deficits in cognition, intrapsychic and interpersonal communication, and the realm of affect, characteristically left behind by the successive developmental phases of early childhood (Gedo, 1979, 1988, 1996). The logical corollary of identifying these developmental disorders is to devise various practical means of instructing patients so that, in these vital realms, they will acquire the skills requisite for better adaptation. Most important are skills essential for tension regulation, affective control, the setting of emotional priorities, reality testing, and the like.

The complex theory of analytic technique I have consequently espoused could be called a "technology of instruction" (Gedo, 1988, Epilogue; see also Wilson and Weinstein, 1992a, b). Obviously, it stands in stark contrast to Gill's exclusive focus on transference interpretation. In my schema, interpretation continues to play a crucial role: it must be used to remove the emotional obstacles (transferences) that interfere with learning—as some would put this, to restore an optimal therapeutic alliance.

When Is Analytic Psychotherapy a Rational Exercise?

Although some commentators have objected to my analytic recommendations on the ground that they depart so radically from accepted practice they yield a process that cannot be called psychoanalysis,[1] nobody has ever argued against their rationality or therapeutic effectiveness. In contrast to the outcomes of the analyses reviewed in the follow-up studies I have cited, the flexible and multimodal technique I have used yields excellent results (Gedo, 1984, Chapter 2; 1991, Chapter 10). To be sure, since I adopted a hierarchical view of mental functioning, I have been alert enough to archaic pathology in prospective patients to have avoided undertaking analyses with persons who might need hospitalization, so that none of my cases conform to Wallerstein's category of those with "heroic indications."[2]

At any rate, it is reasonable to suppose that the close attention I have paid to repairing analysands' apraxias is one factor that has helped to avoid the disappointing results reported in the three follow-up studies. In terms of the developmental considerations highlighted by Schlessinger and Robbins (1983), the epigenetic/hierarchical model requires one to pay equal attention to the pathological derivatives of each phase of development, instead of assuming (as the analysts in the follow-up studies seem to have done) that oedipal resolution would automatically ameliorate the maladaptive legacies of the preoedipal era.

What are the consequences of using the hierarchical model of psychic functioning in the arena of psychotherapy? As Gustafson (1986) has noted, it may serve as a guideline in deciding how to intervene in brief therapies. From a theoretical viewpoint, it calls into question any recommendation to use one standard technique for all patients, such as I understand Gill's (1994) position to be. In a practical sense one can, of course, attempt to instruct patients in procedural skills whatever the frequency of sessions in a treatment may be; in my experience, however, successful learning in long-term psychotherapy is generally obstructed by the emergence of a variety of (usually archaic) transference reactions. Hence, in most psychotherapies, and occasionally in attempted analyses as well, what is actually accomplished is an improvement in adaptation as a result of entering the patient's life as a symbiotic partner, or in Kohut's (1977, 1984) terminology, as a selfobject.[3]

---

[1] For a recent instance, as well as my response, see Druck (1994) and Gedo (1994).

[2] For an instance that came perilously close, see Gedo and Gehrie (1993), chapter 2.

[3] Insofar as in his late work Kohut viewed the need to use selfobjects as expectable

As Tarachow (1963) long ago asserted, one may attempt to suppress transference reactions in psychotherapy by focusing on the difference between the childhood past and the therapeutic present, and such interventions sometimes lead to a new spurt of learning. The difficulty that almost always supervenes, however, is that no sooner is one transference reaction temporarily suppressed than it is succeeded by another; a whole series of transferences may follow each other, often in a circular fashion. This is the reason for the frequency of interminable and inconclusive cases in analytic therapy. In psychoanalysis proper, such vicious circles are somewhat easier to overcome because the specific functions of each transference reaction (and the manner in which these are interrelated) can often be elucidated through reconstruction of the childhood context in which it arose. Such insight, resulting from accurate and timely transference interpretation based on reconstruction, should enable the analysand to learn better ways to cope with the adaptive challenge involved than was the childhood solution thereafter repeated as transference. In other words, because transferences are allowed to flower and attain real intensity (especially as a result of a systematic elucidation of defenses), rather than being suppressed, they may lead to the precise delineation of the childhood apraxia they were originally designed to circumvent. Although transference interpretation is therefore a crucial ingredient of psychoanalysis, in itself it cannot be regarded as mutative.

I regard the dyadic transactions of early childhood that are later repeated as transferences as adaptive solutions that make use of the assistance of caretakers in circumstances for which the autonomous capacities of the child are insufficient. These stop-gap solutions of childhood are perpetuated whenever the individual in question fails to acquire the psychological skills necessary in analogous circumstances in adult life to manage without making a bid for a complementary response from someone else. (I suspect that Kohut [1977, 1984] may have been trying to outline such an idea whenever he referred to the person implicated in transference as a "selfobject.") Of course, "negative" transference reactions seem difficult to understand from this viewpoint as long as they are viewed as isolated phenomena; if, however, the totality of a childhood situation is reconstructed, we can see that the "negative" aspect of the transference merely repeats those childhood transactions in which the symbiotic need at other times satisfied by the caretaker has been frustrated.

It is precisely because in a psychotherapeutic context such inclusive reconstructions are seldom possible (they are difficult even with free association and a maximal frequency of sessions!), that we are unlikely to

---

throughout the lifespan, he has abandoned the analytic goal of maximal control over one's own destiny. In my view, such a compromise is appropriate only in a psychotherapy. If you will, one way to define analysis is that it is treatment in which no such compromise is made.

overcome the propensity of patients to slip from one transference reaction to another in any treatment that fails to use the full armamentarium of psychoanalysis. That is not to say it is impossible to expand the procedural skills of patients in psychotherapy, despite their transference-readiness. If we wish to accomplish this as psychotherapists, however, we cannot adhere to the interpretive model of classical psychoanalysis, as Gill would have us do—on the contrary. In agreement with Tarachow (1963), I believe that in psychotherapy we need to nip transference developments in the bud and, in relatively transference-free intervals, as best we can, attempt to address directly the patient's developmental deficits. I believe these are the conditions most commentators have called a "therapeutic alliance." It is probable that such a state of affairs may also prevail in the presence of a silent idealization of the therapist.

As I noted many years ago (Gedo, 1966, 1967), persons whose problems represent an arrest in development are generally able to profit from such direct instruction; in cases of complex personality disturbances, however, we are more likely to encounter various learning problems (often consisting of archaic transference constellations) that defeat such efforts. In my judgment, in those cases there is no viable alternative to a trial of psychoanalysis—needless to say, best conducted in the manner I recommend (Gedo, 1984; Gedo and Gehrie, 1993). Wherever I have heard or read accounts of long-term, intensive therapies that aim for major personality change, l had to admit that the great majority of cases become interminable or have to be interrupted in mutual disappointment. We would do well to avoid engaging in such overly ambitious and potentially risky ventures.

References

Abraham, K., Ferenczi, S., Jones, E. & Simmel, eds. (1919). *Psychoanalysis and the War Neuroses*. London: International Psycho-Analytic Press, 1921.

Alexander, F. (1956). *Psychoanalysis and Psychotherapy*. New York: Norton.

Alexander, F. & French, T. (1946), *Psychoanalytic Therapy*. New York: Ronald Press.

Basch, M. (1988), *Understanding Psychotherapy*. New York: Basic Books.

Deutsch, F. (1949). *Applied Psychoanalysis*. New York: Grune & Stratton.

Druck, A. (1994). Multiple models and the psychoanalytic stance. *Psychoanal. Inq.*, 14:243–260.

Eissler, K. (1953). The effect of the structure of the ego on psychoanalytic technique. *J. Amer. Psychoanal. Assn.*, 1:104–43.

Erle, J. (1979). An approach to the study of analyzability and analyses: The course of forty consecutive cases selected for supervised analysis. *Psychoanal. Quart.*, 48:198–228.

Erle, J. & Goldberg, D. (1984). Observations on assessment of analyzability by experienced analysts. *J. Amer. Psychoanal. Assn.*, 32:715–38.

Firestein, S. (1978), *Termination in Psychoanalysis*. New York: International Universities Press.

Freud, S. (1914). Recollecting, repeating and working through. (Further recommendations on the technique of psychoanalysis, II). *Standard Edition*, 12:157–174. London: Hogarth Press, 1958.

Freud, S. (1919). Lines of advance in psychoanalytic therapy. *Standard Edition*, 17:157–68. London: Hogarth Press, 1955.

Freud, S. (1926). Inhibition, symptoms and anxiety. *Standard Edition*, 20:87–175. London: Hogarth Press, 1959.

Freud, S. (1933), New introductory lectures on psycho-analysis. *Standard Edition*, 22:3–182. London: Hogarth Press, 1964.

Fromm-Reichman, F. (1957). *Principles of Intensive Psychotherapy*. Chicago: University of Chicago Press.

Gardner, R. (1983). *Self Inquiry*. Hillsdale, NJ: The Analytic Press, 1989.

Gedo, J. (1964). Concepts for a classification of the psychotherapies. *Internat. J. PsychoAnal.*, 45:530–39

Gedo, J. (1966). The psychotherapy of developmental arrest. *Brit. J. Med. Psychol.*, 39:25–33.

Gedo, J. (1967). On critical periods for corrective experience in the therapy of arrested development. *Brit. J. Med. Psychol.*, 40:79–83.

Gedo, J. (1979). *Beyond Interpretation*, rev. ed. Hillsdale, NJ: The Analytic Press, 1993.

Gedo, J. (1980). Reflections on some current controversies in psychoanalysis. *J. Amer. Psychoanal. Assn.*, 28:363–83.

Gedo, J. (1981). Measure for measure: A response. *Psychoanal. Inq.*, 1:289–316.

Gedo, J. (1984). *Psychoanalysis and Its Discontents*. New York: Guilford.

Gedo, J. (1988). *The Mind in Disorder*. Hillsdale, NJ: The Analytic Press.

Gedo, J. (1991). *The Biology of Clinical Encounters*. Hillsdale, NJ: The Analytic Press.

Gedo, J. (1994). Academicism, romanticism, and science in the psychoanalytic enterprise. *Psychoanal. Inq.*, 14:295–312.

Gedo, J. (1995). Working through as metaphor and as a modality of treatment. *J. Amer. Psychoanal. Assn.*, 43:339–56.

Gedo, J. (1996). *The Languages of Psychoanalysis*. Hillsdale, NJ: The Analytic Press.

Gedo, J. & Gehrie, M. (1993). *Impasse and Innovation in Psychoanalysis*. Hillsdale, NJ: The Analytic Press.

Gedo, J. & Goldberg, A. (1973). *Models of the Mind*. Chicago: University of Chicago Press.

Gill, M. (1981). The boundaries of psychoanalytic data and technique: A critique of Gedo's *Beyond Interpretation. Psychoanal. Inq.*, 1:205–32.

Gill, M. (1982). *The Analysis of Transference, Vol. 1. Psychol. Issues,* Monogr. 53. New York: International Universities Press.

Gill, M. (1994). *Psychoanalysis in Transition*. Hillsdale, NJ: The Analytic Press.

Gill, M. & Hoffman, I. (1982), *The Analysis of Transference, Vol. 2. Psychol. Issues,* Monogr. 54. New York: International Universities Press.

Grinker, R., McGregor, H., Selan, K., Klein, A. & Kohrman, J. (1961). *Psychiatric Social Work*. New York: Basic Books.

Gustafson, J. (1986). *The Complex Secret of Brief Psychotherapy*. New York: Norton.

Kohut, H. (1971). *The Analysis of the Self.* New York: International Universities Press.
Kohut, H. (1977). *The Restoration of the Self.* New York: International Universities Press.
Kohut, H. (1984). *How Does Analysis Cure?* ed. A. Goldberg & P. Stepansky. Chicago: University of Chicago Press.
Krystal, H. (1988). *Integration and Self-Healing: Affect-Trauma-Alexithymia.* Hillsdale, NJ: The Analytic Press.
Levin, F. (1991). *Mapping the Mind.* Hillsdale, NJ: The Analytic Press.
Rappaport, E. (1960). Preparation for analysis. *Internat. J. Psycho-Anal.*, 41:626–32.
Schlessinger, N. & Robbins, F. (1983). *A Developmental View of the Psychoanalytic Process.* New York: International Universities Press.
Stone, L. (1954). The widening scope of indications for psychoanalysis. *J. Amer. Psychoanal. Assn.*, 2:567–94.
Stone, L. (1965). *The Psychoanalytic Situation.* New York: International Universities Press.
Tarachow, S. (1963), *An Introduction to Psychotherapy.* New York: International Universities Press.
Wallerstein, R. (1986). *Forty-Two Lives in Treatment.* New York: Guilford Press.
Wilson, A. & Weinstein, L. (1992a). An investigation into some implications for psychoanalysis of the Vygotskian view on the origins of mind. *J. Amer. Psychoanal. Assn.*, 40:357–87.
Wilson, A. & Weinstein, L. (1992b). Language and the clinical process: Psychoanalysis and Vygotskian psychology, Part II. *J. Amer. Psychoanal. Assn.*, 40:725–59.

Transference

Chapter 13

The Interpretation of the Transference: Merton Gill's Contribution

Otto F. Kernberg

Editors' Introduction: *Kernberg discusses the manifold aspects of transference, pointing to his convergences and divergences from Gill's point of view. Thus, Kernberg acknowledges Gill's contribution to technique in the latter's emphasis on transference manifestations occurring with the initiation of treatment. (Silverman emphasizes this point as well.)*

While Kernberg endorses many of Gill's contributions to the conception and technique of transference analysis he points to some gaps and insufficiencies in Gill's formulations. Among Kernberg's main points are (1) Gill could have gone further in explicating the nature of the therapeutic alliance, including the importance of the patient's observing ego. Actually, this point bears on Gedo's critique of Gill's omission of a discussion concerning the patients for whom a therapy featuring transference interpretations is contraindicated; (2) Gill neglected to acknowledge that contemporary Kleinians echo his emphasis on the interpretation of the "here-and-now" transference and the avoidance of early "deep" interpretations; (3) Gill misses the close connection between "transference by displacement and transference by identification" and thus fails to emphasize the "extent to which the patient's transference determines specific countertransference reactions in the analyst"; (4) Gill goes too far in redefining transference as the patient's experience of the relationship without retaining the distinction between appropriate and inappropriate responses (it is central to Gill's conception, however, to avoid the dichotomy of what is realistic and what is distorted, a point also made by Wolitzky in his chapter); (5) neither the patient's nor the analyst's subjective experience is "privileged"; (6) the analytic situation involves three "frames"—the treatment frame, the analyst's technical neutrality, and the split in the analyst between an experiencing and an observing ego, or Kernberg's "third position." These frames allow the analyst to transcend the transference-countertransference situation and enables the patient to identify with "the reflective function of the analyst's third position."

It is easy to imagine Gill taking issue with aspects of Kernberg's position. He would likely have objected to Kernberg's view of the analyst's authority to detect and determine the patient's transference, a concept used by Kernberg in the traditional manner of transference as an exaggerated, inappropriate, distorted response. As Kernberg puts it, "An egalitarian ideology that considers the analyst's perspective as co-equal with the patient's, the countertransference as not more or less pathological than the transference, represents a distortion of the psychoanalytic situation" (Kernberg, 1996). In all fairness, Gill does not propose such an ideology, but privileging the patient's subjectivity may lead to it. Actually, Gill's position, following Racker (1968), was that the analyst's subjectivity should be no more "privileged" than the patient's. He adopted this position as a necessary corrective to the view in which the analyst automatically assumes an attitude of certainty about his or her inferences.

References

Kernberg, O. F. (1996). The analyst's authority in the psychoanalytic situation. *Psychoanal. Quart.*, 65:137–157.

Racker, H. (1968). *Transference and Countertransference.* New York: International Universities Press.

Merton Gill's (Gill, 1982; Gill and Hoffman, 1982) contribution to psychoanalytic technique, summarized in the two volumes of the text *Analysis of Transference,* the second one written jointly with Irwin Hoffman, occupies a central place in the development of contemporary ego psychological psychoanalytic technique. It was a significant step toward the convergence of ego psychology with other major psychoanalytic currents, particularly the American and British object relations approaches and the mainstream contemporary French psychoanalysis (Kernberg, 1993). In addition, Gill's assertion that the transference is a product of the interaction of past and present is a major bridge to the contemporary interpersonal-intersubjectivist-self psychological approach (Kernberg, in press), one that has been fundamentally influential in this country and abroad (e.g., in Thoma and Kachele's, 1987, 1992, approach to psychoanalytic technique).

Furthermore, the sophisticated research methodology presented in the second volume of this work in the form of careful and detailed analysis of transference developments on the basis of recorded sessions of psychoanalytic treatment constitutes a major achievement in relating the findings of formalized research to the practice of psychoanalytic technique. The budding nature of empirical psychoanalytic research, however, has not permitted it to influence psychoanalytic technique to the same extent that observations in clinical psychoanalytic practice have done.

I shall summarize briefly Gill's contributions on transference, together with a critical review of them, including a summary of my own positions regarding several questions raised by his work.

The Prevalence of the Transference

Gill demonstrated convincingly that transference phenomena are ubiquitous from the beginning of the treatment. He differentiated the initial resistance to awareness of the presence of transference from a general resistance to transference development, as well as from the resistance to its resolution. Thus, he described three distinct ways in which transference manifestations are deployed in the psychoanalytic situation. He pointed to the central importance of the transference as the major vehicle by which the infantile neurosis is expressed in the psychoanalytic treatment and convincingly stressed the importance of analyzing transference manifestations from the beginning of the treatment. This position represented a radical change from traditional ego-psychological technique, which at the time was still influenced by the classical overview of psychoanalytical technique of Glover (1955), who divided the psychoanalytic process into an early phase of "the gathering of the transference," a middle phase of the "transference neurosis," and the final phase of the resolution of the transference. Gill rightly criticized and dismantled that traditional position.

Gill might have added the evidence stemming from the psychoanalytic treatment of patients with severe personality disorders, in which blatantly manifest transference always dominates the treatment situation from its very inception. Further, he might have pointed to the fact that the more severe the level of psychopathology, the more premature the dominance of the transference.

Gill emphasized the difference, pointed out earlier by Fenichel (1941), between defenses as intrapsychic phenomena and resistances as interpersonal expressions of defenses in the psychoanalytic situation. In other words, all defenses in the clinical situation are manifest as resistances that, practically, become part of transference expression.

Gill examined the concept of the therapeutic alliance as an expression of the "unobjectionable positive transference," separating the affective aspect of that positive transference from the reality oriented, cognitive aspects of the rational collaboration between patient and analyst. Here, I believe, Gill did not do justice to the concept of the therapeutic alliance, as Deserno did later (1990). Deserno's text, by now a classic (presently being translated from the German), examined this problem fully. The therapeutic alliance, I believe, is now more accurately conceptualized as the alliance between the observing part of the patient's ego and the analyst in his professional role. The observing part of the patient's ego, indeed, is influenced by basic positive transferential dispositions related to the capacity for basic trust, and in this regard, the very capacity for a realistic collaboration with the analyst has a transferential basis. That basis, however, is transformed into the capacity for realistic object investment and commitment, and therefore, warrants being considered as a specific transformational product that corresponds to the realistic relationship between patient and analyst set up as part of the psychoanalytic frame by the initial instructions of the psychoanalyst. Loewald's (1960) definition of that frame, it seems to me, spelled out the conscious and rational contribution of analyst and patient to that realistic relationship, which deserves to be contrasted with the other transferential developments that evolve, as Gill proposed, from the beginning of the treatment. By the same token, the analyst's capacity for a concerned yet technically neutral investment in the patient's well being is also based on the sublimatory transformation of his own basic transferential potential linked to the earliest development of the establishment of the capacity for basic trust.

Gill was aware that in his radical stress on the importance of focusing on the transference analysis from the beginning of the treatment he was coming close to what the British schools, particularly, the Kleinian School (Segal, 1964) had been affirming and practicing for many years. He acknowledged the correctness of that approach but criticized its essential neglect of the reality of the patient/analyst interaction and the Kleinians' tendency to prematurely interpret the transference as related to the earliest and deepest levels of the presumed origin of intrapsychic conflicts, rather than focusing on the interplay between transference and the patient's experiences in the psychoanalytic situation. Gill's critique of the Kleinian position is warranted, I believe, if one refers to Kleinian technique of 30 years ago, but Gill evinced an unfortunate neglect of more recent developments in Kleinian technique (Spillius, 1988) which would have alerted him to the similarity between the developments he proposed and those of contemporary Kleinian authors. Joseph (Spillius and Feldman, 1989) and Segal (1986), for example, stressed analyzing unconscious meanings in the "here and now," avoiding early deep interpretations, and maintaining a consistent focus on the total transference, an approach remarkably similar to Gill's proposals. In fact, this point is one of the major areas of convergence between contemporary Kleinian and ego psychological techniques.

The Nature of the Transference

Gill's observations regarding patients who unconsciously defend themselves against awareness, development, and resolution of the transference point to significant aspects of transference analysis that had previously been underemphasized within the ego psychology literature on technique. The unconscious resistance against the development of an authentic dependency on the analyst, and with it, against all transferential developments characterizes, as we now know, the narcissistic personality disorder and constitutes the narcissistic transference in a specific sense (Kernberg, 1984). This very resistance however, is also a form of transference, a point to which I shall return, in the context of an object relations perspective on the nature of the transference. Gill's emphasis on the resistances to the awareness of the transference led to his stress on the importance of analyzing this type of resistance from the beginning of the treatment. His research cases demonstrated convincingly this technical approach.

The emphasis on the resistance to the resolution of the transference has been a major subject of our technical literature from Freud (1912, 1914, 1937) on, and Freud's analysis of the vicissitudes of erotic transferences and the repetition compulsion in the transference are related subject matters. What Gill, surprisingly, underemphasized are the long stretches of productive analysis of major transference developments, both in their informative and resistive aspects, with gradual deepening of the analysis of unconscious meanings in the here and now followed by tracing them back toward their genetic origins.

Gill illustrated two types of developments in the transference: the displacement of the transference from the original parental object onto the analyst and the unconscious identification of the patient with his parental object. What Gill missed is the intimate, indissoluble linkage between transference by displacement and transference by identification. What is activated in the transference is not simply the representation of a past, internalized object representation, but a relationship between self representation and object representation. What he called displacement refers to the patient's identification with the self representation while projecting the object representation onto the analyst. What he called identification refers to the patient's unconscious identification of himself with his object representation while projecting the corresponding self representation onto the analyst. This basic concept of object-relations theory, namely, that all internalizations are internalizations of a relationship and not of the representation of an object, would flow naturally from Gill's observations, but he probably was unable to make this step because of his view of defenses and drive representatives as relatively independent entities, in other words, a view of impulse/defense configuration predating the revolutionary clarification of this issue by Jacobson (1964) within ego psychology and by Fairbairn (1954) within the British school. Neither of these two authors figure in Gill's 1982 and 1994 reference list.

A consequence of this neglect is Gill's underemphasis of the extent to which the patient's transference determines specific countertransference reactions in the analyst. Gill did mention Racker's (1968) fundamental contribution, the clarification of concordant and complementary identification in the countertransference; but he did not link it naturally to a concept of the transference as the activation of an unconscious internalized object relation of the patient. He also missed, therefore, the analysis of resistances as particular defensively activated object relations in the transference, directed against opposite, repressed, dissociated, or projected impulse-dominated object relations.

The Analyst's Contributions

Gill (1982) came to another major conclusion regarding the transference:

> Rather than regard transference as primarily a distortion of the present by the past, I see transference as always an amalgam of past and present. Insofar as the present is represented in the transference, it is based on as plausible a response to the immediate analytic situation as the patient can muster. This view implies a shift to the position that the analyst is perforce a participant/observer (Sullivan's term) rather than merely an observer. It also implies a shift from the view of the reality of the analytic situation as objectively definable by the analyst to a view of the reality of the analytic situation as defined by the progressive elucidation of the manner in which that situation is experienced by the patient.
>
> From this view that the transference is a result of the interaction between the patient and the analyst it follows that the transference is ubiquitously present from the beginning of and throughout the analysis [p. 177].

I believe this statement contains both valid observations and problematic conclusions. It is true, of course, the patient reacts to realistic observations he makes regarding the analyst's attitude, behavior, and personality, and the expression of the transference crystallizes around these realistic observations. This does not mean, however, that the entire reaction of the patient to the analyst should be attributed to the transference. The realistic reaction of the patient to aspects of the analyst's behavior is just that, an appropriate behavior that has to be differentiated from those inappropriate, exaggerated, or idiosyncratic responses that represent the activation of past, internalized object relations in the here and now. The overextension of the concept of transference to the patient's total behavior blurs and dilutes precisely what needs to be highlighted and clarified. It happens, of course, quite frequently that unacknowledged or defended-against behavior of the analyst may move him to attribute a patient's reactive behavior inappropriately to the transference; this would constitute an authoritarian denial of realistic aspects of the interaction that the analyst has created or contributed to in the psychoanalytic situation.

Gill's stress on the importance of the analyst's honest self-scrutiny to recognize and acknowledge his own contributions to the patient's behavior is very well taken. It is also true, I believe, there are residual aspects of the analyst's countertransference—namely, very early transference dispositions that constitute the counterpart to the patient's transference dispositions linked to basic trust—that never can be fully acknowledged and understood by the analyst. This observation is not in conflict with the analyst's obligation to listen attentively to how the patient experiences him, scrutinize it for whatever realistic aspect it may contain, and differentiate within the patient's response that which is truly transferential. Just as not all behavior of the patient corresponds to the transference, not all behavior of the psychoanalyst can be subsumed under the current concept of countertransference. The observing part of the analyst's ego and his capacity for self-reflection, enriched and reinforced by his training, knowledge, and experience, is not part of the countertransference.

Gill's statement about the transference quoted before implied the analyst cannot study the analytic situation objectively, and that the analyst's view of reality must be defined by "the progressive elucidation of the manner in which that situation is experienced by the patient." Here, Gill can be read as privileging the patient's subjective experience as the basic data for elucidating the reality of the psychoanalytic situation, a major shift in the analysis of the transference/countertransference bind. The shift also has been enthusiastically adopted by the contemporary interpersonal-intersubjectivist-self psychological approach. I question the viewpoint, however, as follows.

The contemporary view of countertransference as the total emotional reaction of the analyst to the patient captures both the patients' contributions to the countertransference (particularly, but not exclusively, by means of the mechanisms of projective identification and omnipotent control) and the potential participation of the analyst's transferential dispositions in the countertransference, particularly under conditions of intense and regressive transferential enactments. I consider the analysis of countertransference in terms of concordant and complementary identifications a key instrument for the analysis of the unconscious conflicts enacted in the form of affectively invested internalized object relations in the transference.[1] The effective analysis of transference and countertransference

[1] The original meaning of "agieren" in Freud's work was not "acting out," but "enactment" or, as rightly translated in French, passage à l'acte.

can only occur in the context of the enactment of the corresponding relationship in the analytic setting.

So far, my approach reflects a focus upon the activation of dyadic object relations in the intersubjective experience of patient and analyst. But I see it as essential to go beyond clarifying the patient's subjective experience to interpret as well what the patient may not yet be aware of, or is avoiding becoming aware of. In fact, the more severe the psychopathology, the more significant information conveyed by the patient's nonverbal behavior. Tactfully confronting and clarifying that behavior is an important aspect of the clarification of the total nature of the transference. In so doing, the analyst also clarifies his own experiences and observations as a different, external object. The combined evaluation of the information derived from the patient's subjective experience, nonverbal behavior, and the countertransference provide a global view of the analytic field. The analyst's subjective experience is not "privileged," but neither is the patient's. The analyst's openness to correct his interpretations as tentative hypotheses is the counterpart of the patients' willingness to correct his own hypotheses about his experience. The analyst both clarifies the intersubjective field and adds a new dimension: an "outsider's" view of it, a reflection on what is experienced by patient and analyst, in addition to conveying his understanding of the patient's subjective experience. Here, the analyst's observing ego, his self-reflection on the nature of his countertransference as well as on the patient's subjective experience of their interaction, and the patient's nonverbal behavior provide a new dimension to the analytic process.

The analyst's interpretive activity validates the patient's subjective experience, broadens the patient's awareness of the object relation activated in the interpersonal field, and fosters internalization of the observing function of an external object, the analyst, that includes the object's own subjective experience.

I believe that the psychoanalytic situation includes three "frames": first, the treatment frame or psychoanalytic setting created by treatment arrangements, including agreements about when, where, and for how long to meet, the respective tasks of patient and analyst; and the like. This frame establishes by design a realistic interpersonal relationship, one that Loewald (1960) defined as the meeting of a person who needs another person to have the knowledge, experience, and good intention to try to be helpful without being omniscient nor omnipotent and that other who wants to help and is aware of the limitations of the effort.

A second frame is created by the analyst's position of technical neutrality and his analysis of the defensive operations that militate against free association and the activation of transference regression. This, the psychoanalytic frame, permits the reactivation and enactment of the patient's world of internalized object relations with their corresponding impulse-defense configurations and the elaboration of the intersubjective field that will become the object of analytic inquiry. Within the facilitating environment of the psychoanalytic frame, enactments of transference and countertransference dispositions immediately begin to distort the realistic relationship of the treatment frame.

A third frame is created by the analyst's internal dissociation into an experiencing part that participates in the transference/countertransference bind and an observing part that includes the analyst's specific knowledge, technical tools, and sublimatory affective investment in the patient. The third frame is essential in the interpretive process. Within it, the analyst immerses himself in the transference and countertransference relationship yet maintains himself outside of it in his interpretive function. This reflective stance constitutes the third position, to use a term from French psychoanalysis.

I believe the third position is an essential precondition for psychoanalytic work. The analyst transcends the transference/countertransference situation and brings in a new perspective that will clarify the unconscious conflict activated in the transference. As a consequence, by the mechanism of introjective identification, the patient is helped to develop a self-reflective function as part of the increase in his ego's capacity to deal with intrapsychic conflicts.

The split of the ego into an observing and acting part as originally described by Sterba (1934) represents the internalization of the reflective function of the caregiver—not simply from mother's empathy with the infant's own experience. Patients develop enhanced capacity for self-reflection not solely from the analyst's empathic response, but also and essentially through identification with the reflective function of the analyst's third position. I propose, in short, we need a "three person psychology," not a one-person or two-person psychology, the third person being the analyst in his specific role.

For example, a patient was impotent with his wife, while fully potent in sexual engagements with other women who submitted to him in a masochistic scenario. He would tie them up and have them carry out self-demeaning acts that symbolically represented their humiliation and his total control. In contrast, he behaved like a shy little boy with his wife. With me, he displayed almost a caricature of submissiveness. He became interested in psychoanalytic ideas, sought out my published papers, and, in an overblown identification with me, used the ideas he found there to argue with his friends and colleagues about alternative psychological theories.

In the course of treatment, the image of a violent father who was sexually promiscuous and a tyrant at home came into focus. The patient gradually became aware of his inhibited behavior as fear of rebelling against the violent father and of the fantasy that the only way to rebel against him would be a violent, bloody overthrow. An underlying fantasy slowly emerged in which he would sexually submit to powerful father representatives and thus solve the conflict with father by becoming his sexual love-object.

What made the analysis of the transference particularly difficult was the surface submission of the patient that protected him against an underlying wish for a dependent, sexual relation with me. The analysis of that underlying wish was interfered with by the patient's guessing my thoughts and immediately accepting what he thought were my theories, fully endorsing them in intellectual speculations. The speculations not only raised serious doubts in my mind about emotional meaning but also disorganized my thinking. Eventually I realized I had become the bound-up victim of the patient's sadistic control in the transference; his ready acceptance of his perception of my train of thought, his way of disorganizing my thinking, paralyzed all work in the sessions. The analysis of that surface quality in his relationship with me eventually induced confusion and intense anxiety in the patient. A fear of me emerged as a threatening father who wanted to keep him in the role of a little child and stood ready to castrate him if he were to penetrate his wife, who represented unconsciously his oedipal mother. It thus became possible to analyze the confusion and paralysis the patient had projected onto me, rather than continuing to enact the pseudosubmissive, father-son relationship.

In this case my early countertransference was one of a somewhat amused curiosity regarding this patient's battles in the defense of psychoanalysis, gradually shifting in the direction of a skeptical concern over his idealization of my viewpoints in psychoanalytic controversies. I had moved from being seduced to becoming a little paranoid to, eventually, confused. It took me quite some time to sort out the actual, deep wishes for a submissive, homosexual surrender from the subtly mocking submissiveness of the patient. The intersubjective quality of the interplay of his attitude ("trust me, I am a totally convinced follower of yours") with my implicit attitude ("I can't tell anymore what, if anything, I can trust") was resolved by my growing awareness that my paralysis and his joyful tranquillity in the hours represented the sado-masochistic scenario of the patient's perversion. My third position facilitated the analysis of the sadistic nature of this transference development and my masochistic submission and led to the activation of his underlying fears of the violent, castrating, oedipal father and the deeper wish for a homosexual submission to him.

There is, of course, the danger that the analyst may misuse or abuse his specific function of remaining outside the transference/countertransference bind by assuming an attitude of arbitrariness, authoritarianism, or indoctrination of the patient. That danger is an intrinsic danger in any work carried out with authority. It is naive, I believe, to attempt to protect the patient against this danger by eliminating the realistic, functional authority of the analyst in the treatment situation. An egalitarian ideology that considers the analyst's perspective as co-equal with the patient's, the countertransference as not more or less pathological than the transference, is a distortion of the psychoanalytic situation (Kernberg, 1996). In all fairness, Gill (1994) did not propose such an ideology, but privileging the patient's subjectivity may lead to it.

Optimally, interpretations should be offered as hypotheses, to be confirmed or disconfirmed by what evolves as a consequence of their formulation. They are enhanced by the use of metaphor, and have at best an "unsaturated" quality not linked to any particular, theoretically assumed, historical moment in the patient's past. They are focused, in short, on the unconscious in the here and now, with the expectation that the interpretive process will gradually deepen and find its genetic direction as patient and analyst follow the associations and observe developments in the transference/countertransference analysis. This view is in contrast to the current questioning of the "objectivity" of interpretations, the denial of the scientific, objective nature of the criteria for the formulation of interpretations, and the potential slippage of a constructivist perspective into a solipsistic relativism. Gill cannot be blamed for this latter day development of privileging the patient's subjectivity.

Gill appropriately, I believe, criticized the defensive denial by the stereotypical silent, passive, and anonymous analyst of his own contribution to the patient's transference regression. That view of the "mirror" psychoanalyst most probably has been unrealistic all along. It was supported, however, by the notion of the analyst's "anonymity," prevalent in both ego psychological and British psychoanalytic traditions in the 1950s and 1960s. The notion led to an unrecognized and unacknowledged idealization of the psychoanalyst, and a defensive protection of that idealization by neglecting to explore countertransference enactments and acting out and their implications for transference analysis.

Anonymity should not be confused with technical neutrality, a crucial concept often misunderstood and exaggerated in clinical practice. Gill (1982) referred to it in the following way: "Neutrality does not mean an avoidance of doing anything, but rather giving equal attention to all the patient's productions, without prior weighing of one kind of material over another, and confining oneself to the analytic task, that is, abstaining from deliberate suggestion. I have elsewhere (1996) described neutrality as including persistent attention to the inadvertent effects of the therapeutic setting and the therapist's interventions on the patient's experience of the relationship." Technical neutrality, as first described by Anna Freud (1936), refers to the analyst's equidistance from the polarities in the patient's intrapsychic conflicts, an equidistance that becomes particularly crucial when such conflicts are activated in the transference. Technical neutrality, thus conceived, I believe, does not imply anonymity but the expectation that the analyst behave in role, while accepting the manifestations of those aspects of his personality that are commensurate with an ordinary professional relationship.

Technical neutrality permits the patient's transference to be carefully differentiated from his realistic reactions determined by the treatment frame and the behavior and manifest expressions of the analyst's personality. The analyst's conclusions, of course, are always subjective in that he operates as a subject utilizing his responses to the patient. The analyst's specific knowledge, experience, and, particularly, attitude regarding countertransference analysis and the introduction of the third position facilitate the analyst's objectivity. The objectivity is not a guarantee of absolute certainty about the truth at any particular moment, but a gradual sorting out of transference from reality, helping the patient identify with the analytic function that eventually will translate into the patient's self-reflective function.

I believe that the French psychoanalytic perspective that conceptualizes the analyst functioning as the third person is an important contribution to this discussion (De Mijolla and De Mijolla Mellor, 1996). Interpreting the nature of the transference/ countertransference relationship from an external perspective symbolically replicates the role of the oedipal father disrupting the preoedipal, symbiotic relationship between infant and mother, thus giving rise to the archaic oedipal triangulation. In the case of patients with neurotic personality organizations, such a function is already available to the patient, whose capacity to split himself into an acting and an observing part indicates a firm establishment of a triangular structure, the advanced oedipal stage of development. Obviously, the analyst's self-reflective exploration of his countertransference also reflects this triangulation.

Patients presenting a borderline personality organization, however, may experience the interpretive behavior of the analyst as a violent disruption of the symbiotic link between patient and analyst. The analyst's interpetive role is strenuously resisted, among other reasons, to avoid the traumatizing effects of the discovery of the relationship of the parental couple, the differences between sexes and generations, the envy of the parental couple, the shock of the primal scene, and the most primitive level of frustration and anxiety in the form of fear and annihilation related to the establishment of triangulation.

The analyst's function as a third person is an important source of reflection and, eventually, self-reflection by the patient, a powerful stimulus for the development of introspection, insight, and autonomy, including autonomy in the search for further understanding of the deeper layers of the dynamic unconscious. I believe that, under optimal circumstances in advanced stages of treatment, the dominance of intersubjective activation of transference/countertransference developments may gradually give way to dominance of the patient's communication of his subjective experience, with internalization of the analyst's reflective function. This is manifest in the patient's capacity to reflect about his own subjective experience so that deeper layers of the unconscious emerge as self-discovery goes beyond the examination of present intersubjective experience.

In contrast, when the entire analytic experience is bound to the analysis of present intersubjectivity, the risk exists of a translation of unconscious conflicts into a more reality based, here-and-now experience that may serve defensive purposes against the deep understanding of the unconscious. Such a defensive fixation at the relative surface level of intersubjective communication may also serve defenses against deep levels of polymorphous, perverse, infantile conflicts, primitive sado-masochism, and conflicts around erotization in general.

The analyst's unconscious will always be present and influencing the patient, but this is no license for discounting the analyst's preconscious elaboration and conscious formulation of interpretive hypotheses. These interventions foster the development of tolerance of separateness between patient and analyst, acceptance of the final impossibility for the patient to totally know the personality of the analyst, and recognition of how the analytic relationship replicates the separation of the generations. The unavoidability of the patient as excluded third person from the oedipal relation of the parents becomes an affirmation of loss, separateness, and autonomy, which includes separateness and autonomy in the erotic realm.

I believe the development of a "real relationship" between patient and analyst as a consequence of consistent transference analysis and working through is a nonspecific, growth promoting aspect of the advanced stages of treatment that leads to partial sublimatory identifications instrumental in working through the depressive transferences and mourning reactions in the termination phase. This process culminates in the capacity for separateness and closeness, difference and loss, and gratitude.

Gill's contribution to contemporary psychoanalytic technique has profoundly influenced the ego psychological approach to transference analysis, established a bridge to other contemporary psychoanalytic schools, and focused the psychoanalytic community's attention upon insufficiently clarified areas, including the nature of anonymity and technical neutrality, transference and countertransference interactions, and the objectivist-constructivist dialectic of transference interpretation.

References

De Mijolla, A. & De Mijolla Mellor, S. (1996). *Psychanalyse*. Paris: Presses Universitaires de France.

Deserno, H. (1990). *Die Analyse und das Arbeitsbündnis*. Munich: Verlag Internationale Psychoanalyse.

Fairbairn, W. R. D. (1954). *An Object-Relations Theory of the Personality*. New York: Basic Books.

Fenichel, O. (1941). *Problems of Psychoanalytic Technique.* New York: Psychoanalytic Quarterly.
Freud, A. (1936). The ego and the mechanisms of defense. In *Writings, Vol. 2.* New York: International Universities Press, 1966.
Freud, S. (1912). The dynamics of transference. *Standard Edition,* 12:97–108. London: Hogarth Press, 1958.
Freud, S. (1914). Observations on transference-love. *Standard Edition,* 12:157–171. London: Hogarth Press, 1958.
Freud, S. (1937). Analysis terminable and interminable. *Standard Edition,* 23:209–253. London: Hogarth Press, 1964.
Gill, M. M. (1982). *Analysis of Transference, Vol. 1.* Madison, CT: International Universities Press.
Gill, M. M. (1994). *Psychoanalysis in Transition.* Hillsdale, NJ: The Analytic Press.
Gill, M. M. & Hoffman, I. Z. (1982). *Analysis of Transference, Vol. 2.* New York: International Universities Press.
Glover, E. (1955). *The Technique of Psycho-Analysis.* New York: International Universities Press.
Jacobson, E. (1964). *The Self and the Object World.* New York: International Universities Press.
Kernberg, O. F. (1984). *Severe Personality Disorders.* New Haven: Yale University Press.
Kernberg, O. F. (1993). Convergences and divergences in contemporary psychoanalytic technique. *Internat. J. Psycho-Anal.,* 74:659–673. Also in *Forum der Psychoanalyse,* 10:296–314, 1994. French translation: Convergences et divergences dans la technique psychanalytique contemporaine. *Revue Belge de Psychanalyse,* 26:1–18, 1995.
Kernberg, O. F. (1996) The analyst's authority in the psychoanalytic situation. *Psychoanal. Quart.,* 64:137–157.
Kernberg, O. F. (1997). The nature of interpretation: Intersubjectivity and the third position. *Amer. J. Psychoanal..* 57:297–312, 1997. Also in *The Annual of Psychoanalysis, Vol. 25,* ed. J. A. Winer. Hillsdale, NJ: The Analytic Press, 1997, pp. 97–110.
Loewald, H. W. (1960). On the therapeutic action of psycho-analysis. *Internat. J. Psycho-Anal.,* 41:16–33.
Racker, H. (1968). *Transference and Countertransference.* New York: International Universities Press.
Segal, H. (1964). *Introduction to the Work of Melanie Klein.* London: Heinemann. (Second ed., London: Hogarth Press, 1975. Reprinted London: Karnac Books & The Institute of Psycho-Analysis, 1988.)
Segal, H. (1986). *The Work of Hanna Segal.* London: Free Association Books/Maresfield Library.
Spillius, E. B. (1988) *Melanie Klein Today, Vols. 1 & 2.* London: Routledge.
Spillius, E. B. & Feldman, M. (1989). *Psychic Equilibrium and Psychic Change.* London: Tavistock/Routledge.
Sterba, R. (1934). The fate of the ego in analytic therapy. *Internat. J. Psycho-Anal.,* 15:117–126.
Thoma, H. & Kachele, H. (1987). *Psycho-analytic Practice, Vol. 1.* Berlin: Springer-Verlag.
Thoma, H. & Kachele, H. (1992). *Psycho-analytic Practice, Vol. 2.* Berlin: Springer-Verlag.

Chapter 14

The Conception of Transference

David L. Wolitzky

Editors' Introduction: *Gill steadfastly held that it was inaccurate and inappropriate to think of the patient's transference as involving a "distortion"; instead it should be seen as a "plausible" construal of aspects of the analyst's behavior. At the same time, he was willing to speak of pathological transference which he (1984) defined as "characterized by the patient's way of rigidly construing and compulsively constructing interpersonal experience" (p. 499).*

The present chapter presents a detailed exposition of Gill's objection to viewing the transference as a distortion. The argument is made that Gill was drawn to this position less for its epistemological virtues than for its function as an antidote to the analyst's potential manipulation and domination of the patient. It is further suggested that in adopting this view Gill placed himself in a dialectical tension between a coherence and a correspondence view of "truth." In the end, Gill eschewed dichotomies (e.g., between a one-person and a two-person psychology) and at the start of the concluding chapter of his last book (1994) he wound up saying that the shifts "from a natural science to a hermeneutic science and from positivism to constructivism embody a new metapsychology that supplants Freud's physicoenergic framework. While these changes favor a coherence rather than a correspondence theory of truth, the dichotomy between the two is often too sharply drawn. A pragmatic view in which one's theory is constructivist but in which one works as though correspondence is possible may seem to

---

I would like to thank several colleagues and friends for their helpful comments on drafts of this chapter: Morris Eagle, Lawrence Friedman, Robert Holt, Evelyne Schwaber, Paul Wachtel, and Jerome Wakefield. Due to space limitations this chapter is a condensed version of an earlier draft. Readers interested in the longer paper can obtain it by writing to me.

be fudging principles, but it is the necessary stance for the clinician" (p. 155). It is argued that Gill was forced to this compromise position by the untenability of an exclusive adherence to a constructivistic framework.

References

Gill, M. M. (1984). Psychoanalysis and psychotherapy: A revision. *Internat. Rev. Psychoanal.*, 11:161–179.
Gill, M. M. (1994). *Psychoanalysis in Transition.* Hillsdale, NJ: The Analytic Press.

In an effort to write a concise introduction to the chapters in this volume of essays in honor of Merton Gill, I started to reread some of Merton's papers, his monograph on transference (Gill, 1982), and his last book (Gill, 1994). I soon found myself writing a separate chapter that grapples with what I regard as problematic and ambiguous aspects of Gill's conceptualization of the transference. I focused particularly on his insistence that it not be thought of as a distortion. As we know, Gill was emphatic in his claim that it is a both conceptual and a technical error to define transference as involving some distortion of the analyst. I believe he arrived at his conceptualization of transference in order to support his clinical conviction that thinking of it as a distortion has authoritarian overtones. I will argue that if one has due regard for the fallibility of clinical inference, particularly with respect to the analyst's unwitting influence on the patient's reactions, it is neither inaccurate nor therapeutically inadvisable to define transference as involving not only a bias but also, at times, some element of distortion. I also will try to show at moments Gill seemed to concede transference could legitimately be regarded as involving a distortion. I think Gill's conflicting statements about distortion in the transference and his attempt to resolve them are expressed in his (Gill, 1994) suggestion that the clinician should work "as though correspondence is possible" while "one's theory is constructivist," although that might seem to "be fudging principles" (p. 155). I wish I had developed these thoughts while Merton was alive so I could have been sure I understood his position and so I would have benefited from the clarification he undoubtedly would have offered.

Gill's Strenuous and Repeated Rejection of the Idea of Transference as a "Distortion"

Gill's Published Writings

One's choice of professional discipline as well as the theory and associated techniques of practice one follows all result from a complex interaction of many determinants. This is perhaps nowhere more true than in psychoanalysis where one's personality is so intimately involved in one's everyday professional functioning. I mention this point at the outset because I agree with observations made by Friedman (in this volume), who, incidentally, referred to Gill as certainly the most vivid and possibly the most eloquent analyst of our time. First, Friedman refers to Gill's hatred of manipulation as a dominant theme in Gill's later work. Second, Friedman notes that "in Gill's paradigm the analyst is wary of all fixed, abstract knowledge and keeps an open mind about every level of the work from the expectations of daily routine, through grand theory of the mind, on up to the notion of a preestablished reality." Gill indeed took this epistemological stance but it seems to me he stopped short of fully and consistently embracing the postmodern version of it that dispenses with a correspondence theory of truth. In a similar but more explicit manner he came to the realization that a comprehensive theory of the therapeutic action of psychoanalysis required both a one-person and a two-person psychology.[1]

In Gill's personal as well as intellectual attitudes one can see how he would find appealing the hermeneutic turn in psychoanalysis and the perspectival outlook that often accompanies it. This view has an affinity with a view of the patient/analyst interaction in which one highlights the idea that the meanings the patient experiences in interaction with the analyst are inevitably, substantially, and constantly influenced by the analyst's personality and behavior. Thus, it was a short step for Gill, who early on in his groundbreaking work on hypnosis with Brenman (Gill and Brenman, 1959) realized the impact manipulating the transference, to stress that unanalyzed interactions in which the analyst's contribution remained

[1] In an interview with Raymond and Rosbrow-Reich (1997), Gill said, "And for a time, I abandoned a central tenet of classical analysis. God be praised, I was able to come back to it. Like in a workshop yesterday, a case was being presented of a woman who blushed uncontrollably whenever she performed. And I said to the group, 'I'm going to take a chance and say something. Do you think it's possible that this blushing . . . ?' You see, the very fact that I'm giving you this illustration means that it ain't all hermeneutics; *I'm still puzzled*. I said, 'Do you think it's possible that the blushing was a displacement to a different part of the body of the engorgement of other parts of the body in preparation for the sexual act?'" (p. 230; italics added).

hidden were antianalytic in that unwitting (or, at times, witting) suggestion was being substituted for insight. Understandings arrived at on this basis would be incomplete, misleading, and based on manipulation.

One major way in which insights would be misleading is that they would place excessive emphasis on the patient's contribution to the ongoing transference-countertransference enactment. Therefore, Gill was zealously attuned to allusions to the transference, stressed that these allusions were stimulated by the analyst's attitudes and behavior, and asserted that these transference allusions, as well as direct expressions of transference, should be made the primary focus of the analysis. Furthermore, in the course of examining these allusions to the transference it was vital to acknowledge the patient's experience was a *plausible* construction based on some aspects of the analyst's behavior and not simply a distortion.[2] This position seems designed to reduce the authoritarian and manipulative aspects of the patient/analyst relationship and, according to Gill, makes it more likely the patient can eventually recognize his or her own bias in the meanings attributed to the analyst's behavior.

From this perspective, Gill's view can be seen as a technical recommendation that resistance to the awareness of transference and its resolution is more effectively dealt with if it is not assumed the analyst is simply a blank screen onto which the patient projects issues uninfluenced by the analyst's personal qualities and subtle as well as blatant interpersonal cues and behaviors. Gill (1982) claimed "psychoanalysis as it is generally practiced is not of good quality technically. In particular, I mean that the analysis of the transference, allegedly the heart of psychoanalytic technique, is not pursued consistently in practice" (p. 1).

Gill noted that resistance to the resolution of the transference requires that the patient needs to become aware of what he or she brings to the situation. He (1982) wrote:

> This is often described as his coming to see how he is distorting the real situation, or how the real situation differs from what he conceives it to be. It would be more correct to say that the patient develops a hypothesis than that he distorts the actual situation. *"Distortion" is an appropriate designation only for those instances in which the influence of the past contradicts the information in the present. If the analyst recognizes that the patient is attempting to be as rational as he can with what he has to work with, he is respecting the patient's sanity.* If, on the contrary, he focuses on the patient's experience of the relationship without looking for something real that the patient may be responding to, he implies that the patient is manufacturing his experience out of whole cloth.

[2] Gill seemed to regard the concept of distortion as implying that the response was created from whole cloth, but a distortion usually is based on something real, by definition.

A more accurate formulation than "distortion" is that the real situation is subject to interpretations other than the one the patient has reached. The analyst suggests that the patient's conclusions are not unequivocally determined by the real situation. *Indeed seeing the issue this way rather than as a "distortion" helps prevent the error of assuming some absolute external reality of which "true" knowledge must be gained.* The analyst need claim only that the situation is subject to various interpretations and that since the patient's conclusions are not unequivocally determined by the features of the situation which can be specified, he would be wise to investigate how his interpretation may in part be influenced by what he has brought to the situation. *While it is in general not an unreasonable presumption that the analyst's view is more objective than the patient's, this may be untrue in a particular instance. In any case, the analyst cannot be certain that he is right, nor can he prove that he is.* A posture of certainty on the analyst's part can only make it more difficult for the patient seriously to consider an alternative interpretation to his original one" [pp. 117–118; italics added].

I have italicized the sentences that seem to me to most clearly convey the dialectical tension in Gill's view of transference and how it should be handled. On one hand, Gill seems ready to accept the traditional view that it is permissible to speak of distortion when the "influence of the past contradicts the information in the present." I think we can take this to mean that the patient is not simply interpreting the present in terms of the past, in which case we could speak of a plausible inference based on past experience. Rather, by virtue of displacement or overgeneralization the patient is misperceiving, that is, distorting, the present in terms of the past, presumably for defensive reasons. Gill clearly is concerned this view carries with it the potential danger the analyst might not be "respecting the patient's sanity."

Although Gill and Hoffman (1982) and Hoffman (1998) explicitly reject the idea of realistic versus distorted perception as a basis for defining transference, they make occasional statements, as in the quote above, that sound like they reluctantly concede some of the patient's responses are distorted. As another example, Hoffman (1998) is willing to retain the "term 'distortion' only if it is defined in terms of the *necessity* that patients attach to what they make happen, and to what they see as happening, between them and their analysts" (p. 104). If a patient is "*compelled* to choose one set of interpretations rather than others" (p. 104), it is hard to see how such biases could be free of distortions or misperceptions, even if the patient's response seems quite plausible. One can readily grant it might often be difficult to confidently assert the patient is engaged in a misperception, but if we regard resistance as defense expressed in the transference, and if defense involves some avoidance of awareness or self-deception, then it follows that transference is not simply a matter of selective attention.

From Gill's (1982) perspective, a major benefit of eschewing the notion of distortion is "it helps prevent the error of assuming some absolute external reality of which 'true' knowledge must be gained" (p. 118). Yet, in acknowledging it is "in general not an unreasonable presumption that the analyst's view is more objective than the patient's" (p. 118), Gill implies that some interpretations are more objective and therefore more accurate than others. That the "patient is attempting to be as rational as he can with what he has to work with" (p. 117) does not preclude the possibility of distortion. Consider the analogy between the ambiguity of the analytic situation and the ambiguity of the Rorschach situation (see Hoffman, 1998). In that context, we deliberately provide a situation with many degrees of freedom for responding. As long as the patient's response does not violate the realistic properties of the ink blot, we do not say his percepts are distorted, only that they are selectively biased and thus reflect the uniqueness of his personality. If, however, the minimal cues offered lead to responses that are measurably deviant in that they do violence to the property of the ink blots, then we say that the patient is showing evidence of perceptual distortions, even though they are not created out of whole cloth.

The analytic situation also is designed to highlight the patient's biased or selective readings of the reality cues unavoidably provided by the analyst. The bias might or might not constitute a distortion. That is, a selective preference for perceiving a Rorschach inkblot in a particular way or a proclivity toward construing the meaning of an interpersonal encounter in a certain manner might constitute one of several nondistorted views in the sense that they do not violate the realistic properties of the situation.

Gill's Unpublished Comments: The Gill-Schwaber Correspondence

Over a period of several years (from the mid-1980s to early 1994), Merton and Evelyne Schwaber engaged in a fairly regular exchange of letters. Dr. Schwaber has graciously agreed to allow Doris Silverman and me to read and to cite these letters for whatever light they might shed on the clinical and theoretical issues that passionately engaged Merton during the last few years of his career. The letters are almost entirely focused on psychoanalytic matters.

It seems to me that there are two major themes that pervade this interesting exchange of letters. First, Gill is trying to understand Schwaber's view of the psychoanalytic process and of the analyst's appropriate role in that process. Second, he is trying to persuade her of the importance of a two-person, interactive perspective and of the analyst's contribution to the patient's transference. Where the two main themes converge, in my opinion, is in their implication of the potential danger the analyst wittingly or unwittingly may impose his views and personality on the patient by virtue of prematurely abandoning the position of an exclusive focus on the patient's intrapsychic reality (Schwaber) or by failing to acknowledge or appreciate his contribution to the patient's transference (Gill).[3]

Much could be said about this issue in their correspondence but I want to focus on Gill's view of analysts' attitudes and of the psychoanalytic situation by simply listing a series of comments from his letters, comments that in their informality convey his position rather explicitly, though with perhaps less precision than in his published works.

From Merton's letter of 16 July 1992:

> Perhaps I should add that I am not only convinced, but messianic in my zeal, to combat what I believe is rife in our field, namely the analyst's imposition of his views on the patient either wittingly or unwittingly. I have often thought that one of the most stupid and unbelievable things that Freud said was his remark in one of his last papers, either "Constructions" or "Terminable and Interminable," that if we make the wrong interpretation no harm is done because there will be no evidence to support it and the patient will simply brush it off, or words to that effect. Or the companion statement, that he believes that he has never been guilty of imposing his views on a patient.

From Merton's letter of 6 August 1992:

> It is with due care not to superimpose our view on the patient, that we acquaint the patient with our view as something for his consideration that we may be enlightening him [about]. . . . I consider neither the patient's nor the analyst's view to be the correct one, but both of them to be selective, plausible, and important views which lead to a kind of "negotiation" between the two participants in an effort to enlarge the understanding of both. . . . Some views are better than others because they are more comprehensive, consistent, and *illuminating of reality insofar as it is given to us to see reality* [italics added].

[3] Schwaber's basic position, as expressed in a series of papers since the early 1980s (Schwaber, 1981, 1983, 1990, 1992, 1995, 1998) is that the essential analytic task is to engage in sustained analytic listening that aims to comprehend the patient's intrapsychic reality. In order to accomplish this arduous task, the analyst must avoid the natural tendency toward premature closure. From Schwaber's perspective, perhaps the most serious espistemological (and technical) error the analyst can make is to emerge too quickly from the mode of sustained inquiry and presume too quickly to know what the patient means by what he or she says.

From Merton's letter of 1 March 1993:

> On that same page Kohut twice speaks of distortions. Once "transference distortions" and once "the selfrighteuosness of a distorted view". . . You see, *there lies my insistence on plausibility rather than distortion*. When patient and analyst disagree there is a "truth" if you will in the point of view of each, but each is being selective. Hence I say "relativistic" or "perspectival" [italics added].

From Merton's letter of 12 February 1992:

> I suspect that many analysts and surely many psychotherapists do "correct" the patient. That is what is meant by calling transference a "distortion." The analyst feels he has to correct the patient. Of course, I am *violently opposed* to that. . . . However the patient experiences the analyst's actions, the analyst has got to see their "plausibility" *rather* than, as I believe is classical analysis, explain that they are "distortions."
>
> My point of view is that it is a two-person relationship in which neither the patient's point of view nor the analyst's point of view is objectively "correct" in their description of any event, whether what takes place between the two of them or something else. All that one can be correct about are such things as facts like the patient's parents were divorced. . . . I believe that it is just as much an error to assume that the patient's point of view is "correct" as it is to assume that the analyst's point of view is "correct" [italics added].

We can see from these selected quotations that when writing informally Merton also expressed quite clearly and forcefully his opposition to the notion of distortion as an element in the transference. He described himself as "messianic" in his "zeal," as "violently opposed" to the idea of correcting a patient's "distortion," as dismayed by Freud's "stupid" remark that a wrong interpretation would do no harm, and convinced that the field is "rife" with attempts of analysts to impose their views on patients. At the same time, he straddled the issue of a coherence versus a correspondence theory of truth by stating in the same sentence that "some views are better than others because they are more comprehensive, consistent, and *illuminating of reality*" (italics added). This statement is consistent with his published statement that the dichotomy between the coherence and the correspondence theory of truth "is often too sharply drawn" (Gill, 1994, p. 155).

Definitions of Transference

Gill (1982) reviewed the literature on transference to support his claim that it should not be regarded as distortion. He cited a definition of transference by Freud (1925): "In every analytic treatment there arises, without the physician's agency, *an intense emotional relationship* between the patient and the analyst *which is not to be accounted for by the actual situation*. . . . This *transference*—to give it its short name—soon replaces in the patient's mind the desire to be cured" (p. 42, italics added). In saying that the reaction arises "without the physician's agency" and that it is not adequately accounted for by the "actual situation," Freud suggests that the excess intensity is a quality that the patient brings to the situation. In this particular definition of transference nothing is said about distortion per se, although it is implied in the phrase "not to be accounted for by the actual situation."

Gill (1982) claimed "that the transference is often defined as 'distorting' a realistic relationship shows a lack of recognition that Freud's inclusion of the conscious, unobjectionable, positive transference in his concept of transference is not an unfortunate lapse but an integral aspect of the concept" (p. 12). On this basis, he argued that Greenson and Anna Freud were in error in their definitions of transference. Gill noted that Anna Freud (1968) defined transference (and countertransference) in terms of "the distortion of a realistic patient-analyst relationship by additions from past unconscious and repressed object relations" (pp. 95–96). He then cited Greenson's (1967) oft-quoted definition: "Transference is the experiencing of feeling, drives, attitudes, fantasies, and defenses toward a person in the present which do not befit that person but are a repetition of reactions originating in regard to significant persons in early childhood, unconsciously displaced onto figures in the present" (p. 171). Although Greenson's definition does not use the word "distortion," the phrase "does not befit that person" could, and probably should, be taken to mean distortion in the sense that it is an unrealistic response to the current situation—inappropriate, for example, in its intensity, tenacity, or capriciousness.

Reactions based on the past, as all reactions are, are not by that fact alone inappropriate or distorted, as for example the so-called unobjectionable positive transference (although as Stein, 1981, astutely showed, there are aspects of the so-called unobjectionable transference that are objectionable in that they can be subtle carriers of resistance). Perhaps we need to distinguish between reactions based primarily on displacement (e.g., erotic transference) and those based mainly on generalization (e.g., the unobjectionable positive transference). Thus, to expect help from the understanding figure of the analyst, based on memories of satisfying childhood experiences of being benignly mentored by an adult to whom one had a significant emotional attachment, constitutes a generalized expectation of kindly assistance based on past, similar experiences. There is nothing distorted, exaggerated, or inappropriate about this attitude (if the analyst is the kind of person assumed). If, however, the patient is in the grips of a blind idealization of the analyst, based on similar tendencies in the past, we are apt to consider this a transference reaction in that there are not sufficient realistic cues in the present situation to justify the patient's positive attitude toward the analyst. In this case it is an unwarranted attribution based on an overgeneralization and to some degree a distortion. If the patient is not simply generalizing his trust in the absence of evidence of trustworthiness on the part of the therapist but is doing so in relation to an untrustworthy therapist, then we would say this is even more of a distortion. Of course, the distinction between an accurate generalization and a failure to discriminate is not always clear.

The fact that the unobjectionable (useful), positive transference is one aspect of transference is one major basis on which Gill rejected the idea of transference as a distortion. In this connection, Freud's (1912) conception of transference rests on the idea of a stereotype plate which influences his later conditions of loving. In other words, the earliest libidinal relationships and their fantasy elaborations are the basis of a working model of what relationships are like. Once formed, this model is relatively impervious to change. It results in the tendency to seek similar relationships and to experience those relationships in accord with the original model (see Luborsky's [Luborsky and Crits-Christoph, 1990] work on the core conflictual relationship theme). Even when the other person is behaving in ways contrary to the original model or is giving ambiguous or minimal cues to support that model, the person might nonetheless invoke the familiar model as it represents the most probable expectation. In this sense one's experience of a new relationship usually feels plausible, unless the person himself reflects on his reaction and finds it inexplicable or unwarranted. Thus, to say that transference is an amalgam of the present and the past (Gill, 1982; 1994) is truistic, since the past inevitably influences our experience of the present. To the extent that past influences the present because of rigid, internal working models that do not take adequate account of the present, the person's response schema is sufficient to invoke the old percept or attribution. Actually, at one point, as noted earlier, Gill (1982) does concede that it is legitimate to use the term "distortion" "for those instances in which the influence of the past contradicts the information in the present (p. 117)," but the overall thrust of his writings on transference runs counter to this statement.

If, following Gill's argument thus far, transference is considered as a repetition in the present of aspects of the past, why then did Anna Freud and others include the idea of distortion in their definition of transference? It is not until later in his monograph that Gill refers to Freud's early definition of transference as involving a "*false connection*" (Breuer and Freud, 1895, p. 302) in which the patient is "re-experiencing emotional relations which had their origin in his earliest object-attachments during the repressed period of his childhood" (Freud, 1925, p. 43). It is here that we have the basis for saying that, as Freud portrayed it, transference (i.e., the erotic and the negative transference) is to a noteworthy degree distorted and unrealistic. In his paper on *The Dynamics of Transference*, Freud (1912) noted aspects of the normal person's way of relating have "passed through the full process of psychical development," are "directed towards reality," and are available to the "conscious personality" (p. 100). This is the basis for the so-called unobjectionable positive transference. At the same time, there are aspects of the patient's manner of relating that have not "passed through the full process of psychical development." Here Freud referred to those aspects that have been repressed. It is the repressed portion that is the basis for the "false connection" and the distorted, unrealistic, inappropriate behaviors that can follow from it. Thus, based on this aspect of transference, Anna Freud and Greenson were correct in including distortion and unrealistic attitudes and behaviors in their definition of transference. At the same time, one can agree with Gill that one should not *automatically* characterize what one regards as the patient's transference reaction as unrealistic or as a distortion.

From a Piagetian perspective, when the influence of the past overrides the present reality one can say that assimilation to preexisting schemata was stronger than the accommodation of the internal working model to the new reality (Piaget, 1954). In assimilation not balanced by accommodation, the person, in a kind of natural, automatic reductionism, is assuming any new experience resembles what happened before and is to be given meaning based on the preexisting schemata. At its extreme, this tendency results in *pars pro toto* thinking in which even a detail of a new experience that has something in common with a previous one determines the overall response. Thus, the response "bat" to an area of the inkblot that, by consensual validation, looks like a bat does not violate the reality of the inkblot but is a biased response in that it reflects a selective preference to an ambiguous stimulus. The response "horse" to the same area of the ink blot would indicate both a bias *and* a distortion.

Based on these considerations, I think the preferred way to conceptualize transference is as a bias[4] or selective preference seen in perception, judgment, attitude, affect, fantasy, behavior, or inference in relation to the analyst (as well as to any another person). The bias might or might not be distorted or unrealistic, meaning it might or might not be a correct or accurate attribution. The bias can be quite plausible in the sense that it is a reasonable, selective preference of a particular reaction over other, more or less equally plausible alternatives. In this definition there is no objection to the notion of distortion; it is just not a necessary feature of the definition of transference. The bias need not be based on

[4] Unfortunately, the terms distortion and bias have a pejorative connotation and perhaps could be replaced by words freer of negative connotations. The term bias might also be problematic in that it implies distortion. "Proclivity" or "selective preference" might be a better term.

repressed wishes, but it does suggest that new experience is being assimilated to a pre-existing model, for emotional rather than cognitive reasons, to the point that it does not take adequate account of the current reality. (See Wachtel's [1980] conceptualization of transference in Piagetian terms.)

The biases and distortions that emerge in the context of the patient's relationship with the analyst often are expressed in reenactments of unresolved, emotionally charged issues from the past. The distortions involved refer both to interpersonal reality and external facts. It is this aspect that differentiates transference from the many selective preferences of everyday life, for example, preferring merlot to zinfandel.

For present purposes, in relation to the definition of transference as motivationally biased and at times distorted reactions, I want to focus on different bases for assimilation to existing schemas by pointing to three ways in which assimilation can predominate over accommodation. First, there may be little if any information to go on. For example, fantasies the patient has before meeting the analyst can only be based on preexisting notions about therapists and the therapeutic process and on the basic information of the analyst integrated with one's schemas about professionals, trust or mistrust of authorities, and so on. Attributions to the analyst on this basis would be based largely on stereotypes and constitute a strong predominance of assimilation because no new reality either supports or contradicts one's schema. Or, one might have some information but go beyond it and fill in the gaps by assimilating the partial information to a preexisting schema. These reactions reflect bias but not distortion. In contrast, when significant, new information plainly contradicts one's preexisting schema, the failure to revise the schema might fairly be considered a distortion in that there is a marked lack of accommodation. That is, the patient does not engage the accommodations necessary to form a realistic appraisal of the analyst.

We can say in making a biased inference, the person is "going beyond the information given" (Bruner, 1973) . If the person is ignoring contradictory information, the bias is also a distortion. With regard to the first case, if there is some similarity between a significant other and a new person and the subject fills in the gaps by assuming that the new person has other qualities possessed by the significant other we have an instance of the operation of a stereotype. The subject is not necessarily wrong in assuming the new person has additional traits possessed by the significant other. But there is no information on which to base such an inference. Using this type of bias as the definition of transference, Andersen and her colleagues (Andersen et al., 1995; Andersen and Glassman, 1996; Andersen and Berk, 1998; Andersen, Glassman, and Gold, 1998; Glassman and Andersen, 1998) have demonstrated this phenomenon in a clever series of laboratory studies. From a social-cognition perspective, our conceptions of significant others operate as chronically accessible constructs, meaning they are always in some state of activation and show a readiness to be activated and applied to new persons. From a psychoanalytic perspective, this is what we mean when we say the patient has a preformed transference or a readiness to exhibit transference when triggered.

Therefore, a central part of the definition of transference should be the idea that new experiences are being assimilated to a pre-existing schema in a potentially maladaptive manner because they do not take sufficient account of the current reality. Thus, perhaps not all failures of accommodation, in the Piagetian sense, should be regarded as instances of transference. That is, there are many instances when assimilation predominates over accommodation that one would not want to regard as transference. For example, if one is shown the word "table" in a tachistoscope followed by brief, barely liminal exposures of the word "chard," one would likely, at least initially, misread it as "chair" based the strong prior association "table–chair." Thus, we might restrict the definition of transference to those instances in which the failure of accommodation pertains to emotionally significant issues, where the inaccuracies in inference, attribution, and such are rigidly maintained as the only appropriate responses to the current reality, and where the reactions are likely to have some maladaptive consequences. That is, insofar as the analytic relationship can be considered to be a microcosm of the patient's other interpersonal relationships one assumes transference reactions in those relationships are bound to create difficulties. Although these discriminations often are difficult to make in the clinical situation, in principle one could still maintain it is possible to distinguish degrees of realism versus distortion and degrees of maladaptation. Otherwise we can only speak of different ways of construing or constructing a personal world.[5]

Gill's Objection to the Transference as a Distortion in Relation to the Social Constructivist View

The main purpose of the foregoing discussion is not to argue for my definition of transference or claim it can be applied with good consensus. Rather, it is to focus on why the notion of transference as distortion was so unacceptable to Gill. It is noteworthy and surprising to me that early in his career, when he was a classical analyst, Gill construed the blank screen metaphor as seriously and literally as he apparently did, for example, as requiring (or justifying) not saying hello or goodbye to patients, as though one was "not supposed to have a relationship with the patient" (Smith, this volume). Although apparently not uncommon in the 1950s

[5] I am grateful to Robert Holt for his careful reading of an earlier draft of this chapter and for pointing out some of the complexities noted above.

and 1960s, this degree of aloof, stilted behavior has long been seen as a caricature of the classical position. After all, as Gill was fond of pointing out, Freud fed the Rat Man herring. Thus, Gill's last position of eschewing the notion of distortion in transference could be considered an attempt to reduce as much as possible the remnants of the analyst's power, authority, and manipulation of the patient (Raymond and Rosbrow-Reich, 1997).

The view of classical psychoanalysis as inherently authoritarian apparently is still strongly embedded in the thinking of some contemporary clinicians. For example, Pizer (1998) writes "Classical technique, based as it is on the adherence to the ideals of neutrality, anonymity, *authority*, and abstinence from enactment is a positional approach to negotiation with the patient (who is then implicitly humiliated by being invited unilaterally to express her interests)" (p. 196, emphasis added). Or, as Mitchell (1998) observed:

> For many, there is a clear analogue between the illegitimate wielding of power in classical psychoanalytic politics and the orthodox analyst's illegitimate claim to a singular scientific knowledge and authority vis-à-vis the patient's mind. . . . It has seemed as if the alternative to the analyst's traditional arbitrary claims to exclusive, objective knowledge is the renunciation of objectivity and the avoidance of truth claims altogether [pp. 6–7].

Mitchell apparently believes this view is not an outmoded caricature of Freudian analysts for he illustrated his claim by citing Brenner's (1996) recent paper. As stated by Mitchell (1998), "Brenner declares that his understanding of psychopathology . . . is empirically derived, objective fact." It follows, argued Mitchell, that:

> Analysts have a perfect right to claim expertise in the conduct of analysis. Any patient in [his] their right mind would cede that authority and knowledge to the analyst. And if patients are not in their right minds in this regard, analysts should hold their ground until patients come to see it their way . . . the analyst, Brenner suggests often, perhaps not always, knows better than the patient what is going on in the patient's mind [p. 13].

It is perhaps, at least in part, in reaction to such a perception of classical analysts that Mitchell prefers a view of the mind as "constructed" rather than "uncovered." It is not that Mitchell claims to be without a preexisting model of psychopathology, but that he maintains "it is one among many possible and *valid*[6] ways of viewing psychopathology"

[6] By using the term "valid" Mitchell would seem to be implying a truth claim rather than meaning valid in the sense of one of several, equally plausible views.

(emphasis added) and one that is not, in contrast to Brenner's model, held to be "empirically derived and objective" (p. 20). Yet, is it not reasonable to suppose that relational and Freudian analysts are equally attached to their preferred narrative story lines concerning what they regard to be the core motives and conflicts of their patients and that representatives of these schools of thought will offer their best guesses of how these preformed narrative structures make intelligible a particular patient's life history and current emotional suffering? To suggest that it is inherently Freudian to claim excessive authority for one's theoretical point of view and one's clinical inferences and interpretations seems to me to be essentially an ad hominem attack that does not advance our understanding. What it does do is swing the pendulum from the belief that we could discover true hidden meanings in the patient's mind to the belief that a negotiated, co-constructed narrative, without any preliminary hunches about what might be *in* the patient's mind, is the only morally and epistemologically legitimate way to conduct an analysis, a view which can be held in an equally dogmatic way.

Like Mitchell, Hoffman also worries about the dangers of thinking the analyst can discover something hidden and preformed in the patient's mind. In a footnote in his paper on *Conviction and Uncertainty in Psychoanalytic Interactions*, Hoffman (1998) wrote, "It is a very short step from a claim that one knows one's own mind to authoritarianism" (p. 168). Hoffman's concern seems linked to his construal of what he refers to as the "positivist or objectivist paradigm" in which "analysts . . . are thought to be capable of standing outside the interaction with the patient, so that they can generate rather confident hypotheses and judgments about the patient's history, dynamics, and transference and about what they themselves should do from moment to moment" (p. 164). Implied in the title of his paper and stated explicitly within it is the claim that the positivist paradigm is associated with an attitude of "conviction" based on allegedly objective knowledge whereas the social-constructivist paradigm is associated with an attitude of "uncertainty," although he allowed the analyst might experience a sense of conviction about his or her subjective experience. Although Hoffman explicitly recognized the possibility of an "open-minded positivism" (p. 169), the overall tone of the paper, as well as of others by Hoffman, is that social constructivists are less apt to impose their own views on the patient.

It should be clear that any insistent claim of certainty, particularly in the realm of motives, whether one's own or another's, can indeed be exploited in the service of wielding power and exercising control. We

---

However, he does not spell out the criteria for judging the accuracy of an inference. It is an ironic, self-contradiction that writers who claim greater validity for the position that they urge tell us that no position has greater validity than another, since all truth is relative.

know, however, from bitter experience that the authoritarianism from the left can be as destructive as the authoritarianism from the right. Thus, constructivism, particularly insofar as it relinquishes hope of arriving at objective knowledge, could be misused to impose one's preferred narrative on the patient just as readily as someone operating from a positivist perspective could seek to impose a preferred theory on the patient. There are arrogant positivists and arrogant constructivists and, let us hope, there are also humble positivists and humble constructivists. Some authors writing from a social-constructivist perspective write as though the idea of a humble positivist is a contradiction in terms.[7] It is also ironic that the constructivist claim of the superiority of the constructivist paradigm is essentially a positivist claim.

Because classical psychoanalysis emerged in a positivist era and because some of its adherents undoubtedly suffered from an excess of theoretical zeal (as well as therapeutic zeal), it is understandable that many critics mistakenly take this historical origin to mean, compared with a constructivist outlook, there is a greater *intrinsic* affinity between authoritarianism and a classical/positivist approach to psychoanalysis. Even if an authoritarian attitude were a common abuse of those with a positivist outlook, it still is not an inherent feature of that epistemological stance.

In sum, if Hoffman is right in warning us that it is a short step from claiming to know one's own mind to authoritarianism it is, sadly, an equally short step from thinking that since the patient does not know his or her mind one can engage in an authoritarian imposition of one's preferred narrative.[8]

Mitchell (1998) wrote "there can be no singular, authoritative version in the patient's mind' about which *either* the analyst or the patient can be right or wrong. Of course, this does not mean that anything goes, that all constructions of conscious experience are equally plausible or accurate" (p. 17). The second sentence suggests a nostalgic nod to a correspondence view of truth and carries the implication that there have to be some criteria for judging the plausibility and degrees of accuracy of clinical inferences. Yet, the thrust of Mitchell's argument is it is dangerous to think the analyst or patient can be right or wrong.

The approach of authors who favor a social-constructivist position often rests on the assumption classical analysts are much more likely than self psychology or object-relations analysts to arbitrate the patient's real-

---

[7] If positivists did not have uncertainty and doubt about the validity of their conclusions, they would not emphasize the importance of experimental controls as a way to trying to eliminate alternative explanations. In this regard, Hoffman's (1998) linkage of positivism and authoritarianism seems puzzling and misleading since positivism is based on skepticism in trusting subjective experience as a basis for conviction about one's inferences.

[8] Schwaber raises similar concerns in one of her letters to Gill (July 19, 1989).

ity, presumably on the grounds that Freudians are more apt to ignore they are participant observers and to think they can operate as pure observers. In my view, there is no inherent theoretical reason for Freudians to think they are arbiters of the patient's reality. Genuine openness to the data and to the interactive experience of the analytic encounter, empathy, avoidance of premature closure, attention to the therapeutic alliance, willingness to abandon a dynamic formulation, and alertness to the countertransference do not seem, on theoretical grounds, to be the exclusive province of object relations and self psychology analysts. I think the excessive technical rigidity of Freudians of the 1950s and 1960s created a chronically maintained image of Freudians as authoritarian. From the perspective of contemporary Freudians, this image constitutes a visiting the sins of the fathers upon the sons. It is also an interesting irony, as Eagle (this volume) clearly noted, that many ardent constructivists are ready to assume if they feel something toward the patient the patient intended them to feel it, and take this as their objective reading of the patient.[9]

I believe Gill's attraction to the social-constructivist paradigm derived in large measure from a *partial* inclination to accept the point of view stated by Mitchell above. At the same time, I believe Gill allowed himself to have ideas, from the start of treatment, about what might "really" be going on in the patient's mind but was careful not to take these ideas too seriously in the absence of confirming evidence. In the end, I think it is fair to say Gill's approach was to be appropriately skeptical about what he thought was going on in the analytic interaction and to be mindful of how he contributed to the patient's experience of him, but not to shrink from having ideas about what might be going on in the patient's mind.

Before he more fully embraced the social-constructivist view, Gill clearly

---

[9] In reflecting on what I regard as Mitchell's (1998) extreme constructivism, I found Wakefield's (1999, personal communication) clarification useful. He draws a distinction between *espistemological relativism* and *ontological relativism*. According to the former position, because we cannot be sure that we know what is going on in the mind of the other we have to be very cautious in our infrerences and receptive to the patient's point of view as a valuable corrective to our initial inference. The latter position maintains that there is nothing we can know independently of what is co-constructed and that there is no real truth other than what is constructed together. I have argued that Gill flirted with the idea of going over the line from espistemological relativism to ontological relativism but wound up straddling the two positions. To the extent that Gill was drawn toward ontological relativism in order to warn us of the temptation to think "I know *better* what is going on in your mind" and to be wary of quickly inferring that the patient was distorting, the issue can be seen as one of emphasis rather than a new paradigm (see, Gill, 1984; Wallerstein, 1984).

As my friend and colleague Morris Eagle humorously put it in coining a phrase during our discussion of Wakefield's comments on this chapter, a "humble espistemologist" is one who has been heard to mutter, "What do *I* know?"

thought there was something to be discovered in the patient's mind, not solely coconstructed. For instance, in his (1983) paper *The Point of View of Psychoanalysis*, he stated, "Interpretation is devoted to discovering hidden meanings. Psychoanalysts surely are occupied with finding such meanings" (p. 533). Even in his last work (Gill, 1994) he was not willing to abandon the traditional view and fully espouse the constructivist perspective. His concluding chapter, after noting the shift from positivism to constructivism favored a coherence theory of truth and "the dichotomy between the two is often too sharply drawn," he wrote, "A pragmatic view in which one's theory is constructivist but in which one works as though correspondence is possible may seem to be fudging principles, but it is the necessary stance of the clinician" (p. 155).

Thus, Gill was drawn to the constructivist position yet ended up with the hybrid view that we should have a constructivist view of transference but operate clinically from a correspondence theory stance. This final compromise, as well as his advocacy of both a one-person and a two-person psychology, seems to me understandable in the following way. On one hand, it preserves the idea of intrapsychically based unconscious fantasies in the patient's mind prior to the start of the analytic encounter. It recognizes that (1) these fantasies can become activated in the course of treatment, (2) some of these fantasies will emerge with any analyst while others might or might not emerge as a function of the particular analyst-patient dyad; (3) these fantasies will, by definition, be based on earlier experiences; (4) they are hidden but discoverable and coconstructed only in the sense that the analytic collaboration contributes to their emergence (but does not create them), and, (5) these fantasies can serve as raw material that can be re-worked in the patient's mind, partly as a function of the unique analytic dyad, and can color and shape the way the patient experiences the analytic interaction, including the creation of relatively new experiences unique to the particular analytic dyad.

Because the analyst is inevitably a participant/observer who emits cues that influence the patient's experience of the relationship, the analyst must recognize and acknowledge, at least silently, the inevitability of participation in the relationship so the patient is not re-traumatized into feeling that he or she is a crazy person creating a perception out of whole cloth. The failure to appreciate the above view can result in an insidiously arrogant stance in which the analyst assumes he has total knowledge of his own unconscious for only then can the analyst judge with authority and correctness that the patient is distorting. Analysts of all persuasions would readily agree that any claim of interpretive infallibility would constitute an egregious display of shameless arrogance.[10]

---

[10] Gill's writings offer fertile ground for further exploration of some of the philosophical dilemmas in contemporary psychoanalysis as well as the subtle ways in which moral issues are intertwined with theoretical ones. My purpose in this chap-

Thus, I agree with Gill that the ready, unreflected-on assumption that the patient is distorting the analyst constitutes a dangerous therapeutic stance. However, the initially tentative inference of distortion says, in effect, one cannot see what about the analyst or the analytic situation gave rise to the patient's reaction. In my view, such an inference is benign if it does not readily become a conclusion and if it stimulates self-reflection in order to detect one's possible self-deception and one's contribution to the patient's reaction. In other words, Gill's emphasis is most useful as a warning for those analysts who might still adhere to a blank-screen model with an asocial ("one-person") view of the analytic relationship that obscures the inevitable, transference/countertransference enactments and assumes the transference unfolds uninfluenced by the analyst and the nature of the interaction.

Thus, I think Gill's semantic and conceptual distaste for the word "distortion" is a reflection of his desire to combat arrogance as much as it is a preferred, well-reasoned philosophical position, although he presented it primarily as the latter. In the end, I think that Gill believed some interpretations of the meanings of the patient's intrapsychic life are likely to be more or less accurate in an objective sense, but we have to be very cautious and humble in our beliefs about these interpretations lest our unconscious blind spots create plausible but inaccurate readings of the patient.

Implications of Gill's View for Analytic Treatment

In my view, contained within Gill's emphasis on interpreting the analytic interaction are some largely implicit assertions about key elements necessary for therapeutic change. Stated most broadly, I suggest Gill believed the quality of the analytic relationship is vital to a positive therapeutic outcome, although I do not recall that he ever expressed it quite this way. More specifically, I read Gill as wanting to promote an egalitarian atmosphere in a situation that otherwise could lend itself to the analyst's exploitation of power. I argue, then, that a primary consequence of (if not motive for) Gill's conception of transference is it helps the patient form a relationship with a significant new object who models a kind of relationship the patient probably did not have in childhood. That experience is the following: the person with a stronger position of power and authority could claim the patient is distorting. Yet, the patient or the patient's psychopathology is not "blamed" for any rupture or difficulty in their relationship. Instead, the analyst understands the patient's responses are a

---

ter is to address these issues in only a limited way as I attempt to articulate the claim that the positions that Gill took in the latter part of his career were heavily influenced by his desire to combat the arrogance he felt too readily accompanied an emphasis on transference as distortion.

plausible construal of their interaction and, furthermore, in the inevitable transference-countertransference enactments, the analyst readily acknowledges there were realistic aspects of his or her behavior that triggered particular emotional reactions in the patient. The analyst thereby shows one can and should seek to take the role of the other and accept responsibility for one's own contribution to the interaction, even when one is in a power position to avoid doing so. The analyst's attitude and behavior are experienced by the patient as fair and respectful of his or her autonomy, freedom, and individuality. Because these new experiences occur in the context of pursuing greater self-understanding as well as mutual understanding, it is difficult to separate the therapeutic value of the new relationship being modeled from the insights conveyed in the interpretations offered.

Gill (1982) wrote that "in the very act of interpreting the transference the analyst behaves differently from what the patient has come to expect and even provoke" (p. 118). In his ensuing discussion of the analyst as a new object (Loewald, 1960), Gill (1982) came closest to a statement of the multiple factors involved in the therapeutic action of psychoanalysis. He said, "The results of any analysis are a mixture in varying proportions of effects due to the analysis of transference, to the accompanying new experience, and to persisting transference" (p. 119). With regard to the last element, Gill maintained the outcome of an analysis "will . . . to a certain extent, be dependent on the gratification of the unanalyzed and persisting transference" (pp. 119–120), a factor that Gill hoped would be kept to a minimum.

In sum, I do not think it is merely a semantic exercise to examine the idea of distortion. It is an issue of interest from a conceptual standpoint and it also reflects important attitudes with respect to the patient. The patient need not, however, experience a suggestion of distortion as a challenge to sanity, just as a slip of the tongue need not mean anything more than the influence of an unconscious idea or wish. But, out of concern that patients might tend to think their sanity was being questioned, Gill felt it safer, appropriately modest, and more in accord with the reality to not think with certainty that our inference is accurate and to consider the patient's construal of the analyst as plausible.

Furthermore, the analyst's alertness for his or her contributions to the patient's view of the relationship implies that the patient can be objective, not just plausible, in construing aspects of the analyst's behavior. This stance on the analyst's part also is less likely to evoke resistance. As Gill (1982) put it, "the clarification of the contribution of the analytic situation to the transference leads to the recognition that the way the patient has experienced the analytic situation is idiosyncratic. The patient must then perforce recognize his own contribution to this experience, that is, the contribution from the past." Here Gill made the empirical claim it is technically preferable to acknowledge *first* the analyst's own contribution to the patient's plausible response, for then the patient will be able to proceed less defensively to the realization that the analyst's contribution is not a sufficient explanation for his or her reaction. It is as though Gill is assuming a model of conflict resolution that states if the analyst models the unilateral, prior acknowledgment of his role in the enactment, the patient will more likely respond in kind.

Although one might argue that the preferred epistemological position should be one of transference coconstruction and an uncertainty about interpersonal reality, I believe Gill was drawn to this point of view less for its philosophical virtues than for what he saw as its compatible implications for the kind of analytic ambience it suggested and the implicit theory of therapeutic action that followed from it. Of course, he also found the hermeneutic, constructivist view appealing as an alternative to the natural-science, Freudian metapsychology. In the end, he (Gill, 1994) advocated that the clinician should work "as though correspondence is possible" while "one's theory is constructivist" although that might seem to "be fudging principles" (p. 155). To argue for the maintenance of a correspondence theory of truth even though the shift to constructivism favors a coherence theory of truth was perhaps his best way of resolving the conflict between the legitimacy of thinking one could accurately infer what was in the patient's mind while at the same time being ever alert to the fallibility of inference. The fallibility results from the automatic assumption that, if the analyst sees matters differently from the patient, the latter is obviously engaged in distortion. It was perhaps the appeal of both the correspondence and the coherence views and the reluctance to surrender either that led him (Gill, 1994) to conclude the "dichotomy between the two is often too sharply drawn" (p. 155). Perhaps the strongest impetus for Gill's position was his desire to safeguard the patient from potential manipulation and exploitation in an asymmetrical power relationship so insight and understanding could flourish in the context of a new, benign interpersonal experience.

References

Andersen, S. M. & Berk, M. S. (1998). Transference in everyday experience: Implications of experimental research for relevant clinical phenomena. *Rev. Gen. Psychol.*, 2:81–120.

Andersen, S. M. & Glassman, N. S. (1996). Responding to significant others when they are not there: Effects on interpersonal inference, motivation, and affect. In: *Handbook of Motivation and Cognition*, ed. R. M. Sorrentino & E. T. Higgins. New York: Guilford Press, pp. 262–321.

Andersen, S. M., Glassman, N. S. & Gold, D. A. (1998). Mental representations of the self, significant others, and nonsignificant others: Structure and processing of private and public aspects. *J. Personal. & Soc. Psychol.*, 75:845–861.

Andersen, S. M., Glassman, N. S., Chen, S. & Cole, S. W. (1995). Transference in social perception: The role of chronic accessibility in significant-other representations. *J. Personal. & Soc. Psychol.*, 69:41–57.

Brenner, C. (1996). The nature of knowledge and the limits of authority in psychoanalysis. *Psychoanal. Quart.*, 65:21–31.

Breuer, J. & Freud, S. (1895). Studies on hysteria. *Standard Edition*, 2. London: Hogarth Press, 1955.

Bruner, J. S. (1973). *Beyond the Information Given*. New York: Norton.

Freud, A. (1968). Acting out. *The Writings of Anna Freud, Vol. 7*. New York: International Universities Press, 1971, pp. 94–109.

Freud, S. (1912). The dynamics of transference. *Standard Edition*, 12:97–108. London: Hogarth Press, 1958.

Freud, S. (1925). An autobiographical study. *Standard Edition*, 20:3–76. London: Hogarth Press, 1959.

Gill, M. M. (1982). *Analysis of Transference, Vol. 1*. New York: International Universities Press.

Gill, M. M. (1983). The point of view of psychoanalysis: Energy discharge or person? *Psychoanal. & Contemp. Thought*, 6:523–551.

Gill, M. M. (1984). Transference: A change in conception or only in emphasis? *Psychoanal. Inq.*, 4:489–523.

Gill, M. M. (1994). *Psychoanalysis in Transition*. Hillsdale, NJ: The Analytic Press.

Gill, M. M. & Brenman, M. (1959). *Hypnosis and Related States*. New York: International Universities Press.

Gill, M. M. & Hoffman, I. Z. (1982). A method for studying the analysis of aspects of the patient's experience of the relationship in psychoanalysis and psychotherapy. *J. Amer. Psychoanal. Assn.*, 30:137–167.

Glassman, N. S. & Andersen, S. M. (1999). Streams of thought about the self and significant others: Transference as the construction of interpersonal meaning. In: *At Play in the Fields of Consciousness*, ed. J. A. Singer & P. Salovey. Mahwah, NJ: Lawrence Erlbaum Associates, pp. 103–140.

Greenson, R. (1967). *The Technique and Practice of Psychoanalysis, Vol. 1*. New York: International Universities Press.

Hoffman, I. Z. (1998). *Ritual and Spontaneity in the Psychoanalytic Process*. Hillsdale, NJ: The Analytic Press.

Loewald, H. W. (1960). On the therapeutic action of psycho-analysis. *Internat. J. Psycho-Anal.*, 41:16–33.

Luborsky, L. & Crits-Christoph, P. (1990). *Understanding Transference*. New York: Basic Books.

Mitchell, S. A. (1998). The analyst's knowledge and authority. *Psychoanal. Quart.*, 67:1–31.

Piaget, J. (1954). *The Construction of Reality in the Child*. New York: Basic Books.

Pizer, S. A. (1998). *Building Bridges: The Negotiation of Paradox in Psychoanalysis*. Hillsdale, NJ: The Analytic Press.

Raymond, L. W. & Rosbrow-Reich, S. (1997). Merton Gill. In: *The Inward Eye*, ed. L. W. Raymond & S. Rosbrow-Reich. Hillsdale, NJ: The Analytic Press, pp. 209–240.

Schwaber, E. (1981). Empathy: A mode of analytic listening. *Psychoanal. Inq.*, 1:357–392.

Schwaber, E. (1983). Psychoanalytic listening and psychic reality. *Internat. Rev. Psycho-Anal.*, 10:379–392.

Schwaber, E. A. (1990). Interpretation and the therapeutic action of psychoanalysis. *Internat. J. Psycho-Anal.*, 71:229–240.

Schwaber, E. A. (1992). Psychoanalytic theory and its relation to clinical work. *J. Amer. Psychoanal. Assn.*, 40:1039–1057.

Schwaber, E. A. (1995). The psychoanalyst's mind: From listening to interpretation: A clinical report. *Internat. J. Psycho-Anal.*, 76:271–281.

Schwaber, E. A. (1998). "Traveling affectively alone": A personal derailment in analytic listening. *J. Amer. Psychoanal. Assn.*, 46:1045–1065.

Stein, M. H. (1981). The unobjectionable part of the transference. *J. Amer. Psychoanal. Assn.*, 29:869–892.

Wachtel, P. (1980). The relevance of Piaget to the psychoanalytic theory of transference. *The Annual of Psychoanalysis*, 8:59–76. New York: International Universities Press.

Wallerstein, R. S. (1984). The analysis of transference: A matter of emphasis or theory reformulation. *Psychoanal. Inq.*, 4:325–354.

Chapter 15

The "Early" Interpretation of Transference: Implications for the Concept of Regression and the New/Old Object Experience in Psychoanalytic Work

Steven H. Cooper

Editors' Introduction: *As Cooper notes, Gill emphasized the desirability of interpretations of the "here-and-now" transference. In presenting this emphasis Gill felt it was important to be aware of those aspects of the analytic situation and the analyst that served as stimuli for the patient's experience of the relationship and to be attuned to the patient's indirect allusions to the manner in which he or she was experiencing the analyst.*

Given this perspective, how early in the treatment should the analyst actually interpret the transference? Cooper considers the issue of early interpretation of the transference in relation to the issue of regression in the analytic setting. He notes Gill's shift in thinking from his classic 1954 Psychoanalysis and Exploratory Psychotherapy to his reconceptualization of 1984 in which he claimed it was neither necessary nor desirable to actively attempt to induce a regressive transference neurosis in the patient. In fact, Gill often cited Macalpine's (1950) paper in highlighting the contribution of the analytic situation itself toward inducing an iatrogenic transference.

Cooper develops the theme of a dialectical tension between the therapeutic value of regression and of experiencing the analyst as a new object. He believes regression can be both useful and problematic, and he is concerned that classical analysts may have a tendency to overvalue regression and thus fail to appreciate the "progressive aspects of so-called regressive phenomena." Cooper aptly reminds us of Gill's (1982) statement that "in the very act of interpreting the transference the analyst behaves differently from what the patient has come to expect and even provoke" (p. 118).

References

Gill, M. M. (1954). Psychoanalysis and exploratory psychotherapy. *J. Amer. Psychoanal. Assn.*, 2:771–797.

Gill, M. M. (1982). *Analysis of Transference, Vol. 1*. New York: International Universities Press.

Gill, M. M. (1984). Psychoanalysis and psychotherapy: A revision. *Internat. Rev. Psychoanal.*, 11:161–179.

Macalpine, I. (1950). The development of the transference. *Psychoanal. Quart.*, 19:501–539.

I met Merton Gill in 1977 while I was a psychology intern. Michael Tansey and Walter Burke organized a study group that was led by Merton in which we each presented tape-recorded psychotherapy sessions for group discussion. Merton was particularly interested in the early interpretation of transference at this time, but in retrospect it's clear that he was rethinking ideas and aspects of technique that would form the body of his work in the last twenty years of his life (e.g., Hoffman, 1996). In broad strokes these ideas focused around his developing dialectic between a one- and two-person psychology.

Merton's last book, *Psychoanalysis in Transition* (1994), was aptly titled. Merton was, to his enormous credit, always a psychoanalyst in transition. Like most areas of practice and study, our field is beset by individuals who for both better and worse, settle into ways of thinking and working. Merton questioned everything. At the time I met Merton, I was getting increasingly interested in becoming a psychoanalyst. After meeting a few times in this study group with Merton, my thinking became solidified. If learning about and becoming a psychoanalyst were anything like what these meetings were like I was signing up. I didn't know at the time what an unusual teacher Merton was, nor did I realize the freedom and playfulness that he was able to engender because of both who he was and the nature of learning outside more formal institutional settings.

Our weekly meetings were characterized by lively debate, argument, laughing, no small measure of intimidation, and learning. I was initially terrified to present my work to older colleagues and especially to Merton, yet this experience remains one of the most rewarding learning experiences I've ever had in connection with psychoanalysis. Merton had an extraordinary ability to teach, though his teaching was not particularly self-conscious; it had the quality of his genuine responsiveness to clinical material and ideas. He taught through a spontaneity of response. One of the things I admired most about his teaching was his willingness to present his own clinical work. Candidates at each of the institutes where I teach are always saying how much they would like to hear the clinical work of their instructors. In our study group Merton probably presented more than any other member. He welcomed criticism about his work. He was always looking to engage in discussion of technique. There were evenings when we wouldn't get much past about five or ten minutes of a psychotherapy session because we all had so much to say about what was happening. At the center of every debate was Merton.

I can now see how much Merton was struggling at the time to integrate various aspects of his interest in the dialectical relationship between intrapsychic and interpersonal processes. He used to laugh about how some of his more classical colleagues called him Sullivanian as though it was a bad thing. I think he was aware of how difficult it was to truly integrate his interest in both one- and two-person psychologies, particularly in the mid-1970s. There is always the tendency in our field to pit notions of interaction in conflict with the understanding of intrapsychic process in ways that Merton was able to counteract.

Before getting into Merton's work on early transference interpretation and its relation to regression and the balance of old and new object experience, I want to recall a few clinical vignettes through which Merton's intelligent, challenging, and charming sensibility became more known to me. Each of these vignettes relate to his work on early transference and how he applied these understandings to clinical process. The first vignette, which I can only very partially recall, was one he presented of a psychotherapy of a young woman at the University clinic where he taught. I believe that the patient was an attractive graduate student 35 or 40 years his junior who had sought treatment looking to better understand her relationships with men. They had clearly developed a beginning alliance, though it was quite early in the treatment. During the tape-recorded session the patient was speaking about liking to be on time with friends and particularly with men, though this posed a conflict—she also didn't want to appear too eager to make contact. In this particular hour she had been a few minutes late as was her growing custom in the therapy. Within the group we began thinking the material contained a number of allusions to the possibility her conflict was also present with Merton. At one point about midway into the hour Merton wondered aloud with her about the possibility she might wish to get to her appointments with him on time and yet fear she might appear too eager with him, too. She laughed nervously a bit and said: "You mean with you?" Merton calmly replied with what I imagine to be a smile on his face: "Well, there's nobody here but us chickens." At this point his patient laughed heartily and began to consider his speculation.

This moment captures for me a number of aspects of Merton's clinical presence I admired. He was always the first to put forward that his interpretations were questions or hypotheses. He was admittedly speculating as we always are and he seemed to enjoy trying to find ways to foster a climate in which this joint inquiry could move forward. Further, this clinical moment obviously exemplifies his idea of interpretation as a form of play. More pertinent to the point of this chapter, transference is, par excellence, a form of play. While Merton's formal theoretical work rarely discussed the work of Winnicott, I always felt the way he worked with transference captured the notion of transference as a psychical region located between reality and fantasy. He always seemed to be "probing" (Ghent, 1992) the object looking for a way to play, a modality through which interpretive play and observation could be developed.

Another moment I recall relates to a case of my own. I was presenting my work with a very likeable and intellllignet man roughly my age who had been unable to integrate his intellectual abilities with work that interested him. He was quite gentle and passive in his presentation, which belied considerable anger, competitiveness, and contempt toward others who were often more successful than he in school and the workplace. He seemed to manage both his longings and his anger through a quite schizoid adjustment. He worked in a store as a merchant and otherwise read and stayed to himself. He was quite engaged with me, however, and intrigued by the idea that someone was taking him seriously and listening closely to his thoughts and feelings. I presented the case because I felt there was something in the material that I wasn't getting. The details are a bit foggy after nearly 20 years, but I recall that as the hour proceeded it became clear that Merton and others were hearing a great deal of this man's longings to be close and fears that I would not like him which he also feared from others. I kept using a phrase I rarely used at the time or now, saying something like, "That would be a whole different ballgame." After I had said this a number of times in various contexts, I began to finish a sentence with the phrase "a whole different ballgame." Merton was smiling and voiced the words with me as I said them. I began to sense more vividly and speak about some of my own fears about my patient's wishes to get close to me as well as his competitiveness and my own fondness and competive feelings toward him.

I found Merton's way of being intellectually aggressive and sometimes sarcastic to be playful, fun, and regularly quite on the mark in terms of what was going on in the dyad. When I began writing, it became fairly customary for me to receive a lengthy letter (one was eight single-spaced pages) critiquing and sometimes praising what I had to say. He read so carefully and thoughtfully it puts most editorial readers to shame. It's interesting to think about the connection between Merton's personal penchant for directness and the theoretical/technical shift in early interpretation of transference he put forward.

I begin here by reviewing some of Gill's work on the early interpretation of transference. I especially relate his work to the role of regression in clinical work because these ideas posed and continue to pose a challenge to psychoanalyst's ways of thinking about construction, reconstruction, and the application of developmental metaphors to analytic process. Regression is related to Gill's original work on the early interpretation of transference because of the problems Gill addressed related to the use of premature genetic reconstruction. As I hope will become clear, Gill, in his own vocabulary and frame of reference, was moving to a much more interpersonally oriented model, but one that maintained his interest in the dialectical tension between a one- and two-person psychology. His work raised many questions about the place of regression in analytic work—questions we are still grappling with. I am particularly interested in the ways in which old and new object experience occur in analytic process.

The Context for Gill's Emphasis on Early Interpretation of Transference

Gill's work on the early interpretation of transference has been incorporated into the fascinating mix of technical changes that characterize contemporary psychoanalysis. Much of current technique focuses more on the increased use of the here-and-now, the interpersonal aspects of the therapeutic relationship, the analyst's contributions to the transference, defenses against transference and transference as defense, and the questioning of linear concepts of development and regression. Gill's contributions to psychoanalysis were so complex and important that, in a sense, the work on the early interpretation of transference contained or summarized many other strands of technical innovation that would unfold over the last 15 years of his work. I believe his writing on the early interpretation of transference was like a textured, complicated musical theme that would be developed through many others, in the rich intellectual strands of American relational models, interpersonal models, and aspects of middle school and Kleinian relational models that have unfolded since the seminal publication of Greenberg and Mitchell (1983).

Interestingly, the area of early transference interpretation as a separate aspect of technique is rarely addressed in contemporary literature. An exception to this observation is Hoffman's (1996) elucidating, scholarly, and detailed account of Gill's evolution as a theorist. This aspect of Gill's work, which received so much controversy when it was published, has become more commonplace in the teaching and practice of psychoanalysis. Those analysts who believe that regression, induced by a relatively more silent analytic stance, is essential to the development of an analytic process are obviously more likely to view the early interpretation as counterproductive toward these ends. At the time Merton was developing his work on the early interpretation of transference, certainly a strong climate opposed the use of early interpretations of any kind. Interpretation itself that was done too early would be seen as a kind of "interaction," a very bad word in those days because it would interfere with the development of a transference neurosis, thereby interfering with the elucidation of unconscious processes. From a more contemporary point of view, however, many analysts don't mention the early interpretation of transference because it is such a widely accepted part of technique. It is accepted because so many have been influenced by Gill's (Gill and Muslin, 1977; Gill, 1982; Gill and Hoffman, 1982) assertion that the analyst is implicated in the transference at every turn, including at the outset of the journey.

The evolution of Freud's ideas about transference has been frequently documented (e.g., Gill and Muslin, 1977; Muslin, 1979; Muslin and Gill, 1978). I only selectively and schematically refer to some of these transitions with a special emphasis on setting a broad background for Gill's emphasis on the early interpretation of transference.

Freud's earliest views of transference (Breuer and Freud, 1895) focused on how distressing ideas connected with the analyst can become an obstacle to the work of analysis. The main work was conceptualized as the lifting of repression and anything that impeded this work needed to be analyzed. This was also the operative model for the case of Dora (Freud, 1905) published 10 years after Freud's earliest publications on transference. As was true in the "Studies on Hysteria," Freud failed to draw the patient's attention to possible allusions to the transference. In the frequently cited postscript following his case report, he regretted not having understood these allusions to the transference. His analysis of Dora as well as the Rat Man involved the avoidance of direct discussion of the relationship between analyst and patient because he was focused on a more unidimensional notion of therapeutic action, namely the recollection of repressed memories.

In "Remembering, Repeating and Working-Through," Freud (1914) focused more on the notion of transference as the revival of infantile imagoes transferred onto the analyst. While Freud (1912) in "The Dynamics of Transference" had begun to develop this idea, he still was primarily focused on the notion of transference as a form of resistance. For example, Freud (1913) stated, "So long as the patient's communications and ideas run on without obstruction, the theme of transference should be left untouched. One must wait until the transference which is the most delicate of all procedures, has become a resistance" (p. 139). Freud (1914) began to emphasize a bit more the importance of transference as an accumulation of repetitive actions and these repetitions require the analyst's attention in the more immediate aspect of patient-analyst relationship. Freud (1914) wrote "One cannot overcome an enemy who is absent or not within range" (p. 152). In that paper Freud also introduced the term "transference neurosis" as an illness brought into the analysis. Gill repeatedly made the point, however, that Freud failed to emphasize the notion of resistance in allusions or indirect references to the transference.

As has been frequently noted, very little of Freud's technique papers and case reports, mostly published before 1909, reflect many of these changes in technique or theory. Much of the case reports are replete with what a contemporary analyst would understand as allusions to the relationship between patient and analyst. Muslin's (1979) study of transference interpretation in the Rat Man demonstrated how Freud (1909) used the transference to help the patient experience episodes from the past. Freud stated, "It was only along the painful road of transference that he was able to reach a conviction that his relation to his father really necessitated the postulation of his unconscious complement" (p. 209). Again and again, however, the transference is not interpreted in immediate and personal terms between patient and analyst. Instead, the transference is seen as a corroboration of the reconstruction of events that led to repressed memories, the formation of obsessional ideas—in short, neurosis. Needless to say, this observation doesn't even begin to address the numerous other points of frank enactment that are so prominent in the case of the Rat Man. At the very least, it led Muslin (1979) to emphasize how the Rat Man was potentially deprived of the opportunity to learn about the past within the present encounter with the analyst.

It was the interactional matrix within which the transference develops and unfolds that was the point of focus for Gill (Gill, 1982; Gill and Hoffman, 1982; Gill, 1983). Gill's work directed analysts to broaden their view of transference, focusing less exclusively on transference as a form of resistance. Gill was also interested in analyzing the constant presence of defenses against the emergence of transference which he believed were frequently being alluded to by the patient from the very outset of treatment.

Gill's emphasis was in many ways a reaction against the use of premature genetic reconstructions. Gill (1982), like Sandler and Sandler (1984), spoke of the problems of reconstructions of the past on the basis of the patient's conscious memories if they are not also interpreted with their potential meaning, often unconscious, in the here-and-now interaction. Gill's method sought to carefully ask about and explore these potential meanings before reconstruction. In some ways Gill sought to explore more surface meanings before attempting deeper reconstructions. Of note with regard to that particular dimension, his technique was similar to recent emphasis by ego psychologists such as Gray (1990) and Busch (1995) to focus on surface factors before interpreting underlying motivation. For the most part, however, these ego psychologically oriented analysts have feared that focusing on the here-and-now might be equated with minimizing unconscious factors determining the nature of the transference. This was never Gill's intent. More importantly, ego psychologists didn't gravitate toward Gill's emphasis because of the much more radical implications of his theoretical and technical contributions. These revolved around the notions that within a perspectivist orientation, the general intent of transference interpretations is to elucidate ways in which the analyst could plausibly be construed as contributing to the patient's experience or perceptions. Through these interpretations, hopefully, the patient is able to understand or become more aware of repetitive aspects of interaction, especially his or her contributions to it.

In my own view, and I think implied by Hoffman (1996) as well, the early interpretation of transference was more an outgrowth of Gill's belief in the ubiquity of allusions to the transference requiring the generally more frequent use of transference interpretation.

Regression and Its Relation to the Early Interpretation of Transference

One of the interesting ways to think about Gill's work on early interpretation of transference is in terms of regression and its role in analytic process. Gill's work changed with regard to how he viewed regression and its relation to analytic process. In 1954, Gill's (1954) frequently cited definition of psychoanalytic technique emphasized regression as one of the central concepts and developments within analytic process: "Psychoanalysis is that technique which, employed by a neutral analyst, results in the development of a regressive transference neurosis and the ultimate resolution of this neurosis by techniques of interpretation alone" (p. 775). In that paper Gill attempted to clarify that he believed regression is not a "spontaneous" occurrence in analytic process. Instead, he stated that "the analytic situation is specifically designed to enforce a regressive transference neurosis" (p. 778). He went on to show how the "trappings" of analysis attempt to induce, accelerate, and deepen the transference.

Hoffman (1996) highlighted some of Gill's major shifts regarding the importance of regression in understanding analytic process: "He ceased to consider the achievement of any particular regressive state, beyond what the patient brings to the analysis, necessary or desirable. The work is then regarded as no less analytic if the issues explored reflect high levels of ego functioning than if they are more overtly primitive, and there is no requirement that they become more primitive for the process to be called an analysis" (p. 38). Gill believed that present interaction partly determines and informs whatever we learn about a patient's neurosis and that the transference is not exclusively determined by impulse, drive, or nerosis. Within this view, the importance of regression is minimized as the defining aspect of analytic experience. The interaction itself is the best way to learn about what people do and repeat doing in organizing interpersonal exchange as well as affective and ideational processes in relation to the self.

It's interesting to think about some of Bird's criticisms of early interpretation of transference (which occurred prior to Gill's publications on the subject) in the context of the issue of regression. Bird (1972) warned it is a mistake to think of early allusions to the transference as "real" transference. He termed these pseudo-transference phenomena. Yet if the analyst were to think of these allusions as more strictly diverting or defensive, then might the patient not be taken seriously by the analyst? I think Bird's position can lead, at times, to iatrogenic regression in which allusions to the patient's experience of the analyst are being overlooked or minimized. Gill's work on early interpretation of the transference opened up vistas for considering everything the patient tells us as an allusion to the patient's experience of the analyst.

It seems to me an outcome of Bird's approach is the analyst may wait for the patient to deliver the "real thing." What is the real thing? In Bird's terms it is the infantile neurosis and until it can be seen and smelled, as it were, in the analytic situation then whatever else the patient reports or alludes to in the transference can be regarded as the prim rose path. Naturally, there is wisdom in Bird's warning not to take every allusion to the transference literally. The patient's conscious beliefs, attitudes, and perceptions of the analyst are often laced with unconscious elements. But there can be nothing as helpful in examining negative and positive transference as the analyst taking it seriously. The interpretation of transference phenomena helps to hold affect, provides a dialogic framework, and helps to analyze further productive regression in which, hopefully, the patient can continue to explore uncharted affective and ideational territory.

Clearly, Bird's view of transference reflects a strong belief in the notion of early allusions to the transference as resistance to the development of the infantile neurosis. This view harkens back to most of Freud's writing on the subject of transference in which the transference is not interpreted in immediate and personal terms between patient and analyst. Instead, the transference is seen either as a form of resistance to the development of transference neurosis or as a corroboration of the reconstruction of events that led to repressed memories.

I believe another position in Bird's remarks regarding transference can lead to iatrogenic regression. Again, however, there is also something to heed in his remarks. Bird warned that what he refers to as the "real help" that an analysis offers can get in the way of the development of transference. Once again he spoke as though the only method of therapeutic action in analysis is through the development of a transference neurosis. When an analyst goes out of his way to be "helpful," it can of course involve avoidance of negative transference or the development of transference. But I believe it borders on perversity to argue a "problem" with the help an analysis offers is that it also contributes to resistance. Transference is so refractory to experience in some ways (which Bird more than anyone since Freud emphasized) that the analyst can interact on a number of levels.

Similarly, Inderbitzen and Levy (1994) have in my view over emphasized how "interaction" is a distraction from learning about the underlying drive derivatives of associations. If this is the goal of analysis then I suppose it might at times, though not necessarily. Certainly, I agree some kinds of interaction can be used to avoid aspects of conflict through either the patient's or analyst's unconscious activity. We can fraternize, make small talk, joke, and even interpret at times with analysands to not deal with hostility or conflict. Conversely, oftentimes joking, interacting, and interpreting facilitate the exploration of hostility and sadism. I disagree that interaction is an opposite to the development of useful aspects of regression. At the same time it would be simplistic for me to argue that silent behavior on the part of the analyst necessarily leads to iatrogenic regression. At times, the relative silence of the analyst can provide a necessary space for the patient to explore affect and unconscious fantasy.

The main problem I have with the understanding of interaction as hindrance is an underlying belief seems to be silence is not a stimulus of some kind. Gill (1994) illustrated quite clearly some of the ways in which silence is an action like any other action. Frustration, if favored over gratification, is a manipulation just as the opposite. Relevant is one of the major points of Gill's work on the interpretation of transference, namely that many objections to the early and frequent use of transference interpretation are set against the background of blank-screen ideals for the analyst. Gill (1982) stated:

> The argument that a transference interpretation intrudes the analyst as a reality into the analytic situation is a persistent remnant of the false precept that the analyst can indeed be only a reflecting mirror. An effort to deny the real impact of the analyst can only result in its remaining implicit so that it exerts its effects without being understood [p. 86].

Gill provided one of the clearest discussions about the effects of silence within the analytic situation. He pointed out how the attitudes the patient holds toward a silent analyst are neither entirely transference nor free from any influence of the present interaction. Gill stated, "An analysis of the patient's reaction will reveal that the analyst's silence is the current stimulus to which the patient responds with more or less plausible attitudes determined by past experience" (p. 88). Gill was always interested in understanding the effects of the analyst on the experience of the patient. He was also interested in questioning the purpose or function of the analyst's technique—this is, the analyst's intentions. For example, he (p. 89) quoted Lipton (1977)—if silence is being used as a technique to influence the patient and is not simply because the analyst is listening, it is most usefully considered excessive silence.

It is a burden for the analyst to carry illusions such as the possibility of not affecting the patient. An analyst must ask, "What are the particular kinds of experiences and perceptions my technical stance might engender? What are the advantages and disadvantages of my technical stance?" There is no technical vantage point that can avoid what Gill referred to frequently as "reality cues."

The most important effect on my work from Gill's technical suggestions involved what I regard as Gill's pioneering efforts to integrate the viewpoints and insights of interpersonal and classical analysis. Gill's exploration of the dialectical tensions between intrapsychic and interpersonal processes helped launch much of the theoretical/technical contributions of American Relational Theory. The specific technical/theoretical contributions implied by this approach are pervasive. Gill's interest in the patient's experience and sense of the analyst partly laid the groundwork for perspectivist and constructivist orientations. Gill, influenced quite heavily by Hoffman's developing theory, developed a keen interest in the patient's plausible feelings and ideas about the analyst's behavior and inner state. Hoffman (1996) summarized the major implications of these changes quite effectively, enhanced by a deep appreciation for the evolution of Gill's thinking on the matter of transference and regression.

Were there problems with his technical suggestions for me? Gill's approach, to some extent, can exacerbate either the patient's or therapist's predilection toward intellectualization. The forms that this intellectualization took are relevant to a discussion of an aspect of technique currently debated. Specifically, Gill was always interested in understanding the effects of the analyst on the patient and most importantly, the patient's speculations about the analyst. For me, for better and worse, I employed what I regard as a heightened deterministic approach gleaned from Gill's interest in the patient's speculations about the analyst. I say "gleaned" because I don't know that I can generalize from my experience to others. I only know that my interest in exploring the patient's plausible speculations about my inner state were at times derailing and avoidant of the "affective urgency" (Strachey, 1934) within the hour. Over time, as my own analytic style developed (as it still is, I hope), I began to fold Gill's emphasis on this dimension into other ways of trying to participate and observe with my patients. To some extent, the act of being always interested in the patient's plausible speculations interfered with the variety of ways in which I try to participate and observe with my patients.

I like Hoffman's position about the effects of ritual and what I would consider the dialectical tensions between a deterministic "faith" and a humility about the limits of our enquiry. Hoffman suggested there are dimensions to the therapeutic action of analysis which include unanalyzed or unanalyzable aspects of the analyst's influence. I have found this viewpoint mitigates or qualifies with a sense of modesty my faith in psychic determinism in ways that make me less prone toward intellectualization in the analysis of transference.

Regression and the Analyst's Blind Spots Regarding New and Old Object Experience

My own views on regression are filled with tension and paradox, far beyond what I can detail in this brief discussion. Like Gill, I believe aspects of regression are useful and inevitable in the process of many analyses; some aspects of regression, however, are highly iatrogenic and problematic. The developmental atmosphere in the analytic setting can be taken too concretely by the analyst in ways that are stultifying and engendering of malignant regression. For some patients, the capacity to not regress is what makes an analysis different and productive in their life. Although the patient needs to be able to experience the analyst as an old object, he needs to be experienced as a new object as well. The attempt to understand the analyst as new object can dilute the patient's experience of the analyst as an old object; conversely, the attempt to repeatedly analyze the patient's experience as an old object can divert from or minimize the ways in which the patient is able to use the analyst as a new object.

It is daunting to integrate the two fundamentally different views of regression that I hold close to my heart. One relates to the value of a developmental atmosphere engendered by the asymmetrical arrangements of the analytic situation in which the patient is likely to attribute to the analyst aspects of parents and earlier caretakers. But the patient can easily be infantalized and opportunities for growth overlooked. Classically trained analysts need ask themselves about potentially destructive aspects of overemphasizing the patient as a naive participant, whereas relationally oriented analysts need ask whether they overemphasize the maturity or pseudomaturity of the patient.

I don't think that it is meaningful to talk about regression as a good or bad thing. Regression occurs both naturally and is induced in analysis. Some analysts with technical stances of greater degrees of silence are probably likely to induce stronger types of regression as are some analysts who take developmental metaphors quite literally in terms of an extreme emphasis on aspects of psychic holding to the exclusion of analyzing complex forms of aggression as it is manifested in analytic interaction. The inevitability of at least some forms of regression was detailed by Bromberg (1979) in a poignant way as he described to interpersonalists both the value of regression and the natural pull for regressive phenomena in the course of analysis. It is my sense that more classically trained analysts are accustomed to useful aspects of regression but unfortunately are not taught to look more for progressive aspects of the patient's communication and even the progressive aspects of so-called regressive phenomena.

Obviously, one of the major differences between classical analysis and relationally influenced approaches is the way in which regression is conceptualized. For the classical analyst, the regression that develops is seen more in terms of the patient's relatively encapsulated conflicts that emerge in the analytic situation. The transference neurosis is promoted through various aspects of the analyst's stance as Gill (1954) systematically analyzed. For the relationally oriented, the analyst's perceptions of regressive phenomena are not usually conceptualized as separate from the analyst's experience and theory imposed on the analytic situation. The analyst is always involved in the development of the patient's plausible speculations and experience as well as the act of conceptualizing the patient's need and wishes within a developmental context (Mitchell, 1991).

The value in talking to patients about simultaneously held old and new experiences of the analyst also interested Gill. In Gill's (1982) discussion of the "new experience" he stated, "It is important to recognize that the resolution of the transference in the here-and-now is accomplished not only by virtue of the examination of the relation between the patient's attitudes and the features of the actual analytic situation which serve as their point of departure, but also because in the very act of interpreting the transference the analyst behaves differently from what the patient has come to expect and even to provoke" (p. 118).

Often experiences of the analyst as an old and new object are held in complex interaction with one another. I believe this relatively ignored aspect of technique may sometimes contribute to prolonged analysis or even more problematical, malignant regression. Most particularly, I will try to focus a bit on the analyst's resistance to seeing something new that the patient is expressing and experiencing, often unconscious in nature.

In its first 80 years, psychoanalysis may have been developed with a particular kind of regrowth fantasy, both consciously and unconsciously held. Particular "developmental tilt" theories (Mitchell, 1988) such as those proposed by Winnicott (1971) and Kohut (1984) focused more on the patient's opportunities for regrowth while many other theories have probably held more implicit expectations about the opportunity for regrowth. Much of psychoanalytic theory operates with the belief that through a regression to points of infantile conflict the patient will be met by the analyst in a different way, one that creates new psychic opportunity. Some would argue more contemporary relational approaches have minimized the "developmental atmosphere" (Stern, 1994) of the analytic situation by emphasizing the maturity of the patient and the patient's capacity to integrate the analyst's subjective reactions as an important aspect of growth during analysis. Those most critical of the relational model may say in conveying and using the analyst's subjectivity, we have gone from a naive or infantalized patient to a "parentified" patient—one who is asked to be pseudo-mature before his time.

I believe, relational and classical models have something to teach each other regarding matters of regression. I don't believe there is value in seeing regression as either present or actually or potentially iatrogenic. From my point of view both are or can be true. I think of analysis partly in a regressive context, like what the art critic Peppiatt (1997) stated about Jackson Pollock's painting: "Pollock's paint-slinging created swirls of color that draw the imagination into a region of boundless space." In some ways the experience of analysis, the experience of subjectivity itself, and particularly someone listening to it invites our imaginations and psyches into a region of boundless space.

Although it is important to say regression occurs descriptively and not prescriptively, it is also useful to distinguish between regression which occurs more naturally and regression brought about by the analyst. Gill (1994) discussed the reluctance of many analysts to seriously consider when we are doing something syntonic for the patient and trying to create a level of discord or curiosity, we are probably to creating a level of regression. What would happen if the patient could stop putting on a happy face when she is angry? What would happen if he could stop acting impulsively whenever he begins to feel tenderness toward another person? Why does my patient ask me so many questions at the beginning of an hour when he is feeling so anxious about whether I really care about him? All of these interventions seem to me quite consistent with the notion of interpreting habitual or characterological defensive configurations and adaptations. These interventions, taken more cumulatively over the course of analysis, can have the effect of stripping away familiar behavioral and psychological modes of adaptation. This kind of regression doesn't happen on its own, it is induced. To be sure, each patient responds in quite different ways to the analyst's actions, but there is a common assumption the analyst is doing what Wittgenstein (1958) and Ricoeur (1977) talked about as a function of interpretation—to take something familiar and make it unfamiliar. People lose their bearings when something is made unfamiliar—and there is also opportunity for learning.

One of the most confusing aspects of regression how it occurs more naturally as a result of analytic process versus its relation to the expectations of the analyst (Mitchell, 1991). For many analysts, particularly those more classically trained, analysis offers many aspects that are more or less analogous to the parent-child relationship. The asymmetrical arrangements of the analytic relationship engender certain aspects of desire, hostility, needs, longings, wishes to be loved, competitive feelings, wishes to rebel, and the like. Within the group of analysts who believe there is a developmental atmosphere to analysis, a general agreement probably exists that what gives analysis its power is both its similarity and difference from the parent–child relationship.

I believe there is little doubt that these observations about the developmental atmosphere of an analysis can never be fully separated from the degree to which the analyst is prepared to see the analytic relationship as an analog of the parent–child relationship. It is useful for any analyst to consider his own assumptions (or observations) about the extent to which the developmental metaphor is operating in his viewpoint or observing stance. How important to the overall success of analysis is it to reconstruct what happened during childhood? How much do we take the developmental metaphor literally?

A fascinating argument has been brewing within the American relational-conflict literature about the nature and importance of regression in clinical psychoanalysis. Stern (1994) suggested that "a developmental atmosphere" is inherent to the analytic setting. This implies the analytic setting engenders certain kinds of regressive pulls related to the hierarchical and asymmetrical arrangement. These include the mobilization of archaic, characterologically constricted modes of relating and complex defenses against reexperiencing early trauma or modes of relating. Stern questions Mitchell's (1991) assumption that the analytic setting is one of two psychological adults.

Mitchell (1994) argued he does not seek to minimize the inevitability of the patient's reexperiencing of early traumas or dependent modes of relating. Mitchell stated he views regression as focused more on earlier interpersonal contexts than to thwarted developmental fixation points. These interpersonal contexts are associated with reparative forms of interaction, new kinds of experience that differ from the earlier types of interaction which were stultifying or traumatic.

It seems there is little or no disagreement about the presence of a developmental atmosphere in the analytic situation, though each analysis obviously differs in this matter. What is a source of disagreement is perhaps how literally we take the developmental analogy. I believe it is not useful to think of analysis as the unfolding of invariant, developmental sequences or fixation points. I am concerned we may lose sight of understanding the person as an adult, not just as a child, and of the person's patterns of relating with others.

A confusing way in which regression is discussed in the literature relates to how it can sometimes be thought of as a transition to earlier periods of development. Gill (1994) posed the question as to whether increased awareness of repressed material indicates deeper levels of regression. If a patient is more able to face distressing issues previously omitted from awareness or repressed then there is some reason to believe that the patient is stronger. Perhaps sometimes we confuse the patient's need for relational contact or accompaniment with the repressed material with the notion of regression to an infantile state. Along these lines, Myerson (1981) pointed out how repressed material always occurs in an interpersonal context. I add that previously repressed material, as it emerges, requires a new interpersonal context, at least a wished-for, newly configured context, which the analyst can attempt to explore. The analyst may also be interested in how the repressed returns in surprising and disguised ways.

I believe there are ways in which we are insufficiently attentive to how the repetition in the transference relates simultaneously to old and new object experience. To put it simply, the transference is often characterized by the way in which a patient selectively perceives and experiences the analyst. Often, in the transference, the analyst resembles an important person from the patient's life, most often a mother or father. Perception and experience discrepant with some of these images are often minimized. Given the power of transference—that is, these tendencies to organize these images that repeat experiences with important others—we sometimes minimize ways in which patients experience and describe different situation with us at the same time they repeat old ones.

One of the reasons we do this is because we don't want to minimize the patient's transference experience. We don't want to avoid a negative transference or divert the patient's attention from important affects. But, as emphasized much more in interpersonal theory, particularly most recently by Bromberg (1979; 1994; 1995), individuals simultaneously try to insure stability and grow. I would characterize this position as overlapping but different than Kohut's assumption that people use defenses to secure the provision of a more empathic object relation than the one that they experienced in childhood.

Gill's continual emphasis on the plausibility of the patient's speculations and the value in trying to understand them can be most helpful in the confusing realm of making sense of old and new object experience. His approach helps the analyst understand and explore both realms of contemporary experience as well as how these contribute to repetitive organizational patterns of behavior.

If the analyst begins with a theoretical bias toward hearing clinical process from the perspective that the old object is clung to for familiarity and safety (Fairbairn, 1952), he might be more likely to minimize instances in which new object experience is sought or expressed. Perhaps the patient engages in "object probing" (Ghent, 1992) in ways that are overlooked by the analyst because the patient's affects or attributions toward the analyst seem familiar when assessed against the patient's parental objects. For example, patients who express negative feelings toward the analyst often seem to be seeing or experiencing something in the analyst that resembles what he has felt toward a parent. However, what can be conspicuously or subtly overlooked in such formulations is the previously unavailable opportunity for expressing feelings with such an object. At other times the analyst is likely to focus on certain ways in which the patient seems identified with the parent in forms such as identification with the aggressor or the victim. While this may provide a useful way of understanding these old and familiar processes, there are also ways in which sado-masochistic identifications occur simultaneously with the new opportunity for communication patterns with others.

Winnicott (1965) and Casement (1991) have each emphasized how the patient creates a "real" or new opportunity in the present to use an analyst to represent old object experience. Winnicott (1965) stated:

> Corrective provision is never enough. What is it that may be enough for some of our patients to get well? In the end the patient uses the analyst's failures, often quite small ones, perhaps maneuvered by the patient . . . and we have to put up with being in a limited context misunderstood. The operative factor is that the patient now hates the analyst for the failure that originally came as an environmental factor, outside the infant's area of omnipotent control, but that is now staged in the transference. So in the end we succeed by failing—failing the patient's way. This is a long distance from the simple theory of cure by "corrective experience" [p. 258].

It is only over time that the analyst can come to see whether a particular kind of enactment of the transference is used in the ways Winnicott described. During this process, however, it is easy to see these forms of repetition as only part of the old object experience. Stern (1994) described this kind of experience with the analyst as the "needed" object experience (even when it appeared initially as a repeated experience), but the problem is that his descriptions can become teleological, as if the patient somehow knows how to work something through that was stuck. An alternative explanation is that as old object experiences are worked through, new object experiences are more accessible over the course of analytic work (Tansey and Burke, 1994; Mitchell, 1994). How much do the analyst's theoretical biases influence how she constructs these experiences and determine what might be new in the patient's expressions?

One complexity related to understanding the new/old object experience is the possibility, sometimes likelihood, that the analyst will repeat painful aspects of the patient's earlier experience. Thus, the old object is reexperienced and repeated in the present. The patient's expectations and tendencies to repeat are forged onto the new experience with the analyst, and the analyst in various ways is likely to respond to or cocreate these repetitions. Enactments often involve the ways in which we unconsciously participate in a repetition of an earlier failure which was close to the patient's experience of an earlier trauma (Casement, 1991). The patient is skeptical to believe the analyst can become a new object partly because she sees the ways in which her analyst is the same as the old object through repetition and enactment.

Our tendency to see repetition may blind us to how new capacities for relatedness are emerging. For example, a patient's ability to feel safe enough with the analyst to criticize, correct, evaluate, and complain can constitute part of a new object experience. This observation is very much in keeping with the notion that negative transference often involves the deepest kind of trust and safety (Greenberg, 1986). Conversely, in many instances positive and especially erotic transferences involve intense sadistic and negative affective experiences, as Stoller (1979) and Gabbard (1994) have observed. Thus, experiences that sometimes appear new can involve disguised aspects of repetition.

It is common and sometimes inevitable for us to repeat aspects of the old object whether we focus ostensibly on what seems to us old or new. For example, if the analyst more rigidly emphasizes the newness in the patient's expression of negative feelings toward the analyst, as something not previously allowed within the parental/child dynamic, the analyst may, unwittingly, repeat aspects of the old. But the relentless interpretation of the patient's attachment to the old object might similarly constitute a repetition of his or her sense of being unrecognized by a parent.

One may question whether or the extent to which the sadism directed toward the analyst derives from the threat from the new object or the expression of feelings toward the old by the new subject. The notion of an object representation containing aspects of self and object helps to understand some of these processes. I have earlier posed the more familiar question raised by Fairbairn's work (Cooper and Levit, 1998), namely, whether the sadism is a response to the threat posed by a new object that disrupts a tenacious gravitating toward the old. Both British and American relational models have emphasized the ways in which the patient may enact aspects of the old object, requiring the analyst to adopt aspects of the patient's self in relation to the object. In these circumstances the question is always whether the analyst will be or can be a new object and/or a new subject. Will the analyst feel beleaguered, helpless, sad, furious, or retaliatory in response to the patient's communications? If the analyst does experience these feelings and expresses them can he do so in a way that differs from the ways the patient had? This can be accomplished through either the analyst's containment and reintroduction of these feelings (speaking from an effectively processed, internal, emotional state) or his judicious analyst-disclosure.

The analyst needs to balance the need to stay with the experience of the analyst-as-old-object in effigy with the attunement to possible ways in which the analyst may emerge from the old object experience. I believe in Freudian analysis there was too much of a resistance or reluctance on the analyst's part to interfere with the development of the old object experience. This position minimized the value of the analyst 1) drawing attention to some of the ways in which the patient might be using him in a new way; 2) using disclosure to differentiate himself at times from the old object experience; or 3) using aspects of his subjectivity as a construction that may allow further interpretation (Cooper, 1997; 1998; Cooper and Levit, 1998). Furthermore, the classical position paradoxically minimized the resilience of transference phenomena—that is, the transference is not necessarily diluted by addressing old and new object phenomena at the same time.

The points of reluctance or resistance for analysts within the relational model involve a potential to too quickly determine the analyst needs do something to act as a new object. Greenberg (1986) drew attention to the potential of both patients and analysts to defensively embrace aspects of the new object. It is quite understandable to seek relief from the unrelenting repetition of problematic relationships. The problems here, well documented by Gill (1983; 1994) and Cooper (Cooper and Levit, 1998) relate to the possibility of either diluting or diverting aspects of transference or similarly being influenced by a number of unconscious factors. There is value in the patient being able to find and create the object (Winnicott, 1971) in the form of the new-object-analyst. If the analyst harps on the theme of newness, the patient's experience may shift to staleness or compliance. Keeping in mind these complexities may help the analyst determine whether interpretations or disclosures by the analyst are more useful in regard to newness or to the patient's experience of the analyst as an old object.

Bromberg (1979) wrote what I regard as a seminal paper addressed to interpersonal psychoanalysts about the value of regression. Regression was seen as a tool, a phenomena that had for too long been ignored or discordant with other foci regarded as central to therapeutic action in psychoanalysis. At around the same time, Gill began developing his interest in the relationship between interpersonal and intrapsychic processes. Gill seemed to push more classical analysts to begin thinking about analytic process in terms of mutual influence and a variety of forms of therapeutic action. Specifically, he began changing his position regarding the necessity for engaging primitive levels of ego functioning and object relations as a defining feature of analytic process. In both classical and contemporary ego psychology and most British relational models, regression was seen as quite central to therapeutic action, though each school has a different model. It is my strong belief that the interpersonal school has had much to teach psychoanalysts of all theoretical persuasions, particularly in the area of regression/progression as forces of change in analytic process. Merton Gill began to realize this and let himself learn and develop a theory consistent with some of this integration between classical and interpersonal models. I will always consider him a role model as a thinker because he was always a psychoanalyst in transition.

References

Bird, B. (1972). Notes on transference. *J. Amer. Psychoanal. Assn.*, 20:267–301.
Breuer, J. & Freud, S. (1895). Studies on hysteria. *Standard Edition*, 2. London: Hogarth Press, 1955.
Bromberg, P. (1979). Interpersonal psychoanalysis and regression. *Contemp. Psychoanal.*, 15:647–655.
Bromberg, P. (1994). Speak! that I may see you: Some reflections on dissociation, reality, and psychoanalytic listening. *Psychoanal. Dial.*, 4:517–548.
Bromberg, P. (1995). Resistance, object-usage, and human relatedness. *Contemp. Psychoanal.*, 31:173–191.
Busch, F. (1995). Resistance analysis and object relations therapy: Erroneous conceptions amidst some timely contributions. *Psychoanal. Psychol.*, 12:43–53.
Casement, P. (1991). *Learning from the Patient.* New York: Guilford Press.
Cooper, S. (1993). Interpretive fallibility and psychoanalytic dialogue. *J. Amer. Psychoanal. Assn.*, 41:95–126.
Cooper, S. (1997). Interpretation and the psychic future. *Internat. J. Psychoanal.* 78:667–681.
Cooper, S. (1998). Analyst-subjectivity, analyst-disclosure and the aims of psychoanalysis. *Psycho. Quart.*, 67:379–406.
Cooper, S. & Levit, D. (1998). The old and new object in Fairbairnian and American relational theory. *Psychoanal. Dial.*, 8:603–624.
Fairbairn, R. (1952). *Psychoanalytic Studies of the Personality.* London: Routledge, 1981.
Freud, S. (1905). Fragment of an analysis of a case of hysteria. *Standard Edition*, 7:7–122. London: Hogarth Press, 1953.
Freud, S. (1909). Notes upon a case of obsessional neurosis. *Standard Edition*, 10:155–318. London: Hogarth Press, 1955.
Freud, S. (1912). The dynamics of transference. *Standard Edition*, 12:97–108. London: Hogarth Press, 1958.
Freud, S. (1913). On beginning the treatment (Further recommendations on the technique of psycho-analysis: I.). *Standard Edition*, 12:123–144. London: Hogarth Press, 1958.
Freud, S. (1914). Remembering, repeating and working through (Further recommendations of the technique of psycho-analysis: II.). *Standard Edition*, 12:147–156. London: Hogarth Press, 1958.
Gabbard, G. (1994). Commentary on papers by Tansey, Davies, and Hirsch. *Psychoanal. Dial.*, 4:203–214.
Ghent, E. (1992). Paradox and process. *Psychoanal. Dial.*, 2:135–160.
Gill, M. M. (1954). Psychoanalysis and exploratory psychotherapy. *J. Amer. Psychoanal. Assn.*, 2:771–797.
Gill, M. M. (1982) *The Analysis of Transference, Vol. I. Psychological Issues*, Monogr. 53. New York: International Universities Press.
Gill, M. M. (1983). The interpersonal paradigm and the degree of the therapist's involvement. *Contemp. Psychoanal.*, 19:200–237.
Gill, M. M. (1994). *Psychoanalysis in Transition.* Hillsdale, NJ: The Analytic Press.
Gill, M. M. & Hoffman, I. (1982). *Analysis of Transference, Vol. II. Psychological Issues, Monogr. 54.* New York: International Universities Press.
Gill, M. M. & Muslin, H. (1977). Early interpretation of transference. *J. Amer. Psychoanal. Assn.*, 24:779–794.

Gray, P. (1990). The nature of therapeutic action in psychoanalysis. *J. Amer. Psychoanal. Assn.,* 38:1083–1099.

Greenberg, J. (1986). Theoretical models and the analyst's neutrality. *Comp. Psychoanal.,* 6:87–106.

Greenberg, J. & Mitchell, S. (1983). *Object Relations in Psychonalytic Theory.* Cambridge, MA: Harvard University Press.

Hoffman, I. (1996). Merton M. Gill: A study in theory development in psychoanalysis. *Psychoanal. Dial.,* 6:5–54.

Inderbitzen, L. & Levy, S. (1994). On grist for the mill: External reality as defense. *J. Amer. Psychoanal. Assn.,* 42:763–788.

Kohut, H. (1984). *How Does Analysis Cure?* ed. A. Goldberg & P. Stepansky. Chicago: University of Chicago Press.

Lipton, S. (1977). Clinical observations on resistance to the transference. *Internat. J. Psycho-Anal.,* 58:463–472.

Mitchell, S. (1988). *Relational Concepts in Psychoanalysis.* Cambridge, MA: Harvard University Press.

Mitchell, S. (1991). Wishes, needs and interpersonal negotiations. *Psychoanal. Inq.,* 11:147–170.

Mitchell, S. (1994). Something old, something new. Discussion of S. Stern's "Needed relationships and repeated relationships: An integrated relational perspective." *Psychoanal. Dial.,* 4:363–370.

Muslin, H. (1979). Transference in the rat man case. *J. Amer. Psychoanal. Assn.,* 27:561–578.

Muslin, H. & Gill, M. M. (1978). Transference in the Dora case. *J. Amer. Psychoanal. Assn.,* 26:311–328.

Myerson, P. (1981). The nature of transactions that occur in other than classical analysis. *Internat. Rev. Psychoanal.,* 8:173–189.

Peppiat, G. (1997). Review of Jackson Pollock show, *New York Review of Books,* March 3.

Ricoeur, P. (1977). *The Rule of Metaphor.* Toronto: Toronto University Press.

Sandler, J. & Sandler, A. (1984). The past unconscious, the present unconscious, and interpretation of the transference. *Psychoanal. Inq.,* 4:367–399.

Stern, S. (1994). Needed relationships and repeated relationships: An integrated relational perspective. *Psychoanal. Dial.,* 4:317–346.

Stoller, R. (1979). *Sexual Excitement.* New York: Pantheon.

Strachey, J. (1934). The nature of therapeutic action of psychoanalysis. *Internat. J. Psycho-Anal.,* 50:275–292.

Tansey, M. & Burke, W. (1994). Transcending interactional tension. Discussion of S. Stern's "Needed relationships and repeated relationships: An integrated relational perspective." *Psychoanal. Dial.,* 4:349–352.

Winnicott, D. (1965). *The Maturational Processes and the Facilitating Environment.* New York: International Universities Press.

Winnicott, D. (1971). *Playing and Reality.* Middlesex, UK: Penguin.

Wittgenstein, L. (1958). *The Brown and Blue Books.* London: Basil Blackwell.

Index